FRANCE GUIDE

YOUR PASSPORT TO GREAT TRAVEL!

ABOUT THE AUTHORS

Robert F. Howe is a veteran journalist, screenwriter, and freelance author who has reported for the *Baltimore Sun* and *Washington Post*. **Diane Huntley** previously worked for *People* magazine and former US Senator Alan Cranston of California. They are the authors of Open Road's *Paris Guide* and currently live in Paris.

HIT THE OPEN ROAD WITH OPEN ROAD PUBLISHING!

Open Road Publishing now has guide books to exciting, fun destinations on four continents, but, oddly enough, some people out there still don't know who we are! We're old college pals and veteran travelers who decided to join forces to bring you the best travel guides available anywhere!

No small task, but here's what we offer:

• All Open Road publications are written by authors, authors with a distinct, opinionated point of view – not some sterile committee or team of writers. Our authors are experts in the areas covered and are polished writers.

• Our guides are geared to people who want great vacations, great value, and great tips for both standard tourist sites *and* fun, unique alternatives.

• We're strong on the basics, but we also provide terrific choices for those looking to get off the beaten path and *experience* the country or city – not just *see* it or pass through it.

• We give you the best, but we also tell you about the worst and what to avoid. Nobody should waste their time and money on their hard-earned vacation because of bad or inadequate travel advice.

• Our guides assume nothing. We tell you everything you need to know to have the trip of a lifetime – presented in a fun, literate, no-nonsense style.

• And, above all, we welcome your input, ideas, suggestions to help us put out the best travel guides possible.

FRANCE GUIDE

YOUR PASSPORT TO GREAT TRAVEL!

ROBERT F. HOWE & DIANE HUNTLEY

OPEN ROAD PUBLISHING

To our parents

First Edition
Copyright ©1995 by Robert F. Howe & Diane Huntley
–All Rights Reserved–

ISBN 1-883323-19-3
Library of Congress Catalog Card No. 95-69848

TABLE OF CONTENTS

SIDEBARS

ACKNOWLEDGMENTS

We would like most of all to thank our parents, whose guidance over the years instilled us with the confidence and daring to realize our dream of living in Paris.

Special thanks also go to our publisher, Jon Stein, who phoned up out of the blue one day and said, "Hey, how would you guys like to write a guidebook to France?"

Our fondness for the Good Life is what drives and shapes this book — at least, that's the way we see it. And no one helped us hone our appreciation for the good things in life more than John Anderson and Molly Moore, with whom we shared some of the best of our French adventures.

Ralph Earl, an unrepentant oenophile who claims to know it all, deserves our appreciation for providing invaluable guidance with the wine section here. (Though we're sure that his wife, Jane, who is the real brains of the family, must have done the heavy lifting.)

Thanks, too, to John Baxter, Christopher Mesnooh, Richard Paxson, Mister Nathaniel J. Queen Jr., Roger Ray, Skye Tallmadge, and Jeri and Andy Turpin for helping us explore and review some of Paris's finest culinary hideaways.

And lastly, thanks to all our friends in Paris (especially Angela Walker, who cared for the cats when we were out of town, Simone Gallo at the American Library in Paris, who helped us with research, and Frederique and Patrick Lallement, who fueled us with an endless supply of magnificent pastries) for putting up with our constant babbling about the book.

See, it was all worthwhile.

1. INTRODUCTION

In terms of overseas destinations, Americans are drawn more to France than any other country in the world. No wonder. It's an extraordinary place, with a charm, grace, and diversity rivaling that of any nation in the world.

France, after all, is the international symbol of the Good Life — of leisurely strolls along grand avenues, of hours spent gossiping over *Pastis* at an outdoor cafe, of inventive meals accompanied by bold vintage wines, of *haute couture* that's actually worn, of paintings that changed the course of art, of soaring monuments celebrating turning points in history, and of captivating men and women who keep their figures despite the pastries and *foie gras*.

And the bewitching landscape is full of promise. You can challenge the treacherous ski slopes that have tested Olympic champions, conquer towering Mont Blanc, shoot the rapids slicing through the Massif Central, steer a barge through the placid canals of Burgundy, or duplicate the famous Tour de France and see the entire country by bicycle.

France also caters to those who want nothing more than to soak up some sun on a fluffy beach or get away from it all in a quaint village clinging to a rocky slope overlooking a valley carpeted with olive groves.

We try to capture that variety in this guide so that you can plan the perfect personal getaway. We describe the major highlights of each region and detail several lesser-known but equally fascinating sights. And we list a range of hotels, from quaint inns to elegant castles.

We also try to give you a sense of the people. We've all heard crazy stories about the French, but what are the people really like? Getting to know the people is half the fun of any visit.

And if you are at all interested in food or wine, we think our food dictionary and wine-buying charts are the best you'll find in any general guide. And that's important. After all, there's no moment quite so poignant during a French holiday as toasting the last drops of a fine wine at the end of an exquisite meal.

Here's looking at you, kid.

2. EXCITING FRANCE!
- OVERVIEW

GETTING ALONG WITH THE FRENCH

The French do not hate Americans, so don't let that image scare you off. Yes, Parisians can get a bit testy, but try not to take it personally. Hey, it's a big city, and residents of big cities all over the world are subject to the same enraging traffic jams, high prices, and general decay.

(Cab drivers and waiters can be the exception. That's not to say that all cabbies and waiters are shifty or snotty, but on the rare occasion when they are, call them on it. And don't be self-conscious about causing a scene. Parisians throw public fits all the time.)

In any case, you will find that the French are generally open and helpful, especially if you can cough out a few spastic phrases of French. People in the countryside have been especially kind to us, taking time to chat about their towns or to tout local wines or just to complain about the current political crises.

You will discover that there is a kind of mutual fascination. Afterall, the special relationship between the Americans and French goes back to the late 1700s, when both countries struggled through national revolutions. And the French culture is fascinating in its veneration of family, tradition, the bounty of the earth, romance, beauty, arts of all kinds, and a glass of fine wine.

All of which is to say that if you can, try to get to know a few locals, even superficially, on your travels through their country. Getting a feel for the people is as memorable as snapping photos of their monuments.

WHEN TO VISIT

Spring and fall. More specifically: May and June, or September and October.

The winters are cold, deary and damp. The much-praised April in Paris is often one long drizzle. And, during the winter holidays, lots of restaurants and shops lock up their shutters for a week or two.

During summer, the weather can become uncomfortably humid in the north and stingingly hot in the south. Plus, there are ten zillion tourists milling around (that's no exaggeration). Also, some hotels and restaurants hike up the prices during the summer months.

And if you've come to see Paris, you could be especially frustrated by August. That's when virtually all the French take their annual vacation. That means Paris shops and bistros by the dozens close down for two to four weeks.

Believe it or not, we have seen hotels in Paris hang a sign on the door announcing that the staff has gone south for August.

FOOD & WINE

French cuisine is deservedly renown, and we talk about it at great length in the Food and Wine chapters later on. But we bring it up here again because we just can't resist talking about food and wine.

Whole trips can be built around food and wine. Not just eating and drinking – though you would certainly do a great deal of both. But you could visit regions where famous cheeses are made, or where the prevalence of garlic and olive oil summons up images of Italy, or where game dishes are treated with an almost religious reverence.

With wines, you could choose a famous wine region and tour the local vineyards, villages, châteaux, and winetasting cellars. You will discover that wine or the wine business permeates every facet of local existence.

Caring cuisine and nurtured wines are integral, maybe even dominant, elements of the French heritage. Because of that, you can learn a great deal about the people by better understanding their food and wine.

For the French, food isn't merely fuel consumed so you can get back to work. It's meant to be fussed over in the kitchen and appraised leisurely in the dining room. Ingredients are usually farm-fresh, even in city restaurants.

You should make an effort to try traditional dishes, such as coq au vin, rabbit in mustard sauce, duck breast (*magret de canard*), snails, onion soup (*grantinée* or *soupe à l'oignon*), goat cheeses (*chêvres*), the breads and pastries, and anything else you can fit under your belt.

And set aside at least one meal for haute cuisine at one of the scores of fine restaurants across the country, where the blend of ingredients is inventive and the presentation on the plate a work of art.

Not surprisingly, there are wines to fit any kind of meal. Bordeaux and Burgundies are the most famous, but try the Alsatian white wines and especially the striking red and white Côtes du Rhône wines.

And when you're in the countryside, try the local wines whatever they are. They are the wines most likely to complement the local cuisine.

A warning: Not every café is going to serve you a memorable meal. In fact, a quick meal in the wrong place can memorable, but for the wrong reason.

Cafés, especially the ones in busy city districts, serve the original French version of fast food, such as grilled cheese sandwiches with ham (*croques monsieur*), omelets which are often overdone, and crêpes made long in advance and reheated. And their wines can sometimes taste something like battery acid. We advise against eating or drinking anything but the most fundamental snack or lunch at almost any café or bistro you find along the major urban avenues.

These are fabulous places to sip an espresso and watch the world pass by, but most of the good food (inexpensive as well as gourmet) is further off the beaten track.

Do a little research before you pick a restaurant for dinner (of course, we highly recommend our picks), make a reservation, and be prepared on occasion to take a cab across town.

BIG CITIES & COUNTRY VILLAGES

If you're used to a place like New York or Los Angeles, you'll probably think France doesn't have any Really Big Cities. Even Paris is manageable. Paris proper has more than two million people, but the core where you will spend your time is surprisingly compact.

The same is true for all the larger cities, whether it's Marseille, Lyon, Nice, Strasbourg, Bordeaux, Nantes, where ever. The reason is simple. You're most likely interested in a city's historic quarter, which is where you'll find the better sights, restaurants, and shops.

Those historic sections (marked by road signs that read *Centre Ville*) have so much culture and history crammed into their narrow lanes that they are somewhat like living museums. They date back hundreds of years to a time when a big city like Strasbourg was little more than a trading village ringed by a river.

Once you've unpacked the trunk, you probably won't need the car again until you head out of town — which, in our view, is a great blessing. We'd much rather stroll leisurely down cobbled lanes than fight traffic.

For a country that's been around as long as France, it's bewildering how open the countryside is. Even from the hustling autoroutes, you will see tiny villages tucked into river valleys or perched on faroff hillsides.

Probably the most famous villages are those in the **Vaucluse** area — places like **Gordes** and **Rousillon**, which seem as old as the stony mountains they occupy. The **Perched Villages** just inland from the Côte d'Azur, such as **Saint-Paul** and **Utelle**, are equally breathtaking.

The villages along the **Alsatian wine route** are picture-postcard perfect, with half-timbered homes and adorable squares spilling over with boxes of geraniums. Villages in the hill country of **Burgundy** are often set in woody enclaves that must look pretty much like they did eons ago. You feel as if you have traveled through time.

And just because you've left the big city behind doesn't mean you won't be able to find a comfortable bed or a decent meal. Far from it.

Almost no matter where you are, you'll be able to find a charming inn or converted castle (converted châteaux are especially common in the Loire Valley). They'll serve local wines and creative haute cuisine, using the freshest possible ingredients.

NORTH & SOUTH

The northern half of the country is the more populated region, in part simply because it's more accessible. It shares borders with Germany and Belgium, and it's just a short trip across (or under, by Chunnel) the English Channel from England.

And, of course, this is where you'll find **Paris**, which is inevitably the first destination for overseas travelers. From Paris, you can reach virtually any corner of the north in one to four hours by car.

Setting aside Paris itself, which is in it's own category, the north is known for its stunning landscapes and magnificent castles.

Beginning in the west, you have the mesmerizing coasts of **Normandy** and **Brittany**. Normandy has amazing broad beaches, verdant rolling hills, and cozy fishing ports. And Brittany is known for its dramatic shoreline and a stark interior inhabitted by a culture distilled in equal parts over the centuries from Britain and France proper. A must-see.

The **Loire River Valley**, just below Paris in the central part of northern France, is the setting for the most famous of the glorious historic castles. There's nothing quite like visiting three or four chÉteaux, then retiring to a converted manor house for a gourmet meal.

And to the east, on the far side of the Vosges Mountains is **Alsace**, a truly beautiful setting, with vineyards and villages of half-timbered homes marching down the slopes of the Vosges to the banks of the Rhine River.

Finally, there is **Burgundy**, which is a real treat for wine-lovers. In the hill country in the northern reaches of Burgundy, you will also find fascinating villages and historic hamlets where monks established heavenly refuges and where Celtic warriors once did battle with the Romans.

The south is best known, and rightfully so, for **Provence** and the **Côte d'Azur**. Provence is one of those rare destinations that lives up to the hype. It is glorious, beautiful, cultured, and largely unspoiled even today.

A perfect vacation would be to rent a house in the Vaucluse region, visit the hillside villages, tour the former Roman fortresses, shop at an outdoor farmer's market in some tiny village, and then retreat to your villa and cook up a massive feast laced with garlic, olives, and rosemary.

The French Riviera (a term more or less synonymous with Côte d'Azur) is also a paradise — though in the height of the summer season it is completely overwhelmed. Slightly off-season, however, and you can revel in the pretty resort towns and the blue, blue waters.

Just above the Côte d'Azur are the **French Alps**, which are eye-popping in their grandeur. Winter sports here among the best in the world.

The southwestern coast is best known for **Biarritz**, an elegant resort just a few kilometers from the Spanish border, and **Bordeaux**, an industrial town at the heart of the most productive and heralded wine region in France.

South central France is probably the least visited. Here, you'll find **Auvergne**, which sits atop an enormous plateau wrinkled with small mountain ranges and river valley. Also, there's the **Dordogne**, which follows the path of the river by the same name and cuts eastward from near Bordeaux through sometimes stirring valleys to the foot of the Massif Central.

THE GREAT OUTDOORS

The French may not cultivate the greatest athletes on the planet, but still they adore outdoor sports of all kinds.

Their beaches are world-famous. There's the Côte d'Azur to the south, with **Saint-Tropez**, **Cannes**, and **Monte-Carlo**, there's chic Biarritz to the southwest, and there are the broad beaches of the Brittany and Normandy coasts to the west and north.

Water skiing, scuba-diving, wind-surfing, sailing, and sunning are available at any of those spots. You can be as busy or as lazy as suits your mood.

Campgrounds are sprinkled all over the country, though some nearer the larger cities looked to us a bit too much like parking lots. But you can find some magnificent camps in the mountains, in the interior, and along the coasts of Normandy and Brittany.

Burgundy is criss-crossed by a network of canals that were used for shipping and that are now available for touring. You can rent part or all of a barge that will float you up and down the region. When you want to touch base with terra firma, just tie up at one of the countless docks and bicycle into the nearest town for fun and provisions.

Biking, by the way, is hugely popular in France (as is obvious by the famous **Tour de France** race). You can bring your bikes and plot your own course along the national grid of bike paths. Or, sign up for an organized tour. While you're biking by day, your belongings are driven ahead to a charming little village where you'll bed down for the night.

Skiing is one of the country's most popular passions. The French Alps have hosted the Winter Olympics several times. **Val-d'Isère** is probably the most famous ski village, but there is also **Val-Thorens**, **La Plagne**, and lots of others.

SPECIAL RECOMMENDATIONS

If you're going to be on the road, pick up a *Michelin Motoring Atlas*. You can find them in the States or in Paris.

They're not cheap, but they are the most thorough collection of maps available. Every tiny road is detailed. Mileage between stops on all major and minor highways is also noted. And especially scenic routes are highlighted in green.

Also, the *Michelin Red Guide* can be a lifesaver. It's not really a travel guide because it doesn't tell you anything about the sights or culture or history of a place. But it does have an exhaustive listing of hotels. That can come in handy if it's getting late in the day and you just don't have the energy to keep going.

The Red Guide also has detailed maps of towns and city centers, thus perfectly supplementing the Motoring Atlas.

**THE CATHEDRAL IN BAYEAUX,
FIRST FRENCH TOWN LIBERATED ON D-DAY**

3. LAND & PEOPLE

LAND

France is ideally located in the center of Western Europe, with Great Britain across the English Channel to the northwest, Spain on the other side of the Pyrénées to the southwest, and Belgium, Luxembourg, Germany, Switzerland, and Italy sharing borders to the northeast and east.

The hexagonally-shaped country, just slightly smaller in area than Texas, boasts a remarkable geological diversity. It is traversed by four major rivers: the **Seine**, which moves westward from the hills of Burgundy through the Paris Basin to the English Channel; the **Loire**, which begins in the south-central part of the country, rises northward to Orléans and the Loire Valley, and then crosses eastward to Nantes and the Atlantic Ocean; the **Dordogne**, which rambles from the Massif Central and spills into the Atlantic near Bordeaux; and the **Rhône**, whose first life trickles out of the Swiss Alps as it flows southbound to the Mediterranean.

The **Saône**, a lengthy river in the heart of France, cuts through Burgundy before joining the Rhône near Lyons.

There are broad, fertile plains around Paris, the Loire Valley, and the southwest section of the country. France's eastern border comprises a series of mountain ranges, beginning in the northeastern corner with the **Vosges**, then the **Jura** east of Burgundy, and finally the **French Alps**, which bear down on the Côte d'Azur (or French Riviera).

The south central section of the country is also heavily mountainous and has several ranges that form what is called the **Massif Central**. And, of course, the southwest foot of France rests on the **Pyrénées**.

Corsica, the large, rugged island south of the Côte d'Azur in the Mediterranean, is also a formal French state (though separatists would like to change that and ignite a few bombs every now and then. There are also several attractive smaller islands off the coasts of the Mediterranean, Brittany, and Normandy. You'll find beautiful beaches along those same coasts, as well as in the southwest near Biarritz.

**SMALLER THAN TEXAS
– BUT THE BIGGEST IN EUROPE !**

• *France is the largest Western European country, occupying 552,000 square kilometers (220,000 square miles). By comparison Texas is 695,000 square kilometers (267,300 square miles).*
• *The French population of 57.2 million is roughly the same as Italy's and, in Europe, is smaller only to Germany's estimated 81 million.*
• *Départements (states) - 96, est. ave. pop. 565,600*
• *Arrondissements (counties) - 335, ave. pop. 167,580*
• *Cantons (cities) - 3,808, est. ave. pop. 14,630*
• *Communes (villages) - 36,560, est. ave. pop. 1,522*

THE PEOPLE

"The French are rude, and they hate Americans."

That hasn't been our experience at all, and we strongly doubt you'll have any problem. Still, it's a common notion — one that's rooted in historic precedent and subtle cultural differences.

Historically, some of the blame goes to Charles de Gaulle, if only because he was the ultimate French role model for decades. He disliked and distrusted Americans and, no doubt, some of that rubbed off.

During the early stages of World War II, France essentially rolled over when the war swept its way. It became largely a nation of collaborators, both through overt support and through the acquiescence of the silent and terrified majority.

When the war ended, de Gaulle, angry with his countrymen, angry with his dependence on American and British might to liberate France, and angry with America's sudden cultural and economic dominance of the free world, distanced himself from the States. He didn't want to be seen, or to see himself, as just a different kind of collaborator — as the man who allowed the Americans to shape the future of France.

Bursting with pride, he sought psychological, social, and economic independence for France. He was so intent on proving that France could stand on its own two feet that he probably went overboard on occasion.

When he pulled his country's military support out of the NATO alliance and met freely with the Soviet leadership during the height of the Cold War, he did so in part as a way to thumb his nose at America and Great Britain. He was saying France did not need help and would forge its own place in the new world order.

No matter how many feathers he ruffled, de Gaulle succeeded in pulling his people out of a mire of despair and destruction. His success at resurrecting a proud economic and military world power is all the more remarkable when one remembers that, aside from certain flashes of cultural and artistic brilliance, things had gone badly for France for a century. The French had been soundly thrashed in the Franco-Prussian war of 1870, the First World War in the Teens, the Second World War in the 1940s, Vietnam in the 1950s, and Algeria in the 1950s and 1960s.

Setting The Record Straight

So let's try to set the record straight. Though there might be a shading of apprehension in the average French person, proud to a fault and wary because America's cultural influence continues to grow thanks to the might of its media, the French do not hate Americans.

In fact, you will find that most people are friendly and some are even eager to help. No doubt, you'll have an easier time as a visitor if you speak some French, just as any foreigner fares better in the States if he speaks some English, or at least tries.

FRENCH FACTOIDS

• *A person can buy a handgun only after first receiving a permit from the police. A person can obtain the permit only if he can prove he is an active member of a shooting club or if he can prove his life is in danger.*

• *Handwritten applications for jobs are required because the applicant's handwriting is analyzed to see if he or she possesses personality traits appropriate to the job.*

• *If you own a television, the government assesses you for an annual tax, the proceeds of which go to subsidize the state run channels of France 2 and France 3.*

• *State subsidies for pregnant women and new mothers can extend as long as to the child's third birthday. The amount is increased if the mother breast-feeds her baby, though a social worker must witness the breast-feeding at least once for the mother to qualify.*

• *Employment classifieds can indicate what age and sex the company seeks in its applicants. The company can also note that it is interested only in physically attractive candidates.*

• *The great majority of employees are paid once a month and are paid by direct deposit into their bank accounts.*

• *You cannot cash a check written to you even if you take it to the bank on which the check was drawn. You can only deposit the amount into your own account.*

• *French women were given the right to vote in 1945.*

• *Jacques Chirac, who became the mayor of Paris in 1977, is the only person ever elected to the post by popular vote. All past mayors had been appointed by the national government.*

Remember also that this is an enormous, busy city, and you will inevitably run into someone who missed the Metro, or just lost their job, or broke up with their girlfriend, and they're going to be cranky. New York, Washington, Chicago, Los Angeles — they're all the same.

The root of so many street-level misunderstandings between American tourists and the locals is that French society is more formal than American. We're used to talking with any stranger who comes along, throwing our arms around their shoulders, and inviting them home to meet the family.

The French don't do that. Strangers are strangers and family is sacred, and never the twain shall meet. You can witness the formality of the French in their language.

Vous, the formal (both singular and plural) word for you, is the preferred choice over *tu*, the familiar form. You would only begin a relationship with *tu* when addressing a child. You would only *tutoyer* an adult (use the familiar form *tu*) after you have known them for months and become pretty good friends. Often even then, a French person might feel uncomfortable using the familiar term.

This is less and less the case with today's French youth, which profited from the social changes brought about in the late 1960s and which is mesmerized by what they see on television as the ease and perks of American society.

With adults, the formality appears in some pretty interesting ways — ways that can affect you during your visit. For instance, when you enter a small shop, it is expected that you would say, *Bonjour, Madame* or *Bonjour, Monsieur* to the shopkeeper. The thinking is that just because they want to sell their products doesn't diminish the fact that this is their space and "guests" should show courtesy. It is also expected that you say, *Au revoir, Madame, merci*, regardless of whether you have purchased anything.

When entering a doctor's office or a small restaurant where there are just a handful of patrons, it is not at all unusual for a French adult to say, *Bonjour Messieurs* or *Bonjour Mesdames*, to the other patients or diners.

Because so many Americans rush in and out of shops, manhandling the merchandise without even glancing at the owner, they are sometimes considered rude and are greeted in kind. French people have told us that they sometimes feel as if American tourists view them and their shops or cafes as nothing more than commodities to be bought and sold.

The Language Barrier

The most obvious barrier is language. While hotel and restaurant employees often speak some English, the French speak a lot less English than is generally assumed. And often, those who do speak passing English feel too ashamed of the poor quality of their English to use it. (Though you are likely to run across several waiters who will answer in English after you have ordered in French — in our view, an annoying habit.)

On the other hand, the French are generally encouraging if you blurt out even the most abysmal phrase of French. It seems sometimes as if they will insist that you speak French well even when you yourself weren't quite sure what you said.

But try anyway. And don't be afraid of accidentally saying something incredibly stupid. That happens to everyone and somehow, whenever you've said something hugely inappropriate, it always seems to have some grotesque sexual connotation.

A real-life example: A friend of ours who has taken a French boyfriend, speaks the language quite well, and has assimilated the culture far better than most was at a party of young French people recently. They were discussing astrology signs and each person identified their sign.

When it came her turn, she meant to say that she was a Virgo. But, for simply having left out a single vowel, she said instead, "I'm a penis." It was several minutes before her friends could pick themselves up off the floor.

But the bottom line is that you will have a more successful trip and have more fun if you attempt a bit of French and fail, than if you had not tried to speak the language at all.

The Money Barrier

Money represents another difference between the cultures that occasional grates. An average middle-class French person is not driven by profit in the same way that so many Americans are. After leaving school, a French person often hunts down a respectable job and willingly (almost unconsciously) settles in for the very long haul.

They might move up the ladder over the years, but the French rarely quit and change jobs without a very compelling reason. They also do not move around the country as often as Americans do in the States, so they are not used to the idea of enormous change.

The net result is that they are relatively secure (or at least not restless) when it comes to money. Their salaries are surprisingly low, but they generally live within their means without fretting about it constantly.

Oh, they regularly bitch and moan about salaries, staging countless work slow-downs and demonstrations. But mostly their beefs against the government are good-natured. (cafés do very well when peaceful demonstrations visit their neighborhoods, and lose lots of glass on those rare occasions when things turn ugly.)

In essence, the French adore the government because of the financial perks built into the system (sort of the adoration of a child toward a parent). The state takes care of virtually all their medical expenses, and employers are obliged by law to pay all or part of their transportation costs. And the law requires that employees receive at least five weeks vacation a year and that they be paid for 13 months work in every 12.

They are not generally comfortable discussing money matters and, in their view, just because a wealthy tourist wants to buy their product or services, that does not mean that they should humble themselves in a cloak of gracious servitude. Quite the contrary. The attitude can be reversed so that the tourist should feel privileged to have access to the shop owner's wares.

Political Hurdles

It's true that the United States and France are often embroiled in some kind of official political squabble. That was true back when de Gaulle pulled French military support out of NATO, as it was recently when the French moaned about the allegedly mercenary dominance of the American film industry during the recent trade negotiations.

What you see is a love-hate relationship. The French are obsessed with Americans and American goods. A big rage in 1994 was for boys to wear caps emblazoned with the names of American sports teams. When asked about the caps, they sometimes admit they don't even know what sport the team plays. For that matter, we've seen caps for teams we've never heard of either.

But there is a fear of American culture, largely because American cultural influences are growing increasingly powerful.

Back to arguments over film: The French, especially politicians, feel that their culture is under attack by the American media. And, truth be told, the French culture and others are under fire — not by a malicious conspiracy masterminded by American CEOs huddled in smoky backrooms, but by naturally evolving market forces and consumer tastes.

As we write this, 14 of the 20 most popular films (judging by ticket sales) over the past 12 month-period in Paris are American-made — topped by *Aladdin*. Five are French, the top one being *Léon* at number 8 (which was a French-American collaboration), and one is British.

Manhattan Murder Mystery, hardly one of Woody Allen's best efforts, is 5th — which demonstrates that Allen could produce a film of nothing more than him standing on his head and the French would fall over themselves in high praise.

The proportions are about the same for the top 20 popular music videos. And the four primary French television stations (TF1, France2, France 3, and M6) are laden with reruns of *Mission Impossible, Beverly Hills 90210, Bay Watch, Miami Vice, Magnum, Quantum Leap, Hogan's Heroes*, and other popular American standard bearers.

Why are there so many American films in French theaters and American television series on French airwaves? Because Americans crank out a huge volume of product, and the European rights are cheap. The French film and television industries simply cannot afford to produce enough original programming to fill the increasing demand of its viewers.

But there is another factor: The French, especially young viewers, are growing accustomed to American sitcoms. They like them. Even French adults, while genuflecting in front of such native film giants as Truffaut, have developed a hankering for the big-budget, action-oriented American pictures.

So what to do? During the recent trade talks, French politicians tried to limit the import of American films and raise tariffs on the films, saying they would use the money to subsidize French productions. The French won the skirmish, but shortly afterward American filmmakers displayed an increasing interest in cooperative ventures with French producers.

This backdoor approach will likely result in increasing French media dependencies on American money and know-how.

Language As The National Soul

In a more extreme effort to slow what is largely seen as an inevitable cultural takeover by American media giants, French politicians in 1994 passed a law that would have made it illegal to use English words in any advertising campaign or notice if a French word existed to express the same thought.

As an example, car ads touting "air bags" would have had to be rewritten to boast about *coussins gonflables de sécurité*, meaning "inflatable security cushions." It doesn't exactly sing, does it?

Essentially, the law was struck down because it violated free speech tenets of the French constitution. The ruling declared that the government could restrict only official use of English. In the most extreme example, this might have required that the government change all the "Stop" signs (which do, in fact, read "Stop") to read *Arretez*.

Not surprisingly, since lawmakers were really only targeting American businesses and French "collaborators" with American businesses, the proposed law was shelved — for now.

We may be somewhat amused by this strutting and fretting, but we should remember how touchy American voters have been every time a proposal is made to institute bilingual English-Spanish ballots or school texts.

Think how you'd feel if two-thirds, or more, of the movies and television you watched in your own home were in French, with subtitles in English or with annoying dubbed voices. And what if your kids were obsessed with Roberto Donadoni of the AC Milan soccer team, but couldn't name a single player on the San Francisco Giants.

MORE FUN FRENCH FACTOIDS

• As of 1990, there were 24,236 Americans living in France.

• When you include the membership subscription and the various taxes, Parisians pay just under 60 percent tax on their electric bill.

• The legal age for drinking, driving, and voting in France is 18.

• The oldest continuous family line belongs to the Capétians, who can be traced back to 852.

• The French pay anywhere from 5 to 56 percent of their income in taxes.

• As of 1991, the average French couple without children and earning only one income made $16,625 after taxes. Couples with three children and two incomes averaged $24,530 per year after taxes.

• The use of contraceptives was legalized in 1967. Abortion became lawful in 1975.

• Women were guaranteed equal rights under the constitution in 1946.

• On average, French women outlive French men, 81.3 years versus 73.1 years.

• The French spend an average of less than two hours a day watching television.

• The highest recorded temperature was 111.2 degrees in Toulouse in southwestern France on August 8, 1923. The lowest recorded temperature was minus 41.8 degrees on January 17, 1985, in the town of Mouthe near the Swiss border east of Dijon.

• There are 82 daily newspapers in France.

• About 75 percent of the power used in France is generated by nuclear plants, the largest such percentage in the world.

• There are four murders per 100,000 people in France a year.

• France has the fourth largest economy in the world.

• France has the highest literacy rate in the world.

• Despite their reputation for eating well, the French rank 30th in terms of how many calories they consume daily.

• The average waiter makes 11,000FF per month. The average manager of a business earns 50,000FF monthly.

• The French consume more medicine per capita than any other nationality in the world.

• The French franc was devalued by 100 fold in 1958, so that overnight, 100 francs became a single franc.

• In France, where Michelin is one of the largest independent corporations, the Michelin man is known as Bibendum.

Maurice Druon, head of the *Académie Française*, the institutional and intellectual keeper of the French language and heritage, noted in an interview published in the summer of 1994 that he wanted to find a way to recapture the French pride in their own language.

"France remains a great power," he said. "We possess a universal language, we are one of the few nuclear powers, we are the fourth largest exporter in the world, we have world's third largest economic maritime sovereignty. But here at home, national pride is taken as bad taste. We welcome all the exotic nationalities, but to embrace our own is to be accused of arrogant nationalism."

He ends up with this plea: "It's necessary to consistently remind ourselves that language gives voice to our souls."

A VILLAGE IN THE CHABLIS WINE COUNTRY, BURGUNDY

4. A SHORT HISTORY

BEGINNINGS (4000 BC-58 BC)

Many people like to think of the French as being nothing more than ... well ... French, as if the people and their culture sprang out of the ground like oaks.

But in truth, the French civilization grew out of a lively stew of Western peoples — the Britons, Greeks, Romans, Vikings, Franks, a variety of Germanic groups, and a host of barbarians, just to name a few.

Their story goes something like this:

It all began with the tribes that occupied the Paris Basin and Dordogne River Valley east of Bordeaux more than 25,000 years ago. The Paleolithic and, later, the Neolithic tribes thrived on France's fertile soil, its game-laden forests, and the watery highways of the Seine, the Loire, and the Rhône rivers.

Especially around southern Brittany, great stone monoliths laid out in patterns predicting the paths of the sun and moon show us that a highly organized and contemplative race called France home as far back as 4,000 BC.

The unborn nation's attraction as a fertile and geographically central destination became increasingly evident in the few hundred years before Christ. The warriorlike Celts filtered down from the north and took charge of the upper half of contemporary France for 700 years or more.

At roughly the same time, the Greeks arrived in the south, establishing an outpost that would one day become the thriving port of Marseille. The Greeks, beset by marauders in the 2nd century BC, called on their allies, the Romans, to aid them.

The Romans did and, liking what they saw of the south of France (and who wouldn't), settled in, ultimately establishing bustling cities at Aix, Nimes, Arles, and other spots along the Rhône and Saône river valleys extending north into Burgundy. That Roman influence in the South of France survives even today.

When the Celts in the north were assaulted by Germanic tribes from the northeast, they too called on the Romans. A big mistake. Left to their own devices, the Celts, led by their epic chief **Vercingétorix**, might ultimately have made mincemeat out of the Teutonic tribes who were trying to gain a foothold in Burgundy.

Instead, the great **Julius Caesar** himself answered the Celtic plea for help. Literally, he came, he saw, he conquered, turning on his Celtic allies and adding the northern climes, including Paris, to the Roman empire for a good 500 years.

Though Vercingétorix skunked Caesar in an initial skirmish, he later and inevitably succumbed to the greater power of the Roman forces and was hauled off to Rome, where he was executed.

ROMAN RULE (58BC-476AD)

Despite their military brutality, the Romans planted the first seeds of an organized national identity for the French peoples. Under Roman guard, peace reigned and, because of that, trade, education, and the arts flourished.

Even Paris, which had already become a trade center under a Celtic tribe known as the **Parisii**, profited.

The tribe's name, said to be derived from a Celtic word meaning "boat," was tribute to their skill as traders. And being traders, they had sought out a home on a major river — in this case the Seine, where there also happened to be a well-traveled north-south highway.

Savvy, too, about the ways of war, the Parisii were drawn to the natural protection offered by an island in the middle of the Seine. That island became known as the **Ile de la Cité** and is still today at the very heart of Paris.

Thus, Paris truly sprang from the serpentine river that now divides the city roughly in half from the east toward the west.

The Romans arrived in 52 BC, bringing order to the tribal chaos in their typically aggressive but efficient fashion. They soundly defeated the Parisii in a battle on the Left Bank not far from where the Ecole Militaire (7th arrondissement) now stands, and, by the first century AD, they had rebuilt the settlement on the Ile de la Cité and renamed it **Lutètia**.

The Romans were the first to significantly expand the town off of the island and onto the Left Bank. In the neighborhood later called the Latin Quarter, they built temples, a forum, baths, and an amphitheater known as Arènes, the remains of which can be found off of the rue Monge (5th arrondissement).

The Roman years, up through to the 5th century, were noted by an expanding wine trade (what a surprise), a devastating barbarian occupation, and the heroics of two Christian saints.

Romans objected when **Saint Denis**, Paris's first Christian bishop, attempted to convert Parisians en masse. For his troubles, he was beheaded on a Right Bank hilltop later named Mons Martyrium, or **Montmartre** (18th arrondissement). Legend has it that Saint Denis retrieved his severed head and marched to where the cathedral by his name now stands six miles north of Paris's Porte de la Chapelle.

Sainte Geneviève won the hearts of Paris in 451. At the time, the settlement had been abandoned by Roman troops who feared Attila the Hun, who was marching through France. But Geneviève, a 15-year-old of intense religious conviction, persuaded Parisians not to flee the city, saying Attila would not come.

Fortunately, Attila chose for his own reasons to steer clear and Geneviève was later canonized. In her honor, the hill on which the Sorbonne and the Panthéon now stand became known as **Mount Sainte-Geneviève** (5th arrondissement).

THE DARK AGES (476-987)

The next several centuries were rough ones, marked by war, floods, epidemics, and mere neglect. No wonder it was called the Dark Ages.

The mid-400s were particularly unpleasant, with the ailing Roman hierarchy being pounded by a series of barbarian tribes, including the **Huns**, who plundered much of the north, and the **Visigoths**, who swarmed over the Aquitaine region of southwestern France.

The late-400s saw the ascent of the Franks, whose roots were in modern-day Belgium and who were led by **Clovis I**. In some ways, the imperious Clovis was the first true king of France. It wasn't that he ruled all of what would become France, but he certainly ran roughshod over a mighty chunk of it.

He was also a clever politician, marrying a Gallic princess from Burgundy and adopting the Roman Catholic faith. The two moves enabled him to preside more peacefully and to bring the increasingly influential powers of Christianity onto his side of the fence.

Clovis is also credited with adopting Lutètia as his capital and renaming the city Paris.

Unfortunately, Clovis's heirs fought viciously over the empire and ultimately ripped it apart. In the late 700s, **Charlemagne**, a Frank himself, inherited the throne from his father, Pepin I, and consolidated power again.

It was during Charlemagne's time that feudalism emerged on a more formalized basis. He and rulers that followed began to award fiefs to loyal warriors and aristocrats. He also allowed these vast properties to be passed on to heirs, thus beginning what would become the herditary lines of a propertied class that hired other classes as laborers.

During this period, when dukes and marquises often battled one another over what belonged to whom, a wave of immigrants from Britain occupied Brittany and, later, throngs of **Vikings** invaded Normandy.

The powerful and cunning Vikings threatened the French crown until king Charles the Simple proved he wasn't so simple after all and coopted the Viking chief by naming him count of Rouen and Normandy in 911.

The Vikings settled in for good.

CIVILIZATION TAKES HOLD (987-1335)

After a quick succession of nominal kings with such unflattering sobriquets as "the Bald," "the Stammerer," and "the Fat," **Hugh Capet** took the throne in 987, declaring Paris his base and setting in motion a period of magnificent growth.

Civilization began to take hold in the 11th century. Guilds for river traders, butchers, and other craftsmen were established. These organizations grew increasingly influential over time, laying the groundwork for citizen participation in government.

It was also during this time that Philippe II built a wall around Paris and constructed a small fortress at the western edge named the **Louvre** (1st arrondissement). It was not until the late 1300s that the Louvre was expanded and transformed into a grand palace.

Notre-Dame (4th arrondissement), which would become the gem of Parisian Gothic architecture, was begun on the Ile de la Cité in 1163, followed not long afterward by the elegant **Sainte-Chapelle** cathedral a stone's throw away. In the 1200s, the University of Paris and the still famous **Sorbonne** college were established on the Left Bank in the Latin Quarter (5th arrondissement).

The city center had begun to take a now recognizable shape, with government based on the Ile de la Cité, intellectual pursuits on the Left Bank, and business concerns on the Right.

The church also grew more powerful during this era, giving kings a special cachet by blessing them and pushing various supposedly noble Crusades (Louis IX became the only French king to be sainted in thanks to his daring deeds during the religious quests). The mighty Benedictine abbey at Cluny nurtured its version of separate but equal clout by opening hundreds of dependant houses across Burgundy.

At the same time, a sort of political maelstrom rocked the fledgling nation, with dukes and marquises bickering and sometimes warring with one another and the king. Nothing illustrates the bizarre and divisive politics quite so well as the fact that **William the Conqueror**, duke of Normandy, went off on his own in 1066 and conquered England, becoming king of the British isles while remaining only a duke in the Viking warrior's adopted home of France.

Over the decades, William's successors added to London's holdings in France, expanding from Normandy to Aquitaine (southwestern France), Brittany, and Gascony. The illustrious and devious dukes of Burgundy then declared an alliance with the British. In essence the British throne controlled the entire western half of France and bracketed Paris on the east through its political ties to Burgundy.

The French throne was near collapse. All-out war was near.

WAR & RENAISSANCE (1336-1598)

The 14th and 15th centuries were predictably rocky. There was natural havoc, in the form of the Black Death in the mid-1300s. And there was political upheaval, including internal unrest over high taxes, peasant uprisings (the precursors to the Revolution itself 200 years later), and what became a seemingly interminable war with England.

In 1336, Edward, king of England and duke of Gascony (southwestern France), renounced his allegiance to Philippe VI, king of France. He claimed that as grandson to the French king Philippe IV, he was the heir to the French throne, not Philippe, who was grandson to Philippe III. (Well, you can see that this was sort of an ugly family squabble fought on an epic plain.)

The result of their tensions was what became known as the **Hundred Years War**, which formally endured for 138 years. The French were mauled for decades, their cities burned to the ground, and their people massacred. The French throne was finally seized by the English in 1418 and would not be recaptured until 1437.

The turning point of this war came at the hands of **Jeanne d'Arc**. She is credited with having rousted Charles VII out of exile, as well as out of his stuporous failure to lead. Given troops by the king, she then retook the pivitol Loire valley city of Orléans from the British in 1429.

While enabling the French king to resume command, Jeanne herself was captured by the Burgundian dukes who still sympathized with the English. In fact, they sold their precious prisoner to the English, who tried her and burned her at the stake in Rouen in Normandy.

Louis XI, the successor to Charles VII, not wanting to witness a repeat of the near disintegration of the French monarchy, set about in the late 1400s to subdue all the formerly independent dukes and to establish a unified nation at last.

The Renaissance of the 16th century was somewhat kinder to France. King François I was the champion of the movement, having voyaged to Italy and gained an uncommon appreciation for arts and letters. He brought Leonardo da Vinci to France, and either built or vastly remodeled a slew of magnificent castles that still dot the Loire Valley. He also undertook the expansion of the Louvre in Paris.

In fact, Paris thrived during this era. Reflecting Italian architectural inspiration, a magnificent **Hôtel de Ville** (4th arrondissement), or city hall, was built on the Right Bank across from Notre-Dame. In 1564 Catherine de Medicis ordered the **Palace of the Tuileries** and a magnificent garden be constructed just west of the Louvre.

At the close of the century, the classical **Pont Neuf** was constructed, connecting the western tip of the Ile de la Cité with both banks, as it does today. It was the first bridge without houses on its sides and is the oldest of the more than thirty bridges in the city.

Thanks to the money of the bourgeois class, the intellect of French universities, and the reputation of such writers as Rabelais, Paris gained a reputation as a European center of the arts and highbrow debate. Unfortunately, one of those debates, fueled in the later 1500s by new-fangled printing presses humming overtime in Paris, led to the next major war and undid a great deal of the unity the kings had sought after the Hundred Years War.

This debate centered on religion and, catalyzed by Martin Luther in Germany and Jean Calvin in France, pitched the Catholic power structure against an increasingly aggressive tide of Protestantism.

The result: more bloodshed, probably the worst of which occurred in Paris in August 1572 when, on Saint-Bartholomew's day, thousands of Protestants known as Huguenots were slaughtered in accordance with a devious plan arranged by Charles IX, Catherine de Medicis, and others. Bodies littered the Seine. The story is partially told in the epic 1994 French film, *La Reine Margot*.

Religious war flamed on for 36 years before Henri IV, desperate to bring an end to the internal strife, converted to Catholicism, was welcomed back to Paris in 1594, and enacted the **Edict of Nantes** in 1598 in an effort to stabilize Catholic and Protestant relations.

EXPANSION & THE SUN KING (1598-1788)

For awhile, things were better. Under Henri IV and later under Louis XIII's able "manager," **Cardinal Richelieu**, internal political order was largely restored, the monarchy benefited by a more centralized management of taxation and bureaucracy, various marriages were arranged with foreign powers to keep possible invaders at bay, and a renewed national pride swelled up in the country.

The 16th and 17th centuries were also a time of imperialist expansion, as France set sail for Africa, the New World, India, and other far off lands, claiming many of them for herself and the king.

In Paris in the mid-1600s, growth continued rapidly on the Right Bank. The elegant **Place des Vosges** (4th arrondissement) was built in the Marais (meaning "marsh") district, the Louvre and Tuileries palaces were linked, and the Palais Cardinale (later **Palais Royal**) was constructed for Cardinal Richelieu.

On the river, the **Pont Royal** was built to span the Seine west of the Ile de la Cité, and the Ile Saint-Louis (4th arrondissement) was fashioned out of two tiny islands just east of the Ile de la Cité. On the Left Bank, the luxurious **Jardin des Plantes** (5th arrondissement) was established, as was the marvelous **Luxembourg Palace** (now home to the French Senate, in the 6th arrondissement) with gardens that still attract locals by the thousands.

The stage of prosperity was therefore set for **Louis XIV**, who ruled from 1643 to 1715 and would become France's most memorable king.

Louis XIV continued the orgy of intellectual pursuit, architectural oppulence, and imperialist growth with the invaluable aid of **Jean-Baptiste Colbert**, his superintendent of buildings and finance minister. In Paris, broad avenues replaced ramparts, the early version of the **Champs-Elysées** (8th arrondissement) was laid out just west of the expanding city, the **Place des Victoires** was built, then the **Place Vendôme**.

The **Hôtel des Invalides** (7th arrondissement), to the west on the Left Bank, was erected for destitute military veterans, and even further west, eight miles from the current Porte d'Auteuil, **Versailles** went up. Construction of this palace of palaces, with such luxuries as 1,400 fountains, required the efforts of 36,000 dedicated builders and artisans.

The era during and just after Louis XIV saw some of the nation's most brilliant minds flower. **Voltaire**, **Rousseau**, **Diderot** and others were the cream of the crop. Arts and literature blossomed, as did the bourgeois class that seemed always to profit no matter how many wars the country continued to wage.

Politically, Louis pressed hard for a stronger centralized government and indulged a craving to increase his monarchal sway by declaring war on Holland, Spain, the Germans, and the English. Louis lost most of the wars and ran up a horrendous national debt. He and his successors, Louis XV and Louis XVI, unwisely sought to staunch the flow of royal funds by raising taxes time and again.

The gap between the rich and the poor grew ever wider, especially around Paris, where the suburbs were bursting with a working class made desperate by hunger and abuse. Food shortages spurred riots from 1775 through 1788. Local parliaments then began to balk at the crown's efforts to raise taxes that would dig into their own bourgeois pockets.

In short, the seeds of revolution had been planted and were about to blossom.

REVOLUTION & THE EMPIRES (1789-1870)

Revolution came knocking on the door to the 400-year-old **Bastille** prison July 14, 1789. In truth, there were only a handful of prisoners at the Bastille (12th arrondissement), but the raid and its subsequent destruction symbolized what the populace thought would be a new order. The Revolution also galvanized Paris as the indisputable centerpoint of French existence, whether viewed in political, economic, or artistic terms.

Violence became a way of life for several decades. The Revolution claimed 1,200 lives in the September massacres of 1792, the first year of the formally declared First French Republic (France is now on its Fifth, meaning it has had five constitutions in little more than 200 years). Many of the dead were true loyalists to the crown, and many happened simply to have been in the wrong place at the wrong time.

The following January, **Louis XVI** was taken to the guillotine in the Place de la Concorde (8th arrondissement) and executed, followed the next autumn by **Marie Antoinette**, his enormously unpopular queen from Austria.

The thirst for blood worsened during the **Reign of Terror** in 1793 and 1794, when the National Assembly passed the Law of Suspects. According to this expedient edict, anyone suspected of treason was automatically judged guilty. Consequently, another 20,000 people in Paris alone were guillotined.

In the countryside, things were just as bad. Local revolutionary committees slaughtered landowners, tax collectors, and just about anyone else they didn't cre for. Terrified aristocrats handed over their estates to "The Nation" and mobs ripped down castles and even some churches.

The damage to historic religious properties was awesome and, though many were skillfully repaired, the blind visciousness of Revolutionary gangs is still evident in cracked tombs and toppled towers.

The newly proclaimed national republic saw several political parties seize power, each of which in turn was found guilty of some heinous crime and each of which was quickly toppled (along with their leaders' heads). The Girodins, Danton, Robespierre, all of them ultimately fell victim to the chaos they had nurtured in an effort to rid the country of the monarchy and the aristocratic regime.

The Directory, a bumbling conservative faction, was the last to try their hand at governing before a young Corsican soldier took charge at gunpoint in 1799. The horrifying national bloodletting was finally quelled by one of the most violent men of all, **Napoleon Bonaparte**.

This was a good news-bad news proposition. The good news was that he ended the mindless violence, dictated a largely workable constitution, instated a legal framework called the **Code of Napoleon** (many of whose legal tenants still gird French law), and reduced inflation.

The bad news was that he had a vision of French supremacy akin to that of Hitler's dreams for Germany a century later. Napoleon immediately marched off to war.

At the height of Napoleon's power, he had dealt the Holy Roman Empire a fatal blow and ruled a huge swath of western Europe stretching from the heel of Italy up through Switzerland, Germany, and Belgium to Holland. Poland too was annexed.

Only Britain and, later, Russia eluded his tyrannical grasp. Ultimately Napoleon was defeated by the Russians in 1814 and then, after he escaped exile, he was bested again by the British in 1815. France was stripped of its new lands and ordered to pay costly restitution.

After Napoleon's final exile to the island of Saint Helena, the task of governing the nation bordered on the impossible. Paris reeled from economic strain. A cholera epidemic wiped out 19,000 residents in 1832, and two more revolutions, one in 1830 and a second in 1848, transformed the streets of Paris into a battleground between the classes.

Once again the people looked for a savior and once again they turned to a Bonaparte. Profiting from the General Assembly's decision in 1848 to hold the first national presidential election, **Louis Napoleon Bonaparte**, Napoleon's ambitious nephew, won by a landslide.

Three years later, under the pretext that the General Assembly was attempting to strip the people of the right to vote, Napoleon shut down the Assembly and, exactly one year later, declared himself **Napoleon III**, Emperor. (Clever man.)

Surprisingly, it was a good thing he took charge. Ultimately, his wisdom triumphed over his hunger for pure power.

Over time, he enlarged the powers of the Assembly and the Senate, allowed for a freer press, increased the country's industrialization (which began several decades after that in Britain), improved banking institutions, pressed for new colonial acquisitions in Indochina and Africa, and even made a temporary ally of Britain in successful efforts to defeat the Russians in the Crimea.

Most importantly for Paris proper, Napoleon III put **Baron Georges-Eugène Haussmann**, the local prefect, in charge of a total facelift for the city. Haussmann is largely responsible for the lasting grandeur of Paris, having ruthlessly cleared slums, opened up the grand avenues, vastly improved the water and sewage systems, constructed new docks, and developed parkland. Under his watch, Paris bloomed into an enviable world capital.

THE THIRD REPUBLIC (1870-1914)

Then Napoleon III made a fatal mistake, allowing himself to be duped by duplicitous German politicians into going to war against Prussia in

1870. His ill-equipped army was crushed, he himself was captured, and, less than a year later, the Prussians marched down Haussmann's beautiful avenues. The Second Empire was over and the Third Republic began its long reign.

The last of the 1800s and the years leading up to World War I were politically chaotic for the French, with the government changing prime ministers as often as if it were trying on new hats in a boutique.

Conservatives and even bigoted right wingers took control for some time, the worst of the lot instigating the dreaded **Dreyfus Affair**, which caused a deep divide in the French political landscape at the turn of the century. Alfred Dreyfus, a captain in the army, had the misfortune to be Jewish at a time when anti-Semites controled the army.

In an effort to stigmatize Jews nationwide, a group of conspirators framed him, convincing the courts that he had sold military secrets to the Germans. He was quickly carted off to Devil's Island, and it was many years before he was finally exonerated.

Fortunately, during these bleak political times, the architectural and cultural forces of France thrived. Some historians even suggest that it was a century of violence, defeat, and corruption that spurred a Romantic era capable of works like the **Eiffel Tower** (built in 1889) and the Impressionist movement.

Literature, music, and the art world flourished like never before, led by giants such as Gustave Flaubert, Emile Zola, Charles Baudelaire, Maurice Ravel, Claude Debussy, Edouard Manet, Henri Matisse, Pierre-Auguste Renoir, and Vincent Van Gogh. The list goes on and on.

Emile Zola's magnificent Rougon-Macquart series of novels, written from 1871 to 1893, are probably the most profound literary chronicles of a culture ever composed. In them, he captures virtually every facet of French life, from tramps and railroad engineers to high society and the Dreyfus Affair.

The artistic and literary world continued to flourish into the early 1900s. One of the most notable achievements was Marcel Proust's haunting *Remembrance of Times Past*, the first volume of which came out in 1913.

But the following year, the arts were put on hold and the whole world held its breath as the melange of European political alliances, all meant to somehow keep all the potential tyrants politically bound into passivity, came completely unraveled.

THE WORLD WARS (1914-1945)

Ugly reality and international crisis returned in 1914, when the German army slogged its way through Belgium to within a few miles of Paris. The French government fled to Bordeaux and the French army threw everything they had at the Kaiser's crew, even using taxis to rush troops to the front.

The Germans were held in the battle of the Marne, but the French lost hundreds of thousands of men in the first few months of what would become history's most gruesome exercise in military futility.

The Germans were effectively defeated four years later at Verdun, by General Philippe Pétain (who would later run the traitorous Vichy government during World War II). But the cost of trench warfare was huge. The French lost more than 1.3 million men, and suffered another 3 million wounded. Almost half of the young men were gone, industries were crippled, farms were laid waste, inflation boomed, and the national debt grew to ominous proportions.

It wouldn't be until the late 1920s that the French economy began once again to pick up speed. But this momentum too was quickly lost in the Great Depression that began in 1929 with the New York Stock Exchange crash.

The hideous economy brought out the most fanatical right wingers in both France and in Germany, where the Nazi party grew quickly and Hitler began to undo the binders placed on his country by the Treaty of Versailles that had ended World War I.

France essentially stood by as Hitler marched on Czechoslovakia, then Austria, then Denmark, Holland and Belgium. War was at hand and the French, having hidden their heads in the sand, were ill prepared mentally, politically, and militarily to defend themselves against the storm of German tanks and bombers that swept across French borders.

On June 14, 1940, Hitler's rejuvenated German troops occupied Paris. A turncoat French government was established in the central spa town of Vichy with Pétain as its head. It was a disgraceful government, rooting out Jews, executing resisters, and providing laborers to the German armies. (Recent research suggests that François Mitterand, the Socialist president of France from 1981 to 1995, had more intimate ties to the Vichy government than was originally believed and maintained relations with some former Vichy leaders up through the 1980s. He responded that his relationship was necessary during the war years to aid resistance fighters.)

Finally, American, British, Canadian, and a token band of French troops landed on the beaches at Normandy on June 6, 1944. At great cost of lives, both military and civilian, the war was turned. In the following weeks, Allied armies devastated several French cities — an unfortunate necessity in flushing the German army out of France.

Members of the French resistance, sensing that the end of war was near, increased their harassment of the German occupation forces and, a little more than two months later, Paris was freed.

The liberation of Paris was both the city's most exhilirating and terrifying moment. True, the Allied troops seemed sure to drive out the Germans, but at Hitler's orders bombs had been placed under most of the significant Paris monuments. Level the city, Hitler demanded.

But German General von Choltitz, based in Paris, could not bring himself to carry out the orders. Thus, when American troops and a French garrison led by General Jacques Leclerc drove into Paris on August 19, they found the city intact.

General Charles de Gaulle, having marshaled the free French forces from exile in England, returned to his capital in a triumphant march down the Champs-Elysées August 26, 1944.

The Vichy government was instantly dissolved, Paris resumed its rightful place as the seat of power, an estimated 9,000 collaborators were executed, and, in a disturbingly brutish attempt to purge the nation of its demons, women who had shown favors to German troops were stripped naked and paraded with shaved heads up and down the streets.

POSTWAR GUILT

Despite reveling in a giddy atmosphere of regained freedom, France was also emotionally and politically troubled immediately after the war.

Plainly put, the French felt a stinging and well-deserved sense of guilt. They were intimately aware that collaboration with the Nazis had been painfully commonplace and that the famed Resistance forces, though active throughout the war, had not received the unwavering popular support they should have.

Even today, in discussions with French families, you are likely to hear tirades against the rampant corruption and empty denial of those who did nothing to thwart the German occupation forces. At the same time, without fail, these families proclaim that their own fathers or grandfathers were numbered among the few unerringly loyal Resistance members.

(This phenomenon of reconstructive memory is not unlike that seen more recently in the United States. A huge majority of Americans remember voting for John F. Kennedy in 1960, even though Kennedy could not possibly have won all those votes in his squeaker against Richard Nixon. The collective, self-healing memory shifted after Kennedy was shot, when the nation suffered an overpowering and unifying sense of grief and guilt.)

Jean-Paul Sartre, Simone de Beauvoir, Albert Camus, and other writers were at the heart of France's postwar intellectual debate, and it is easy to sense their discomfort in virtually all their writings from the time.

Sartre's *Troubled Sleep*, written in the late 1940s and de Beauvoir's *The Mandarins*, published in 1954, are especially keen in their dissection of the wartime struggle with collaboration and the postwar turmoil during which the past actions of even the dearest friends were held to the unforgiving scrutiny of hindsight.

These themes were also debated at length in articles pubished in *Les Temps Modernes*, a periodical founded by Sartre in 1945.

THE ECONOMIC BOOM

Economically, France was in very sad shape after the war. It had lost thousands of factories, hundreds of miles of roads and train tracks, and a staggering number of farms and homes. If there was a silver lining, it was that the nation's needs meant there would be jobs and, with jobs, relative prosperity.

Like the United States, France enjoyed an economic boom, especially in the 1950s and 1960s and especially in Paris, as younger generations abandoned small farming towns for the promise of education and better-paying jobs in the big city.

The coal and electric industries were nationalized, as were the country's largest banks and transportation companies. The government fashioned a remarkable net of social and health services and made them available to everyone. And schools sprang up everywhere to cope with the soaring population.

High tech industry took off. The French, having once lagged far behind other European states in industrialization, gradually assumed a leadership role in the latter half of the century.

They developed supersonic passenger planes (the SSTs, produced jointly with Britain), the 200 mph **TGV** (*train grande vitesse*, meaning "very rapid train"), an enviable network of toll highways criss-crossing the nation, and a phone system that offers users a free home computer called a Minitel. With a Minitel (if you can get your fingers to fit those tiny keys), you can look up phone numbers, reserve theater or plane tickets, consult psychics, join a singles club, or just about any other task you can complete by phone.

Despite occasional slow-downs, such as during the 1973 worldwide oil crisis caused by steep increases in the price of Arab crude, the French economy continued to grow, finally surpassing the British. Today in Europe, its economy is second only to Germany's.

France also played a key role in the creation of the **Common Market**, an increasingly powerful political tool that would bind European neighbors in an economic alliance that would theoretically prevent future wars. The alliance began in 1957, with the signing of the **Treaty of Rome** by France, Western Germany, Italy, Belgium, Holland, and Luxembourg.

Initially hesitant nations, impressed with the lower tariffs of unification and pressured by the increasing globalization of modern industry, later joined. Today, the European Community numbers fifteen countries and leaders have discussed the possibility of expanding into Eastern Europe.

POSTWAR PARIS

Paris itself grew like crazy after the war.

In the period from 1945 to 1959 alone, more than 60,000 housing units were built in the city. Paris expanded so quickly, in fact, that by the early 1960s, the government decided it was once again time to clear some slums and modernize.

To attract profitable tourists and improve the national image as a world power, classic monuments and buildings, black with soot after years of neglect, were also encased in scaffolds and blasted cleaned.

In the 1970s and 1980s, the government improved the local transportation system with a freeway (the *Périphérique*) that circled the city and with a network of commuter trains (the **RER**) that branched out into suburbs in all directions.

New monuments also rose, though they sometimes introduced unwelcome modern elements to revered neighborhoods. In the 1970s, for example, the food markets that had occupied Les Halles for centuries were replaced by a largely unpleasant multi-level mall sinking several stories into the ground.

Under President Georges Pompidou's watch, a hugely unpopular Montparnasse office tower (15th arrondissment, visible from anywhere in the city) was erected in the name of "Progress" in the neighborhood near the Select Café and other Left Bank landmarks.

For some, the last straw of modernism was the **Pompidou Arts Centre** (4th arrondissement), completed just north of the Hôtel de Ville. A monstrous tribute to Pompidou (who followed de Gaulle in the early 1970s), the center and its fine museum of contemporary art was designed with the ductwork, escalators, and other unsightly organs on the exterior of the structure.

Still, the Pompidou (or *Beaubourg* as many locals call it in reference to its immediate neighborhood) has defied its critics and become the most visited building in Paris.

POLITICS: DE GAULLE & COMPANY

Politically, postwar France had a somewhat dicey start. De Gaulle, having formed the provisional government, put a formal end to the Third Republic and gave women the vote for the first time ever.

Still, he did not like the look of the various parties squabbling for power and, pouting mightily because they did not accept him as the obvious national father-figure, entered political semi-retirement in 1947.

What immediately followed was not a pretty sight. Domestically, barely-contained chaos reigned. Prime ministers were supplanted on average every six months.

Internationally, the Vietnamese (led by Paris-educated Ho Chi Minh) stomped the French at Dien Bien Phu in 1954, then drove them out of the country (thus setting the stage for American "intervention").

In Africa, France granted independence to Tunisia and Morocco in 1956, but failed to move quickly enough in Algeria. The subsequent Algerian fight for independence was so fierce that France committed as many as 350,000 troops at a given time to quell the rebellion, and still they failed. Algeria became the French counterpart to America's Vietnam.

Algerian-backed terrorist acts became commonplace in Paris. Worse, in the late 1950s, a handful of French military leaders actually switched sides, invading Corsica in 1958 and threatening a military coup over their own nation.

As the French looked to Louis Napoleon for peace and stability in the mid-1800s, they now pleaded for de Gaulle's return. He was allowed to draft a new constitution giving the president enormous powers and, in short order, to assume the presidency himself.

Still, it would be 1962 before de Gaulle granted Algeria independence. Even today there are Algerian hostilities toward the French, this time led by Muslim extremists who object to Algeria's subservient economic relationship with the "infidels" of mother France.

The beginning of the end of de Gaulle's 10-year "reign" came in May 1968. Students, enraged over their antiquated university system, the war in Vietnam, and an assortment of often vague anti-establishment issues, staged violent riots in Paris that quickly spread throughout the country.

The date is hailed as a political turning point by the political left, which insists that the student demonstrations and subsequent sympathy strikes by millions of labor union members brought France into the modern era in terms of social awareness and political equality.

There was change in substance as well, especially in what had been a hugely overcrowded and impersonal university system. The massive universities were decentralized, students were granted a role in school management, and the student-professor ratio was eased. Labor unions also won concessions on unemployment, low wages, and job safety.

De Gaulle's initial response to the demonstrations was to dismiss the boisterous students as a minor and insignificant nuisance. Only after several days passed and after unions joined students in the streets did de Gaulle address the nation over the radio, rallying support from the right with platitudes about national pride.

In an obvious backlash to the violence of the riots, de Gaulle supporters staged their own demonstrations and, within weeks, reelected

Gaulist members to the National Assembly by a huge majority. It looked initially as if de Gaulle had maintained his political hold.

In reality, however, the war hero's allure had dimmed. For many, he was suddenly viewed as someone to be placed, with eternal thanks, on a pedestal in a museum. He was a symbol of the past at a time when the French were increasingly hungry for a progressive and prosperous future.

In 1969, de Gaulle floated a referendum in front of the voters, proposing various government reforms that included greater regional autonomy and reforms in the French Senate. He was a great believer in the political utility of referendums, having bypassed political opponents in the past by taking his cause to the people, who had shown him unquestioning support.

This time, things were different. The referendum was soundly defeated.

Once again pouting mightily, de Gaulle skulked off the job. He never formally resigned. He said he was going off to write his memoires and he died a year later.

THE POST-DE GAULLE ERA

De Gaulle was followed by other conservatives, first Pompidou, who had once served as de Gaulle's prime minister and who died in office of cancer, and then, in 1974, **Valery Giscard d'Estaing**. A dashing younger man, Giscard shocked the staid older generations and won favor with younger supporters by lowering the vote to 18 and making abortion and contraceptives more easily available.

But the significant national political shift that some had predicted right after the May 1968 strikes did not come until 1981, when a coalition of French intellectuals, liberals, and Communists backed socialist **François Mitterand** for president and he won.

The election was fascinating in that de Gaulle and Mitterand had sparred for decades. Mitterand had actually worked for the Vichy government during the war, while de Gaulle had fled to exile. Mitterand was ever the intellectual, while de Gaulle had capitalized on a military career base.

In the years after the war, Mitterand had staked out the moderate left, while de Gaulle symbolized the conservative right. In 1965, the only year de Gaulle was elected president by popular vote, Mitterand was his challenger, winning 45 percent of the vote.

Thus, the election in 1981 of Mitterand seemed to signal the final rejection of de Gaulle and his stodgy political principles. But for all their placard-waving activism, the French are wary of sudden change.

As a result, Mitterand's leftist visions were quickly dulled by compromise and practicality. Voters insured he would toe a moderate line in 1986 and again in 1991 when they elected a conservative majority in the

General Assembly, forcing him to recommend equally cautious prime ministers.

Giscard would have liked another shot at the presidency, and **Edouard Balladur**, Mitterand's most recent prime minister, had clearly positioned himself for the top spot. Balladur was polling strong, despite having caved weakly in the face of demonstrations by employees of Air France and by students seeking future job guarantees. Balladur's government was also staggered in late 1994 by the resignation of three ministers under clouds of corruption.

But no one wanted the job more than **Jacques Chirac**, a conservative who served briefly as prime minister under Giscard and Mitterand, and became Paris's first popularly elected mayor in 1977 (those in the 1800s had been appointed and a federal ministry had governed Paris since). Despite having also simulataneously served as prime minister, Chirac remained a very popular mayor, holding highrises at bay, opening new squares, refurbishing the Champs-Elysées, and hiring a green-clad army of workers to scour the streets of Paris daily.

There is even a motorcycle-bound dog-doo patrol (though here Chirac and his patrol seem clearly to be losing the battle). It all seems to have paid off, because in May 1995 Jacques Chirac was elected president of France.

POSTWAR FRENCH PRESIDENTS

Fourth Republic
- *Vincent Auriol (socialist) 1947-1954*
- *René Coty (conservative) 1954-1958*

Fifth Republic
- *Charles de Gaulle (Gaullist) 1959-1969*
- *George Pompidou (Gaullist) 1969-1974*
- *Valéry Giscard d'Estaing (conservative) 1974-1981*
- *François Mitterand (socialist) 1981-1995*
- *Jacques Chirac (conservative) 1995-present*

5. PLANNING YOUR TRIP

WHEN TO VISIT - CLIMATE & WEATHER

You're not likely to come to France for the climate, and it's a good thing.

Oh, there are plenty of nice days during the spring and fall, when the temperatures hover in the mid-60s and the chill of the evenings can be warded off with a light sweater. But the winters are dark and cold (temperatures plop down in the 20 to 30 degree range) and the heavy summer days in the north feel much hotter than the 75 degree norms.

And then there's the rain. Lots of it, say the experts, because winds and fronts off the blustery Atlantic and warmer Mediterranean collide over France, causing all sorts of meteorological grief.

April, despite what you may have heard, is often one long brooding storm. Floods are commonplace in the south. And it's not uncommon during winter and early spring for three or four vicious hailstorms to tear through places like Brittany and Normandy during the course of a single afternoon, or for clouds to sit atop whole sections of the country for days on end.

The exception, of course, is the southeastern quarter of the country, which enjoys a warmer climate and a dryer kind of heat. At times in the summer, the heat can be sharp and stinging, but you can always jump into the nearest available pool or refreshing cove.

Bottom line, the best months for a visit are May, June, September, and October (except for skiers, who arrive in droves in December, January and February). And not just because of the weather. During the winter holidays, many restaurants and shops close down. And during July and August, many hotels and restaurants hike up their rates, and the south of France is elbow-to-elbow tourists from all over the world.

The very worst time for a visit is August, when the French abandon Paris and the northern cities en masse. Literally thousands upon thousands of them rush off on holiday to the South of France and the United States.

If you want to visit Paris, the exodus may seem as if it's good news. But the bad news is that before the French leave, they padlock their shops, bakeries, and bistros for two to four weeks.

Believe it or not, we have seen hotels hang a sign on the door announcing that the staff has gone south for August. So your shopping, dining and hotel options are limited for the month, especially if you want to escape the most touristy and congested quarters of the northern cities.

PASSPORTS & VISAS

You will, of course, be obliged to show a current passport. No special visas are currently required of American visitors who stay less than three months. If you are staying longer, you need to contact a French consulate to ask how to apply for a long-stay visa, which is a somewhat tortured process brought to you by the nation who invented the word "bureaucracy." *The French Embassy is in Washington at 4101 Reservoir Rd. NW, Washington, D.C. 20007; 202-944-6200.*

No vaccines are required. (A health note: Though France has nationalized medicine, little if any free assistance would be available to you as a tourist, so be sure that you have proper health insurance.)

CUSTOMS

Arriving

Customs probably won't be a factor for you until you return to the States. Nonetheless, when you arrive in France you will be funneled through a French Customs area, where signs will lead you to one line if you have something to declare, and another line if you don't. Usually, you sail right through. On occasion, French authorities will stop someone and check their bags. Mainly, they do it to keep up appearances.

And once inside the terminal, DO NOT leave your baggage unattended. We have seen bags scooped up quickly and blown up in the parking lot by police bomb squads who worry probably a bit too much about terrorists. And it must be quite embarrassing to gather up your charred underwear in front of a crowd of curious strangers.

Returning

At some point during your flight home you will be given a small Customs form to complete. You are supposed to declare the total value of all the items you acquired that were gifts or purchases (even from duty-free shops) and that are in your possession. Only one form is required per family.

As a United States resident, you are allowed, duty-free, no more than one liter of booze (no matter what type), and no more than 200 cigarettes or 100 cigars (no Cuban cigars at all, for the obvious reason). Though baked goods and cured cheeses are allowed, other fresh food is forbidden. All plants (even cuttings and seeds) must be declared. If you are carrying more than $10,000 in currency of any kind, that too must be declared.

You are allowed a total exemption of $400 worth of items. If you exceed your $400 exemption, you will be asked to pay a flat 10 percent duty on the next $1,000 worth of goods. After you pass the $1,400 plateau, each item you bring in is assessed a duty that applies to that particular type of item (there are countless incomprehensible formulas).

Duty can be paid by cash, check and, in some locations, credit cards. Traveler's checks can be used if the checks do not total more than $50 more than your assessed duty (they dislike giving change).

For more information, phone (703) 318-5900 in the Washington D.C. area, or 011.33.1.42.96.12.02 in Paris.

ARRIVALS & DEPARTURES
By Air
Aside from one or two flights (Delta Airlines) that take you directly to Nice, flights originating in the States head for Paris. Paris has two principle airports: Orly, a few miles south of the city, and Roissy-Charles-de-Gaulle, a few miles to the north. Both have all the conveniences and frustrations of a large urban airport.

There are plenty of duty free shops where you can find everything from silk scarves to CDs a little cheaper than they are in Paris stores (though they will probably still be more expensive than you can find in U.S. retail stores). Often, there are long lines at the ticket counters, so when your airline suggests you show up for a departure two or three hours before boarding time, they're not kidding.

Stepping off the plane, you will be guided en masse down various hallways and corridors until you reach small glass booths where you present your passport for what will probably be a cursory glance and stamp of arrival. From there, you move on to the luggage area and, afterwards, through customs (see above).

For information about Charles de Gaulle, phone 1.48.62.22.80 or 1.48.62.12.12. For information about Orly, phone 1.49.75.15.15. or 1.49.75.52.52.

Airlines
Some airlines have non-stop service from American cities to Paris. It's usually a bit more expensive, but, in our view, it's worth the money. If you

have had to wait around to switch planes in the States, you will be dog-tired when you arrive here and your first day will be lost in a fog of exhaustion.

Travel agents can help you find charter services. The **Alliance Française**, which is a Paris-based language school with tiny campuses in many major American cities, is one of many cultural organizations that offer worthwhile package deals. If you want to do a bit of comparison pricing, which we recommend highly, here are some airlines to try:

• **Air France** *(Paris 1.42.99.23.64)*
• **American** *(U.S. 800-433-7300, Paris 1.42.89.05.22)*
• **Continental** *(U.S. 800-525-0280, Paris 1.42.99.09.09)*
• **Delta** *(U.S. 800-221-1212, Paris 1.47.68.92.92)*
• **Northwest** *(U.S. 800-225-2525, Paris 1.42.66.90.00)*
• **TWA** *(U.S. 800-221-2000, Paris 1.49.19.20.00)*
• **United** *(U.S. 800-241-6522, Paris 1.48.97.82.82)*
• **USAir** *(U.S. 800-772-4368, Paris 1.49.10.29.00)*

From the Airport to the City

If you have a layover or are stopping in Paris, splurge and take a cab into the city. It will cost 100 to 200FF, but it will get your vacation off to a smoother, happier start. Remember that you will probably have flown through the night, gotten very little sleep, and will be tired and probably cranky. Your cab fare will be a bit higher than what the meter says because you will be charged extra for bags that go in the trunk.

You can save some money by taking the Air France bus into town. Regular buses are also available, but they are much slower and are not really equipped to handle lots of luggage.

Air France buses leave Charles de Gaulle for Porte Maillot, then the Arc de Triomphe about every 15 minutes, from 6 a.m. to 11 p.m. The ride can take a half hour to an hour, depending on traffic. From Porte Maillot or the Arc de Triomphe, both of which are on the Right Bank, you will have to continue to your hotel by cab or Metro.

Air France buses from Orly will drop you off at either the Gare Montparnasse or the Invalides Air Terminal, both of which are near the center of the Left Bank. Both Air France bus lines also work in reverse and can be taken to the airports at the end of your stay.

For Air France bus information, phone 1.43.23.97.10.

RER trains can also bring you into town from the airports. From Charles de Gaulle catch a short connector bus from the airport to the Roissy RER station, where you will take the B3 RER line into the very heart of Paris. There are several stops, running north to south through the city. From Orly, catch the C2 RER line, which will stop at several stations along the Seine on the Left Bank.

Trains run frequently from before 6 a.m. to just after midnight.

GETTING AROUND FRANCE

Air Travel Inside France

Air Inter, a subsidiary of the state-owned Air France, is your best bet. When they're not on strike (an annoyingly regular occurrence), they fly to just about anywhere in France you'd like to go and their rates are reasonable. *For information, phone 1.45.46.90.00 in Paris.*

Train Service

The French train service made headlines years ago when it introducted the **TGV**, which stands for *Train Grande Vitesse* or Very Rapid Train. One of the nation's most brilliant technological innovations, the TGV is a bullet-shaped train that offers speed, comfort and affordable fares.

The national **SNCF** train network, which combines the TGV and regular trains, is so reliable that one of the rote phrases taught in schools here is: *Les trains en France ne sont jamais en retard.* Which means, "The trains in France are never late." And it's true.

As with airlines, the center of the French train universe is Paris, which has six train stations: Montparnasse and Austerlitz on the Left Bank, and Saint-Lazare, Gare du Nord, Gare de l'Est, and Lyon on the Right Bank. The Paris station where you arrive or depart is determined by your place of geographic origin. For instance, if you are leaving for Brittany along France's west coast, you will depart from the Gare Montparnasse. If you are arriving from Burgundy to the southeast of Paris, you will be deposited at Gare de Lyon.

For information about SNCF destinations and fares, call 1.45.82.50.50 or 1.45.65.60.60. Travel agencies in the U.S. and Paris can also help with train schedules and ticket purchases.

All six SNCF stations are on Metro lines, so it is fairly easy to continue to your hotel by Metro. Taxi stands are also located at train stations.

- **Gare d'Austerlitz**, *55 quai d'Austerlitz (5th, M:Gare d'Austerlitz)*, serving southern France, southwestern France, Spain, and Portugal.
- **Gare de l'Est**, *place du 11 Novembre, 1918 (10th, M:Gare de l'Est)*, serving eastern France, southern Germany, Luxembourg, northern Switzerland, and Austria.
- **Gare de Lyon**, *20 boulevard Diderot (12th, M:Gare de Lyon)*, serving southern France, southeastern France, central France, Italy, Switzerland, and the Alps.
- **Gare Montparnasse**, *17 boulevard Vaugirard (15th, M:Montparnasse)*, serving western France.
- **Gare du Nord**, *18 rue de Dunkerque (10th, M:Gare du Nord)*, serving northern France, northern Germany, Belgium, Great Britain, and Holland.

• **Gare Saint-Lazare**, *13 rue d'Amsterdam (8th, M:Saint-Lazare)*, serving Normandy and Great Britain.

> ## TRAIN PASSES
>
> *If you want to do a lot of train travel in France, you can purchase a* **France Vacances Pass** *offering unlimited travel for particular lengths of time. Air France and SNCF also offer some package deals combining air and train travel. For information, contact Air France (see above), SCNF (see above), or the main French Tourist Information office at the address nearest you (see For More Information below).*
>
> **Eurorail passes**, *which are good for most of Europe, can also be used as extensively as you like in France. The passes must be purchased in the United States. For information, phone the offices in New York at (212) 308-3103.*

Car Rentals

All the major airports and train stations have the usual array of car rental agencies eager to separate you from your money. But if you're only visiting Paris, just say no to a car. Parking is expensive and often non-existent. The rules of the road are different than in the United States and accidents are stunningly common and complicated to resolve.

However, to really get a feel for other sections of the country— especially if you want to wander off the beaten path — you must have a car. To rent a car, you will need your American driver's license or an International Driver's License, which you can buy at AAA.

Some credit card companies provide car insurance when you pay for the rental with their card, but it is still a very good idea to buy all the basic coverage from the rental company. (Often you can get them to include the insurance free of charge.)

Rules of the road you must remember: one, the car coming from the right always has the right of way; two, stop signs are routinely ignored by other drivers; and three, seatbelts are required by law, even in the backseat.

Your travel agent can arrange for a rental car or you can do it yourself by phoning the 800 numbers of the rental agencies listed below. *For 800 directory assistance in the U.S., dial 800-555-1212.*

If you are already in Paris, car rental agencies can be found in the *Location* section of the Paris Yellow Pages. In fact, you will be better off if you avoid the central number and call the office nearest your hotel.

Car Rental Agencies in Paris
• **Avis**, *1.46.09.92.12, Fax 1.40.71.81.81.*
• **Car Rental**, *1.48.08.31.31.*

- **Eurodollar**, *1.49.38.77.77, Fax 1.49.38.77.72.*
- **Europcar**, *1.30.44.90.00 or 1.30.43.82.82.*
- **Eurorent**, *1.45.67.82.17, Fax 1.40.65.91.94.*
- **Hertz**, *1.47.88.51.51.*
- **Prestige Limousines**, with chauffeur, *1.42.50.81.81.*

WHAT TO PACK

You'll probably want to bring at least one semi-formal or business-like outfit (ties, dresses, that sort of thing) for the better restaurants. It's not that formal attire is required, but you will feel more at ease if you don't look like country bumpkins.

A lot of hotels have hair dryers, but they don't work very well, so you should toss one into your bag. And don't forget a converter and an adapter for the 220 volt power here. Converters and adapters can easily be found at Radio Shacks and travel shops.

If you're traveling extensively outside Paris, you will also want to find a store where you can buy a Michelin Atlas and the current Michelin Red Guide, which lists thousands of hotels and restaurants. The Red Guide's city maps complement the Atlas and can help guide you directly to the center of town and to your hotels. A bit of trivia: The **Michelin Man** — you know, the tubby guy composed of a pile of tires — is known in his home country of France as **Bibendum**. More trivia: Bibendum is also the name of one of London's hippest restaurants and is set in ye olde tyre shop in the Knightsbridge section of town.

FOR MORE INFORMATION

Write or call the **French Tourist Office** nearest you:
- *610 Fifth Avenue, Suite 222, New York, New York 10020; (212) 757-1125*
- *645 North Michigan Ave., Suite 630, Chicago, Illinois 60611; (312) 337-6301*
- *2305 Cedar Spring Road, Suite 205, Dallas, Texas 75201; (214) 720-4010*
- *9454 Wilshire Boulevard, Suite 303, Beverly Hills, California, 90212; (310) 272-2661*

6. BASIC INFORMATION

ELECTRICITY

The current in France runs at a menacing 220 volts and the plugs are shaped differently. If you have an electric razor or a hair dryer or whatever, you will need a current converter and a plug adapter. Even so, say many electronic whiz-kids, machines with motors will eventually burn out. Message: bring cheap hairdryers.

HEALTH SERVICES

Health care in France is first-rate and completely modern, which is not to say French doctors do everything exactly the way American doctors do. There is nationalized health care and, on occasion, this will cover emergencies. But you are still much better off having your own medical and especially dental coverage. Your forms will be completed in French and you will be billed in francs. Your Stateside carrier will convert the francs to dollars when they reimburse you.

Paris has an **American Hospital** with mostly American doctors and a bilingual staff *at 84 boulevard de la Saussaye, in Neuilly-sur-Seine, a close-in suburb to the west, not far from the Pont de Neuilly Metro stop and at the end of the no. 82 bus line. Phone 46.41.25.25.*

A comprehensive listing of English speaking doctors can be obtained from a women's organization known as **WICE**, *at 20 boulevard du Montparnasse, 75015 Paris (15th, M:Montparnasse), 45.66.75.70.* Another listing is included in *Bloom Where You're Planted*, a helpful book for local Americans published by **The American Church in Paris**, *65 quai d'Orsay, 75007 Paris (7th, M:Invalides), 47.05.07.99.*

Various emergency medical phone numbers are listed later in this section under "Essential Phone Numbers." Help is available around the clock. Pharmacies are clearly marked with green neon crosses. Medicines, including common aspirin, can only be purchased at a pharmacy.

Some pharmacies in Paris where you are likely to find someone who speaks English:

- **British & American Pharmacie**, *1 rue Auber (9th, M:Opéra), 47.42.49.40.*
- **Pharmacie Drugstore Saint-Germain**, *149 boulevard Saint-Germain (6th, M:Saint-Germain-des-Prés), 42.22.80.00.*
- **Pharmacie Dhery** (24 hours), *84 avenue des Champs-Elysées (8th, M:George V), 45.62.02.41.*
- **Pharmacie Opéra**, *6 boulevard des Capucines (9th, M:Opéra), 42.65.88.29.*
- **Pharmacie Swann**, *6 rue Castiglione (1st, M:Concorde), 42.60.72.96.*

IN PRINT IN ENGLISH
Library
- **The American Library**, *10 rue du General Camou, 75007 Paris (7th, M:École Militaire), 45.51.46.82.*

Newspapers
- *The International Herald Tribune*, which is largely a blend of pieces from the paper's owners: The Washington Post and The New York Times. 9FF, daily except Sunday.
- *USA Today*
- The European edition of *The Wall Street Journal*
- *The Financial Times, of London*
- *The European*

Magazines
A variety of the usual is available in the big cities, including *Time, Newsweek, Vanity Fair, Glamour, Rolling Stone*. There are also several local products in Paris, where more than 20,000 Americans are said to live:
- *Boulevard*, a glossy bi-monthly for the chic and wanna-be chic. 20FF.
- *France USA Contacts* (FUSAC), a bi-weekly advertiser which is quickly becoming the Bible of classified ads for Americans in Paris. Free.
- *Paris Voice*, a monthly tabloid. Free.
- *Pariscope*, an essential weekly listing every cultural and nightlife event in town. Has an English section. 3FF.
- *TimeOut, Paris Guide*. Free.

PEEING IN FRANCE
The three most important things in the life of a tourist are: one, appropriate attire for the weather; two, comfortable footwear; and three, a place to answer nature's call.

Layering and the willingness to sacrifice some style in favor of comfort will probably get you through the first two. But what about number three? In a strange city? In a foreign country, where they don't have the same standards about these things that we do?

It takes a little knowledge, that's all. And, on occasion, strong thigh muscles.

Every café and restaurant has a bathroom. Usually they're in the basement (*sous sol*) and usually there's one sink in a common area, often with a telephone.

If you're a woman and haven't traveled much you may one day open the door with the silhouette of a woman on the it, look at the hole in the floor inside, and think there's been some mistake or that someone stole the toilet. But no. It's called a Turkish toilet and it requires balance and good quads.

As a general rule, French bathrooms (*toilettes*) are not as clean as those back home. Paper towels are rare (we'd love to have the hot air dryer concession). And it's not uncommon for women to have to walk past a urinal to get to the ladies' room.

Where to go (so to speak):
• Those hulking green cabins you sometimes see half-blocking the sidewalk represent the current incarnation of the streetside pissoir and they are better than you might imagine. The 2FF cost is minimal compared to extreme discomfort. They are heated and surprisingly clean for what they are. (They clean themselves seconds after you've stepped out.)
• All first class hotels have immaculate rest rooms. Keep your eyes peeled for the sign, look like you're registered, and see how the other half lives.
• Department stores almost always put the bathrooms on an upper floor, the theory being that you'll be tempted by all their fine wares to and from.

POST OFFICES

Whether you're visiting large cities or tiny hamlets, there is a post office near you. Look for the yellow *Poste* signs. There are often markers on city streetcorners, pointing the way to the nearest **Bureau de Poste**.

Offices are open from 8 a.m. to 7 p.m. Monday through Friday, and 9 a.m. to noon on Saturdays. The main post office in Paris, at 52 rue du Louvre (1st, M:Louvre) is open 24 hours a day for telegrams, phone calls, and general delivery (poste restant).

Air mail letters with one or two pages are 4,30FF to the United States.

Tabacs (bars which also carry tobacco) also sell stamps. In fact, the lines in a *tabac* are often shorter and quicker than they are in the post office, where the French do everything from pay their utility bills to conduct their banking.

Helpful phrase: *Je voudrais des timbres pour les êtats-Unis, s'il vous plaît.* Just hold up your fingers for how many you want.

MONEY & BANKING

You can't get more basic than money and, like Sally Bowles says in *Cabaret*, money makes the world go around. For France, and especially Paris, bring lots. You will spend more than you expect, and probably more than you want. But what's the point of coming all this way if you have to remember it as a time when you deprived yourself of the available pleasures just because things cost a bit much.

French **francs** come in coins for 1, 2, 5, 10 and 20FF, and in bills for 20, 50, 100, 200 and 500FF. *Centimes*, the French equivalent of cents, come in coins for 5, 10, 20 and 50 centimes.

Changing Money

The French Prime Minister Edouard Balladur, who is just aching to become president in 1995, has done an admirable job over the past year of propping up the French franc. As a result, the franc, like the French economy, has managed to level off after its tailspin during the recession of 1992 through 1994.

The franc has consistently traded at somewhere between five-to-one and six-to-one on the dollar. The financial section of your newspaper or your local bank should be able to tell you where it stands on any given day.

So, you ask, where do you pick up a few hundred francs? Some, but not all, American banks will have a modest amount of foreign currency in the vault. Likewise, some, but not all, French banks will exchange francs for dollars. Those that do will have a sign reading *Change* outside the door. Some of the upper crust hotels will help you out, but only if you are a guest and only at a crummy rate.

Whether you have cash or travelers checks, the most common way to change money in the larger towns and cities is at a *Change* bureau — usually a tiny storefront with signs outside showing the going rates of about twenty currencies.

Change bureaus often brag that they don't charge you for the change. Nonsense. They give you less than the full market value of your currency (compare their posted exchange rate with currency tables in that morning's *International Herald Tribune*), so there is a charge built into the exchange. You can sometimes find better exchange rates if you shop around a bit.

In the smaller towns and villages, it can sometimes be difficult to change money, so you should plan ahead, making sure you have enough cash to get you through.

Credit & ATM Cards

Most banks will give you a cash advance on a credit card.

Or — and this is the easiest method of all — if your ATM card is hooked into one of the major electronic banking systems, just do what you do at home: Find an ATM (they look just like they do in the States), punch in your secret four-digit personal identification code, and count the cash when it comes out the slot.

Banks will charge you a flat fee for these transactions (as they do in the States), or charge you a percentage by giving you a lower-than-market-value exchange rate, or both, depending on how greedy your bank is. (If you charge an advance at a French bank, it too will factor in a small cut.)

Important: You can save the cost of conversion fees by using your credit cards for meals and purchases because your bank will give you the full market value when it exchanges your charge in francs for its payment in dollars.

American Express

I was ticked off when I learned that even preferred customers are charged a conversion fee at **American Express**. What's the point of being preferred if you have to pay all the fees anyway.

However, American Express still does business bigtime in converting dollars to francs and issuing travelers checks to American tourists. The main offices in Paris are: *11 rue Scribe (9th, M:Opéra), 42.66.09.99*; and *12 Rond Pont Champs-Elysées (8th, M:Franklin-Roosevelt), 42.25.15.16. The offices are closed Sundays.*

A Special Tip

Another way to save conversion fees is to join the **American Automobile Association** in the United States and to buy travelers checks in French francs instead of dollars.

AAA gives you virtually the full market value on your exchange, has no service charge, and supplies you with French franc traveler's checks that will be honored at the full face value by virtually any bank or change bureau, as well as by most French stores, hotels and restaurants.

Sure, you still have to pay the membership fees for AAA, but that will come in handy next time you get a flat tire in the middle of the night.

SAFETY & TAKING PRECAUTIONS

France, even downtown Paris, experiences nothing approaching the violent crime that plagues American cities. This does not mean you should not be on your guard. Wallets and purses do get stolen, vandals do break into cars, and people are occasionally mugged.

Avoid empty dark streets late at night, watch out for pickpockets on crowded buses and subway cars, and keep your cool if those around you are losing theirs. Of the primary tourist neighborhoods in Paris, Pigalles and Les Halles are the only two where we sometimes feel a bit uncomfortable.

Police are often nearby. The emergency police phone number is *17*. *The central police station is at 208 rue Faubourg Saint-Honoré (8th, M:Ternes), 42.89.55.78.*

SOCIAL ORGANIZATIONS

- **American Center**, *51 rue de Bercy, 75012 Paris (12th, M:Bercy); 44.73.77.77.* Various American cultural programs and contacts.
- **American Women's Group in Paris**, *22bis rue Pétrarque, 75016 Paris (16th, M:Trocadéro); 47.55.87.50 or 47.55.87.51. Also at 49 rue Pierre-Charron, 75008 Paris (8th, M:Franklin-Roosevelt), 43.59.17.61.*
- **Association of American Residents Overseas**, *42.04.09.38.*
- **WICE**, a women's organization, (see above), *20 boulevard du Montparnasse, 75015 Paris (15th, M:Montparnasse); 45.66.75.70.*

TELEPHONES

France, which not long ago had an absolute disgrace of a telephone system, has now advanced beyond most countries.

Virtually any country in the world can be dialed direct, though you must tap into an international line by dialing 19, then the country code. For the United States, you would dial: 19, then 1, then the area code, then the phone number you want.

Other country codes can be found in the front of a French phone book (yellow or white pages). Or, if your French is good, dial 12 for directory assistance.

If you want to use an AT&T credit card or speak with an American operator, dial 19, then 0011, then wait for the recorded instructions.

If you are in Paris and want to phone a hotel or restaurant somewhere else in France, dial 16, then the number of the party. If you are outside Paris and want to phone a hotel in Paris, dial 1, then the number.

If you are in the U.S. and want to call a number in Paris direct, dial 011 for the international line, 33 for the country code, 1 for the city code of Paris, then the eight-digit number you want.

By the way, France does not have a touch tone system, so you won't be able to dial your bank's computer back home to check your balance. And, you'll be sad to know, you cannot dial 800 lines from France. You can only reach 800 lines by calling the operator and charging the call on a credit card as if it were a regular phone number.

Public Telephones

Though there are still coin-operated public phones in some bars, France was one of the first countries to eliminate coin-operated public phones on the streets. Hoping to discourage vandals who kept breaking into public phones in search of a few francs, the French devised phones that use cards that resemble credit cards.

These cards can be purchased most easily in **Tabacs** (which are bars which also sell tobacco — look for the *Tabac* sign outside), Metro stations and post offices. They are available for 40FF and last seemingly forever.

These can even be used to phone the United States from a pay phone.

In a rare burst of marketing genius, makers of the cards have circulated a myriad of designs and they are now collected in France the same way baseball cards are collected in the States.

Helpful phrase: *Je voudrais une télécarte, s'il vous plaît.*

TIPPING

In hotels, if someone carries your bags to your room, it is common to give a small tip of 10 or 20FF, depending on the amount of luggage, the character of the hotel, and whether the porter accidentally drops your luggage down two flights of stairs. It is also common to leave small loose change in an ashtray in the room in the morning as a tip for the maid who cleans your room — though this is often done only at the end of your stay.

In restaurants, the tip is included in the price of the meal (*servis compris*). If you have enjoyed a fine meal, it is common to leave an additional tip of 5 to 50FF, depending on the meal and the restaurant.

In the now rare case where the tip is not included, that fact will be prominently noted on the menu (*servis n'est pas compris*). If that is the case, a 10 to 15 percent tip is normal.

Five to 10FF should cover the cloak room attendant. Bathroom attendants expect 2 to 5FF.

For taxis, tip is included, though you might offer another 5 to 20FF, depending on the distance and your mood.

TOURIST OFFICES

Even small towns usually have an Office de Tourisme or a Syndicat d'Initiative. When you enter a town look for signs with a big "I" on them. They will guide you to the office.

We list at least one tourist office for every region we cover in the following regional chapters. Just look up your destination and then look under the "For More Information" subheading.

If you are visiting Paris, the **central tourist office**, *open during the week from 9 a.m. to 8 p.m., is located at 127 avenue des Champs-Elysées, 75008 Paris (8th, M:George V); 49.52.53.54, or fax 49.52.53.00.* Smaller offices are also found at the Eiffel Tower and all the train stations except Gare Saint-Lazarre.

WATER

Yes, you can drink the water. In fact, virtually every bistro or restaurant will want to know if you would like bottled water with or without bubbles (*gazeux ou sans gaz*) with your meal. However, you can save a few francs simply by requesting a small pitcher of tap water (*un pichet d'eau* or, in hip Paris parlance, *Chateau Chirac*, which is a reference to the revered Paris mayor).

If you want to be extra cautious, as many people recommend (especially our close friends John and Molly, who live in India — gee, I wonder why they worry about drinking water), order bottled water and avoid any brush with local waterborne germs.

ESSENTIAL PHONE NUMBERS

- *Information: 12*
- *Medical Emergency: 15*
- *Police: 17*
- *Fire and Any Emergency: 18*
- *Poison Center in Paris: 1.40.37.04.04*
- *American Hospital in Paris: 1.46.41.25.25*
- *Ambulance in Paris: 1.40.44.43.45*
- *SOS Medecins (medical emergency) in Paris: 1.47.07.77.77*
- *SAMU (medical emergency): Left Bank 1.45.67.50.50*
      Right Bank 1.42.45.50.50
- *24-Hour House Calls in Paris: 1.45.45.31.03*
- *24-Hour Pharmacy in Paris: 1.45.62.02.41*
- *Dental Emergency in Paris: 1.43.37.51.00*
- *SOS Help (crisis line) in Paris: 1.47.23.80.80*
- *SOS Avocats (legal help) in Paris: 1.43.29.33.00*
- *American Embassy in Paris: 1.42.96.12.02*
- *American Consulate in Paris: 1.42.96.12.02*
- *American Consulate in Marseilles: (16) 91.54.92.00*
- *American Consulate in Nice: (16) 93.88.89.55*
- *American Church in Paris: 1.47.05.07.99*
- *American Express (for stolen card) in Paris: 1.47.77.72.00*
- *American Express (for stolen checks): 05.90.86.00*
- *Visa (for stolen card) in Paris: 1.42.77.11.90*
- *Information in U.S.: (19) 1+Area Code+555-1212*

7. THE CUISINE OF FRANCE

It was hearty country cooking that first made a name for French cuisine – dishes like a cassoulet made with sausage, preserved duck, and white beans, or a *petit salé* of pork in a pool of lentils, or *coq au vin*, a free range chicken stewed in red wine laden with onions, carrots, and herbs.

The ingredients were fresh off the farm and the results enough to warm the coldest toes on the most bitter winter night.

Haute cuisine came along ages ago and jazzed things up with marvelously rich sauces. When many people think of French cuisine, they still envision plates drenched in heavy cream sauces. Not so.

About a decade and a half ago, culinary superstars lightened the cholesterol load, combined ingredients that had never before shared a plate, invented clever new sauces based on wines and natural meat juices, and refined the presentation on the plate to an art form that was dubbed *nouvelle cuisine*.

Today, the best chefs say that nouvelle cuisine, with its characteristically puny portions, is dead. Well, yes and no.

The current end-all, be-all is a kind of haute cuisine that often combines the best of traditional dishes with the inventiveness of nouvelle ingredients. Sort of the best of both worlds.

You should make it a point to try both traditional and haute cuisine. Bistros and brasseries are usually home to the traditional, while full blown restaurants are more likely to offer creative menus with unexpected, sometimes bizarre, combinations of ingredients.

In both cases, you will note that, as on the farm, no food product is tossed carelessly into the waste bin. Browse through one of the city's many amazing market streets and you'll see what we mean. Vendors hawk everything from celery root and fresh beets, to trays of brains, intestines, feet, and ears. During game season in the fall, butchers showcase entire pheasants, small deer, hares, and even whole wild boars.

What you see in the marketplace is exactly what might end up on your plate that night. So, for instance, if you're squeamish about organ meat, read the menu very carefully. *Ris de veau* is not a tender veal medallion. It is veal sweetbreads, which are very popular, but may not be to your taste.

And *andouilette*, a staple at good restaurants and bad, is a sausage stuffed not with ground pork, but with chewy strips of a pig's small intestines – not one of our favorites.

Even with game, which we absolutely love, take some care. Most is truly game, which is to say wild, and we've had fine pheasant in quality restaurants where we've picked shotgun pellets out of the meat.

EATING OUT

No matter how many times you've eaten in French restaurants in the United States, you are likely to find yourself at a loss from time to time here. Bring along our guide with its *Food Dictionary* (see below) and be prepared to ask questions.

There are dishes – not just organ meat, but certain types of fish – that rarely appear on American menus. And the names given the dishes often reflect the style of preparation, which is something even the best dictionary may fail to explain. You may recognize a word or two, but still have no idea what you're ordering unless you ask.

Though chicken and beef are available in several forms, you should sample other staples of French cuisine, such as rabbit, duck, lamb, and veal. Rabbit roasted in a mustard sauce can be miraculous. *Magret de canard*, the breast of a duck, is served medium rare like a good steak. *Gigot*, or leg of lamb, and *blanquette de veau*, a veal stew in white sauce, are both standard fare worth your attention.

Well-known appetizers include *escargots* (snails steeped in butter and garlic), a salad with rounds of warm goat cheese (*chèvre*), *patés* of all kinds, and herring with warm potatoes.

Of course, the French are also famous for their sweet tooth. Dessert menus offer a dizzying variety of pastries, fruit tarts, and sorbets.

Reservations are highly recommended and few restaurants (especially decent ones) will seat you before 7:30.

We've listed many of our favorite bistros and restaurants in the *Where to Eat* sections accompanying the regional guides in this book. But window shop as you stroll the streets during the day and you're likely to find a gem or two. Menus even for the best restaurants are posted outside so you know what you're getting into.

Often you will see a *formule* or *prix fixe* selection noted on a menu. Those selections offer fewer options, but are usually ten to thirty percent cheaper than if you were to order the same dishes *à la carte*. Some *prix fixe* menus even offer a half bottle of wine per person.

And don't forget that the French adoration for food extends beyond their native cuisine. Paris especially is liberally seeded with restaurants featuring dishes from all over the world – Italian, Chinese, Vietnamese, Lebanese, Spanish, just about any kind of food you can imagine.

You wouldn't go to Chicago just to gnaw on ribs. Likewise you should branch out in France.

TYPES OF RESTAURANTS

Auberge - A term that has taken on an alluring cachet in recent years. Once referring strictly to a country inn with a few rooms and hearty home-cooking, the term is now used by city restaurants that want to lure customers keen on a blend of gourmet and country cuisine.

Bistro - A small, usually informal neighborhood restaurant which is often family-owned and where the food is traditional country cooking.

Brasserie - A term that once referred to a beer pub, where the action was mostly at the bar. Now many brasseries have been transformed into bistro-like restaurants, though brasseries are often larger and less intimate.

Café- Small informal establishment that offer coffees, teas, alcoholic beveridges, and simple meals, such as omelets or salads. Often with outoor seating, this is where you can sit for as long as you like, reading a good book, contemplating the future, or watching the people.

Restaurant - This name is supposed to signal a more serious and formal dedication to food, complete with linen tablecloths. You cannot wander in for a quick café.

Tabac - A French-style bar, serving coffee and booze of all kinds, and with a counter near the door where you can buy cigarettes, payment cards for public phones, lottery tickets, and Metro tickets.

THE THREE MEALS

Petit Dejeuner – **Breakfast**

Breakfast is served at hotels and cafés from about 7:30 to 10:00. It is usually a light meal with coffee or tea (for types of coffee, see *café* below under Beverages) and a small basket of bread and pastries with butter and jam. Orange juice is common, but is usually extra. Cereals can be found at some hotels, and, on rare occasions, so can eggs and a kind of Canadian-style bacon. Eggs are normally considered a lunch food.

Common breakfast patries include *chansons aux pommes* (flaky pastries with apple filling), *croissants* (crescent-shaped rolls), *pains au chocolat* (flaky pastry with a small amount of chocolate in the middle), and *tartines* (small half baguettes with butter and, if you ask jam).

A brief aside: If you want jam or preserves, ask for *confiture*. We've had friends request *préservatifs*, which is a good way to cause a sudden silence in the room. *Préservatifs* are condoms.

Dejeuner – **Lunch**

Lunches generally stretch from about 11:30 to 2:30, after which many places refuse to serve any food at all until dinner.

For ages, lunch was the major meal of the day, but that custom has grown more and more outdated as the French work day grows busier. Fewer people are ordering steaks and more are choosing the *salades composées*, such as the *salade Niçoise* with tuna or a *salade paysanne* with egg and small bits of bacon called *lardons*.

Omelets and fries are still very popular, as are *croques monsieur* and *croques madame*, which are similar to grilled cheese sandwiches, but with ham, chicken or an egg. You won't find many hamburgers, and even if you do, you'll probably be disappointed by them.

If you're on a march through the city and don't want to sit for lunch, **crépe stands** offer an alternative. A crépe with strips of ham, shredded Guyère and an egg will fuel your fires for a couple of hours at least.

Delis (*traiteurs*) are scattered around and offer pastas, prepared meats, and salads to go for reasonable prices. Bakeries also prepare cheap baguette sandwiches or tiny quiches and pizzas that you can wolf down while sitting on a park bench. They're not haute cuisine, but they'll keep you on your feet and they're cheap.

FOOD STORES

When you want to put together a meal on your own, you can go to various small supermarkets or, better yet, do it like the natives do: one specialty shop after another.

alimentation - *small food store*
boucherie - *butcher's shop*
boucherie chevaline - *horsemeat butcher*
boulangerie - *bakery*
cave - *wine shop*
charcuterie - *like a deli*
confiserie - *candy shop*
crèmerie - *dairy products*
emporter - *carry-out*
épicerie - *general store*
fleuriste - *florist*
fromagerie - *cheese shop*
marchand de légumes - *vegetable store*
poissonerie - *fish shop*
traiteur - *prepared foods*
triperie - *tripe shop*
volailler - *poultry shop*

Diner – **Dinner**

Some bistros and brasseries will serve dinner as early as 7:30, but most patrons arrive between 8:30 and 10:00. Service continues up until close to midnight.

No matter when you arrive, your meal should be savored. Most French restaurants expect only one sitting per table per night, so don't feel as if you need to rush to make room for the next guy. Sit as long as you like.

Dinner in France can be akin to a religious experience – that is, if you choose your restaurants carefully and take time to study the menu so that you order what you think you're ordering.

Don't be rattled if the waiter comes by almost instantly to take your order. (The French often order very quickly.) Simply say, *Pas encore. Deux minutes, s'il vous plaît.* This means, "Not yet. Two minutes, please."

No matter how many French restaurants you've frequented in the States, you're going to come over here, sit down at a table in a nice restaurant, open the menu, and panic. Afraid to ask questions, you'll take your best guess and order what you think will be a tender veal medallion. Instead you'll get a plate of sizzling sweatbreads or a hulking veal kidney.

It's inevitable. Everyone we have ever met in Paris has a story like that. And, for the most part, guides just don't help much when it comes time to order a nice meal with a worthy bottle of wine. Until now, that is.

Below you will find what we think will be an indispensable Food Dictionary. French restaurants routinely invent names for new ways of preparing foods (or invent new names for old ways of preparing foods– good marketing), so you will still run across lots of mysterious words. When in doubt, ask for an explanation.

FOOD DICTIONARY

Vegetables, Fruits, Herbs, Meat, Fish, Bird, Seafood, Game, Desserts, Terms, Preparations and Dishes:

à la - in the manner of, indicating preparation style
abricot - apricot
abats - organs
agneau - lamb
aiguillettes - long thin slices
ail - garlic
aïoli - mayonnaise suffused with garlic
Albert - sauce of cream and egg yolk with mustard and horseradish
ali baba - same as baba au rhum
alose - shad
alouette - lark
amandes - almonds

ananas - pineapple
anchoiade - anchovy paste with herbs, for fried bread
anchois - anchovy
andoillette - sausage of strips of pig's small intestines
anguille - eel
araignée - a long-legged crab
artichaut - artichoke
   coeurs d' - artichoke hearts
   fonds de - artichoke bottoms
   vinaigrette - cold artichoke with vinaigrette on the side
   violet - small red-tinged artichoke
asperges - asparagus
   d'Argenteuil - large white asparagus
   pointes d' - asparagus tips
assiette - a plate of something
assiette de crudités - plate of raw vegetables, such as tomato, shredded carrot
   (carotte râpée), celery root
assorti - assorted
aubergine - eggplant
aulx - plural of ail, or garlic
avocat - avocado
baba au rhum - small molded sponge cakes soaked in rum or rum flavoring
bacon - a Canadian-style bacon
baigné - bathed
bananes - bananas
bar - sea bass
barbue - brill, similar to sand dab or sole
barde - thin rasher of bacon, larded
baudroie - angler fish
bavette - flank steak
Béarnaise - creamy white sauce with egg yolk, butter, white wine, shallots,
   tarragon and other herbs
bécasse - woodcock
bécassine - snipe
béchamel - white sauce with butter, flour and milk
beignet - a fritter
belon - one of finest types of oyster
betterave - beet
beurre - butter
   blanc - butter sauce with shallots and vinegar
   noir - browned butter
bifteck - common steak
bigorneaux - spiral-shelled sea mollusc

MORE TIPS FOR EATING OUT

• The word *"Entrées"* on the menu indicates the appetizers. *"Plats"* are the main courses.

• *"Garçon"* for *"waiter"* is no longer appropriate or amusing. *"Monsieur"* is more polite.

• Water is not automatically served at the table. You can avoid the cost of bottled water, which is what the waiter will suggest, by ordering *"un carafe d'eau,"* which is a small pitcher of tap water. The water's just fine, though purists insist that bottled water is the safest for travelers going anywhere outside their own country.

• When ordering meats, the French word for rare is *"saignant,"* and very rare is *"bleu."* Medium rare is *"à point,"* and medium well is *"bien cuit."*

• Traditional French cooking calls for green salads (*"salades vertes"*) to be served between the main course and dessert, but it is no longer unthinkable to request a salad as an appetiser. Salads are rarely included with a meal.

• Cheese can be ordered between the main and dessert courses, and you should take advantage of the fabulous choices here. French cheese, especially the amazing variety of goat cheeses (*"chèvre"*), has not been processed the same way as cheese is in the States and, consequently, is generally fresher and richer.

• Coffee (*"un café"*) is espresso and is served in a demitasse. A *"café creme"* is espresso with steamed milk. Some places serve American coffee (*"café filtre"*). Your coffee will not be served until you have finished eating. (You can ask, but nine times out of ten, your request will be ignored.)

• When asking for the check, say, *"L'addition, s'il vous plaît."*

• The tip and tax are included in the price, though with a good meal it is customary to leave the waiter another five to fifty francs depending on the service and the bill.

biscuit - cookie
bisque - creamy soup, usually with seafood
    de crevettes - with shrimp
    de hommard - with lobster
blanquette - veal stew in heavy white gravy
blettes - Swiss chard
blini - small Russian-style pancake with sour cream, smoked salmon and
    caviar
boeuf - beef
bolet - wild mushroom
bombe - ice cream lined, molded frozen dessert

Bordelaise - brown sauce with pan juices, red wine, shallots, bone marrow, thyme, bay and other herbs

bouchée - mouthful

boudin - pork blood sausage

bouillabaisse - a fish stew rich with lots of olive oil, garlic, tomato and other herbs

bouilli - boiled

bouillon - broth, usually of beef or chicken

bouquet - large shrimp served cold

Bourguignon - beef cubes stewed in red wine sauce with bacon, onions, and herbs

boudin - blood sausage

braisé - braised

Brillat Savarin - hollow cake

brioche - a soft egg bread

brochet - pike

brochette - meat cubes grilled on a spit

brocoli - broccoli

cabillaud - codfish

cacahuète - peanut

caille - quail

calamar - squid

canapé - small round of toast, usually as a base to a topping of cheese, eggs, etc.

canard - duck

caneton - duckling

canette - small duck

câpres - capers

caramel - burned sugar

caramvlisé(e)(s) - near-burned in a broiler

cardons - edible thistles

carotte - carot

carpe - carp

carré - ribs

    d'agneau - rack of lamb

carrelet - similar to a flounder

cassoulet - casserole with white beans and herbs, with duck, pork, sausage, and/or other meats

caviar - fish eggs

céleri - celery

céleri-rave - celery root

cendre chemisée - cloaked with ash, smoldering

cépe - wild mushroom

cerises - cherrys
   jubilé - cherries poached and flamed with kirsch, often served with ice
      cream
cervelas - a baloney-like sausage
cervelle - brains
champignons - mushrooms
   croûte aux - mushrooms in a pastry shell
chanson aux pommes - flaky pastry with an apple filling
chanterelle - wild mushroom
chantilly - whipped cream used in toppings
chapon - capon, or castrated rooster
charcuterie - sampling of sausages
charlotte - pudding
Charolais - prized breed of French cattle
chasse - game
châtaignes - chestnuts
châteaubriand - beef tenderloin or Porterhouse cut
chaud(e) - hot
chausson - turnover
cheval - horse
chèvre - goat cheese
   fraîche - only a day to a few days old
   seche - dried somewhat with age
chevreau - baby goat
chevreuil - small deer, roebuck
   forestière - roasted with strips of pork fat, and served with onions,
      mushrooms and fried potatoes
chicorée - chicory
chiperons - squidlike cuttlefish
chipolatas - small-diameter sausage
choix - indicating you have a choice
chou - cabbage
chou à la crème - cream puff
chou-fleur - cauliflower
chou-frisé - kale
chou-rouge - red cabbage
chou de Bruxelles - Brussels sprouts
choucroute - sauerkraut, also referring to various types of pork served on
   a bed of sauerkraut
ciboulettes - chives
cigales - clam with distinctive long shell like a razor clam
citron - lemon
citron vert - lime

clafouti - a tart made by pouring batter over fresh fruit and then baking the mixture

claires - a good quality type of oyster

clémentine - kumquat

cochon - pig

cocotte - hen

coeur - heart

coeurs de palmier - hearts of palm

coings - quinces

colin - a whiting or hake

compote de fruits - stewed or poached fruits

concombres - cucumbers

confit - preserved meat

    de canard - preserved duck meat

    d'oie - preserved goose meat

confiture - preserves

consommé - usually meat stock

coq - rooster

coquelet - young rooster

coquillages - shellfish

coquilles - shells

coquilles Saint-Jacques - scallops

Cordon bleu - veal slices with slices of ham and Guyère in between, breaded and fried in butter

cornichons - pickles

côte - rib or chop

côtelettes - chops

coulis - stewed meat juice

courgette - squash

couscous - steamed cracked wheat pilaf with lamb or chicken

crabe - crab

crème - cream

    Anglais - light custard sauce

    d'asperges - cream of asparagus soup

    brulée - light custard with a very thin layer of burned sugar on top

    caramel - custard prepared in a small mold with a light caramel sauce

    champignons - cream of mushroom soup

    fraîche - a very heavy cream commonly used instead of ice cream as a topping for tarts

    glacée - ice cream

    de poireaux - cream of leek soup

    de poulet - cream of chicken soup

cramic - an egg bread with raisins

crêpe - a large thin pancake, served with a variety of fillings, including meats, cheeses or preserves

cresson - watercress

cressonière - watercress soup

crevettes - shrimp

croissant - crescent shaped flaky roll

croquant - crisp

croque madame - a croque monsieur with an egg cooked into the middle of the top slice of bread, or with chicken instead of ham

croque monsieur - a type of grilled cheese sandwich, often with a slice of ham inside

croustade - a pastry shell
    de champignons - mushrooms in a light pastry shell

croûte - crust

croûtes - croutons

cru - raw cured meat

crudités - cut and shredded raw vegetables

crustacés - shellfish

cuisse - thigh

cuit - cooked

datte - date

daube - a stew of beef in wine and vegetables
    Provencal - gravy laced with garlic, anchovies and capers

daurade - sea bream

déglacée - warmed up

délices - delights, meaning just about anything

demi - half

diable - brown meat sauce with pepper, shallots, herbs

dinde - turkey

dorade - sea bream

échalote - shallot

éclair - oblong puff pastry filled with chocolate or coffee custard and topped with icing

écrevisses - crayfish

effilé(e) - flaked (as in almonds), oven-ready

émincé(e) - cold roast meat reheated in a sauce

émulsionné(e) - liquified

endive - endive

entier(e) - whole

entrecôte - common rib steak

entrées - appetizers

épaule - shoulder

éperlans - smelts

épices - spices
épinard - spinach
escalopes - thin slices of a meat
escargots - snails
escargots de mer - sea snails
escarole - green bitter lettuce
estouffade - stew of beef cubes braised in red wine, herbs, onions, bacon,
    mushrooms
estragon - tarragon
étuvé(e) - stewed
façon - in the manner of
faisan - pheasant
farci(e) - stuffed
fenouil - fennel
fermier - indicates poultry raised on farm
feuilles - leaves
feuilles de vigne - grape leaves
    farcies - grape leaves stuffed with rice and herbs
feuilleté - broad pastry leaf or shell
fèves - broad beans
figue - fig
filet - a tenderloin cut
fine herbs - fresh chopped parsley, tarragon, chervil
flageolets - beans resembling small green limas
flambé(e) - flamed
flétan - halibut
fleurette - small flower
Florentine - often a preparation using cooked spinach
foie - liver
    gras - goose liver, either whole or ground into a pâté
    de volaille - chicken liver
fondu(e) - melted
    Bourguignonne - cubes of meat cooked and eaten individually at table
    in a pot of hot oil
    Savoyarde - pot of melted cheese used as dip
forestière - often indicates sautéed mushrooms, sometimes with bacon and
    small potatoes
four (au) - baked
frais - fresh, cool
fraîche - fresh, cool
fraise - strawberry
    de bois - wild strawberry
fraboise - raspberry

fricassée - stew of meat, vegetables and herbs in which the meat is partially cooked in butter before being added to stew
frit(e) - fried
frites - French fries
froid(e) - cold
fromage - cheese
    blanc - mild fresh cheese with heavy cream
    de tête - head cheese
fruits - fruits
fruits de mer - mixed seafood
fumé(e) - smoked
gambas - large Mediterranean prawns
garni(e) - garnished
garniture - garnishes
gateau - cake
gelée - in aspic
genièvre - juniper berry
gibelotte - fricassee
gibier - wild game
gigot - leg
girolle - wild mushroom
glaces - ice cream
goujon - small carplike freshwater fish
gratin - a dish sprinked with bread crumbs and grated cheese and then browned
gratin dauphinois - scalloped potatoes
gratiné - prepared with bread crumbs
gratinée - French onion soup with croutons
grenade - pomegranate
grenadine - pomegrante syrup
grenouilles - frogs
    Provencal - pan fried in olive oil, garlic and tomatoes
grillades - grilled meats
grillé(e) - grilled
grive - thrush
groseilles - currants
    a maquereau - gooseberry
grumes - heavy skin or coatings
Guyère - a Swiss-like cheese
hamburger - often a thin patty and little else
hareng - herring
    avec pommes à l'huile - salad with herring and potatos on friseé lettuce vinaigrette

haricots - beans
    blanc - white lima beans
    rouge - kidney beans
    vert - green beans
hérissons de mer - sea urchins
hollandaise - white sauce with egg yolks, butter, lemon juice
hommard - lobster
hors d'oeuvres - appetizers
hot dog - a reheated foot-long dog of mediocre pork stuffing, packed in a
    baguette with melted guyere on top
huile - oil
    d'arachides - peanut oil
    de noix - walnut oil
    d'olive - olive oil
huitres - oysters
    douzaine d' - a dozen oysters
ile flotant - floating island, an ice cream dessert
jambon - ham
    de Pari - cooked ham
    de Parme - Italian prosciutto
jambonneau - lower leg of ham, boned and usually cold
jeune - green, unripe
jour (du) - that day's offering
julienne - thin cut strips of vegetables
jus - juice
juteux - juicy
kebab - marinated meat and vegetables grilled on skewer
kramic - an egg bread with raisins
laitue - lettuce
lamelles - small strips, slivers
lamproie - lamprey
langouste - spiny lobster
langoustine - sea crayfish
langue - tongue
lapereau - young rabbit
lapin - rabbit
lard - with bacon
lardons - American-style bacon bits
léger - light
legumes - vegetables
lentilles - lentils
lièvre - wild hare
lotte - angler or frog fish

loup - sea bass
macarons - macaroons
macédoine de legumes - diced mixed vegetables cooked and served with
    mayonnaise
mâches - lamb's lettuce, corn-salad
madeleines - shell-shaped tea cakes
Madère - indicates sauce with Madeira wine
magrets - slices of breast meat, usually duck
mais - corn
maison (à la) - prepared in the house style
maître d'hôtel - creamed butter with parsley and lemon
mandarine - between an orange and a tangerine
maquereau - mackerel
marcassin - young wild boar
marennes - type of oyster
mariné(e) - marinated
marrons - chestnuts
    glacés - candied chestnuts
mateolote - fish stew with wine, onions and mushrooms
mayonnaise - mayonnaise
médaillon - round cut of meat
mélange - mix
melba - usually a poached fruit with syrup on ice cream
melon - melon
    de Cavaillon - like a cantaloupe
    d'eau - watermelon
    au porto - with Port
    a l'Italienne - with thin slices of Italian ham
menthe - mint
meringues - stiff shell of sweet egg white
merlan - a whiting
merlu - a type of hake
meunière - often flour-coated filets pan-fried in butter and served with
    parsley and lemon butter
meurette - poached eggs on toast rounds drenched with red wine sauce with
    shallots, garlic, and herbs
miel - honey
mignon - tenderloin cut
mijotè(e)(s) - simmered
mille feuille - flaky layered pastry with creamy filling
mirabelle - small yellow plum
moelle - beef bone marrow
Mont Blanc - small peak-shaped dessert of sweetened chestnut meat

topped with whipped cream or powdered sugar
moka - coffee-flavored
morille - morel, a wild mushroom
mornay - white sauce with bÇchamel and grated Gruyère and Parmesan
   cheeses
morue - dried codfish
moules - mussels
   farcies - stuffed
moussaka - ground lamb mixture with eggplant and tomato
mousse - a whipped but creamy dessert usually made with egg and
   chocolate; also a rich meat pâté whipped with cream and egg whites
mousseline - hollandaise sauce with whipped cream
mousserons - small wild mushrooms
moutarde - mustard
mouton - sheep, mutton
mulet - mullet
museau - beef face or snout
myrtilles - bilberries
Napolitaine - slice of frozen ice cream with vanilla, chocolate, and strawberry
nappé - covered with gravy
natur - plain
navarin - lamb stew with potatoes, onions, tomatoes, herbs
navets - turnips
Newburg - creamy lobster and wine sauce
noisettes - hazelnuts, or small disks of tenderloin
noix - nuts, top round in veal, nuggets of something
   de coco - coconut
nougat - a burned sugar almond crunch
nouilles - noodles
oeufs - eggs
   a l'Americaine - fried
   brouillés - scrambled
   chemise - poached
   a la coque - soft-boiled
   durs - hard-boiled
   durs avec mayonnaise - hard-boiled with mayonnaise
   Florentine - with spinach and cheese sauce
   en meurette - poached on garlic toast with red wine sauce
   mollets - medium boiled eggs
   plat - fried
   poché - poached
   de saumon - salmon eggs

oie - goose
oignons - onions
oiseau - bird
olives - olives
    noires - black olives
    vertes - green olives
olivettes - type of grape
omble - a charr, similar to trout
omelette - plain omelet
    avec jambon - with ham
    avec fromage - with cheese, usually guyere
    complète - with ham and cheese
    et frites - with French fries
    natur - plain omelet
onglet - skirt steak
orange - orange
ortolan - small game bird
os - bone
oseille - sorrel
oursin - sea urchin
pain - bread
    d'epice - spice bread
    de campagne - country-style bread, usually with some wheat flour
pain au chocolat - flaky pastry with a small amount of chocolate in the
    middle
palombe - type of wild pigeon
palourdes - clams
pamplemousse - grapefruit
pané(e) - pan fried
papillote (en) - when something is marinated, then sealed in paper or foil
    and baked
parfum - flavor
parfumé(e) - flavored with
pâté - pate â
pavé - tenderloin cut
pays (du) - a dish from the area
paysanne - mix of bacon pieces and cooked vegetables
pêches - peaches
perche - perch
perdreau - young partridge
perdrix - partridge
Périgueux - rich meat sauces with truffles
persil - parsley

persillé(e) - sprinkled with chopped parsley
petit salé - poached slightly salted meat
petits fours - tiny cakes
petits pois - peas
pied de cochon - pig's foot
pigeon - pigeon
pigeonneau - young pigeon
piments doux - pimentoes
pintade - Guinea fowl
pintadeau - young Guinea fowl
piquante - spicy
pistache - pistachio nut
plat - plate, dish of something
plateau - tray
   de fromage - cheese plate
plie - flat fish with brilliant orangish-red spots
poché(e) - poached
poëlé(e) - pan fried
poire - pear
   Belle Hélène - poached pear in syrup on ice cream with chocolate sauce
poireaux - leeks
pois chiches - garbanzos
poissons - fish
poitrine - chest
   fumée - American-style bacon rashers
poivre - pepper
   vert - green pepper
poivrons - bell peppers
pomme - apple
pommes de terre - potatos
   allumettes - thin French fries
   chips - chips
porc - pork
porcelet - suckling pig
poularde - roasting chicken
pot au feu - a stew with beef, chicken and vegetables
potage - soup
poulet - chicken
poulpe - octopus
praline - roasted almonds in carmelized syrup
pré salé - refers to lamb fed on salt tidal grasses
profiteroles - small pastry balls filled with ice cream or custard, then doused
   with chocolate sauce

Provencal - indicates preparation with olive oil, white wine, garlic, tomato, anchovy and other ingredients

prune - plum

pruneau - prune

purée - mash, thick soup

quenelle - light dumpling with sauce

quetsche - small purple plum

queue - tail

queue de boeuf - oxtail

quiche - an egg pie, with various ingredients
    lorraine - with cream and bits of ham or bacon

râble - back, usually of rabbit

radis - radish

raie - stingray or skate

raifort - horseradish

raisin - grape
    sec - raisin

râpées - shredded, grated

ratatouille - a Provencal casserole with eggplant, squash, onions, tomatoes, garlic, and herbs

rémoulade - a mayonnaise sauce with mustard, capers, anchovies and herbs

rubarbe - rhubarb

rillettes - cold shredded meat pastes

ris de veau - veal sweetbreads

rissoles - breaded fritters stuffed and deep-fried

riz - rice

rognons - kidneys

rollmops - pickled herring wrapped around a piece of onion

romarin - rosemary

rosbif - roast beef

rosette - small round piece

rôti(e) - roasted

rôtis - roasts

rouget - Mediterranean red mullet

rouille (a la) - thick sauce of garlic, chili, pimento

rumsteack - sirloin cut

safran - saffron

salade composée - large lunch salad
    Niçoise - usually with tuna, egg, green beans, bell peppers, and anchovy on bed of lettuce, served vinaigrette
    verte - common green salad

Saint-Jacques - scallops

Saint-Pierre - John Dory fish of the mackerel family

salami - salami
sandre - a pike-perch
sandwich - baguette sandwich
    au jambon - with ham
    au jambon et fromage - with ham and guyere
    au thon - with tuna
    au thon et crudités - with tuna, lettuce, tomato and egg
sanglier - wild boar
sardines - sardines
saucisses - cooked sausage
saucisson - uncooked sausage
saumon - salmon
sauté(e) - sauteed
sauvage - wild
scampis - prawns
sec, sèche - dried
sèche - cuttlefish, a squidlike creature
sel - salt
selle - saddle, as in lamb
sirop - syrup
sole - sole, flat fish
sorbet - sherbet
soufflé - beaten egg whites suffused with various flavorings and baked in
    a mold
soupe - soup
    à l'oignon - French onion soup
    gratinée - French onion soup
    pêcheur - fish soup
spumoni - ice cream with candied fruit
steake - steak
    au poivre - with crushed peppercorns pushed into meat
sucre - sugar
suivant le marché - what's available and fresh at market
suprême de volaille - boneless chicken breast poached and served in cream
    sauce
tartare - mayonnaise sauce with egg, pickle, caper, parsley and herbs
tartare - raw meat, usually either beef or salmon
tarte - tart, open-faced pie
    à l'onion - onion and cream tart
    aux pommes - apple tart
    aux framboise - raspberry tart
    citron - lemon tart
tartelette - inidivual-sized tarts

tartine - a small half baguette with butter
   avec confiture - with jam
   avec miel - with honey
terrine - strictly speaking, the vessel in which paté is made, but also refers
   to heavily ground meat with herbs
thon - tuna
thym - thyme
tiède - slightly warm
tiramisu - a bit of liqueur-soaked sponge cake topped with rich custard and
   chocolate powder
tomates - tomatoes
tortue de mer - turtle
   véritable - turtle soup
tournedoes - quality beef tenderloin
tourte - hot meat pie
tranche - a slice
tripe - stomach lining
triperie - tripe (stomach lining) shop
truffes - truffles
truffé - a dish with truffles mixed in
truite - trout
turbot - turbot, flounder-like fish
vanille - vanilla
vanneau - a small game bird
varié(e) - assorted
veau - veal
velouté - creamy white sauce with veal or fish stock
ventre - stomach
viande - meat
vichyssoise - light leek and potato cream soup, served cold
vigneronne - indicates a sauce or stuffing with grapes and wine
vinaigre - vinegar, literally soured wine
vinaigrette - a dressing of oil, vinegar and herbs
volailles - fowl, usually chicken
yaourt - yogurt

BEVERAGE DICTIONARY

apératif - before meal drinks
   Kir - mixture of white wine and crème de cassis
   Kir Royale - mixture of champagne and crème de cassis
   Pastis - a popular licorise-flavored drink
   Ricard - a Pastis

bière - beer
   à la pression - draft beer
   blonde - lager
   brune - dark beer
   légère - light
café - espresso
   café au lait - espresso with a pitcher of steamed milk
   café crème - espresso with steamed milk
   café filtre - an American coffee
chocolat chaud - hot chocolate
Calvados - alcoholic cider
Cassis - black currant liqueur
cidre - cider
citron pressé - lemon juice served with water and sugar
Coca - Coke
   Coca Light - Diet Coke
Cognac - Cognac
Cointreau - orange-flavored liqueur
eau - plain water
   avec gaz - with bubbles
   Château Chirac - tap water (named after Paris mayor)
   de vie - very strong brandy-like liquor
   natur - tap water
   sans gaz - without bubbles
glace - ice
Grand Marnier - orange-flavored liqueur
jus - fruit jus
   d'orange - orange juice
   de pamplemousse - grapefruit juice
   de pomme - apple juice
   de tomate - tomato juice
kirsch - clear cherry brandy
lait - milk
limonade - a clear tart style of lemonade
Orangina - soft drink with tangerine and orange
Porto - port
rhum - rum
thé - tea
vin - wine (see following chapter on Wine)
   blanc - white
   de maison - house wine
   rosé - rosé
   rouge - red

whisky - Scotch
Williamine - pear brandy

COURSES OF A FORMAL DINNER
(in order)
entrée - appetizer
plat - main course
salade - salad
fromage - cheese
dessert - dessert
café - coffee (only after, not during, dessert)

FOOD GROUPS
fruits - fruits
herbs - herbs
légumes - vegetables
oeufs - eggs
pain - bread
pâte - pasta
patisseries - pastries
poissons - fish
viandes - meats

OBJECTS AT THE TABLE
assiette - plate
bouteuille - bottle
cendrier - ashtray
chaise - chair
couteau - knife
cuiller - spoon
fenêtre - window
fourchette - fork
nappe - tablecloth
sel et poivre - salt and pepper
serviette - napkin
table - table
verre - glass

SAMPLE MENU
From: Bernard & Martine Morillon in Beaune

NOS ENTREES

Bouchée Souvaroff Baignée de sa Petite Sauce Truffe
Noix de Coquilles Saint-Jacques Poàlées, Jeunes Epinards,
    Fleurette de Safran, Foies de Pigeonneaux Rôtis
Truffe Fraîche de chez Pebeyre cuisinée sous la Cendre
    Chemisée dans sa Barde le Lard
Foie Gras de Canard servi en Pot au Feu, Jeune Bouillon,
    Sauce Crème à la Truffe, Petits Légumes Fanes
Jeune Salade de Mâche Coquille, Poitrine Rôtie de Canette
    Sauvage Tiède Rosée en Aiguillettes, Huile de Noisettes,
    Vieux Vinaigre
Oeufs Brouillés aux Huîtres Plates de Belon en Profiterolles
    Purée de Cresson, Nappés au Coulis d'Oursins
Huîtres Plates de Belon Chaudes, Oeufs de Caille Pochés
    en Meurette, Quenelles de Crème de Dattes
Jambon Frais Persillé, Petite Gelée de Meursault
Escargots Cuisinés À la Bourguignonne servis cans la Maison
Jeune Consommé de Volaille à la Demidoff

NOS POISSONS

Huîtres Plates de Belon Marinées, Vinaigre de Vin en
    Ravioles de Bar de Ligne Petit Bateau, Jus d'Huîtres
    crèmé Emulsionné
Queues de Langoustines, Noix de Saint-Jacques Rôties,
    Caviar Oscietre, Moussette de Poivrons Rouges
Bar de Ligne Petit Bateau de Guilvinec Rôti au Chou Vert,
    au Chou Rouge, Petit Jus de Veau
Blanquette de Saint-Pierre Breton, Huîtres Plates de Belon,
    Goujonnettes de Sole Grumes de Raisins Blancs, Riz
    Sauvage Canadien
Rougets Petit Bateau en Filets Poàlés, Poitrine de
    Pigeonneau de la Ferme, Effilade d'Endives Caramélisées,
    Petit Jus à la Saveur Pain d'Epice
Queues de Langoustines de Guilvinec Faáon Brillat Savarin,
    Chiffonnade de Laitue
Homard Pàché sur les Côtes du Finistère, Gratiné à la Faáon
    de la Mère Brazier
Ventre de Dorade, Dés de Moelle, Fumet de Vin Rouge

NOS VIANDES

Foie de Veau Franáais à la Casserole, Baigné de sa Petite
    Sauce de Veau aux Herbes Hérissons de Betteraves Rouges
Charlotte de Ris de Veau Braisé à la Truffe Fraîche
    Emulsion de Foie Gras, Salsifis Juteaux de la Vallée
    de la Saône, Jus Réduit à la Crème, Pistil de Safran
Volaille de Bresse Mijotée au Gevrey-Chambertain
    sélectionné par le Baron Cairol, Tagliatelles de
    Courgettes, Julienne de Poitrine
Pigeonneau de Ferme de la Bresse Souvaroff, Cuit à la
    Cocotte, Figues Fraîches Rôties
Côtelettes de Pigeonneau Cuites à la Cocotte, Mijotées
    aux Salsifis, Eminvé de Poires Cuites au Vin Rouge
Rognon de Veau Franáais, Cuisiné à la Mode d'Alexandre
    Dumaine
Coeur de Charolais en Croûte d'Artichauts, Sauce Foyot
    Emulsionnée, Cardons Grantinées à la Moelle

8. THE WINES OF FRANCE

INTRODUCTION

It sounds crazy to recommend that you drink wine when you visit France. Nothing could be more obvious. But then you'd be surprised how many Americans arrive in Paris and order Jack Daniels, neat, with a Bud back.

Most hard liquor is available, though bourbon is sometimes hard to find. But the price of a mixed drink will make your head spin long before the booze will. Why bother?

There is plenty of beer, some of which is quite good and some of which is truly awful. Kronenbourg, the Budweiser of France, is a refreshing, safe choice, and you should be able to afford a second glass.

But wine is an integral part of the national heritage in France. Check any bistro at lunch time and you'll find stuffy businessmen and grimy laborers alike quaffing — not sipping — wine with their midday meal. At home, even the children are given a small glass with the family feast.

And just as wine is part of any meal, so it is the economic and cultural backbone of communes throughout the country. Literally, grapes are grown and wine is made everywhere in France. There is even a tiny vineyard in Paris proper (see *Paris: Seeing the Sights* chapter).

The range of available wines is staggering, swinging wildly from bone dry to sickly sweet and from dirt cheap to impossibly expensive. Of course, that raises the question: How do you choose?

Here are a few pointers:

• Drink what you think tastes good. Sounds dumb, but then so many people spend small fortunes drinking wines that snobs tell them they're supposed to like.

• When possible, drink the local wine. Regional French wines marry well with the local cuisine because they've grown up together over the past 2,000 years.

• Don't be afraid to ask for advice. Especially outside the major tourist regions, most restaurant owners and maîtres d'hôtels take pride in helping you find the right wine.
• Establish your price range. For the *crème de la crème*, you'll have to cash in your IRAs. There is, however, an unlimited number of outstanding wines at reasonable prices.
• Splurge occasionally. A great wine is a unique sensory pleasure. It comes at a price, but then so do so many memorable experiences.
• Match the wine with the food and the setting. A $75 bottle of Meursault would no doubt be a real treat on a picnic lunch. But then, if you're gazing across a golden valley to the river below and the mountains beyond, a $6 bottle of Muscadet would probably be just as good.
• Experiment. With the sea of wines available, you are sure to make some discoveries on your own, and those will probably be the most memorable wines of all.
• Have fun. Nothing ruins a good bottle of wine faster than a know-it-all who doesn't know enough to shut up and enjoy.

WINES IN A RESTAURANT

The nuts and bolts of what you're likely to see in a restaurant:

Red and white wine will be available in 25 and 50 centiliter carafes at most bistros and brasseries for anywhere from 30 to 60FF per 50 cl. carafe. These wines will be the equivalent of jug wine and, on occasion, you'll wish it had come from another jug. But with an omelet or nondescript lunch steak, a carafe is a smart choice.

Brasseries and smaller restaurants usually stock a limited selection of bottled wine, with a list that indicates the type of wine (e.g. Burgundy, Bordeaux) but not necessarily the maker or the vintage. These won't be great wines, and are likely to be the same or slightly better than what you can order by the carafe.

The real fun begins when you're ready to spend nearly as much time choosing a wine as you do selecting your main course. The two are, in fact, usually chosen together so that they complement one another.

Wine lists run anywhere from a half page in your menu to a separate menu of twenty pages or more. For oenophiles, the wine lists of the top-ranked restaurants will be as engrossing as a good novel. But if you don't know wine well enough to request precisely what type you want and from what year, the longer lists can be mind-boggling.

Whether the list is short or long, don't hesitate to ask for advice. We've discovered several memorable wines we never knew existed just by asking.

Several good restaurants offer bottled wine with a house label. It may not be the finest wine available, but it is often a safe and satisfying choice.

Afterall, they know that unless they've picked a decent wine, the patrons won't come back.

IDENTIFYING FRENCH WINES

What follows here is a somewhat over-simplified description of French wines that should help you get started on what could easily become an obsessive new hobby.

To begin with, in France, the wines are usually named for the region they came from, not for the grapes used in the process (the exception is the Alsace region, where wines take the names of the dominant grape used to make the wine, as in California).

For instance, in the most general sense, a **Bordeaux** is any wine that comes from the Bordeaux region along the Atlantic Coast where the Gironde spills into the sea.

There are, however, many types of Bordeaux, each of which takes its name from the sub-section of Bordeaux where the grapes were grown. The micro-climates and soil content of each subregion can make two wines surprisingly different, even if they were made a couple of miles apart and from the same type of grape.

Several types of grape are grown in Bordeaux and other regions, and winemakers often blend juice from different grapes in varying proportions to give their wine its distinctive bouquet and flavor.

WHITE VERSUS RED

White wines are usually drunk younger than red wines, are served chilled, and are generally thought to complement white meats, such as fish or chicken.

Made in the western end of the Loire Valley, **Muscadet** is a simple but refreshing dry white wine. It is so simple, in fact, you don't generally have to worry too much about when it was made or by whom.

Sancerre is another pleasant white, from the opposite end of the Loire. An **Entre Deux Mers** from the Bordeaux region is also a refreshing white wine that is usually drunk quite young.

The white **Rieslings** and **Gewurztraminers** from the Alsacian region of northern France are more carefully made. They are fuller and fruitier than a Muscadet. They are, in fact, vastly underrated by Americans, who usually assume they are the same syrupy sweet wine as is made from the same types of grapes in Germany.

Just the opposite is true. The Alsacian Rieslings are, in fact, quite dry and age well. Two very good recent vintages were 1989 and 1990.

For the driest of the dry, try a white **Graves** from the Bordeaux region. Another fine dry white is the **Pouilly-Fuissé** from the Mâcon area of Burgundy.

White Burgundies, in fact, are thought to be the finest white wines in France, maybe in the world. There is a range here, in part because the Burgundy region stretches south more than 100 miles, beginning roughly in the Chablis area southeast of Paris.

Chablis itself is quite good, and not at all like the mediocre chablis that American restaurants served twenty and thirty years ago. **Meursault** is even better, and the **Puligny** and **Chassagne Montrachets** are thought to be the best white Burgundies of all. When made properly, these are wonderfully intense and flavorful dry wines. Excellent years include 1978, 1982, 1985, 1986, 1989, 1990, and 1992.

A word about rosé: We're not fans. In the grossest general terms, rosés too often taste to us like wimpy reds. The exception: **Tavel** from the Côtes du Rhône.

Ultimately, red wine is the greatest treat. There are larger differences among red wines than there are among whites. That means you'll experience more surprises as well.

Some reds are meant to be lightly chilled, but many are served at room temperature (though never warm). And generally, reds will complement red meats, from beef and lamb to gamey birds or duck.

Beaujolais is probably the most delightfully fresh and fruity red wine, and is often served chilled. It's the standby of most bistros. The release of the **Beaujolais Nouveau** in mid-November is a big occasion throughout the country. It's the first wine produced in the current year, so it is very, very young. And it is very, very popular.

Bottles labeled simply Beaujolais or Beaujolais Villages can be good, but they are blends of juices and grapes from across the Beaujolais region. The better Beaujolais are the *crus*, which take their names from specific subregions, such as Juliénas, Fleurie, and Régnié.

The Languedoc region in the south and the Loire Valley produce a variety of inexpensive reds, many of which can be the perfect thing for a simple lunch. To generalize, however, they are mostly table wines with neither the bouquet nor the lasting power of the country's better wines.

The Côtes du Rhône in the south is noted for its outstanding **Châteauneuf-du-Pape** and **Hermitage** wines, both of which boast a great deal of character. They may be too bold for some, but they're often a good value and once you get a taste for them, you'll wonder why you didn't always have some on hand. Wines bottled simply as a Côtes du Rhône can be a very good value. Good years were 1985, 1988, 1989 and 1990.

Unfortunately, really horrible cheap red Burgundies swamped American markets years ago. If you're one of those people who cringe at the memory, it's time to wipe the slate clean because you are missing some of the best wine around.

True Burgundies, meaning the wines that come from Burgundy, are made exclusively from Pinot Noir grapes, age extremely well, and have a rich but rarely overpowering taste. The danger here is that the quality is all over the map. Even if something is labeled *Premier Cru*, that doesn't mean the wine is going to be any good.

In Burgundy more than any other region in France, the growers are the key. We list several respected growers in the following charts.

In general, the best red Burgundies are thought to be the **Côte de Nuits**, which are a heavier, almost gamey wine, and the **Côte de Beaunes**, which are a bit lighter and softer.

Chambolle-Musigny, **Gevrey-Chambertin**, **Vougeot**, and **Vosne-Romanée** are considered the best subregions of the Côte de Nuits, and **Volnay**, **Pommard**, and **Savigny-lès-Beaunes** are the best of the Côte de Beaunes. Good years: 1978, 1979, 1983, 1985, 1988, 1989 and 1990.

Bordeaux is the accepted pride and joy of French wine. That is not to say that if you order a bottle labeled simply *Bordeaux*, which indicates a blend, that it will be good. Judicious selection and a willingness to experiment and occasionally to loosen the pursestrings are musts.

A complex ranking system was set in place more than a hundred years ago to identify the châteaux that consistently produced the best wines. The big, big names include **Château Margaux, Château Latour, Château Lafite-Rothschild, Château Haut-Brion, Château Pétrus.** (A lot of experts scoff at the rating system, saying it's outdated. But it is still a very good indicator of the better producers.)

You may not be able to afford the best of the Bordeaux, but there are many very good châteaux that produce excellent wines at reasonable prices. Again, don't hesitate to ask questions. If you want to make the choice yourself, you will want to weigh four factors: the subregion (the *Cru*, or vineyard) where the wine was made, the maker of the wine, the vintage, and the price.

Wines from the subregions of Margaux, Saint-Julien, and Pauillac are luxuriously rich and mellow when aged properly — and they can age well for decades. The **Graves** are particularly bold and the **Saint-Emilions** and **Pomerols** are wonderfully earthy. The more generic **Médocs** and **Haut-Médocs** are often rich and heavy, perfect for game. Good years: 1970, 1975, 1978, 1979, 1982, 1983, 1985, 1986, 1988 and 1989.

WINETASTING

If you're visiting any of these wine regions, be sure to stop at a few chÉteaux and sample their wares. Some major cellars and producers are listed in the "Winetasting" sections in the chapters on Alsace, Burgundy, and the Loire Valley.

MAJOR FRENCH WINES
With Selected Vintages & Producers

ALSACE

Alsatian winemakers complain that too many people confuse their wines with the sweet white wines the Germans make across the Rhine River from Alsace.

It's too bad because the comparison isn't fair. Yes, the Alsatian wines can taste fruity. But the good ones are dry and crisp — perfect for the often heavy Alsatian cuisine.

Alsace differs from other major French wine regions in two important ways. One, it is almost wholly dominated by white wine, producing a large share of the country's whites (the reds, in fact, are generally poor). Secondly, the wines are not named for the region or village where they are made. Instead, as in California, the wines are named for the grapes used to produce them.

Strong Vintages: *1976, 1981, 1983, 1985, 1988, 1989, 1990*

TYPES OF ALSATIAN WINE

There are seven principal grape varieties used in Alsatian wines.

• *Gewurztraminer* - *A spicy, flowery wine, the best of which ages extremely well.*

• *Muscat* - *A dry, heavily-scented wine that is not produced in much quantity. An acquired taste.*

• *Pinot Blanc* - *One of the less interesting wines, with much of it rising only to the level of acceptable table wine.*

• *Pinot Noir* - *It's hard to imagine this is the same grape that produces the best Burgundies because, here, the wine is mostly a rosé. Still, these rosés often have good flavor.*

• *Riesling* - *In general, the best and most sophisticated of the Alsatian wines. Medium-dry with a solid finish.*

• *Sylvaner* - *You'll find lots of this available in pitchers in restaurants. Straight-forward, good taste, cheap.*

• *Tokay* or *Pinot Gris* - *A warm and rich wine, with more body than most regional wines and good aging prospects.*

Vendage Tardives & the Grand Crus

In the last 20 years, Alsatian producers searched for ways to compete with other wine growing regions and came up with two effective ideas. One, to promote their *vendage tardives* and, two, to establish a set of quality guidelines and to award *Grand Cru* status to those vineyards whose wine measures up.

Vendage Tardive translates essentially to "late harvest" and refers to wines that were made from grapes harvested unusually late in the season. That's good because the grapes are bursting with natural sugars, and that means more taste and more alcohol. The good ones also age especially well and are served as very sweet dessert wines. But, of course, because the weather must cooperate, vendage tardives don't come along very often.

As of 1986, there were 47 vineyards whose wine and production standards measured up to *Grand Cru* guidelines. Producers who make wine from grapes in these vineyards can, and often do, add that vineyard's name to their label.

So the label would likely include: the grape from which the wine was made, the Grand Cru (or vineyard) where the grapes were grown, the words "Grand Cru," and the name of the producer. For example: Gewurztraminer, Altenberg de Bergheim, 1983, Lorentz.

THE ALSATIAN GRAND CRUS
(and the nearby village in case you want to visit):

Altenberg de Bergbieten (Bergbieten)
Altenberg de Bergheim (Bergheim)
Altenberg de Wolxheim (Wolxheim)
Brand (Turckheim)
Eichberg (Eguisheim)
Engelberg (Dahlenheim)
Frankstein (Dambach-la-Ville)
Froehn (Zellenberg)
Geisberg (Ribeauvillé)
Gloeckelberg (Rodern)
Goldert (Gueberschwihr)
Hatschbourg (Hattsatt)
Hengst (Wintzenheim)
Kanzlerberg (Bergheim)
Kastelberg (Andlau)
Kessler (Guebwiller)
Kirchberg de Barr (Barr)
Kirchberg de Ribeauvillé (Ribeauvillé)
Kitterlé (Guebwiller)
Mambourg (Sigolsheim)
Mandelberg (Mittelwihr)
Markrain (Bennwihr)
Moenchberg Andlau)

Muenchberg (Nothalten)
Ollwiller (Wuenheim)
Osterberg (Ribeauvillé)
Pfersigberg (Equisheim)
Pfingstberg (Orschwihr)
Praelatenberg (Orschwiller)
Rangen (Thann)
Rosacker (Hunawihr)
Saering (Guebwiller)
Schlossberg (Kaysersberg)
Schoenenbourg (Riquewihr)
Sommerberg (Niedermorschwihr)
Sonnenglanz (Beblenheim)
Spiegel (Bergholtz)
Sporen (Riquewihr)
Steinbrubler (Wettolsheim)
Steinert (Pfaffenheim)
Steinklotz (Marlenheim)
Vorbourg (Rouffach-Westhalten)
Wiebelsberg (Andlau)
Wineck-Schlossberg (Katzenthal)
Winzenberg (Blienschwiller)
Zinnkoepflé (Westhalten-Soultzmatt)
Zotzenberg (Mittelbergheim)

RESPECTED ALSATIAN PRODUCERS

Albert Boxler
Albert Mann
Alfred Wantz
André Thomas et Fils
Anstotz et Fils
Antoine Stoffel
Barmes-Buecher
Bernard et Robert Schoffit
Cave Vinicole de Hunawihr
Charles Schleret
Dirler
Einhart
Emile Schwartz
Ernest Burn
Gerard Wagner
Herbinger
Hugel
J.B. Adam
Jean Becker
Jean Huttard
Jean Schaetzel
Jean Sipp
Jean-Martin Spielmann
Jean-Pierre Dirler
Joseph Gsell
Josmeyer
Julien Meyer
Klein aux Vieux Remparts
Kuehn

Kuentz-Bas
Leon Heitzmann
Lucien Albrecht
Marc Kreydenweiss
Marcel Deiss
MaterneHaegelin et Ses Filles
Meyer-Fonne
Mittnackt Klack
Muré
d'Orschwihr
Ostertag
Paul Schneider
Paul Schwach
Pierre Arnold
Pierre Frick
Pierre Sparr
Pierre et Jean-Pierre Rietsch
Raymond Renck
Roland Schmitt
Rolly-Gassman
Schlumberger
Sick Dreyer
Sipp-Mack
de la Tour
Trimbach
Weinbach
Weingarten
Willy Rolli-Edel
Wittmann Fils
Zind-Humbrecht

BORDEAUX

Bordeaux is no doubt the most famous of the French wines. That is due in part to the wizardry of the most accomplished châteaux and in part to the fact that a flood of table red and white wines are produced here and shipped all over the world.

Reports are that 500 million bottles of wine are produced out of the Bordeaux region's 100,000 hectars. The famous wines — the **Margaux**, **Pauillac**, **Saint-Julien**, and others — account for only a small pool of this sea of wine.

The most famous châteaux generally specialize in red wines, but Bordeaux is also well known for its whites. The **Graves** region produces some beautifully subtle and elegant dry white wines. And **Sauternes** are among the most famous sweet white dessert wines in the world.

This embarrassment of riches constitutes a bit of a challenge for you. How do you pick a single bottle of Bordeaux from a wine list 20 pages long?

As we say in virtually every section here, you will need to weigh four factors: the producer of the wine, the subregion of Bordeaux where the vines were grown and the wine was made, the year or vintage that the wine was made, and the price.

MAJOR RED BORDEAUX

As in most French wine regions, these wines take their names from the location (or appelation), not from the grape used in making the wine. All the wines below are made mostly of Cabernet Sauvignon, Merlot, and Cabernet Franc grapes. In general, Cabernet Sauvignon is the dominant grape, though the wines from Saint-Emilion and especially Pomerol often focus on the Merlot.

The selection in the Bordeaux region is a wee bit simpler than in the Burgundy area. In Burgundy, a single vineyard may be divided among a dozen or more owners who produce wildly varying wines. In Bordeaux, châteaux often own large homogeneous vineyards.

Also unlike Burgundy, where a wine maker may produce wines from grapes grown in several vineyards scattered all over the Côte d'Or, the châteaux generally produce wine from a single large vineyard.

Graves

Location: The large area immediately to the west and southwest of the city of Bordeaux.

Type of Wine: A complex, but lighter red usually made with a blend of juices from the Cabernet Sauvignon (about half), Merlot, and small amounts of Cabernet Franc. Can be a bit overpowering for those who prefer the feathery touch of a good Margaux. The winemakers of Graves agreed on an independent quality control and rating system some time ago, and there are currently 13 red and 9 white Crus Classés.

Strong Vintages: *1975, 1978,1979, 1982, 1983, 1985, 1986, 1988, 1989, 1990*

THE GRAVES RED CRUS CLASSÉS

Bouscaut
Carbonnieux
Chevalier
Fieuzal
Haut-Bailly
Haut-Brion
Latour-Haut-Brion
Latour-Martillac
Malartic-Lagravière
Mission-Haut-Brion
Olivier
Pape-Clément
Smith-Haut-Lafitte

Other Respected Producers
Archambeau
Beau-Site
Bichon Cassignols
Brondelle
Chantegrive
Doms
Fleur Jonquet
Gravières
Louvière
Mission-Haut-Brion
Rahoul
Saint-Robert
Vieille France

Margaux

Location: About 20 kilometers (12 miles) north of Bordeaux.

Type of Wine: One of the most famous, sophisticated, and subtle reds. Though delicate, it has a full-bodied bouquet and taste. The Margaux are subject to the controls and rating system established for Médocs in 1855.

Strong Vintages: *1978, 1979, 1982, 1983, 1985, 1986, 1988, 1989, 1990*

THE MARGAUX GRANDS CRUS
(See Grand Cru Médocs chart)

Other Respected Producers
Berlande
Gurgue
Labergorce
Labergorce Zede
Larruau
Marsac Seguineau
Martinens
Monbrison
Pichecan
Rausan-Ségla
Siran
Tayac
Tour de Mons

Pauillac
Location: About 40 kilometers (25 miles) north of Bordeaux.

Type of Wine: Another highly sophisticated and rich red. Though sometimes tannic, rarely enough to intrude on the supple taste. The Pauillacs are subject to the controls and rating system established for Médocs in 1855.

Strong Vintages: *1975, 1978, 1979, 1981, 1982, 1983, 1985, 1986, 1988, 1989, 1990*

THE PAUILLAC GRANDS CRUS
(See Grand Cru Médocs chart)

Other Respected Producers
Baron Philippe
Becasse
Bellegrave
Bernadotte
Fleur Milon
Fleur Peyrabon
Fonbadet
Pibran
Tour du Roc Milon
Tourette

Pomerol

Location: Just to the east of the town of Libourne, about 30 kilometers (18 miles) east of Bordeaux.

Type of Wine: Made almost totally with Merlot, these reds can be richer and softer. Though they age well, they are often drunk younger than wines heavy with Cabernet Sauvignon. There is no formal Grand Cru status awarded Pomerols, though that should be seen more as a sort of political decision and should not reflect on your interest in the wine.

Strong Vintages: *1975, 1981, 1982, 1983, 1985, 1986, 1987, 1988, 1989, 1990*

RESPECTED POMEROL PRODUCERS

Bon Pasteur
Certain de May
Clinet
Clos des Litanies
Conseillante
L'Eglise-Clinet
L'Evangile
Fleur Pétrus
Gazin
Grave-Trigant de Boisset
Gravette de Certan
Lafleur
Lagrange
Latour à Pomerol
Montviel
Petit-Village
Pétrus
Pin
Plincette
Rève d'Or
Trotanoy
Vieux Château Certan
Vray Croix de Gay

Saint-Emilion

Location: Just a few kilometers east of the town of Libourne, about 35 kilometers (22 miles) east of Bordeaux.

Type of Wine: Sometimes infused with a larger percent of Cabernet Franc, these reds are generally heartier and fleshier, and are often drunk within a few years of production. Has its own ranking of 11 Premiers Grands Crus Classés and 61 Grands Crus Classés.

Strong Vintages: *1975, 1982, 1983, 1985, 1986, 1988, 1989, 1990*

PREMIERS SAINT-EMILION GRANDS CRUS

Ausone
Beauséjour
Belair
Canon
Cheval-Blanc
Clos Fourtet
Figeac
Gaffelière
Magdelaine
Pavie
Trottevieille

Other Respected Producers

Angelus
Belle Rose
Bernateau
Cadet-Bon
Canon-la-Gaffelière
Cantin
Carrillon de l'Angelus
Carteau Pin de Fleurs
Carteau-Matras
Clos Larcis
Commanderie
Corbin Michotte
Dassault
Dominique
Fleur Cardinale
Fonroque
Franc Pipeau Descombes
Grand Corbin Despagne

Grand Mayne
Grand-Pontet
Haut-Cadet
Haut-Nauve
Haut-Rocher
Jean Voisin
Lamarte
Larmande
Moulin Saint-Georges
Pavie Decesse
Petit Val
Robin des Moines
Rose Blanche
Saint-Hubert
Tertre-Roteboeuf
Tonnelle
Tour Figeac
Trolong-Mondot
Vieux Château l'Abbaye

Saint-Estèphe

Location: Just above the Pauillac subregion in the heart of what is called the Haut-Médoc, where many of the most famous wines are made.

Type of Wine: These may not have the class of other Bordeaux, especially those of neighboring Pauillac or Saint-Julien, but they are still rich and full of character. The Saint-Estèphe wines are subject to the controls and rating system established for Médocs in 1855.

Strong Vintages: *1975, 1978, 1979, 1981, 1982, 1983, 1985, 1986, 1988, 1989, 1990*

THE SAINT-ESTÈPHE GRANDS CRUS
(See Grand Cru Médocs chart)

Other Respected Producers
Andron Blanquet
Capbern Gasqueton
Chambert-Marbuzet
Crock
Domeyne
Haut-Marbuzet
Lavillotte
Lilian Ladouys
Marbuzet
Meyney
Ormes de Pez
Phelan Segur
Saint-Estèphe
Segur de Cabanac
Tronquoy-Lalande

Saint-Julien

Location: About 35 kilometers north of Bordeaux in the Haut-Médoc region.

Type of Wine: A personal favorite of ours, with much of the seductive richness of the slightly more expensive Margaux and Pauillacs. Saint-Julien wines are subject to the controls and rating system established for Médocs in 1855.

Strong Vintages: *1975, 1978, 1979, 1981, 1982, 1983, 1985, 1986, 1988, 1989, 1990*

THE SAINT-JULIEN GRANDS CRUS
(See Grand Cru Médocs chart)

Other Respected Producers
Bridane
Gloria
Lalande-Borie
Moulin de la Rose
Terry-Gros-Cailloux

The Grand Cru Médocs

Way back in 1855, Napoleon III, wanting to promote his nation's fine wines, ordered the Bordeaux makers to devise a ranking system that would acknowledge the best producers of the great red wines of the region.

Judging as much by the price of the wines as any qualitative judgments, the makers came up with a five-tiered system of Premiers Crus, followed by Deuxièmes, Troisièmes, Quatrièmes, and Cinqièmes (which translates easily into First, Second, Third, Fourth and Fifth).

All the hotshots in the wine world agree that the rankings are woefully outdated. There are, they say, some producers who should have fallen from the list and many who should have been added. Still, the list is a formidable one, with the top two or three levels still cranking out one magnificent wine after another.

Over the past 10 years, almost all the ranked wines have begun producing what is called a "second" wine. The second wines are made from grapes on the same vineyard as the primary wine and are often similar to the primary wine. However, they can be purchased for half the price or less. (Remember, though, that the seconds are seconds because the don't quite measure up or come from younger vines, so it is possible to find an occasional dog.)

Premiers Crus
Haut-Brion (Graves)
  2nd: Bahans Haut-Brion
Lafite-Rothschild (Pauillac)
  2nd: Moulins de Carruades
Latour (Pauillac)
  2nd: Les Forts de Latour
Margaux (Margaux)
  2nd: Pavillon Rouge
Mouton-Rothschild (Pauillac)

Deuxièmes Crus

Brane-Cantenac (Margaux)
    2nd: Notton
        de Fontarney
Cos-d'Estournel (Saint-Estèphe)
    2nd: Marbuzet
Ducru-Beaucaillou (Saint-Julien)
    2nd: La Croix
Durfort-Vivens (Margaux)
    2nd: de Curé-Bourse
Gruaud-Larose (Saint-Julien)
    2nd: Sarget de Gruaud-Larose
Lascombes (Margaux)
    2nd: Segonnes
        La Gombaude
Léoville-Barton (Saint-Julien)
    2nd: Lady Langoa
Léoville-Las-Cases (Saint-Julien)
    2nd: Clos du Marquis
        Grand Parc
Léoville-Poferré (Saint-Julien)
    2nd: Moulin-Riche
Montrose (Saint-Estèphe)
    2nd: La Dame de Montrose
Pichon-Longueville-Baron (Pauillac)
    2nd: Les Tourelle de Pichon
Pichon-Longueville-Comtesse-de-Lalande (Pauillac)
    2nd: Réserve de la Comtesse
Rausan-Ségla (Margaux)
    2nd: Lamouroux
Rauzan-Gassies (Margaux)

Troisièmes Crus

Boyd-Cantenac (Margaux)
Cantenac-Brown (Margaux)
    2nd: Canuet
        Lamartine
Calon-Ségur (Saint-Estèphe)
    2nd: Marquis de Ségur
Desmirail (Margaux)
Ferrière (Margaux)
Giscours (Margaux)
    2nd: Cantelaude

d'Issan (Margaux)
    2nd: Candel
Kirwan (Margaux)
Lagrange (Saint-Julien)
    2nd: Les Fifes de Lagrange
Lagune (Haut-Médoc)
    2nd: Ludon-Pomiès-Agassac
Langoa-Barton (Saint-Julien)
    2nd: Lady Langoa
Malescot-Saints-Exupéry (Margaux)
    2nd: de Loyac
        du Balardin
Marquis d'Alesme-Becker (Margaux)
Palmer (Margaux)
    2nd: Réserve du Général

Quatrièmes Crus
Beychevelle (Saint-Julien)
    2nd: Amiral de Beychevelle
        Réserve de L'Amiral
Branaire-Ducru (Saint-Julien)
    2nd: Duluc
Duhart-Milon-Rothschild (Pauillac)
    2nd: Moulin de Duhart
Lafon-Rochet (Saint-Estèphe)
    2nd: Le Numéro 2 de Lafon-Rochet
Marquis-de-Terme (Margaux)
    2nd: de Gondats
Pouget (Margaux)
Prieuré-Lichine (Margaux)
    2nd: Clairefont
Saint-Pierre (Saint-Julien)
    2nd: Clos de Uza
        Saint-Louis-le-Bosq
Talbot (Saint-Julien)
    2nd: Connétable de Talbot
Tour-Carnet (Haut-Médoc)

Cinqièmes Crus
d'Armailhac (Pauillac)
Batailley (Pauillac)
Belgrave (Haut-Médoc)
Camensac (Haut-Médoc)

Cantemerle (Haut-Médoc)
  2nd: Villeneuve de Cantemerle
Clerc-Milon (Pauillac)
Cos-Labory (Saint-Estéphe)
Croizet-Bages (Pauillac)
  2nd: Enclos de Moncabon
Dauzac (Margaux)
  2nd: Laborde
Grand-Puy-Ducasse (Pauillac)
  2nd: Artigues-Arnaud
Grand-Puy-Lacoste (Pauillac)
  2nd: Lacoste-Borie
Haut-Bages-Libéral (Pauillac)
Haut-Batailley (Pauillac)
  2nd: La Tour d'Aspic
Lynch-Bages (Pauillac)
  2nd: Haut-Bages-Averous
Lynch-Moussas (Pauillac)
Pédesclaux (Pauillac)
Pontet-Canet (Pauillac)
  2nd: Les Hauts de Pontet
du Tertre (Margaux)

Other Red Bordeaux

Wines from these appelations are less well-known, but that doesn't mean you might not find some real gems at very reasonable prices (especially among the Haut-Médocs). In any case, there are scores of fine table wines bottled with under these regional names:

Bordeaux AOC	*Lussac Saint-Émilion*
Bordeaux Clairet (rosé)	*Listrac*
Bordeaux Supérieur AOC	*Médoc*
Bordeaux-Côtes de Castillon	*Montagne-Saint-Émillion*
Canon Fronsac	*Moulis*
Côtes de Bourg	*Moulis-en-Médoc*
Côtes de Francs	*Parsac-Saint-Emillon*
Fronsac	*Premières Côtes de Bordeaux*
Graves de Vayres	*Premières Côtes de Blaye*
Haut-Médoc	*Sainte-Foy-Bordeaux*
Lalande de Pomerol	*Saint-George Saint-Émilion*

MAJOR WHITE & DESSERT BORDEAUX

Though the red Bordeaux receive most of the international praise, there are superior whites as well, especially those from the Graves and Sauterne regions. The Graves can be exceptionally light and dry. The Sauternes are famous sweet dessert wines.

Entre-Deux-Mers

Location: Generally refers to the large delta-shaped region east of Bordeaux between the Dordogne and Garonne Rivers.

Type of Wine: True connoisseurs will take exception with us listing this as a major white Bordeaux. It's true that Entre-Deux-Mers is really a white table wine, but it is equally true that it is bright, reasonably priced, and exported in massive quantities.

Strong Vintages: *Meant to be drunk quite young.*

RESPECTED ENTRE-DEUX-MERS PRODUCERS

Bonnet
Candeley
Chevaux des Girondins
Ducla
Fleur
Gammage
Grangeneuve
Haut-Rian
Hauts de Fontaneau
Jamin
Launay
Peyrières
Reynier
Saint-Florin
Tour de Mirambeau
Tuquets

Graves

Location: Same general area as where the bold reds are made, immediately to the west and southwest of the city of Bordeaux.

Type of Wine: Some truly exquisite dry-as-a-bone white wines made from the Sémillon and Sauvignon Blanc grapes. No doubt the best of the non-Chardonnay dry whites made in Bordeaux. The Graves have an independent rating system identifying 9 white and 13 red (see above) Crus Classés.

Strong Vintages: *1982, 1983, 1985, 1986, 1988, 1989, 1990*

THE WHITE CRUS CLASSÉS

Bouscaut
Carbonnieux
Chevalier
Couhins
Couhins-Lurton
Latour-Martillac
Laville-Haut-Brion
Malartic-Lagravière
Olivier

Other Respected Producers

Belon
Brondelle
Caillou
Chantegrive
Clos Floridene
Fieuzal
Gravallas
Haut-Brion
Haut-Mayne
Louvière
Magneau
Millet
Pont de Brion
Pontac Monplaisir
Respide
Saint-Jean-des-Graves
Smith Haut Lafitte
Vieux Château Gaubert

Sauternes

Location: Generally, an area about 35 kilometers (22 miles) southeast of the city of Bordeaux.

Type of Wine: (Also look for Barsac, another dessert wine made next door to the Sauterne area.) World-class sweet wines, made from a blend of Sèmillon, Sauvignon, and Muscadelle grapes. It is the sweet wine like a Sauterne in which the "noble rot" comes most into play. Noble rot is caused by the "Botrytis cinerea" fungus, which eats through the skin of a grape, ultimately turning the grape brown. The rot also concentrates the sugars. Sauternes are so valued that they, too, have a ranking system identifying the most highly prized vineyards (or crus). It has three tiers: Premier Crus Supèrieur, Premiers Crus, and Deuxièmes Crus.

Strong Vintages: *1975, 1976, 1980, 1981, 1983, 1985, 1986, 1988, 1989, 1990*

MEMORABLE SAUTERNES

Premier Crus Supèrieur
d'Yquem

Premier Crus
Climens (a Barsac)
Clos Haut-Peyraguey
Coutet
Guiraud
Lafaurie-Peyraguey
Rabaud-Promis
Rayne-Vigneau
Rieussec
Sigalas-Rabaud
Suduiraut
Tour-Blanche

Deuxièmes Crus
d'Arche
Broustet
Caillou
Doisy-Daëne
Doisy-Dubroca (a Barsac)
Doisy-Vèdrines
Filhot
Lamothe (Despujols)
Lamothe (Guignard)
Malle
Myrat
Nairac
Romer
Romer-du-Hayot
Suau

Other Strong Producers

Coutet-Cuvée Madame (Barsac)	*Haut-Claverie*
Fargues	*Liot*
Gilette	*Raymond-Lafon*
Haut-Bergeron	*Remparts de Bastor*
	Suduirant-Cuvée Madame

Other White Bordeaux
 Like the minor red Bordeaux listed before, these are minor whites, meaning they're not the best of the lot. Still, you might discover a magnificent little wine under one of these labels:
• *Barsac* (sweet)
• *Cadillac* (sweet)
• *Cérons* (sweet)
• *Côtes de Bourg*
• *Graves de Vayres*
• *Loupiac* (sweet)
• *Premières Côtes de Blaye*
• *Saint-Croix-du-Mont*
• *Sainte-Foy-Bordeaux*

BURGUNDY

 Generally a **Burgundy** is any wine produced in the Burgundy region of France, whether the wine is white, rosé or red. Burgundy is an enormous geographical region, snaking through four French *départements* and beginning about 125 kilometers (77 miles) southeast of Paris and extending down the Yonne and Saône River valleys almost to Lyon 460 kilometers (285 miles) southeast of Paris.
 Many world-class white and red wines are produced in the region because controls are tight and growers try to maintain their reputation for quality (in part so they can justify the often screamingly-high prices).
 In general, the best white Burgundies, all from the Chardonnay grape, are the **Chablis** from around the village of Chablis; **Meursaults**, **Puligny-Montrachets**, and **Chassagne-Montrachets** from the Côte de Beaune; and the **Pouilly-Fuissé** near Mâcon.
 The best reds, all from the Pinot Noir grape, are said to be the **Gevrey-Chambertins**, **Vosne-Romanées** and **Chambolle-Musignys** of the Côte de Nuits, and the **Pommards** and **Volnays** of the Côte de Beaune. The lighter and fruitier **Beaujolais**, made from the Gamay grape in the southern stretch of Burgundy, are the most affordable and internationally popular wines.

Choosing a Burgundy
 Choosing a good Burgundy is a challenge, in part because there are umpteen different vineyards, growers, and producers.
 Even if you recognize the name of a wine you like (e.g. Meursault or Côte de Nuits), that doesn't mean that just any Meursault or Côte de Nuits will good. There are just too many mediocre producers seeded through these valleys. And just because they're mediocre doesn't mean they won't charge you an arm and a leg.

So what do you look for on a label? Again, four things: one, the name of a respected producer; two, a good price; three, the words *Grand Cru* or *Premier Cru*; and, four, a good vintage.

Crus & Labels

In general, the Grand Crus are rated the best of the wines, and Premier Crus are the second rung. To earn either title, wines from those crus (or vineyards) are tasted by regional panels of wine experts before being released.

Reading the labels can be a bit tricky. Again, the French generally define a wine by its point of origin (*appellation d'origine*). This is very much the case with good Burgundies. Here's why:

A bottle labeled merely "Burgundy" is probably not going to be very good. It may not even be a vintage wine. It may even contain juice from grapes grown in several regions and during different years.

A recognized Burgundy AOC (the popular abbreviation for *appelation d'origine contrôlée*), which has been found to meet several regional control standards, may add the region or even village name to their wine. For example, *Beaune* or *Nuits-Saint-Georges*, both of which are small towns.

Next on the ladder of quality Burgundy come the Premiers Crus and Grands Crus. The word *Cru* is the same as *climat* and usually refers to a particular vineyard in a recognized and controlled region or village. For instance, in the Chablis region there are dozens of vineyards lining the valleys, but only 7 vineyards (or Crus) are recognized as Grand Cru quality and another 12 are said to be of Premier Cru quality.

Back to reading the label: A Premier Cru can adopt a hyphenated name, combining the name of the village or subregion where the wine was produced (e.g. *Beaune*) with the name of the vineyard where the grapes were grown (e.g. *Cent-Vignes*). So you might find a wine that is labeled a *Beaune-Cent-Vignes, Premier Cru.*

To further complicate matters, each vineyard can be divided between several producers (e.g. **Château de Meursault, Michel Pont, Domaine René Monnier**, and others make wines from parcels of the Cent-Vignes vineyard). The name of the producer will also appear on the label.

So, to continue our example, you would be able to find a Premier Cru whose label reads *Beaune-Cent-Vignes, Premier Cru, Château de Meursault* — which happens to be a very fine wine.

The few Grands Crus can take their names solely from the vineyard where they are produced, such as the famous **Clos-de-Vougeot**. But again, there are usually many producers making wines from parcels of Grand Cru vineyards, so it is still best to choose one of the better winemakers.

What all this boils down to is that there are hundreds of names of Burgundy wines. We try to simplify things below for each of the major regions so that you can spend more time enjoying the wine than in fretting over which to choose.

RED BURGUNDY WINES
Côte de Nuits
Location: The narrow northern section of the Côte d'Or, beginning just south of Dijon and extending 20 kilometers (12 miles) toward Beaune.

Type of wine: Almost exclusively heavier red wines produced from the Pinot Noir grape. The best age very well.

Strong Vintages: *1976, 1978, 1983, 1985, 1987, 1988, 1989, 1990, 1991, 1992*

Below you'll find the major red Côte de Nuits:

CÔTE DE NUITS-VILLAGES
Wines made from grapes picked in the communes of Brochon, Comblanchien, Corgoloin, Fixin, and Prissey. Wines made strictly from grapes from Fixin can also include the name Fixin on the label.

CHAMBOLLE-MUSIGNY
Respected Producers

Antonin Guyon	Hudelot-Noëllat
Barthod-Noëllat	Jacques-Frédéric Mugnier
Chambolle-Musigny	Joseph Drouhin
Christian Clerget	Leymarie
Christian Confuron	Leroy
Comte Georges de Vogüé	Lionel J. Bruck
Denis Mugneret	Louis Jadot
Faiveley	Michel Serveau
Georges Roumier	Michelle Galley
Ghislaine Barthod	Moine-Hudelot
Henri Perrot-Minot	Pierre Betheau
	Robert Groffier et Fils

FIXIN
Respected Producers
Berthaut
Bruno Clair
Clavelier et Fils
Faiveley
Gelin-Moulin
Pierre Gelin

GEVREY-CHAMBERTIN
Respected Producers
Alain Burguet
Armand Rousseau
Bernard et Pierre Dugat
Bourée Père et Fils
Charles Mortet et Fils
Chézeaux
Christian Serafin
Claude et Maurice Dugat
Denis Bachelet
Drouhin-Laroze
Dufouleur Pere et Fils
Faiveley
Geantet-Pansiot
Goillot-Bernollin
Humbert Frères
Jean et Jean-Louis Trapet
Lucien Boillot et Fils
Maume
Michel Esmonin et Fille
Pierre Damoy
Joseph Drouhin
Joseph Roty
Leroy
Louis Jadot
Lucot-Javelier
Philippe Leclerc
René Leclerc
Varoilles

MOREY-SAINT-DENIS
Respected Producers
Armand Rousseau
Bruno Clair
Dujac
Georges Bryczek
Guy Castagnier
Heresztyn
Hubert Lignier
Michel Serveau
Nicolas Rossignol-Trapet
Pierre Aimot
Ponsot
Robert Groffier et Fils
Truchot-Martin

NUITS-SAINT-GEORGES
Respected Producers
Alain Michelot
Caves des Hautes-Côtes
Chevillon
Clos de l'Arlot
Clos Frantin
Daniel Rion et Fils
Emanuel Rouget
Faiveley
Georges Chicotot
Henri Gouges
Hospices de Nuits
Jacques et Patrice Cacheux
Jean Chauvenet
Lecheneaut
Leroy
Lionel J. Bruck
Machard de Gramont
Max et Jean-François Ecard
Poulette

VOSNE-ROMANÉE
Respected Producers
Arnoux Père et Fils
Bertrand Machard de Gramont
Château de Vosne-Romanée
Gerard Mugneret
Gros Frère et Soeur
Haegelen-Jayer
Henri Jayer
J. Confuron-Côtetidot
Jacques et Patrice Cacheux
Jean Faurois
Jean Grivot
Jean Méo-Camuzet
Jean Tardy
Leroy
Lupe-Cholet
Mongeard-Mugneret
Mugneret-Gibourg
Pascal Chevigny
Pernin-Rossin
René Engel
Robert Arnoux
Romanée-Conti
Vaucher Père et Fils

VOUGEOT
Respected Producers
Chantal Lescure
Château de la Tour
Denis Mugneret
Drouhin-Laroze
Faiveley
G. Roumier
Gros
Henri Rebourseau
Hudelot-Noellat
Jean Grivot
Joseph Drouhin
Louis Jadot
Méo-Camuzet
René Engel

Côte de Beaune/Reds

Location: Extends from just a couple of kilometers north of Beaune (the wine capital of Burgundy) south about 28 kilometers (17 miles) just past Santenay.

Type of Wine: Some of the Burgundy region's finest reds, from the Pinot Noir, and whites, from the Chardonnay grape.

Strong Vintages: *1976, 1978, 1983, 1985, 1988, 1989, 1990, 1991, 1992*

Below you'll find the major red Côte de Beaunes:

CÔTE DE BEAUNE-VILLAGES

Wines from the 16 communes of Auxey-Duresses, Blagny, Chassange-Monrachet, Cheilly-lès-Maranges, Chorey-lès-Beaune, Dézize-lès-Maranges, Ladoix, Meursault, Monthélie, Pernand-Vergelesses, Puligny-Montrachet, Saint-Aubin, Saint-Romain, Sampigny-lès-Maranges, Santenay, and Savigny.

ALOXE-CORTON

Respected Producers
Antonin Guyon
Cachat-Ocquidannt et Fils
Capitain-Gagnerot
Charles et Michelle Muller
Christian Gros
Maillard Père et Fils
P. De Marcilly
Robert et Raymond Jacob

AUXEY-DURESSES

Respected Producers
Jean-Pierre Prunier
Jean-Pierre Diconne
Jessiaume Père et Fils

BEAUNE

Respected Producers

Albert Morot Hospices de Beaune
Arnoux Père et Fils
Besancenot-Mathouillet
Château de la Velle
Coron Père et Fils
Charles Allexant et Fils
Jean-Marc Bouley
Jessiaume Père et Fils
Lois Dufouleur
Louis Jadot
Louis Violland
Moingeon
Mommessin
P. Misserey
Pierre Bouzereau-Emonin
Philippe Bouzereau
Prosper Maufoux
René Monnier
Xavier Bouzerand

CHASSAGNE-MONTRACHET

Respected Producers

Bernard Bachelet et Fils
Jean-Nöel Gagnard
Philippe Bouzereau
Prieur-Brunet
Roger Belland

CHOREY-LÈS-BEAUNE

Respected Producers

Château de Chorey-lès-Beaune
Guyon
Jacques Germain
Jean-Luc Dubois
Pascal Laboureau
Tollot-Beaut et Fils

MEURSAULT
Respected Producers
Comte Lafon
Doudet-Naudin
Jacques Prieur
Pierre Boillot

POMMARD
Respected Producers
A.F. Gros
André Mussy
Armand Girardin
Bichot
Caves des Hautes-Côtes
Comte Armand
Courcel
Crea
Cyrot-Buthiau
Gabriel Billard
Henri Delagrange et Fils
Hospices de Beaune
Jean Garaudet
Jean-Luc Joillot
Lahaye Père et Fils
Lejeune
Leroy
Michel Gaunoux
Michel Rebourgeon
Parent
Picard Père et Fils
Pothier-Rieusset
Rossignol-Fevrier Père et Fils

SAINT-AUBIN
Respected Producers
Sylvain Langoureau
Vincent Prunier

SANTENAY

Respected Producers
Buissière
Château de Mercey
Capuanao-Ferreri
Maison Jean Germain

SAVIGNY-LÈS-BEAUNE

Respected Producers
Camille Giroud
Capron-Charcousset
Cornu
Dubois d'Orgeval
Martin-Dufour
Maurice Ecard et Fils
Michel Gay
Rogert et Joel Remy

VOLNAY

Respected Producers
Antonin Guyon
Boigelot
Doudet-Naudin
François d'Allaines
Jacques Prieur
Jean-Marc Bouley
Joseph Drouhin
Olivier Leflaive Frères
Pousse d'Or
Robert Ampeau et Fils

Other Red Côte de Beaunes

Minor wines that may include some bargains:
- *Cheilly-lès-Maranges*
- *Monthélie*
- *Pernand-Vergelesses*
- *Saint-Romain*
- *Sampigny-lès-Maranges*

Challonaise & Mâconnaise Wines
Location: Two very large regions extending 80 kilometers (50 miles) south from the town of Chagny just past the city of Mâcon.
Type of Wine: These two areas crank out an enormous amount of decent table wine. Most of the better wines are whites, but there are some reds, again from the Pinot Noir grape, but often lighter than the Côte de Beaune and Côte de Nuits reds.
Strong Vintages: *Most of the reds here are meant to be drunk in the first few years.*
Below you'll find a list of selected Challonaise & Mâconnaise reds:

GIVRY
Respected producers
François Lumpp
Gardin
Joblot
Michel Sarrazin et Fils
Sauleraie
Thenard
Thierry Lespinasse

MERCUREY
Respected producers
Antonin Rodet
Bordeaux-Montrieux
Cellier Meix Guillaume
Chamerose
Charles Vienot
Château de Chamirey
Château de Mercey
Croix Jacquelet
Emile Juillot
Jeannin-Naltet Père et Fils
Maurice Protheau et Fils
Meix Foulot
Michel Briday
Michel Juillot
Michel Raquillet
Monette
Pierre Gruber
Renarde
Yves de Launay

RULLY

Respected Producers
Chapitre
Charles Gruber
Château de Davenay
Château de Rully
Eric Suremain
Folie
Jaffelin
Jean-Claude Brelière
Lheritier
Maurice Protheau et Fils
Michel Briday
Paul and Henri Jacqueson

Beaujolais

Location: Rhône département in the southern section of Burgundy region east of the Saône River, running about 35 kilometers (22 miles) from Mâcon almost to Lyon.

Type of Wine: Not really a Burgundy in that, geographically, it lies just outside the southern flank of the Burgundy départements. Still, guides always include Beaujolais here, so we have followed suit. These fruity reds made from the Gamay grape and generally meant to be drunk within a few months to no more than four or five years.

Strong Vintages: *1989, 1990, 1991*

The Beaujolais Wines

Being such a young wine there are not the same complex rating systems as with other, more sophisticated red Burgundies. There are about 4,000 growers in the area, though many merely grow the grapes, then sell them to large producers. You will note below that Georges Duboeuf, a large company that generally makes very good wines, owns a piece of many of the better growers in the area.

• **Beaujolais AOC** - Probably grapes taken from various places in the southern stretch of Beaujolais country and used for a blended wine.

• **Beaujolais Supérieur AOC** - Also probably a blend made from grapes from various spots in the southern Beaujolais, but resulting in a wine with a slightly higher alcohol content than Beaujolais AOC.

• **Beaujolais Villages AOC** - Wines made from grapes scattered across 40 villages in the northern section of Beaujolais. Considered generally a bit better than the Beaujolais AOC.

• **Beaujolais Nouveau** - This wine is released by Beaujolais producers in increasingly enormous quantities on the third Thursday in November, when it is still as young as a kitten. Served chilled, it is fruity, delightful, and sinfully drinkable. (Keep aspirin handy.)

The 10 Crus

There are 10 villages in Beaujolais that have been recognized for producing a higher quality wine — though it is still very reasonably priced. The experts tout **Moulin-à-Vent** and **Fleurie**, though we personally like **Juliénas** and **Brouilly** a great deal as well.

BROUILLY

Respected Producers

Château de Nervers (Duboeuf)
Grandes Vignes (J.C. Nesme)
Jean-Paul Ruet

CHÉNAS

Respected Producers

Benon
Brureaux
Charvet
Château Chévres
Combe-Remont (Duboeuf)
Darrous (Duboeuf)
Guy Braillon
Hubert Lapierre
Jean-Louis Santé
Louis Champagnon
Manoir des Journets (Duboeuf)
Robin

CHIROUBLES

Respected Producers

Bouillard
Château de Javernand (Duboeuf)
Cheysson-Les-Fargues
Desmeures (Duboeuf)
Fourneau
Georges Boulon
Georges Passot
Raousset

CÔTE-DE-BROUILLY

Respected Producers
Alain Bernillon
Château Delachanel
Château Thivin
Chavanne
Guy Cotton
J.C. Nesme
L. Bassy

FLEURIE

Respected Producers
Bachelard (Duboeuf)
Chapelle des Bois
Château de Fleurie
Château de Grand Pré (Pierre Ferraud)
Château des Deduits (Duboeuf)
Clos de la Roilette
Guy Depardon
Michel Chignard-lès-Moriers
Quatre Vents (Duboeuf)
René Berrod-Les Roches du Vivier

JULIÉNAS

Respected Producers
André Pelletier
Bottière Domaine de la Seigneuries de Juliénas (Duboeuf)
Château de Juliénas
Château des Capitans
Château des Vignes (Duboeuf)
Château du Bois de la Salle
Mouilles (Duboeuf)

MORGON

Respected Producers
Aucoeur
Château de Bellevue
Château de Pizay
Desvignes
Georges Brun
Jacques Trichard
Janodet
Jean Descombes (Duboeuf)
Lapierre
Princess Lieven (Duboeuf)
Vatoux (Duboeuf)

MOULIN-À-VENT

Respected Producers
Bruyère
Château de Moulin-à-Vent-Jean (Pierre Bloud)
Château des Jacques
Chauvet (Duboeuf)
Diochon
Héritiers-Tagent (Duboeuf)
Jacky Janodet
René Berrod
Teppe (Chanut Frères)
Tour du Bief (Duboeuf)

RÉGNIÉ

Respected Producers
Georges Duboeuf
Jean Durand
Jean-Paul Ruet
Joel Rochette
Ponchon (J. Durand)
Potet (Duboeuf)

SAINT-AMOUR

Respected Producers
Champs Georges Trichard
Grilles
Janin
Pirolette (Duboeuf)

WHITE BURGUNDY WINES
Chablis

Location: Yonne departement in the northwest section of Burgundy region east of the Yonne River.

Type of Wine: Dry, almost steely, white wines made from Chardonnay grape.

Strong Vintages: *1978, 1982, 1983, 1985, 1986, 1988, 1989, 1990, 1992*

The Different Wines
- **Petit Chablis** - Inexpensive, light and meant to be drunk quite young. Not up to standards of the Crus.
- **Chablis AOC** - Wines that may be made from grapes grown in several different vineyards or in vineyards that have not earned Premier or Grand status. Still, they have been judged to meet various criteria and should be good wines.
- **Premier Crus** - There are 12 vineyards that have earned Premier Cru status.
- **Grand Crus** - There are seven recognized Grand Cru vineyards: Blanchots, Bougros, Les Clos, Grenouilles, Preuses, Valmur, and Vaudésir.

RESPECTED CHABLIS PRODUCERS

Château Grenouilles	Jean Defaix
Château de Maligny	Jean-Luc Aegerter
Château de Vivier	Jean-Paul Droin
Colombier	Jean-Pierre Grossot
Conciergerie	Laroche
Cooperative la Chablisienne	Laurent Tribut
Daniel Dampt	Long-Depaquit
Denis Race	Louis Michel
Durup	Maison Blanche
Duvergey-Taboureau	Malandes
Edmond Chalmeau	Marcel Duplessis
Eglantière	Meulière
Eglise	Michel Barat
Etienne Defaix	Pascal Bouchard
François et Jean-Marie Raveneau	Philippe Testut
	Pierre André
Guy Robin	Robert Vocoret et Fils
Herve Azo	René et Vincent Dauvissat
Jean Collet et Fils	Servin
Jean Goulley et Fils	William Fèvre
Jean Dauvissat	

Côte de Beaunes/White
   Location: Extends from just a couple of kilometers north of Beaune (the wine capital of Burgundy) south about 28 kilometers (17 miles) just past Santenay.
   Type of Wine: Some of the Burgundy region's finest white wines from the Chardonnay grape, as well as red wines, from the Pinot Noir. The rich full-bodied whites are said to challenge any white wine in the world.
   Strong Vintages: *1978, 1979, 1981, 1982, 1983, 1985, 1986, 1989, 1990, 1992*
   Below you'll find the major white Côte de Beaunes:

ALOXE-CORTON
Respected Producers
Pierre Marey et Fils

BEAUNE
Respected Producers
Château de Beaune
Château de la Velle
Goupil de Bouille
Joseph Drouhin
Louis Jadot
Louis Latour
Louis Violland
Remoissenet Père et Fils

CHASSAGNE-MONTRACHET
Respected Producers

Amiot-Bonfils	*Fontaine-Gagnard*
Bernard Moreau	*Georges Déleger*
Blain-Gagnard	*Jean Pillot et Fils*
Chartron et Trebuchet	*Jean-Nöel Gagnard*
Château de Chassagne-Montrachet	*Marc Collin*
	Michel Niellon
Colin-Deleger	*Moillard-Grivot*
Duc de Magenta	*Morey*
Fernand Coffinet	*Ramonet*
	René Lamy-Pillot

BUYING WINE IN PARIS

Some of the best spots to shop for that special bottle.

• *L'Amour du Vin*, 48 avenue de la Bourdonnais (7th, M:Ecole Militaire), 45.55.68.63. Also, 94 rue Saint-Dominique (7th, M:Ecole Militaire), 45.56.12.94. Very good wines at shockingly good prices chosen by owner Patrick Dussert-Gerber, author of "Le Guide Dussert-Gerber des Vins de France." Currently our favorite stores.

• *CCA*, 128 rue Vieille du Temple (3rd, M:Saint-Sébastien), 48.87.55.67; 84 rue Monge (5th, M:Monge), 45.35.71.93; 37 boulevard Malesherbes (8th, M:Saint-Augustin); and 51 avenue La Motte Picquet (15th, M:La Motte Picquet), 43.06.26.65. A small chain that offers a variety of smart recent vintage wines at reasonable prices. Look for several of the "second" wines produced by the major Bordeaux Châteaux.

• *Caves Estève*, 10 rue de la Cerisaie (4th, M:Bastille), 42.72.33.05; 292 rue Saint-Jacques (5th, M:Port Royal), 46.34.69.78; and 32 avenue Félix Faure (15th, M:Lourmel), 44.26.33.05. A very good small chain that offers regular tastings and stocks of reasonably priced, carefully selected alternatives to the obvious Grand Crus. Popular with the locals.

• *Cave Jean-Baptiste Besse*, 48 rue de la Montagne Sainte-Geneviève (5th, M:Maubert-Mutualité), 43.25.35.80. A trusted neighborhood wine shop for more than 60 years.

• *Les Caves Taillevent*, 199 rue du Faubourg Saint-Honoré (8th, M:Saint-Philippe-du-Roule), 45.61.14.09. Though only open since 1987, this shop profits from its association with the famous restaurant by the same name.

• *Nicolas*. A large chain with shops everywhere. Popular, though we've never been terribly impressed with their selection.

• *Au Verger de la Madeleine*, 4 boulevard Malesherbes (8th, M:Madeleine), 42.65.51.99. A family-run enterprise since 1937, with a large selection of rare wines.

MEURSAULT

Respected Producers

Albert Grivault
Château de Meursault
Coche-Dury
Comte Lafon
François Jobard
Guy Roulot
Henri de Villamont
Lahaye Père et Fils
Latour-Giraud
Michel Bouzereau
Michel Dupont-Fahn
Michelot
Michelot-Buisson
Patrick Javillier
Pierre Boillot
Pierre Morey Robert Ampeau
Roger Caillot et Fils
Roux Père et Fils

PULIGNY-MONTRACHET

Respected Producers

Charles et Paul Bavard
Coron Père et Fils
Leflaive
Etienne Sauzet
Gerard Thomas
Paul Pernot

SAINT-AUBIN

Respected Producers

Maison Jean Germain
Roux Père et Fils

SANTENAY

Respected Producers

Herve de Lavoreille
Olivier Père et Fils

Other White Côte De Beaunes
- *Auxey-Duresses*
- *Cheilly-lès-Maranges*
- *Chorey-lès-Beaune*
- *Pernand-Vergelesses*
- *Saint-Romain*
- *Sampigny-lès-Maranges*
- *Savigny-lès-Beaune*

Challonaise & Mâconnaise/White
    Location: Two very large regions extending 80 kilometers (50 miles) south from the town of Chagny just past the city of Mâcon.
    Type of Wine: These two areas crank out an enormous amount of decent table wine. Most of the better wines are whites, again made from the Chardonnay grape.
    Strong Vintages: *Most wines here are meant to be drunk in the first few years.*
    Below you'll find a list of selected Challonaise & Mâconnaise whites:

MÂCON-VILLAGES

Respected Producers

André Bonhomme
Auvigue-Burrier-Revel
Bongrand
Bouchard Père et Fils
Cave de Prisse
Cave de Vivre
Château Berze
Château de Loche
Chenevière
Dominique Vaupré
Girard
Granges
Guffens-Heynen
Honoré Lavigne
Louis Jadot
Manciat-Poncet
Perelles
René Michel
Talmard
Valanges
Vieux Saint-Sorlin

POUILLY-FUISSÉ
Respected Producers
André Forest
Cave de Chaintre
Chapelle
Château Fuissé
Daniel Barraud
Cordier Père et Fils
Corsin
Ferret
Gilles Noblet
Guffens-Heynen
Lorton et Fils
Manciat-Poncet
Plantes
Roger Lasserat
René Guerin
Soufrandise
Thibert Père et Fils
Vessigaud Père et Fils

RULLY
Respected Producers
André Lheritier
Château de Davenay
Folie
Michel Briday
Eric de Suremain
Henri et Paul Jacqueson
Jaffelin
Martial Thevenot
Rully Saint-Michel

CÔTES DU RHÔNE WINES

Wines from the **Côtes du Rhône** region, which begins just past Lyon and trails down both sides of the river to about Avignon, are among the best values you'll find in good French wines and are among most underestimated by the average American consumer.

One obvious reason is that they are not available in the kinds of export quantity and variety that the Bordeaux and Burgundies are. But another reason is that some people, especially those who prefer the soft and refined qualities of a good Bordeaux, are a bit shocked by the relatively bold tastes of the **Hermitages** and even the **Châteauneuf-du-Papes**.

It's true that Hermitage is about as muscle-bound a wine as you're likely to find. Still, when it's good, it will knock your socks off. And the Châteauneuf-du-Papes, which range from rich and round to fruity and refreshing, are among our very favorites for just about any occasion. The robust **Gigondas** and **Côte Rôtie** wines also rank high in our books, and are well worth a try for anyone who enjoys a full-bodied, but rarely obnoxious, red.

This long region snaking along the river is almost completely dominated by red wines, with the dominant grape of the best products being the Syrah. Still, the supple and sophisticated whites from **Château Grillet** and **Condrieu** are said to be among the finest in all of France (they are hugely expensive as well). And the white Châteauneuf-du-Pape and Hermitage may surprise you for how good they are.

We even have to break our prejudice against rosés and recommend that you sample a **Tavel**, which many critics tout as the very best rosé around.

Below you'll find a list of major red Côtes du Rhône wines:

Châteauneuf-du-Pape

Location: An area just south of the city of Orange and north of Avignon in the heart of the southern half of the Côtes du Rhône wine region.

Type of Wine: Probably the best known of the Côtes du Rhône wines. There is incredible diversity in the wines because 13 varieties of grape are allowed. In general, the better wines are full-bodied, though rarely overpowering. They age well.

Strong Vintages: *1978, 1979,1981, 1983, 1985, 1986, 1988, 1989, 1990*

RESPECTED CHÂTEAUNEUF-DU-PAPE PRODUCERS

Beaucastel	*Guigal*
Beaurenard	*Haut des Terres Blanches*
Bosquet des Papes	*Henri Bonneau*
Cabrières	*Janasse*
Chante Cigale	*Lucien Barrot*
Chante Perdrix	*Lucien et André Brunel-Les Cailloux*
Chapoutier Barbe Rac	*Marcoux*
Charvin	*Modorée*
Château de la Gardine	*Moulin-Tacussel*
Château la Nerthe	*Nerthe*
Clefs d'Ors	*Paul Autard*
Clos des Papes	*Pegau*
Clos du Caillou	*Pierre André*
Clos du Calvaire	*Pierre Jacumin*
Clos du Mont-Olivet	*Rayas*
Durieu	*Rays Pignan*
Eddie Féraud	*Reviscoulado*
Font de Michelle	*Roquette*
Galet des Papes	*Saint-Benôit*
Gardine	*Solitude*
Gérard Charvin	*Vieux Donjon*
Grand Jean	*Vieux Télégraphe*

Côtes du Rhône
   Location: The growing region for this general wine extends over an enormous area through the Rhône River valley.
   Type of Wine: All but a tiny percent are red and there are many accepted grapes, meaning quality varies enormously. Generally hearty wines meant to be drunk young.
   Strong Vintages: *These are meant to be consumed within five years or so.*

RESPECTED CÔTES DU RHÔNE PRODUCERS

Amouriers
Andezon
Berthete
Bouche
Brezeme
Champ-Long
Château la Croix Chabrière
Château Saint-Estève d'Uchaux
Fuzière
Mordorée
Rigot
Romarins
Vieux Chàne
Vignerons d'Estezargues

Côtes du Rhône-Villages
   Location: Applies to 17 villages in the southern half of the Rhône Valley in the départements of Drôme, Gard, and Vaucluse.
   Type of Wine: The next step up from the recognized Côtes du Rhônes, therefore with a bit more body and character.
   Strong Vintages: *1985, 1986, 1988, 1989, 1990*

RESPECTED CÔTES DU RHÔNE-VILLAGES PRODUCERS

Brusset
Cabasse
Château du Grand Moulas
Coriancon
Parpaiouns
Presidente
Rabasse Charavin
Saint-Etienne
Sainte-Anne
Vieux Chêne

Côte-Rôtie

Location: An area near Vienne, about 30 kilometers (18 miles) south of Lyons.

Type of Wine: At least 80 percent from the Syrah grape, the rest from the Viognier. Full-bodied and one of the best, most prestigious of the Côtes du Rhône wines.

Strong Vintages: *1978, 1979, 1982, 1983, 1985, 1987, 1988, 1989, 1990, 1991*

RESPECTED CÔTE-RÔTIE PRODUCERS

Bernard Burgaud
Chapoutier
Clusel-Roch
Gilles Barge
Guigal
Henri Gallet
Jamet
Levet
Marius Gentaz-Dervieux
Michel Ogier
Pierre Gaillard
Pierre Barge
René Rostaing
Robert Jasmin
Vallouit Vagonier
Vidal-Fleury
Vincent Gasse

Crozes-Hermitage

Location: The area on the opposite side of the Rhône River from the city of Tournon

Type of Wine: Another bold red made from the Syrah grape, though not as finished as the Hermitage. Ages moderately well, but you'd want to drink it before a decade passes.

Strong Vintages: *1978, 1979, 1982, 1983, 1985, 1987, 1988, 1989, 1990, 1991*

RESPECTED CROZES-HERMITAGE PRODUCERS

Alain Graillot	*Pavillon-Mercurol*
Albert Belle	*Paul Jaboulet*
Château Curson	*Thalabert*
Entrefaux	*Vallouit*
Meysonniers	

Gigondas

Location: In the Montmirail hills 16 kilometers (10 miles) east of the city of Orange.

Type of Wine: A personal favorite. A rich, potent, somewhat sassy and reasonably priced red made mostly from the Grenache grape with touches of Syrah and Cinsault to round out the taste.

Strong Vintages: *1978, 1979,1981, 1983, 1985, 1986, 1988, 1989, 1990*

RESPECTED GIGONDAS PRODUCERS

Cayron
Chapelle
Château du Trignon
Clos du Joncuas
Close des Cazaux
Daniel Brusset
Delas
Edmond Burle
Font-Sane
Gouberts
Gour de Chaule
Guigal
Longue-Toque
Moulin de la Gardette
Paul Jaboulet
Pesquiers
Piaugier
Raspail
Redoitier
Saint-Gayan
Santa Duc
Tourelles

Hermitage

Location: Around the town of Tain l'Hermitage in the central part of the Rhône Valley.

Type of Wine: Probably the boldest, toughest, most tannic wine of the region. Can be absolutely superb, unless you prefer more gentle wines. Made from the Syrah grape and needs a few years before you dip in.

Strong Vintages: *1978, 1979, 1982, 1983, 1985, 1987, 1988, 1989, 1990, 1991*

RESPECTED HERMITAGE PRODUCERS

Albert Belle
Bernard Faurie
Cave de Tain l'Hermitage
Chapoutier
Chave
Henri Sorrel
Jaboulet
Vallouit Greffières

Saint-Joseph

Location: A large area on the western banks of the Rhône around the city of Tournon.

Type of Wine: Though made entirely from the Syrah grape, the same as Hermitage, the Saint-Joseph reds are much lighter, fruitier, and less expensive.

Strong Vintages: *1988, 1989, 1990*

RESPECTED SAINT-JOSEPH PRODUCERS

Alain Graillot
André Perret
Bernard Faurie
Cave de Sarras
Chapoutier
Chave
Chêne
Cuilleron
Fauterie
Gachon
Grippat
Guy Veyrier
Jean Marsanne
Monteillet
Pascal Perrier
Paul Jaboulet
Pierre Gonon
Raymond Trollat
Roche Paradis
Vallouit

Tavel

Location: Just a few kilometers northwest of Avignon, on the opposite side of the river from Châteauneuf-du-Pape.

Type of Wine: Okay, so we've included a rosé. In general, we're not fans, but these are very seductive.

Strong Vintages: *Meant to be drunk in the first couple of years.*

RESPECTED TAVEL PRODUCERS

Carabiniers
Château d'Aqueria
Maby
Mordorée
Vignerons de Tavel

Other Red Côte du Rhône Wines

- *Cornas*
- *Côteaux du Tricastin*
- *Côtes du Luberon*
- *Côtes du Ventoux*
- *Côtes du Vivarais*
- *Lirac*
- *Muscat de Beaumes-de-Venise*
- *Rasteau*
- *Vin de Pays Côteaux de l'Ardèche*
- *Vin de Pays Collines Rhodaniennes*

Below you'll find a list of major white Côtes du Rhône wines:

Château Grillet

Location: A single vineyard located in the Condrieu area opposite the Rhône from Vienne.

Type of Wine: Said to be a remarkable dry white wine made only from the finicky Viognier grape. Supposed to be one of France's finest whites, made by the same family for three centuries. We're still looking for our first bottle.

Strong Vintages: *1976, 1978, 1979, 1981, 1982, 1985, 1986, 1987, 1988, 1989*

RESPECTED CHÂTEAU GRILLET PRODUCERS

Only the one, Château Grillet

Châteauneuf-du-Pape

Location: An area just south of the city of Orange and north of Avignon in the heart of the southern half of the Côte du Rhône wine region.

Type of Wine: Very few white Châteauneuf-du-Papes are made, and it's a shame because the best of them are a real treat. A fresh but textured wine made from Grenache Blanc and Clairette grapes.

Strong Vintages: *Meant to be drunk within a few years.*

RESPECTED CHÂTEAUNEUF-DU-PAPE PRODUCERS

Chante Perdrix
Charbonnière
Château de Vaudieu
Château la Nerthe
Château Mont-Redon
Font de Michelle
François Laget
Janasse
Juliette Avril
Paul Autard
Père Anselme
Saint-Benoit

Condrieu

Location: A small 57-acre area opposite the Rhône and southwest a few kilometers from Vienne.

Type of Wine: Like Château Grillet, the Condrieu wines are made from Viognier grapes and are very highly prized. They are often described as exotic and floral wines. We're still shopping for our first bottle of Condrieu as well.

Strong Vintages: *Meant to be drunk within a few years.*

RESPECTED CONDRIEU PRODUCERS

André Perret	Georges Verney
Côteau de Chery	Gilles Barge
Cuilleron	Guigal
Delas Frères	Herve Richard
Dumazet	Philippe Pichon
Faviere	Robert Niero
	Yves Cuilleron

Crozes-Hermitage

Location: The area on the opposite side of the Rhône River from the city of Tournon

Type of Wine: A respectable white made from Marsanne and Roussanne grapes. Not much is produced and the white has nothing like the muscular flavor of the reds.

Strong Vintages: *Meant to be drunk in the first few years.*

RESPECTED CROZES-HERMITAGE PRODUCERS
Château Curson
Remizières

Hermitage

Location: Around the town of Tain l'Hermitage in the central part of the Rhône Valley.

Type of Wine: As with the white Crozes-Hermitage wines, the Hermitage whites are made from the Marsanne and Roussanne grapes. These are generally richer and fuller than the white Crozes-Hermitages, though they still possess nothing like the aggressive character of the red Hermitages.

Strong Vintages: *1985, 1987, 1988, 1989, 1990, 1991*

RESPECTED HERMITAGE PRODUCERS
Chante-Alouette
Chave

Saint-Joseph

Location: A large area on the western banks of the Rhône around the city of Tournon.

Type of Wine: A light, fruity and refreshing white wine made from Marsanne and Roussanne grapes.

Strong Vintages: *Meant to be drunk in the first few years.*

RESPECTED SAINT-JOSEPH PRODUCERS
Cave de Saint-Desirat
Cave de Tain l'Hermitage
Chapoutier
Delas
Jean-Louis Grippat
Maurice et Dominique Courbis
Pierre Gonon
Vallouit

Other White Côte du Rhône Wines
- *Clairette de Die* (sparkling)
- *Côtes du Rhône*
- *Côtes du Rhône-Villages*
- *Lirac*
- *Saint-Péray* (sparkling)

THE EXPERTS

We've compiled a lot of information for you, but we're still not experts. If you want to dig really deep, turn to the genuine gurus. Here are just a handful of invaluable resources to help you along in your newfound hobby. Parker and Johnson, both mentioned below, have several very smart books on various facets of the wine trade.

- *Anglade, Pierre (ed.)* **Larousse Wines and Vineyards of France** *(New York: Arcade Publishing, 1990 translation).*
- *Barbey, Adélaide (ed.),* **Le Guide Des Vins** *(French only), (Paris: Hachette, updated annually).*
- *Johnson, Hugh,* **Pocket Encyclopedia of Wine** *(New York: Fireside Books, Simon & Schuster Inc., updated annually).*
- *Millon, Marc and Kim,* **The Wine Roads of France** *(London: Grafton Books, Harper Collins Publishers, 1994).*
- *Parker, Jr., Robert M.,* **Wine Buyer's Guide** *(New York: Fireside Books, Simon & Schuster, 1994).*
- *Wine Spectator magazine, P.O. Box 50462, Boulder CO 80322-0462; (800) 752-7799.*

9. PARIS
- INTRODUCTION

Paris has mesmerized Americans since Benjamin Franklin snapped up the assignment as America's first ambassador to France. His portrait still hangs in the freshly redecorated Ambassador's residence on rue du Faubourg Saint-Honoré and, judging by the picture, he was pretty pleased to be here.

Who can blame him? Paris is among the world's most accessible and exhilarating cities. You can get from one end of the city center to the other in a manner of minutes – even by foot.

But you would never do that, of course, because you'd be distracted dozens of times by the sight of majestic bridges arching over the Seine, or by the splash of color in a public garden, or by the lure of an historic exhibition in a world-famous museum.

Even though Paris is a large city, you rarely feel rushed or pressed. It's simply too seductive to take an empty seat at a local café and sip a glass of vin ordinaire while you watch the people strolling by or eavesdrop on the half dozen conversations spoken in as many languages around you on the sidewalk terrace. Then, finally, you're up and off again, sampling the city as if it were an extraordinary cultural buffet, with international artworks, restaurants, music, and movies at every turn.

In the course of a single day, you can admire Impressionist master-pieces at the Musée d'Orsay, sip an afternoon Pastis at yet another café, dine on classic dishes in a bustling neighborhood bistro, take in an extravagant cabaret, and nurse a nightcap in a Left Bank boite featuring some cool jazz.

We also highlight our favorite sights, urging you to skip some of the most obvious (therefore crowded) stops because there are so many museums, monuments, and parks with more character and charm.

And eating ... well, we hope you like eating and sampling wines as much as we do because we think we've found some absolutely fabulous restaurants. Some may be a bit off the beaten track, but the memories will be well worth the price of a cab.

Paris, said to be the third most densely populated city in the world, doesn't feel like it at all.

Yes, in spots the narrow streets are made virtually impassible by legions of residents and tourists on foot, and there are traffic jams to rival any ever seen on the Cross-Bronx Expressway. But, miraculously, Paris feels more like a gathering of modestly-sized neighborhoods, each with its own distinct charm and character.

That's why we've organized the heart of the Paris section of this guidebook – the hotels, restaurants and sights – by neighborhoods. If you picture this magnificent city as a collection of communities with diverse personalities, rather than as a massive stockyard for monuments and museums, we think you're more likely to come away with a more affectionate appreciation of Paris and Parisian culture. More to the point, we think you'll have more fun.

The division into neighborhoods is a practical one as well. Most of your visit is likely to be on foot (if you're doing this trip properly, your feet should ache at the close of every day), so you'll probably want to tour the city in manageable sections.

This guide should help you choose which sections to visit. And, at the end of the day, if you just don't have the energy to travel across town for dinner, this guide will also identify a good restaurant near your hotel.

Important: You'll notice that with each of our listings of hotels, restaurants and sights, we have included the address and, beside it in parentheses, the number of the arrondissement and the name of the nearest Metro stop. Whenever you ask for directions or grab a cab, it will help matters enormously if you can identify the arrondissement of your destination.

WHAT'S AN ARRONDISSEMENT? YOU NEED TO KNOW

The divisions and neighborhoods we've created for the purposes of this guide roughly parallel the Parisian **arrondissements**.

What's an arrondissment? Glad you asked, because it's an essential bit of knowledge, whether you're following our guide, reading a local map, or trying to locate a shop you saw advertised in the newspaper.

The Paris arrondissements are essentially political wards whose current boundaries were established in the 1800s. There are 20 arrondissements, beginning at the western half of the Ile de la Cité and spiraling outward and clockwise, crossing the Seine several times and resembling, as "they" say, the chambers of a snail's shell.

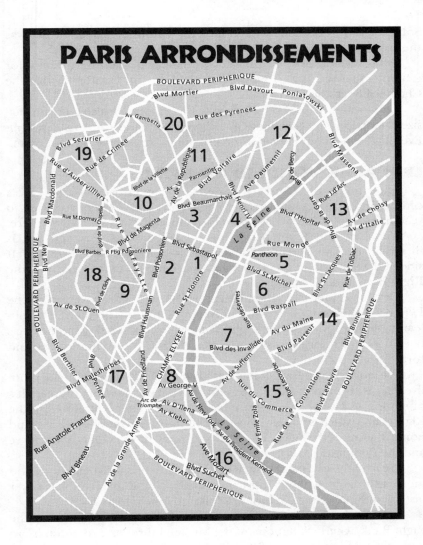

Each arrondissement has its own city hall and independently elected mayor – though, in truth, the executives of all 20 arrondissements are political puppets whose strings are pulled by Jacques Chirac, the longtime conservative mayor of Paris who has made no secret of the fact he wants to preside over all of France some day.

But the arrondissements are more than expedient political devices. The borders were drawn largely where distinct neighborhoods already existed – communities defined over time by their proximity to a religious enclave, or their role as a center of government, education or commerce.

Some are largely residential developments that sprang out of the fields as the city expanded.

After a couple of days, you'll get the hang of it, realizing instantly, for example, that the 5th arrondissement is the Latin Quarter or that the Champs-Elysées bisects the 8th.

Our locator maps should help you, but you should also buy a pocket-sized book available just about anywhere titled *Paris par Arrondissement*. Even Parisians (even Paris policemen) don't leave home without them.

LEFT BANK VERSUS RIGHT BANK

Later on, in the *Paris – Where to Stay* chapter, we describe Paris's central districts in greater detail to help you choose where you want to search for a hotel, but we also want to get in a quick word of advice here.

The Left and Right banks are so-named because – and this is incredibly obvious when you think about it – the **Left Bank** is on the left side of the Seine as it flows westward toward the Atlantic Ocean, and the **Right Bank** is on the right side. Voila!

Of course, long ago, the names also took on political overtones. The Left Bank, being home to the universities and intellectuals, was left-leaning politically, while the Right Bank, which is where big business has been conducted for centuries, was considerably more conservative and further right politically.

We much prefer the Left Bank. It's less stuffy, less crowded, and more liveable, with more small shops and more parks and open areas. It's humming with activity, but it's not as frenzied as the central part of the Right Bank, which is doubly congested because it is a business district and home to some of the bigger tourist attractions – most notably, the Louvre and the Pompidou Arts Center.

We find the cafés and bistros on the Left Bank more neighborly and more affordable, without forsaking quality. The Right Bank has fewer bistros and many cater to business folks on lunch breaks.

On the other hand, if you're looking for luxury, you'll find that on the Right Bank, where all but one of the Michelin three-star restaurants are located, and where all five of the palace-style hotels can be found. Haute couture and pricey shops also abound on the Right Bank, especially along the rue du Faubourg Saint-Honoré and rue François-Ier, both of which are in the 8th arrondissement.

An important exception to these generalizations is the area around the Bastille on the Right Bank. After the Bastille Opera House opened in 1989, that area blossomed with hip clubs and restaurants, becoming the Soho of Paris. It has a much more Left Bank feel to it than other Right Bank neighborhoods.

GETTING THE MOST OUT OF YOUR VISIT

There is so much to do in Paris it's sometimes tough to decide where to start. There are the museums, the monuments, the cafés, the shops, the parks, the open markets, the cabarets, the jazz clubs, the boats on the Seine, the gardens blazing with blossoms, and on and on and on.

One thing you should accept before you drive yourself crazy is that you can't see it all in one visit. Too many people try and end up racing from one museum to another to the point that all the paintings and sculptures begin to look alike. Then they climb aboard the plane home and realize that they never really saw the city or the people.

Our advice: Tour the city on foot and don't try to wedge in more than three or four sights a day. Also, take time to windowshop and people-watch. You learn a lot about the culture that way, plus the live theater of daily life here is as entertaining as in any city in the world.

And from time to time, just set the maps aside and wander. You'll be amazed what fascinating little streets, shops and bistros you'll discover purely by accident.

SPECIAL RECOMMENDATIONS

Two things you should do even if you're the kind of person who hates doing the obvious touristy things: Take a boat tour along the Seine and see a cabaret. They may seem hokey just because everyone does them. But they're not. They are a lot of fun.

And for listings of events going on in town pick up a copy of *Pariscope*. It costs only 3FF and is remarkably comprehensive, whether you're interested in high brow performances, low-brow movies, or puppet shows for the kids. This little marvel of a publication even has a small English-language section produced by the TimeOut folks who made their name publishing a first-rate weekly guide to events in London.

10. ITINERARIES

••• FOR THE PERFECT PARIS HOLIDAY

Here are three suggested itineraries, for three, four, and seven day vacations in Paris. You'll find each hotel, restaurant, and activity described in the pages that follow. Simply check out the relevant chapters or look them up in the index and go to town – literally!

For each, we recommend the same four choices for your hotel: for special occasions, the Hôtel Le Relais Saint-Germain or Duc de Saint-Simon, or, for the budget conscious traveler who still wants something special, the Hôtel des Grands Ecoles or the Hôtel des Grands Hommes.

We suggest you just stop by several of the monuments, admiring them from the outside. For others, we suggest you take time for the full tour. You can always check our listings to see which days museums and other sights might be closed, but keep in mind that times may change.

You'll probably want to catch a cab to most of the dinner restaurants; you will be very glad you did. And remember, as with any itinerary, no matter how perfect, set it aside from time to time and follow your own instincts and appetites.

THE PERFECT THREE DAYS

Day 1
• Check into hotel
• Tour Notre-Dame de Paris
• Stroll through the Square de l'Île de France behind Notre Dame overlooking the Île Saint-Louis
• Lunch – The Brasserie Balzar
• Stroll through Luxembourg Gardens
• Stop by Saint-Sulpice
• Window-shop at the galleries and boutiques along all the tiny side streets between the boulevard Saint-Germaine and the river
• Rejuvenating coffee or cocktail – Aux Deux Magots
• Back to your hotel to freshen up
• Dinner – Le Petit Marguery

Day 2
- Tour the Musée d'Orsay Café
- Lunch – The Musée d'Orsay Café
- Tour the Musée National Auguste Rodin
- Ride to the top of the Eiffel Tower
- Take a one-hour cruise on the river
- Rejuvenating coffee or cocktail – choose an outdoor café along the avenue de la Bourdonnais
- Back to your hotel to freshen up
- Dinner – L'Assiette

Day 3
- Stop by the Arc de Triomphe
- Stroll down the avenue des Champs-Elysées
- Peek into the Virgin Megastore
- Stop by the Place de la Concorde
- Tour the Madeleine
- Lunch — l'Écluse
- Tour the Opéra Garnier
- Stop by the Musée National du Louvre
- Stop by the Flower Market on Île de la Cité
- Stop by the booksellers who line the banks of the Seine
- Rejuvenating coffee or cocktail – Choose an outdoor café by the Seine near the boulevard Saint-Michel
- Back to your hotel to freshen up
- Dinner – Le Bistro d'à Côté

THE PERFECT FOUR DAYS

The same three days outlined above, plus:

Day 4
- Stop by the Georges Pompidou Center
- Tour the Musée Picasso
- Lunch — Jo Goldenberg
- Stop by the place des Vosges
- Stop by the place de la Bastille
- Stroll down the main street of the Île Saint-Louis
- Rejuvenating coffee or cocktail – Choose an outdoor café on the Quai d'Orleans on the Île Saint-Louis
- Back to your hotel to freshen up
- Dinner – Chardenoux

THE PERFECT SEVEN DAYS

Day 1
• Check into your hotel
• Tour Notre Dame de Paris
• Stroll through the Square de l'Île de France behind Notre Dame overlooking the Île Saint-Louis
• Lunch – The Brasserie Balzar
• Stop by the Panthéon
• Stroll through the Jardin des Plantes
• Rejuvenating coffee or cocktail – The rooftop café of Institut du Monde Arabe
• Back to your hotel to freshen up
• Early dinner – Polidor

Day 2
• Tour La Musée de Cluny
• Stroll through Luxembourg Gardens
• Lunch – La Coupole
• Stop by Saint-Sulpice
• Window-shop at the galleries and boutiques along all the tiny side streets between the boulevard Saint-Germain and the river
• Rejuvenating coffee or cocktail – Aux Deux Magots
• Back to your hotel to freshen up
• Dinner – Le Petit Marguery

Day 3
• Tour the Musée d'Orsay
• Lunch — The Musée d'Orsay café
• Tour the Musée National Auguste Rodin
• Tour the Hôtel des Invalides
• Rejuvenating coffee or cocktail — the outdoor section of the cafe Vauban almost directly across the street from the entrance to Napoleon's tomb
• Back to your hotel to freshen up
• Dinner – L'Assiette

Day 4
• Ride to the top of the Eiffel Tower
• Take a one-hour cruise on the river
• Early lunch – Au Bon Accueil
• Stop by the Trocadéro
• Stop by the Arc de Triomphe

- Stroll down the avenue des Champs-Elysées
- Peek into the Virgin Megastore
- Stop by the Place de la Concorde
- Rejuvenating coffee or cocktail – Angelina
- Stroll through the Jardin des Tuileries
- Back to your hotel to freshen up
- Dinner – Le Bistro d'à Côte

Day 5
- Stop by the Château de Vincennes
- Tour the Parc Floral
- Lunch – at the crèperie in the park
- Tour the Musée National du Louvre
- Rejuvenating coffee or cocktail – try one of the new underground cafés at the Louvre
- Stop by the Flower Market on Île de la Cité
- Stop by the booksellers who line the banks of the Seine
- Back to your hotel to freshen up
- Dinner – Tan Dihn

Day 6
- Tour the Opéra Garnier
- Tour the Madeleine
- Lunch – l'Écluse
- Tour the Montmartre neighborhood
- Rejuvenating coffee or cocktail – choose an outdoor café at the Place de Tertre near Sacré-Coeur
- Back to the hotel to freshen up
- Early dinner – Perraudin
- Go to a cabaret – The Lido or Crazy Horse

Day 7
- Stop by the Georges Pompidou Center
- Tour the Musée Picasso
- Lunch – Jo Goldenberg
- Stop by the place des Vosges
- Stop by the place de la Bastille
- Stroll down the main street of the Île Saint-Louis
- Rejuvenating coffee or cocktail at one of the outdoor cafés on the Quai d' Orleans on the Ile Saint-Louis
- Back to your hotel to freshen up
- Dinner – Chardenoux

11. PARIS - BASICS

INTRODUCTION

Though Paris is one of the world's largest and most densely populated metropolises, it is surprisingly easy to navigate. The central core of Paris, where you will no doubt spend the bulk of your time, is relatively compact.

You can, and should, cover a huge amount of ground by foot. And when your feet begin to ache, the Metro system, which is both extensive and safe, will save the day. Shops, newsstands, change bureaus, and cafes are always within easy reach, and, despite what you've heard, most Parisians are helpful and friendly – especially if you attempt even a tiny bit of poorly phrased French.

ORIENTATION

Paris, the capital of France, occupies a series of gently rolling hills in the north-central part of the country and is divided into **Left Bank** and **Right Bank** halves by the **Seine River**, which spills into the Atlantic Ocean 200 kilometers (125 miles) northwest at the port of Le Havre. The city is within easy reach of London to the northwest, Brussels to the north, Munich to the east, Geneva to the east, and Milan to the southeast.

Paris proper has a population of roughly 2.1 million people, with a metropolitan total hovering around 10 million. The climate is not exactly sensational, but it rarely grows cold enough to snow and or hot enough to melt the pavement under your feet.

France is six hours ahead of the East Coast of the United States – though, for a few days each spring and fall, the difference is seven hours (spring) or five hours (fall) because the French do not follow the same timetable for switching back and forth from daylight savings time.

GETTING AROUND TOWN

Maps, A Must

Because this city follows no grid and a single street can change names several times, a good map is essential. Printemps, Galeries Lafayette, and other local department stores circulate very useful free maps in hotels, some restaurants, and travel bureaus. Their maps also contain lots of helpful information.

If you stay more than a few days, however, you need to pick up a copy of *Paris par Arrondissement* for about 60FF. This tiny book is the Bible of Paris maps, even for Parisians. It includes every tiny street in Paris proper as well as many of the close-in suburbs. It also has Metro and bus maps, and notes various landmarks, open markets, and government offices.

Virtually any bookstore, many newsstands, and most hotel-based shops carry this book.

By Foot

Bring comfortable shoes because Paris, with its grand avenues, countless shops and bistros, and beautiful parks, is made for walking. You will walk and walk and walk, then stop for a leisurely coffee or Pernod, and then walk some more.

One strategy is to choose a neighborhood that you want to explore thoroughly, take the Metro to the heart of that neighborhood, and then walk the day away. In this guide, we divide Paris into manageable and logical neighborhoods, or quarters.

Oh, and watch out for dog droppings.

By Metro

The **Metro** system is remarkable – so remarkable that you will note that every time we give you an address for a hotel, a museum or whatever, we include the arrondissement and the Metro stop.

Rarely will you wait more than five minutes for a train. The Metro's 13 lines criss-cross the city, making every neighborhood accessible. All lines run from 5:30 in the morning to just past midnight.

And it's cheap. You can buy single tickets, but it makes much more sense to ask for a *carnet*, which is a packet of 10 tickets for only 41FF. You can travel anywhere in the city, changing as many times as you like, on a single ticket. When you buy the carnet ask for *un plan* also, which is a free map of the Metro system. Tickets and maps are also available at *Tabacs* which display a sign outside resembling the green Metro tickets. These same tickets are good for the buses.

Metro stations are clearly marked at the street level so they are easy to find. Sometimes you will spot a big yellow M in a circle. Other times, you will see the wonderful green metal Art Deco stations.

The drawbacks: the system can get crowded, especially along central lines like the number 1 that runs beneath the Champs-Elysées; the system shuts down at 12:30 a.m.; and you sometimes have to walk what seems like a long block underground to transfer lines.

By Rail

The **RER**, or *Reseau Express Regional*, is a system of four light rail train lines that are used primarily to ferry commuters into Paris during the day and back to the suburbs at night. However, there are inner city stops, so that the RER supplements the Metro. And there are several suburban sights, including Versailles, within reach of the RER system.

Prices vary according to the distance you cover, but they are reasonable. If you use the RER only to cover a few stops inside the city, simply use one of your Metro tickets. Otherwise you must find a ticket window and tell the cashier where in the suburbs you are going. The cashier will charge you accordingly. If you want a round-trip ticket (usually two tickets), ask for *aller-retour*.

By Bus

The Paris bus system, with more than 40 lines, is even more comprehensive than the Metro system. The advantage, of course, is that you are above ground and can watch the scenery sail by.

The 69 line, for instance, is like a tour bus. It begins near the Eiffel Tower, crosses the Seine near the Musée d'Orsay and the Louvre, and whisks past the Hôtel de Ville and Bastille all the way to Päre Lachaise and beyond.

Disadvantages are that traffic can slow you down and buses are often quite crowded. The Parisian sense of space is different from an American's, so don't be surprised if you are pressed in tightly on all sides.

The bus system uses the same tickets as the Metro. But if you travel some distance, you have to use two tickets. Check the diagrams posted at the bus stop to determine whether you need one or two tickets. People are occasionally stopped by the bus authority in mid-ride and ordered to pay a fine right there because they rode too far on a single ticket.

When you step on the bus there will be a small machine behind the driver. Simply push your Metro ticket into the slot and it will be properly punched. (You can buy tickets from the driver, but life is a lot easier for everyone if you've already purchased tickets at a Metro or Tabac.)

Bus service begins at 6:30 a.m. and ends around 9 p.m., with some lines working until just after midnight.

Bus Tours

There are a bunch of them. Some specialize, offering everything from art-related tours to late-night tours of live sex shows. Prices run from 100-400FF a day, depending on the type of tour.

• **Les Cars Rouges**, *3 rue Talma (16th, M:La Muette); 42.30.55.50.*
• **Cityrama**, *4 place des Pyramides (1st, M:Tuileries); 42.60.30.14.* One of the most popular.

• **Excursions Parisiennes**, *51 rue de Maubeuge (9th, M:Notre Dame de Lorette); 42.80.42.54.*
• **Paris-Vision**, *214 rue de Rivoli (1st, M:Tuileries); 42.60.30.01. Also at 1 rue Auber (9th, M:Opéra); 47.42.85.84.* One of the best and most popular.
• **Paris Bus Service** (minibus from hotel by special arrangement), *20 avenue Franklin Roosevelt, 94300 Vincennes; 43.65.55.55.* Based in the suburbs.
• **Tax Voyages** (minibus from hotel by special arrangement), *7 rue Jules Verne, 93400 Saint-Ouen; 40.12.88.08.* Based in the suburbs.

By Boat

Yes, you can actually get around town by boat – well, sort of. There is a service called **BatOBus**, which has five stops along the Seine, stretching from the Eiffel Tower to the Ile de la Cite. *Single trips are 12FF, or you can hop on and off all day with passes for 60FF.*

There are also several boat tours that swing up and down the Seine day and night for hour-long narrated tours. Boats depart about every half hour beginning in midmorning and ending at about 10 p.m. Prices run 25 to 40FF per person. Most of the boats are huge, but these brief cruises are still somehow romantic.

There are dinner tours as well, though they are said to have disadvantages – dinner distracts you from the sights and the sights distract you from a pretty expensive dinner.

• **Bateaux Mouches**, *Pont de L'Alma (7th, M:Alma-Marceau or Pont de l'Alma); 42.25.96.10.*
• **Bateaux Parisiens**, *Tour Eiffel/Pont d'Iéna (7th, M:Alma-Marceau or Pont de l'Alma); 44.11.33.44. Also at Notre-Dame/Quai Montebello (5th, M:Saint-Michel); 43.26.92.55.*
• **Vedettes de Paris**, *Port de Suffren (8th, M:Bir-Hakeim or Pont de l'Alma); 47.05.71.29 and 45.50.23.79.*
• **Vedettes du Pont Neuf**, *Square du Vert-Galant (1st, M:Pont Neuf); 46.33.98.38.*

For tours of the Paris canals that cross the northeast section of the city:
• **Canauxrama**, *13 quai de la Loire (19th, M:Jaurès); 42.39.15.00.*
• **Paris Canal**, *19 quai de la Loire (19th, M:Jauräs); 42.40.96.97.*

By Taxi

Taxi stands marked by white signs with blue lettering are scattered throughout the central part of the city, primarily at major intersections, circles, or monuments. You can also hail a cab from the sidewalk, though they are not supposed to stop if there is a taxi stand close by. You can also order a cab by phone, though there is an extra charge to summon the car to your door.

Rates should be posted on the left side window. If you have baggage there is an additional fee, and rates are a bit higher after 10 p.m. Tip is included in the fare, though it is common, even expected, that you offer 5 to 20FF depending on the length of the trip and whether the driver imperiled your life.

You know the cab is available if its bright roof light is on. If the small light beneath that sign is on, the cab is occupied or on call.

Complaints should be addressed to Service Taxi-Préfecture de Police, 36 rue des Morillons, 75015 Paris; 45.31.14.80.

Some taxi services that will get you to the airport or around town:
• **Aero Taxi**, *47.31.30.30.*
• **Alpha Taxis**, *45.85.85.85.*
• **Artaxi**, *42.41.50.50.*
• **G7**, *47.39.47.39.*
• **Taxis Bleus**, *49.36.10.10.*
• **Taxis Radio Étoile**, *42.70.41.41.*

By Car

A very successful and intelligent attorney friend of ours drove his family into Paris not long ago and became so thoroughly confused so quickly that he hailed a cab and paid the driver to lead him caravan-style to his hotel.

Paris does not have a logical street grid, there are many tricky traffic circles, even relatively straight streets change names every three or four blocks, and French drivers are statistically dangerous.

In short, there is little we can offer in terms of advice or solace if you tour Paris by car – except to find your destination as quickly and safely as possible, then park your car for as long as you can. Your hotel will show you the nearest garage, though there are not many.

If you park on the street, you will see that most spaces are marked with the word *Payant*. This means the space is metered and that somewhere nearby on the sidewalk you will see a four-foot electronic meter with a P on top that asks you how much time you would like. After you pay, the meter spits out a small receipt with the expiration time printed prominently. This slip goes on your dashboard. Parking tickets are very expensive.

Do not park in a space marked *Livraisons*. This means "deliveries."

Car rental agencies abound, but, as we've said several times now, to see Paris by car is to hate Paris. Driving is not fun, parking is a hassel and expensive, and statistically the French have truly horrible road records. Once a week there is an accident on our relatively open and safe street.

If you just absolutely must have a car, see *Car Rental* in the *Planning Your Trip* chapter.

By Bicycle

Limited use of bicycles could be fun, but stay away from crowded streets and keep your eyes wide open at all times. Rental agencies, some of which have bicycle tours, include:

- **Autotheque**, *80 rue Montmartre (2nd, M:Montmartre); 42.36.87.90.*
- **La Maison du Velo**, *11 rue Fénelon (10th, M:Gare du Nord); 42.81.24.72.* A popular one.
- **Mountain Bike Trip**, *6 place Etienne-Pernet (15th, M:Felix-Faure); 48.42.57.87.*
- **Paris-Velo**, *2 rue du Fer-à-Moulin (5th, M:Censier-Daubenton); 43.37.59.22.*

PLACES OF WORSHIP

The *International Herald Tribune* publishes a weekly list of services. Or, for information about services, *phone 46.33.01.01 Monday through Friday.* A few churches and temples where services are conducted in English:

- **Adath Shalom**, *22bis rue des Belles-Feuilles (16th, M:Porte Dauphine); 45.53.84.09.*
- **American Cathedral** (Episcopal-Anglican), *23 avenue George V (8th, M:George V); 47.20.17.92.*
- **American Church in Paris** (Protestant), *65 quai d'Orsay (7th, M:Invalides); 47.05.07.99.*
- **Church of Christ**, *4 rue Deodat-Severac (17th, M:Malesherbes); 42.27.50.86.*
- **International Baptist Fellowship**, *123 avenue du Maine (14th, Mouton-Duvernet); 47.49.15.29.*
- **Saint-George's Anglican Church**, *7 rue Auguste-Vacquerie (16th, M:Kléber); 47.20.22.51.*
- **Saint-Joseph's Catholic Church**, *50 avenue Hoche (8th, M:Charles-de-Gaulle); 42.27.28.56.*
- **Saint-Michael's Church** (Anglican), *5 rue d'Aguesseau (8th, M:Madeleine); 47.42.70.88.*

LOST & FOUND

Anything that is lost is likely to stay that way. However, if you're lucky your belongings might show up or be reported to the **Lost and Found Bureau**, *36 rue des Morillons (15th, M:Convention). The office is open Monday to Friday from 8:30 a.m. to 5 p.m. For information, phone 45.31.14.80.*

FOR MORE INFORMATION

The **central tourist office**, *open during the week from 9 a.m. to 8 p.m., is located at 127 avenue des Champs-Elysées (8th, M:George V); 49.52.53.54, Fax 49.52.53.00.* Smaller offices are also found at the Eiffel Tower and all the train stations except Gare Saint-Lazarre.

City Hall has an information office *open Monday through Saturday from 9 a.m. to 6 p.m. at 29 rue de Rivoli (4th, M:Hôtel de Ville); 42.76.43.43.*

For an English version phone recording of current entertainment and events, *call 49.52.53.56.*

There are other guide books as well. Of course, they are not nearly as good as ours, but if you insist on a second opinion you could try the Michelin Paris Guide.

12. WHERE TO STAY IN PARIS

Your first challenge is to decide where to stay. To make that decision, you need to know a bit about the various central neighborhoods of Paris — which has more character, which has better restaurants or more sights to see, which is historic and which is relatively new, that sort of thing.

Choosing a hotel recalls the old rule of thumb about the three most important things in shopping for a house. Answer: location, location, location.

So what follows here are what we think of as the seven primary neighborhoods in central Paris and an accompanying list of hotels. Each neighborhood is home to several very pleasant hotels.

For the most part, the hotels we've included here are ones in which any American would feel comfortable. Unless otherwise noted, all have private bathrooms. Virtually every room also has a television (most with cable) and a direct dial phone, and, in many cases, a hair dryer, a minibar and a small safe for your valuables.

Even in the better hotels, rooms are often on the small size by American standards. But that is rarely a problem because you won't spend much time in the room anyway. But if you do want something larger, ask for a "junior suite." It will be slightly larger than the average double and will have a small sitting area at one end. A full suite, called an *appartement*, will have a separate sitting room.

The management and reception staff at the better hotels (most three stars and all four stars) are university trained. Hotel management is a respected profession in Europe and the men and women who practice it are quite serious about providing quality service. You may have heard lots of horror stories about the rudeness of the French, but if you feel a victim of that attitude at your hotel you should change hotels.

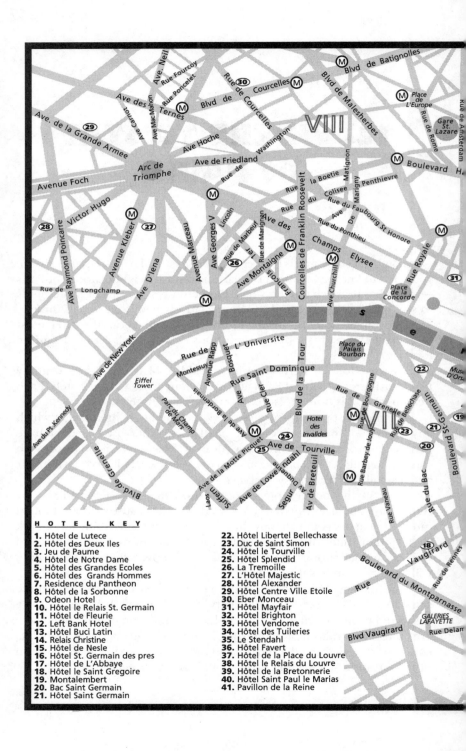

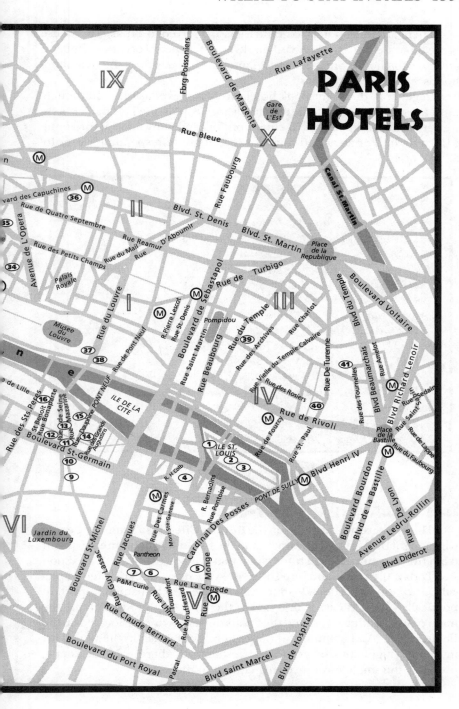

There are some hotels so grand they're referred to as palaces. We list those separately in case your visit marks an extra special occasion. But our advice is to choose one of the nice, mid-sized hotels near the neighborhoods you most want to visit.

In general, the Right Bank hotels are more expensive, even though most are no better (and some are clearly worse) than the Left Bank hotels we list. You should be able to enjoy comfort and convenience for about $100 a night. For an added touch of class, figure on spending closer to $200 a night.

THE FAB FIVE

Some call them palaces. These are the places a fairytale princess would stay, or an industry giant, or a major movie star on a promotional tour for his latest release. They are sumptuous and chic in every way. Fit for a fantasy, if you can foot the bill. Personally, we just stop by for a glass of Chablis every now and then. (Rates are for doubles. Suites run from 10,000 to 50,000FF.)

LE BRISTOL, *112 rue du Faubourg Saint-Honoré (8th, M:Miromesnil), 42.66.91.45, Fax 42.66.68.68. Rates: 2,500 to 3,600FF.*

LE CRILLON, *10 place de la Concorde (8th, M:Concorde), 44.71.15.02, Fax 44.71.15.02. Rates: 2,300 to 3,800FF.*

HÔTEL GEORGE V, *31 avenue George V (8th, M:George V), 47.23.54.00, Fax 47.20.40.00. Rates: 2,100 to 2,400FF.*

LA PLAZA ANTHENEE, *25 avenue Montaigne (8th, M:Franklin-Roosevelt), 47.23.78.33, Fax 47.20.20.70. Rates: 2,700 to 4,700FF.*

THE RITZ, *15 place Vendome (1st, M:Tuileries), 42.60.38.30, Fax 42.60.23.71. Rates: 2,700 to 4,100FF.*

THE ISLANDS

ÎLES DE LA CITÉ & SAINT-LOUIS

This is where it all began — on the **Île de la Cité** with a primitive people who sought proximity to the water and the fish, and who wanted to profit from the busy north-south trade route that crossed the Seine at this spot.

Today, the two islands are still at the very heart of Paris. Geographically, they are almost dead center. They have also remained important politically. Though City Hall is across the river on the Right Bank, the **main police headquarters** and the **Palais de Justice** are still located on the Ile de la Cité. And culturally, though there's not much in the way of art museums, nightclubs or even great restaurants, there is **Notre Dame**, probably the single most inspiring church in the land.

An appropriate spot to begin any tour of Paris, whether its your first trip or your fiftieth, is **Ground Zero**, a marker in the square facing Notre Dame from which all mileage counts to Paris are measured. From here, on foot, you can reach most of Paris proper within 30 minutes.

The **Île Saint-Louis**, which began as a residential real estate venture centuries ago, is much more hospitable for overnight stays than the area around Notre Dame, which is crawling with tourists night and day. You'll also find better food and some tiny shops and galleries worth visiting along the main street that divides Saint-Louis east to west.

WHERE TO STAY

1. HOTEL DE LUTECE, *65 rue Saint-Louis-en-l'Ile (4th, M:Pont-Marie), 43.26.23.52, Fax 43.29.60.25. Rooms: 23. Rates for doubles: 810FF. Breakfast: 43FF. No restaurant. Note: No credit cards. Traveler's checks are accepted.*

The Lutece is owned by the same people who own the Deux-Iles a few doors down (see our next entry). Like the other, it is small, having been carved out of a 17th-century apartment house, and is well-located for both Left and Right Bank expeditions.

This is not as bright and cheery as its sister inn, though there is a warming, well-used fireplace in the entry. A cozy three-table breakfast nook is also located off the main foyer.

The hallways are quite narrow, most rooms have beamed ceilings, and bathrooms come either with a somewhat cramped shower or a tub with hand-held shower (request the latter). The staff is friendly and English is spoken here. Remember: no credit cards.

2. HOTEL DES DEUX-ILES, *59 rue Saint-Louis-en-l'Ile (4th, M:Pont-Marie), 43.26.13.35, Fax 43.29.60.25. Rooms: 17. Rates for doubles: 810FF. Breakfast: 43FF. No restaurant. Note: No credit cards. Traveler's check are accepted.*

A delightful little hotel, despite their infuriating policy of not accepting credit cards.

Set among the small shops that line the main street of the Ile Saint-Louis, the Deux-Iles is a cheery and warm hotel fashioned out of a 17th-century apartment building. It offers a very good location (close to Left and Right Bank attractions and restaurants) at a reasonable price.

The lobby, with its glass-enclosed garden, is the most colorfully decorated space in the hotel, though the smallish rooms are comfortable and pleasing. There is plenty of closet space, and bathrooms are outfitted sometimes with showers and sometimes with tubs equipped with hand-held showers. English spoken here.

3. JEU DE PAUME, *54 rue Saint-Louis-en-l'Ile (4th, M:Pont-Marie), 43.26.14.18, Fax 40.46.02.76. Rooms: 32. Rates for doubles: 795-1,270FF. Breakfast: 75FF. No restaurant.*

Only six years old, this fascinating hotel was once an indoor tennis court, where members of Louis XIII's royal entourage thrashed out a few sets in the mid-1600s. You can still see the loft where friends and fans watched the matches in progress.

Enter off of the shop-lined rue Saint-Louis-en-l'Ile, through a short stone passageway, past a small garden, and into a captivating lobby with a beamed ceiling, red-tiled floor, leather couches and a small bar. Beyond a glass elevator that takes you up to your room is the breakfast area, with glass-topped wrought-iron tables, original rough stone walls, and a lattice of timbers that support both walls and ceiling.

Rooms are a decent size, with blond wood furnishings, fabric on the walls, beamed ceilings, minibars and gray marble bathrooms. If you're worn out by your flight or a few days of energetic sightseeing, relax in the free hotel sauna. The closets are disappointingly small.

Book long in advance.

LEFT BANK

THE LATIN QUARTER
5th Arrondissement

The **Latin Quarter** is just like you would imagine it to be. This is where the Romans expanded the early city of Lutetia, building arenas, baths and homes up the slopes of the hill which later became known as **Mount Sainte-Geneviève**, and where today stands the gravely majestic **Panthéon**, a last resting place for many of France's greatest artists and politicians.

Roman and medieval remains can still be seen here, both at the **Arènes de Lutece** and the **Cluny museum**. The **rue Mouffetard** with its colorful open market was once the primary Roman road to the south.

It was also on these slopes that the **Sorbonne** and **University of Paris** were established. They naturally attracted students and scholars who once walked the streets with their noses in the air speaking Latin — thus Latin Quarter.

Today, there are even more schools, students and professors, often lending the narrow old streets the gaiety of their youth and enthusiasm. Bookstores, cafés, small clubs and restaurants abound and are among the more affordable in the city. There is a dash of elitism as well: The 5th arrondissement is also home to the famous **Tour d'Argent** restaurant and ex-President François Mitterand.

WHERE TO STAY
4. HÔTEL DE NOTRE DAME, *19 rue Maître-Albert (5th, M:Saint-Michel or Maubert-Mutualité), 43.26.79.00, Fax 46.33.50.11. Rooms: 34. Rates for doubles: 690-750FF. Breakfast: 40FF. No restaurant.*

As it's name suggests, the Notre Dame is just a block from the river just opposite Notre Dame. It also happens to be a couple of blocks from Mitterand's home (just in case you want to drop by to offer him a bit of advice).

Though this hotel is near the heart of the busy Latin Quarter, it is on a tiny street that doesn't get much traffic. As a result you have a pretty and tranquil hideaway.

The rooms are, as with most hotels here, on the smallish side. They have been redecorated in the past four years in a kind of unobtrusive contemporary style, with blond wood desks, fabric wall coverings, and beige faux-marble bathrooms, which are separated from the bedrooms by frosted glass partitions. Bathrooms all have tubs, many of which are the three-quarter length variety, where you sit rather than lay yourself out.

Minibars and cable television are the rule. A tiny breakfast room is just past the front desk, and the staff is very friendly and speaks good English.

5. HÔTEL DES GRANDES ECOLES, *75 rue du Cardinal Lemoine (5th, M:Cardinal Lemoine), 43.26.79.23, Fax 43.25.28.15. Rooms: 48. Rates for doubles: 330-600FF. Breakfast: 40FF. No restaurant.*

Charming with a capital 'C.'

The Grandes Ecoles, built as a private home back in 1760, takes its name from the quarter, which is liberally seeded with schools of all kinds for all ages. Though the hotel is just a stone's throw from the Panthéon and the busy, but charming, Place de la Contrescarpe, it is set off the street in a garden courtyard that is unusually tranquil for this neighborhood.

The three main buildings, three stories high, flank the cobbled courtyard, where many of the visitors take breakfast or sip an afternoon drink. Most rooms, which are smallish to average size, look out on the courtyard and reflect the garden motif in floral and pastel decor.

In fact, tranquillity is considered so important here that though the owners outfitted every room to receive cable television, guests said they wanted no such thing. Result: no televisions at all.

The Grands Ecoles could use a splash of paint here and there, but the ambiance and the staff are very welcoming. Book at least a month in advance because regulars quickly claim all the rooms.

6. HÔTEL DES GRANDS HOMMES, *17 place du Panthéon (5th, M:Luxembourg or Sorbonne), 46.34.19.60, Fax 43.26.67.32. Rooms: 32. Rates for doubles: 730-760FF. Breakfast: 35FF. No restaurant.*

The Grands Hommes offers elegance and a stunning location at a relatively reasonable price. The hotel dates back to the 18th century and looks directly out onto the majestic Pantheon, the handsome City Hall for the 5th arrondissement, and the expansive place du Panthéon. In fact, rooms on the second, fifth and sixth floors have small terraces where you can gaze transfixed or, in some cases, even take your breakfast.

Rooms are all decorated differently, though many have the same type of beamed ceiling, brass beds, antique (and antiqued) armoires, and colorful prints covering the walls. Minibars, radios and television with cable come with each room. Bathrooms have tubs and are tiled.

The breakfast room is the converted wine and storage cellar downstairs from a well-lit, warmly decorated lobby and sitting area. Very well located, near the Luxembourg Gardens, and popular with business types. Book ahead. If you find the hotel booked, see Résidence du Panthéon below.

7. RÉSIDENCE DU PANTHÉON, *19 place du Panthéon (5th, M:Luxembourg or Sorbonne), 43.54.32.95. Rooms: 34. Rates for doubles: 730-760FF. Breakfast: 35FF. No restaurant.*

The same owner and largely the same hotel as the Grand Hommes detailed above.

8. HÔTEL DE LA SORBONNE, *6 rue Victor-Cousin (5th, M:Luxembourg or Sorbonne), 43.54.58.08, Fax 40.51.05.18. Rooms: 37. Rates for doubles: 400-470FF. Breakfast: 35FF. No restaurant.*

A no-frills kind of place, but very reasonably priced, clean and well located for Latin Quarter adventures.

The Sorbonne is on a tiny street facing one of the many entrances to, yes, you guessed it, the Sorbonne. If you stay here, you should go around the corner to the square fronting the Sorbonne entrance and have a coffee at one of the small cafés — it's great people watching as you spy on the life of a French student.

The hotel has small rooms outfitted in a kind of nondescript contemporary style, and small bathrooms, many with showers. All rooms have cable television.

The breakfast nook off of the entry on the main level has but four tables and a somewhat intimidating African totem. But again, it's perfectly serviceable and the staff is well used to foreigners.

SAINT-GERMAIN & MONTPARNASSE
6th & 14th Arrondissements

An interesting blend of student, commercial and residential interests, this quarter is at the center of the Left Bank and is probably best known to Americans as the favored stomping grounds for Lost Generation literary giants such as Hemingway and Fitzgerald.

Their old haunts are still very much alive — the cafés especially still profit from the Lost Generation mystique. Along the boulevard Saint-Germain and, further south, the boulevard du Montparnasse, you'll find such familiar sounding places as the **Deux Magots**, the **Café Flore**, the **Select**, the **Coupole**, the **Polidor**, and the **Closerie des Lilas** (see "Literary Legacies" in *Where to Eat in Paris*).

The **Luxembourg Gardens** in this quarter are Paris's favorite, and rightly so. The grounds are beautifully kept with vibrant beds, tranquil hideaways, and a busy central pool where children sail toy boats. The **Saint-Germain-des-Prés** and **Saint-Sulpice** churches are also in this quarter.

Between the boulevard Saint-Germain and the river is a bustling commercial neighborhood that includes dozens of galleries with original art — much of it overpriced, but still worth a look.

There are several very good hotels here, allowing you to profit from the variety of the neighborhood, its many restaurants and clubs, and its proximity to the rest of the city. In fact, if you're a Left Bank type, this is probably what you're looking for.

WHERE TO STAY

9. ODÉON HÔTEL, *3 rue de l'Odéon (6th, M:Odéon), 43.25.90.67, Fax 43.25.55.98. Rooms: 34. Rates for doubles: 850-1,100FF. Breakfast: 55FF. No restaurant.*

The Odéon Hotel is in a terrific location and would be a dream come true for those whose vision of early Parisian architecture is beamed ceilings. The 16th-century building was renovated a few years ago and, though the beams are a nice touch, the designers might have done something to enlarge the narrow hallways and tiny rooms.

The rooms do, however, have plugs adaptable to American computers and two telephone lines so you won't have to miss that important client while you're on the phone with your partner.

Rooms are air-conditioned, which is uncommon in Paris despite the summer humidity. English is spoken.

10. HÔTEL LE RELAIS SAINT-GERMAIN, *9 carrefour de l'Odéon (6th, M:Odéon), 43.29.12.05, Fax 46.33.45.30. Rooms: 10. Rates for doubles: 1,450-1,580FF. Suite available. Breakfast included. No restaurant.*

This is hotel heaven.

If you want good taste, style, elegance, period furniture, big rooms, huge closets and storage space where you can keep your luggage and purchases, breakfast any time of the day in a sunny setting that allows for lots of people-watching, great service, and even a small library in case you finish the book you brought, then you definitely want to be one of the lucky people to get a reservation at the Hôtel Le Relais Saint-Germain. Some rooms even have terraces.

The hôtelier, Monsieur Laipsker, is justifiably proud of his creation, which he continues to improve all the time. The one drawback: English is only just barely spoken. If you have a spirit of adventure, a love of charm, and some money to spend, this is a marvelous spot to settle in.

11. HÔTEL DE FLEURIE, *32-34 rue Gregoire de Tours (6th, M:Saint-Germain-des-Prés), 43.29.59.81, Fax 43.29.68.44. Rooms: 29. Rates for doubles: 610-1,200FF. Breakfast: 50FF. No restaurant.*

This is a charming hotel on the other side (away from the river) of the boulevard Saint-Germain. Its location makes it much quieter than other hotels in the area, but it is still just steps away from the action. The 18th-century building was completely renovated in 1989 and the result of the work is a lovely setting with many modern and practical features (such as individual room controls for heat and air conditioning).

A light touch in the traditional furnishings is matched by the light color of the textured fabric wall covering and the marble in the baths, which come with mounted towel warmers (the rooms available for 610FF have more modest bathrooms with showers only). Each room also has a valet-pants presser.

The staff is friendly and English is spoken.

12. LEFT BANK HÔTEL, *9 rue de l'Ancienne Comédie (6th, M:Odéon), 43.54.01.70, Fax 43.26.17.14. Rooms: 31. Rates: 990-1,090FF. Breakfast: 30FF. No restaurant.*

Just a few doors up from **Le Procope** (one of the oldest restaurants in Paris), the Left Bank Hotel welcomes you into a lobby that is pure charm. Although the decorators were somewhat heavy-handed in their application of the Empire style, many of the rooms are good sized and a few come with day beds that would be ideal for a couple traveling with a child. Some of the rooms have a delightful roofline view of Notre Dame.

A fun location, where English is spoken and service is as important to the staff as it is to you. And surprise: this is part of the American Best Western chain.

13. HÔTEL BUCI LATIN, *34 rue de Buci (6th, M:Mabillion), 43.29.07.20, Fax 43.29.67.44. Rooms: 27. Rates for doubles: 850FF. Suites available. Breakfast included. Restaurant: coffee shop open until 6 p.m.*

Designed with a capital 'D' from top to bottom by a young Frenchman, Alain Perrier (whose work echoes that of Philippe Stark), the Buci Latin seems to have been created on the principle that both fun and form follow function.

The stairway is painted floor to ceiling with graffiti and the door to each room has its own distinctive paint job. Inside, the rooms are a nice size with lots of beautiful light wood and Haitian cotton spreads and wall hangings. The rooms on the street side are air conditioned (so you can close the windows on hot, noisy nights), but those on the court are not.

The duplex and the junior suite are something to write home about. The upstairs bathroom in the duplex has a clawfooted tub, a gorgeous tiled stall shower, a double sink and a rattan vanity that will make you feel you're spending quality time in the tropics. All this on a mezzanine that overlooks the king size bed downstairs. The junior suite has a huge bedroom, a large circular whirlpool bath and a tiny private terrace.

The English-speaking staff prides itself on offering excellent service, and the hotel is well-located in the beating heart of the Saint-Germain-des-Prés quarter.

The Buci also offers something very rare in Paris: rooms accessible to people in wheelchairs. Although management failed to install the rails that would make the shower and toilet areas of the bathroom safer, the rooms are larger, they're on the ground floor, they have extra wide doors and the showers are completely open.

14. RELAIS CHRISTINE, *3 rue Christine (6th, M:Odéon), 43.26.71.80, Fax 43.26.89.38. Rooms: 51. Rates for doubles: 1,520-1,650FF. Breakfast: 95FF. No restaurant.*

On a quiet street in one of Paris's most historic and picturesque Left Bank neighborhoods, the Relais Christine offers guests comfort, style and top quality service — for a price, of course.

The building, a 16th-century cloister, has been transformed into a contemporary four-star luxury hotel without losing its historic charm. Each room is decorated slightly differently in a charming melange of traditional French styles. In addition, each looks out onto a flower-filled courtyard.

The marble bathrooms are fit for royalty, which seems only appropriate since the street and the hotel are named for the second daughter of Henri IV and Marie de Medici. (Be sure to ask for the brochure—available in English — relating the history of the neighborhood, the street and the hotel.)

The breakfast room, a converted basement with stone walls, vaulted ceiling and suit of armor, vibrates with a sense of history. And bacon (or ham) and eggs are available for those on special high cholesterol diets.

The staff speaks English and is extremely eager to help. A suite and a duplex are available, as is a private garage.

15. HÔTEL DE NESLE, *7 rue de Nesle (6th, M:Odéon or Saint-Michel), 43.54.62.41. No fax. Rooms: 20. Rates for doubles: 260-450FF. Breakfast: included. No restaurant.*

The Hôtel de Nesle is not for everyone. For one thing, they don't take reservations (just show up around 10:30), they don't speak English, and not a single member of the staff has benefited from a degree in hotel management.

But what the hotel does have are happy, satisfied customers who have enough money left over after they pay their hotel bill to enjoy Paris as they see fit. The hotel is located in as chic a neighborhood as the Left Bank offers. (Indeed, it's a stone's throw from the four-star Relais Christine.) The street is quiet, some of the rooms look out on a rose garden (two live ducks, no extra charge), and the sheets on the freshly made beds are immaculately white.

The place is charming, but funky. Almost all of the rooms are painted with nearly life-sized murals depicting various scenes from French history. All have sinks, and many also have toilets and tubs and showers. It's possible to share a two-bed room with a stranger and pay only 130FF per night, breakfast included. A couple of large rooms will accommodate four people for only 450FF.

If you're young or young at heart and on a shoestring budget, you'd feel at home.

16. HÔTEL SAINT-GERMAIN-DES-PRÉS, *36 rue Bonaparte (6th, M:Saint-Germain-des-Pres), 43.26.00.19, Fax 40.46.83.63. Rooms: 30. Rates for doubles: 750-950FF. Breakfast: included. No restaurant.*

Just steps away from Les Deux Magots and the lively center of Saint-Germain, this pleasant hotel has a lovely, antique-filled lobby to welcome you and a cozy breakfast room to help you start each day. The reception staff is English-speaking and, while not warm and fuzzy, they are efficient and clearly want to be of service.

The rooms are generally small, but are bright and gay thanks to the color schemes and patterns of the wallpaper, rugs and bed spreads. The large armoires have enough space for clothes and suitcases. While the sitting rooms of the suites (1,300-1,600FF) are on the small side, the bedrooms are spacious and comfortable.

Many guests are repeat customers, so clearly the Hôtel Saint-Germain-des-Prés is doing something right.

17. HÔTEL DE L'ABBAYE, *10 rue Cassette (6th, M:Saint-Sulpice), 45.44.38.11, Fax 45.48.07.86. Rooms: 46. Rates for doubles: 920-1,450FF. Suites available. Breakfast included. No restaurant.*

This 18th-century residence gets more and more charming as time goes by. The standard rooms are not huge, but the others are very comfortable and the four duplex suites come with private terraces. Room number four, a large one, has its own private lovely garden. And the view from the terraces of the suites is quintessentially Parisian. In fact, you can see the top of Saint-Sulpice's bell towers.

In good weather, you can enjoy breakfast in the slate courtyard at the center of the hotel. Or you can order room service for breakfast or light meals any time you like.

The decor of the rooms is not wildly distinctive— no antiques, for example — but they are very pleasant. The real draw, aside from the charm of the common areas and the extremely friendly and helpful staff, is that the Hôtel de l'Abbaye, while situated in the heart of Saint-Germain, offers an oasis of tranquillity in one of the world's most frenetic cities.

18. HÔTEL LE SAINT-GREGOIRE, *43 rue de l'Abbé-Gregoire (6th, M:Saint-Placide), 45.48.23.23, Fax 45.48.33.95. Rooms: 20. Rates for doubles: 760-1,290FF. Suite available. Breakfast: 60FF. No restaurant.*

Although in the heart of Paris and near many of the 6th arrondissement's most famous attractions, the Hôtel Le Saint-Gregoire is tucked away in a quiet corner where few tourists (other than hotel guests) venture.

The decorating style in the larger than average rooms relies on a pleasant mix of antiques and modern pieces. Some rooms (890-1,290FF) have wonderful private terraces. The junior suite (excellent for a party of three, at 1,290FF) has a small terrace on the courtyard. When asked what made his hotel different from all the others, François de Bene, the manager, replied that "the Saint-Gregoire is more like a home than a hotel." Given his friendliness and eagerness to please, it's easy to believe.

An added advantage is that the hotel is near a few off-price retailers. Look for the words "stock" and "dégriffé" in the windows.

NEAR THE EIFFEL TOWER
7th Arrondissement

At a little more than 27,000FF per square meter, this is the priciest real estate in the city. It's surprising in a way because so much is residential and because the character is not nearly as stuffy or snooty as two or three Right Bank neighborhoods.

Maybe in part because of the real estate, this neighborhood is pleasant and easy to explore, except for the government agencies that clog up the eastern half with walled-off buildings, official cars and armed guards.

The **Eiffel Tower** (*La Tour Eiffel*) is here, of course, as is the **Hôtel des Invalides**, which is the golden dome under which you will find Napoleon's tomb. The **Musée Rodin**, dedicated to the sculptor, and the **Musée d'Orsay**, the converted rail station where the best of the country's Impressionist works are housed, are must-sees on any itinerary.

This is also where many of the enormous barge-like tour boats leave on their hour-long trips up and down the river. Taking a boat may sound a bit touristy, but the experience is well worth the price (see Chapter 11, *Paris – Basics*, p. 153).

There are a handful of very good restaurants and some trendy hotels near the Musée d'Orsay and the Eiffel Tower. And, whether it's for better or worse, you're likely to bump into a bunch of Americans here — and not just tourists. This is where a large part of Paris's American population has nested.

WHERE TO STAY

19. MONTALEMBERT, *3 rue de Montalembert (7th, M:Rue du Bac)*, *45.48.68.11, Fax 42.22.58.19. Rooms: 51. Rates for doubles: 1,550-1,980FF. Suites available. Breakfast: 95FF. Restaurant.*

It's your honeymoon, your anniversary, your special gift to yourself. Whatever the occasion, the Montalembert will make it memorable and make you feel special.

This well-located luxury hotel offers a range of services not usually found outside the grand hotels such as the Ritz or Crillon. (The Montalembert also has the added benefit of being less stuffy ... er, *formal*, than the deluxe hotels.)

The special pluses include 24-hour room service, air conditioning, VCRs and a video library, valet service, two private rooms, which can be used for meetings or private dining, and convenient parking. These pluses make up for the less-than-huge (but not small) rooms.

In addition to the tangible services, an energetic and English-speaking staff is available to respond to your every need.

The one warning here involves the choice between rooms appointed in what management calls "the traditional French style" or the modern style. Go traditional. If you do, you'll feel like you're living a Parisian dream. If you choose modern, you might as well be at a Hilton in any city in the world.

20. BAC SAINT-GERMAIN, *66 rue du Bac (7th, M:Rue du Bac)*, *42.22.20.03, Fax 45.48.52.30. Rooms: 21. Rates for doubles: 590-890FF. Breakfast: 79FF. No restaurant.*

Don't be put off by the unimposing entrance of this well-located small hotel (virtually on the corner of rue du Bac and boulevard Saint-Germain). Take the elevator up one flight to the reception and lobby area and you'll be in good hands with the friendly staff that speaks excellent English.

The rooms are good sized and the double windows keep the noise from the street to a minimum. The real prize here is the eighth-floor terrace, part of which is glass enclosed and which offers a classic view of the Paris roofline.

Breakfast is served on the terrace and the staff is amenable to its use by guests at virtually any hour. Stop at a local wine store, make a special selection, and take the elevator to the top. You'll feel like a native in no time.

21. HÔTEL SAINT-GERMAIN, *88 rue du Bac (7th, M:Rue du Bac)*, *45.48.62.92, Fax 45.48.26.89. Rooms: 24. Rates for doubles: 400-680FF. Breakfast: 40FF. No restaurant.*

Apparently there are more than a dozen hotels with this same name in Paris, so if you want to avoid ending up somewhere other than where you're staying, memorize your address. This particular Hôtel Saint-Germain combines a reasonable price, good location, and a touch of elegance. The best bets are the rooms on the courtyard. This isn't because they're quieter (double panes on all the windows take care of that problem), but because all these bathrooms have been renovated and are quite stunning. The baths in the other rooms are cramped and, by American standards, pretty old-fashioned.

This Hôtel Saint-Germain has been a hotel for thirty years, and the building has been in the same family for two hundred years. English, Spanish, and German spoken – probably even some French.

22. HÔTEL LIBERTEL BELLECHASSE, *8 rue de Bellechasse (7th, M:Solférino), 45.50.22.31, Fax 45.51.52.36. Rooms: 43. Rates for doubles: 650-750FF. Breakfast: 60FF. No restaurant.*

If you plan to make an extensive visit to the **Musée d'Orsay** (which we score as the city's best large art museum), this is the hotel for you. It's half a block down from that bright jewel in Paris's cultural crown.

Recently renovated, the hotel's public areas offer lots of glass and chrome. The rooms are small and, if you happen to get one of those decorated in a deep gray wallpaper, a little on the dark side. Ask for a yellow room and your visit will seem sun-filled even if the weather doesn't cooperate (which it frequently doesn't).

The staff is friendly and English is spoken, which is helpful because most guests are American.

23. DUC DE SAINT-SIMON, *14 rue de Saint-Simon (7th, M:Rue du Bac), 42.22.07.52, Fax 45.48.68.25. Rooms: 29. Rates for doubles: 1,000-1,500FF. Suites available. Breakfast: 70FF. No restaurant.*

More than half of the Duc de Saint-Simon's guests are American, so it's hardly undiscovered. But that fact also attests to how exquisite this small hotel is.

Although the rooms are not large, they are decorated in style. Each bedstead and dresser appears to have been personally selected, as if it were meant to decorate the home of an individual with discerning taste. Indeed, the sitting rooms of the suites (1,500-1,900FF) are amazing.

Four regular rooms (numbers 14, 24, 25 and 42) come with private terraces that would be the ideal spot for a romantic rendezvous.

You can enjoy breakfast in your room, or in what was, in the 17th century, a coal and wine cellar. Room service is also available for light meals all day. The reception staff speaks excellent English. Reservations as much as a month in advance are necessary in peak season.

If you're lucky, one of the Americans you will run into will be one of America's most famous actresses. We're told she stays at the Duc de Saint-Simon frequently. At first, you may not see her. You may just hear that unforgettably husky voice.

24. HÔTEL LE TOURVILLE, *16 avenue de Tourville (7th, M:Ecole Militaire) 47.05.62.62, Fax 47.05.43.90. Rooms: 30. Rates for doubles: 760-1,390FF. Suites available. Breakfast: 50FF. No restaurant.*

The owners of the Hôtel Le Tourville are committed to making their hotel the best it can be, and their quest for quality shows. The average-size rooms are warmly decorated in soft colors (yellow, sand or pink schemes), and the well-outfitted bathrooms have classy marble touches. Antique armoires and dressers add a touch of elegance to the modern bed and nightstand arrangements.

Easily the nicest double rooms are the four with private terraces. But at 1,390FF, they're not exactly a bargain, especially if you happen to come during a stretch of wet or cool weather. The two junior suites (1,990FF) are good for families, with beds enough to sleep four. They also have whirlpool baths, stall showers and double sinks.

The Tourville, which was renovated in 1993, is charming, the staff seems eager to help and the location is very good (near sights, the Metro and a cab stand). But it seemed a wee bit overpriced. Perhaps the pricing is in anticipation of the fourth star the hotel has been told it will receive in the fall of 1994 from the French hotel board.

25. HÔTEL SPLENDID, *29 avenue de Tourville (7th, M:Ecole Militaire), 45.51.24.77, Fax 44.18.94.60. Rooms: 48. Rates for doubles: 670-790FF. Suites available. Breakfast: 42FF. No restaurant.*

Of all the hotels we visited, the newly renovated and spiffy Splendid is the only one that conceded up front that it would negotiate its rates. So, if you hate to pay full price, here's your chance to bargain.

Located in the heart of the 7th arrondissement, the Splendid offers guests an excellent example of a "Haussmann" style building (Haussmann was the brilliant city planner who redesigned the city in the late 1800s and whose name is often used to describe the classic architectural style the city is best known for) with the most modern of interiors.

Renovated in 1992, the Splendid's furnishings are reproductions of simple Art Deco pieces. The feel of the hotel is very new, so if you're after Old World charm you might want to consider another place.

If a room with a view of the **Eiffel Tower** is something you've dreamed of, then you'll want Room 307. There are also three suites (980FF, and two have views of the Tower) that are well-suited for the business traveler who needs a Fax and computer-adaptable plugs.

The Splendid's staff is friendly and ready to serve.

RIGHT BANK

NEAR THE CHAMPS-ELYSÉES

8th & 16th Arrondissements

Chic and historic. And often expensive.

First for the chic. Below the famous Champs-Elysées is the **Golden Triangle**, formed by the **Champs-Elysées**, **avenue George V**, and **avenue Montagne**. Here are several of the very finest and most expensive upper crust hotels. And along François 1er, which cuts the triangle in half, are the clothing designers you've always read about.

Window-shopping is a passionate pastime here, and the largely residential avenues themselves are some the most handsome in all of Paris.

Above the Champs-Elysées, the streets are a bit less grand, but still affluent, with lots of restaurants and clubs that are generally trendier with the tourists than they are with the locals.

Unfortunately, the Champs-Elysées itself is a tragic disappointment, with overpriced shops, fast food outlets, car dealerships, and largely unthinking, unfriendly crowds. Still, at either end, you will find some of the city's most memorable sights – the **Arc de Triomphe** to the west and the **Place de la Concorde** to the east.

The grand **Trocadéro**, always humming with rollerskaters, mimes, artists and strollers, is also in this quarter, as is the **Grand Palais des Beaux Arts**, the magnificent **Madeleine church**, the **American Embassy** and even US Ambassador Pamela Harriman's residence.

WHERE TO STAY

26. LA TREMOILLE, *14 rue de la Trémoille (8th, M:Alma-Marceau), 47.23.34.20, Fax 40.70.01.08. Rooms: 108. Rates for a double: 1,950-2,930FF. Breakfast: 100FF. Restaurant.*

If you have four legs, a tail, ears that fold over and you answer to the name of Norton, then you have stayed at this dream-come-true four-star luxury hotel. Yes, this is where *The Cat Who Went to Paris* stayed. The hero of Peter Gethers' charming (to cat lovers, that is) book is fondly remembered here.

In the heart of the ultra rich Golden Triangle area of the ritzy Right Bank, the Hôtel de la Trémoille seems to have everything a four-star luxury hotel should have without the snooty formal atmosphere that permeates some others. The rooms are enormous and beautiful and each one is different. The suites (2,780-7,410FF) are quite literally breathtaking.

The common areas of the hotel are the very definition of elegance, the restaurant offers a varied menu at surprisingly low prices (relative to the cost of the rooms), and the hotel has full conference facilities.

But it is the staff that truly distinguishes the Tremoille. Management and reception teams are graduates of Europe's finest hotel management programs. Each and every person who works here strives to learn the names, as well as the tastes of each guest.

27. L'HÔTEL MAJESTIC, *29 rue Dumont d'Urville (16th, M:Kléber), 45.00.83.70, Fax 45.00.29.48. Rooms: 30. Rates for doubles: 1,150-1,450FF. Suites available. Breakfast: 60FF. No restaurant.*

The Hôtel Majestic is unlike any other hotel we visited, and what distinguishes it from the competition may or may not be your cup of tea.

Both the common areas and the rooms in this four-star hotel seem more like the bedrooms and salons of a private home than a place where strangers stop off briefly. The furnishings, the carpeting, even the color schemes reflect a personal rather than a calculating professional eye.

Of course, that's exactly what many travellers would prefer. The caveat is that the Majestic's rooms look like they were decorated by one's formal, affluent, French aunt. They're charming, but in a way that may not be to everyone's taste.

What would be to everyone's liking is the size of the rooms. The standard doubles (1,150FF) are roomy, the doubles with a "lounge combined" (1,450FF) are spacious, the suites (1,800FF) are enormous, and the Penthouse (2,000FF), which also has a big balcony, is out of this world.

The reception staff speaks English, the street is extremely quiet but close to the action.

28. HÔTEL ALEXANDER, *102 avenue Victor Hugo (16th, M:Victor Hugo), 45.53.64.65, Fax 45.53.12.51. Rooms: 62. Rates for doubles: 1,190-1,300FF. Breakfast: 70FF. No restaurant.*

Just off of the charming Victor Hugo circle, the Hôtel Alexander is something of a surprise. From the looks of the tasteful, but tiny lobby, the Alexander doesn't seem like many other four stars. Although it's in a chic neighborhood, it's nothing like the Trémoille, for example, or even the Relais Christine on the Left Bank.

But it does have advantages. The rooms are a good size and are tastefully decorated. The bathrooms are enormous and each shower/tub combination has a shower curtain. This isn't really the petty thing it might seem. Very few French shower/tubs have curtains and most Americans, unfamiliar with how to use a hand-held shower without something protecting the rest of the bathroom, end up swimming from the tub to the door after they've bathed.

The curtain, we're told, is also evidence that the management knows what Americans expect and aims to please. In addition to the large bathrooms, the Alexander offers large televisions and roomy armoires. Another small plus is the courtyard where you can take your breakfast in good weather and onto which some of the rooms face.

The reception staff speaks excellent English. Well-located if you prefer the Right Bank.

29. HÔTEL CENTRE VILLE ÉTOILE, *6 rue des Acacias (17th, M:Argentine), 43.80.56.18, Fax 47.54.93.43. Rooms: 16. Rates for doubles: 650-1,000FF. Breakfast: 55FF. No restaurant.*

This small hotel is pleasant and appears to be well-managed, but really doesn't have a whole lot to distinguish it. The common areas and the rooms are so modern that you could be anywhere and, because not a single room faces the street, you can't even soak up Parisian ambience staring out the window.

The fact that all the rooms are on a courtyard also tends to keep them pretty dark throughout the day.

The location, however, is not bad if you like the Right Bank. The **Arc de Triomphe**, for instance, is right around the corner — as is one of the main Air France bus terminals, from which you can be quickly whisked away to the airports.

30. EBER MONCEAU, *18 rue Léon Jost (17th, M:Courcelles), 46.22.60.70, Fax: 47.63.01.01. Rooms: 18. Rates for doubles: 580-630FF. Breakfast: 50FF. No restaurant, but an arrangement with a restaurant a couple of doors down allows for full room service until 10 p.m.*

Maybe you've always dreamed of coming to Paris but you've put it off because you don't speak French or you get lost in big cities. If that's the case, this is the hotel for you. Jean-Marc Eber, the owner, lives to ensure that his guests have the most outstanding Parisian vacation possible. He maintains a library of guide books which he loans out. He recommends restaurants, makes reservations, and runs interference because he genuinely likes his guests.

The standard doubles are fine without being exceptional. The three *appartements* (1,000FF) and the two suites (1,100-1,300FF) are ideal for families. Some rooms have terraces, some skylights. All have a French-style sofa bed in the sitting room that is called a *clic-clac* and makes an surprisingly comfortable bed. In addition, they have enormous closet space for stashing luggage as well as hanging clothes.

Not far from the **Arc de Triomphe** and the lovely **Place des Ternes**, the Hôtel Eber is a real find.

NEAR THE LOUVRE
1st & 2nd Arrondissements

This quarter is steeped in history and culture, led, naturally, by the **Musée du Louvre**. We're still not fans of I.M. Pei's glass pyramid and the shallow surrounding fountains that hose down visitors at the slightest breeze. But the new **Richelieu wing** is a great triumph, as are the below-ground shops where you can find everything from Lalique glass to affordable antique prints.

The **Jardin des Tuileries** is here, of course, running west out of the mouth of the Louvre — though a good deal of restoration is being done now on the gardens. The **Palais Royal**, with its enormous enclosed garden, is just north of the Louvre, and the truly elegant **Place Vendôme** is a few blocks west. The fabulously sumptuous **Garnier Opera House** is also just north of the Vendôme.

Lots of Americans stay in the high end hotels on and just off the **rue de Rivoli** here, and there's no question they are elegant, usually with fine dining no further than just off the lobby. You'll have no trouble finding jewels, antiques, and *haute couture* here either.

On the down side, this is largely a business quarter (in fact, this was the first neighborhood in the city to be dominated by commerce), made even more congested by zillions of tourists. And the prices of just about everything are unusually steep.

WHERE TO STAY

31. HÔTEL MAYFAIR, *3 rue Rouget-de-l'Isle (1st, M:Tuileries), 42.60.38.14, Fax 40.15.04.78. Rooms: 53. Rates for doubles: 1,214-1,414FF. Suites available. Breakfast: 80FF. No restaurant.*

The Mayfair has some of the feel of a palace-style hotel. Huge Oriental rugs and plush green furnishings greet you in the reception area. The salon/bar has a parquet floor and red leather-tiled ceiling. The small elevator is nicely appointed with fabric wallcoverings.

The rooms are also quite nice, with fabric wallcoverings, king-sized beds, and roomy off-white marble bathrooms. Safes, minibars, cable television, towel-warmers, and air-conditioning are standard. Two floors are also designated non-smoking floors, which is daring for a hotel in Paris, where many locals still smoke like fiends.

The service is attentive and the location is convenient to most of the major Right Bank sights. On the down side: For a hotel of this stature and at this price, it could do with a little sprucing up. Some of the common areas especially are beginning to look a bit overused and tired.

32. HÔTEL BRIGHTON, *218 rue de Rivoli (1st, M:Tuileries), 42.60.30.03, Fax 42.60.41.78. Rooms: 70. Rates for doubles: 550-850FF. Breakfast included. No restaurant.*

The rooms on the rue de Rivoli side of this large hotel overlook the **Tuileries gardens** and open up onto a view that stretches from I.M. Pei's **glass pyramid** at the center of the Louvre to the **Arc de Triomphe** and, on clear days, the **Grande Arche** of **La Défense** beyond. At night, the view gets even better, with the **Eiffel Tower** across the river bathed in light.

A Japanese firm bought the Brighton about four years ago and refinished the lovely salon with its striking marbled columns and coffered ceiling off of the entry. Many of the rooms have also been spruced up.

In general the rooms are especially large, with high ceilings, lots of period furnishings, chandeliers and ample closet space. And most of the rooms with views have a small balcony. Room 216 is particularly grand.

The bathrooms, too, are enormous by Paris standards. Though often done in a rather sterile white tile, they feature large tubs with hand-held showers, sometimes double sinks, bidets, and convenient small benches.

Even the location is good — especially for a Right Bank hotel. True, the rue de Rivoli is a mob-scene of tourists, but you can easily stroll to just about any Right Bank attraction from here.

Remember to request a room with a view.

33. HÔTEL VENDOME, *1 place Vendôme (1st, M:Tuileries), 42.60.32.84, Fax 49.27.97.89. Rooms: 46. Rates for doubles: 950FF. Suites available. Breakfast included. Small restaurant.*

A very well-known hotel with a stunning address, just a few paces off the magnificent **Place Vendôme**. If you want to shop for a few expensive baubles, maybe a diamond tiara or two, this is the perfect neighborhood.

The hotel puts on a show of elegance as well, with high ceilings, elaborate molding on the ceilings and walls, and several period pieces and chandeliers in the rooms. Even brass beds and marble fireplaces are available in some rooms. And some bathrooms have double sinks and most are about as roomy as you'll find in Paris.

Still, the common areas could use a little freshening up. And the salon, where you can grab a sandwich, sip a cocktail or even dine on various unimaginative pasta dishes, seemed a bit grim with its black leather banquettes and aging red carpet. An amusing historical detail: this building, constructed in 1699 by the architect to Louis XIV, housed the **Republic of Texas Embassy** in 1842–1843!

34. HÔTEL DES TUILERIES, *10 rue Saint-Hyacinthe (1st, M:Tuileries), 42.61.04.17, Fax 49.27.91.56. Rooms: 26. Rates for doubles: 790-990FF. Breakfast: 50FF. No restaurant.*

Located just above the **Tuileries**, near the **Louvre**, the **Opéra Garnier**, the **Place Vendôme** and other Right Bank sights, this hotel is a bit like someone's private residence. Each room is decorated differently (wallpapers change room to room). Sometimes the concept is a great success; sometimes you wonder what the decorator was thinking.

Still, this is a very friendly hotel converted from an 18th-century residence. It is run by an attentive staff and boasts several extra features—air conditioning, a trouser press in every room, large closets and space underneath to stow your bags, and double-glazed windows to subdue the noise. Room number 1 even has a jacuzzi-tub.

Pleasant common areas, with a small sitting area on the main floor and a breakfast room in the former basement.

35. LE STENDAHL, *22 rue Danielle Casanova (2nd, M:Opéra), 44.58.52.52, Fax 44.58.52.00. Rooms: 21. Suite available. Rates for doubles: 1,500-1,900FF. Breakfast: 80FF. No restaurant.*

Let's start with the bad news: this hotel is extremely expensive. In every other way, it is a magnificent small hotel.

The location on an uncrowded street near the elegant **Place Vendome** is just a few blocks from the **Opéra Garnier**, the **Madeleine**, the **Place de la Concorde** and the **Tuileries**. Every room is immaculate and filled with light, and the general decor is stylish and classy — down to the matching curtains and bedspreads and the sophisticated tile chosen for the bathrooms (bathrobes are also included). The hotel even offers wooden hangers in its large armoires, which are also fitted out with drawers for your socks and other items.

Air conditioning, minibars, cable television and small safes are standard. A folder in each room advises guests where to eat and shop, as well as how to get around and use the public telephones. Last but not least: the inviting salon/bar has been decorated as a small library featuring copies of every volume Stendahl ever wrote.

36. HÔTEL FAVART, *5 rue Marivaux (1st, M:Richelieu-Drouot), 42.97.59.83, Fax 40.15.95.58. Rooms: 37. Rates for doubles: 620FF. Breakfast included. No restaurant.*

A plaque affixed beside the entrance to this hotel proudly proclaims that the master Spanish painter Francisco Goya stayed here in the summer of 1824. The Favart also faces the historic **Opéra Comique**, a fabulous classic performance hall.

The Favart was redecorated only five years ago, and the entry area still looks fresh and welcoming. The *trompe l'oeil* behind the reception desk and another up the staircase, which also has a handsome wrought-iron railing, are extremely well executed.

The rooms are rather large, with beamed ceilings, fabric on the walls, good-sized closets, and bathrooms with tubs equipped with hand-held showers. The furnishings aren't exactly chic, but neither are they dowdy.

The location is just a few blocks above the **Opéra Garnier** and the **Madeleine**. Up sidestreets to the north, you'll spot the imposing elongated onion domes of **Sacré-Coeur**. The Metro stop is a few doors away, giving you easy access to the rest of the city.

37. HÔTEL DE LA PLACE DU LOUVRE, *21 rue des Prêtres Saint-Germain l'Auxerrois (1st, M:Louvre), 42.33.78.68, Fax 42.33.09.95. Rooms: 20. Rates for doubles: 670-800FF. Breakfast: 40FF. No restaurant.*

In honor of its proximity to the **Louvre**, this hotel has named each room for a famous French painter and decorated each room with prints of that painter's work (though the painters are from the modern era, which is poorly represented at the Louvre). The hotel's proximity to the Louvre is one of its big selling points. Rooms in the front of the building can get a glimpse of the Louvre and look out on a sideview of the **Saint-Germain l'Auxerrois** church.

The hotel occupies a tiny street located virtually in the heart of Paris, so the **Ile de la Cité**, the **Musée d'Orsay**, the **Opéra Garnier**, the **Pompidou Center** and other attractions are a short walk away.

The decor, redone in 1988, is *très* modern. The foyer is dominated by a pastel mural along one rippling stone wall. The faint colors suggests Cubist shapes and shadows. Even the decor of the downstairs breakfast room, the 14th-century Cellar of the Musketeers, is mod.

Rooms are on the smallish size and have minibars and televisions (no cable). Bathrooms are also a bit small, but are comfortable and have baths with hand-held showers.

38. HÔTEL LE RELAIS DU LOUVRE, *19 rue desPrêtres Saint-Germain l'Auxerrois (1st, M:Louvre), 40.41.96.42, Fax 40.41.96.44. Rooms: 20. Two suites. Rates for doubles: 780-890FF. Breakfast in your room only: 50FF. No restaurant.*

This is a gay and charming little hotel located on a tiny street directly behind the **Louvre**. Though the street itself is a bit dull, its central location puts you within an easy walk of several major monuments and museums — **Notre Dame**, the **Palais Royal**, and **Pont Neuf** among them. The famous **Samaritaine** department store, with its rooftop terrace, is just a few doors away as well.

Only a few years old, the Relais du Louvre has a fresh, bright and welcoming feel about it. The foyer is decorated in salmon pink, with forest green doors, a large Oriental rug, and colorfully-upholstered furnishings. The rooms themselves follow that lead.

Each room is decorated slightly differently, though they all have bright, light color schemes and floral patterns on the beds, sofas and curtains. They have good-sized closets, which can come in very handy. Bathrooms all have tubs with hand-held showers.

THE MARAIS & BASTILLE
3rd, 4th, & 11th Arrondissements

This is a fascinating area steeped in history and dripping with character. Long, long ago the area around the elegantly restored **Place**

des Vosges was a marshy tract. It's hard to picture today because any stroll along tiny neighborhood streets just north of the rue de Rivoli uncovers an endless number of hip art galleries, coffee houses, and clothing shops.

There is also a thriving Jewish quarter, with all the wonderful food you might imagine, and a popular gay neighborhood, with all the clubs you might imagine.

A few blocks further east, you'll find the **Place de la Bastille**, site of the prison that played so formidable a symbolic role in the Revolution. That square is now home to the palatial **Bastille Opera House**, which opened in 1989 on the 200th anniversary of the Revolution. That opening also helped bring about a transformation in the blocks to the east of the opera house. This area has become the Soho of Paris, with increasingly popular clubs and small restaurants.

First time visitors might find this area a little bit off the beaten track. Still, it is so easy to get around on the Metro, that shouldn't be a concern.

WHERE TO STAY

39. HÔTEL DE LA BRETONNERIE, *22 rue Sainte-Croix-de-la-Bretonnerie (4th, M:Hôtel de Ville), 48.87.77.63, Fax 42.77.26.78. Rooms: 30. Rates for doubles: 620-730FF. Breakfast: 42FF. No restaurant.*

The Bretonnerie is a popular hotel in the middle of the 4th arrondissement, not far from the **Georges Pompidou Center**, the **Place des Vosges** and the **Ile de la Cité**. Lots of small shops and clubs dot the immediate neighborhood, which is also quite near the Jewish quarter and such fabulous eateries as **Joe Goldenberg's** (see Chapter 8, page 101).

The hotel itself, with its stone walls, ceiling beams and period furnishings, was a 17th-century residence. The decor of the common areas, dominated by heavy browns and a sort of startling turquoise, is a bit grim.

The rooms themselves are somewhat brighter (still too much brown) and are of a decent size — many have especially high ceilings, which is somewhat unusual for Paris hotels in this quarter. Bathrooms come with tubs and hand-held showers and give you plenty of room to maneuver.

40. HÔTEL SAINT-PAUL LE MARAIS, *8 rue de Sevigne (4th, M:Saint-Paul), 48.04.97.27, Fax 48.87.37.04. Rooms: 27. Rates for doubles: 510-670FF. Suite available. Breakfast: 45FF. No restaurant.*

This five-year-old hotel is just down the street from the **Place des Vosges** and about three blocks from the marvelous **Musée Picasso**. A few blocks south, you run into the Seine.

The owners chose a contemporary decor, with some touches of the original 16th-century frame showing through, such as the beams in the foyer and the exposed stone in the cellar where breakfasts are now served.

There is a small bar on the main floor and a small patio in back, away from the noise of rue de Sévigné.

Overall, the accommodations are adequate and the furnishings are generic contemporary stained woods. Cable television and safes for your belongings are available in all the rooms.

41. PAVILLON DE LA REINE, *28 place des Vosges (3rd, M:Chemin Vert), 42.77.96.40, Fax 42.77.63.06. Rooms: 50. Rates for doubles: 1,300-1,950FF. Suites available. Breakfast: 90FF. No restaurant.*

Just off the **Place des Vosges**, one of most elegant historic squares in Paris, the Pavillon is likewise one of the most elegant hotels in Paris — especially at the price, which is expensive, but is still half the cost of the snooty *grandes dames* near the Champs-Elysées. And this is a much more interesting neighborhood.

Built only in 1986 – and owned by the same people who run the Relais Christine (reviewed above) – the Pavillon is set in a private courtyard with a vibrant garden blends flawlessly into its historic surroundings. A large sitting room off the foyer is outfitted with huge leather couches and chairs, massive Oriental rugs and various artworks recalling the 1600s when the Place des Vosges was built as residences for various royal families. A marvelous detail: the *trompe l'oeil* concealing the elevator.

Rooms are generous, with varying decors, though almost all have fine fabric walls, king-sized beds, air-conditioning, minibars, large closets and spacious bathrooms (terry cloth bathrobes included). There is even a private garage.

The company motto: "Know How to Live." Book months in advance.

FINDS & FAVORITES

Of the spots we've reviewed in the preceding pages, we'd recommend the following hotels to those who want something special without signing away the farm.

3. JEU DE PAUME, *54 rue Saint-Louis-en-l'Ile (4th, M:Pont-Marie), 43.26.14.18, Fax 40.46.02.76.*

5. HÔTEL DES GRANDES ÉCOLES, *75 rue du Cardinal Lemoine (5th, M:Cardinal Lemoine), 43.26.79.23, Fax 43.25.28.15.*

6. HÔTEL DES GRANDS HOMMES, *17 place du Panthéon (5th, M:Luxembourg or Sorbonne), 46.34.19.60, Fax 43.26.67.32.*

10. HÔTEL LE RELAIS SAINT-GERMAIN, *9 carrefour de l'Odéon (6th, M:Odéon), 43.29.12.05, Fax 46.33.45.30.*

15. HÔTEL DE NESLE, *7 rue de Nesle (6th, M:Odéon or Saint-Michel), 43.54.62.41. No fax.*

23. DUC DE SAINT-SIMON, *14 rue de Saint-Simon (7th, M:Rue du Bac), 42.22.07.52, Fax 45.48.68.25.*

26. LA TRÉMOILLE, *14 rue de la Trémoille (8th, M:Alma-Marceau), 47.23.34.20, Fax 40.70.01.08.*

30. EBER MONCEAU, *18 rue Léon Jost (17th, M:Courcelles), 46.22.60.70, Fax: 47.63.01.01.*

32. HÔTEL BRIGHTON, *218 rue de Rivoli (1st, M:Tuileries), 42.60.30.03, Fax 42.60.41.78.*

41. PAVILLON DE LA REINE, *28 place des Vosges (3rd, M:Chemin Vert), 42.77.96.40, Fax 42.77.63.06.*

13. WHERE TO EAT IN PARIS

INTRODUCTION

In our view, dining out in Paris is one of the great pleasures in life.

No doubt, part of that attitude comes from the sheer romance of the idea. But there's more to it than starry-eyed visions of clinking crystal goblets and gazing across the Seine toward the illuminated Eiffel Tower.

In France, food isn't just fuel meant to be burned off quickly at the shop the next morning. It's one of the foundations of French culture. A good meal is equal, if not superior, to a profitable day at the office.

That's been so for centuries. Cuisine is revered in France more so than in just about any other country in the world (with Italy following as a close second).

And it's not just haute cuisine that tantilizes the French. In fact, we'd say most of the locals prefer traditional, country-style cooking. But whether the restaurant specializes in roast chicken and boiled potatoes or boned quail breast in a light pastry served with baby grilled squash, French patrons give the meal their undivided attention.

The dining table is also where they catch up on all the local gossip. And it would never occur to them to leave the table until not only all the food has been vacuumed up, but until all their tales are told. That table is theirs and theirs alone for the night.

Dining in Paris is also a pleasure because of the extraordinary variety that you can find in local restaurants. Corner bistros offer a blend of neighborly boisterousness and simple country cooking. Or you can settle into an intimate booth at one of the elegant three-star establishments where the presentations on the plate are as artful as anything you've seen on a canvas.

And don't forget that you can find some marvelous Vietnamese, Italian, Lebanese, and other ethnic restaurants. There are even American-style steak houses if you're dying for a T-bone or a decent bowl of chili.

Our choices below try to capture that variety, both in terms of ambiance and cuisine. Again, most restaurants on the main boulevards, such as the Champs-Elysées or Saint-Germain, are likely to be disappointing. Those places tend to toss together mediocre meals, soak up your hard-earned money, and show you the door.

Be patient, look around, and be willing to walk a few blocks or grab a cab.

THE BAD NEWS

You may lose your appetite when you see some of the prices. In fact, you might consider every restaurant but the corner crêperie to be expensive.

However, don't forget that the 15 percent tip and 18.6 percent tax are included. Also, unlike in the States, where restaurants profit by two or three seatings per table per evening, French restaurants expect patrons to linger as long as they like.

At the better restaurants your bill will never appear before you request it. At smaller bistros, they may drop off a register receipt for each course or round of drinks you order, then tally them up at the end when you ask to pay.

For our purposes here, we created three price categories for meals, not including wine: inexpensive, for meals costing less than 150FF per person; moderate, for 150 to 300FF per person; and expensive, for more than 300FF per person. You'll note a couple of "very expensive" restaurants as well. It's quite easy to spend 1,000FF per person.

And don't forget to call to find out if the restaurant is open (many close on Sundays or Mondays, and sometimes all of August) and to make reservations.

Bon appetit!

THE ISLANDS

ILES DE LA CITÉ & SAINT-LOUIS

1. AUBERGE DE LA REINE BLANCHE *(traditional/inexpensive), 30 rue Saint-Louis-en-Ile (4th, M:Pont-Marie), 46.33.07.87.*

A tiny bistro for a tiny island — appropriately decorated with miniature pieces of furniture hanging from the walls. The prix fixe of 140FF offers an unusually wide range of choices. Some examples: a leek tarte, mussels in garlic, grilled quail, saddle of lamb, veal scallops with a cream and mushroom sauce. The food here is quite decent, but, in part, we include this spot because it's cute and the crowd, though touristy, is often friendly.

2. BERTHILLON *(ice cream), 31 rue Saint-Louis-en-Ile (4th, M:Pont-Marie), 43.54.31.61.*

Ice cream and sorbets — guava (Wow!), pink grapefruit, pear, tea, Grand-Marnier (Excellent!), glazed chesnut, and on and on and on. Even vanilla, but the kind of vanilla that could lead to serious addiction. Several places on the Ile Saint-Louis sell Berthillon now. Just look for long lines.

LEFT BANK

THE LATIN QUARTER
5th Arrondissement

3. TOUR D'ARGENT *(haute cuisine/very expensive), 15 quai de la Tournelle (5th, M:Maubert-Mutualité), 43.54.23.31.*

Top of the line. Some say the food is not the best Paris has to offer. Maybe. But it's close, and with its army of attentive waiters and its view of the Seine and Notre-Dame, it is difficult to imagine a more complete dining experience. Try the house specialty, pressed duck, with a crêpe Suzette for desert. Tour d'Argent also boasts the most extensive wine list in all of France. Ask for a tour of its cellar. And brace yourself for the tab. Think of it as an investment in your memories.

4. AU BEAUJOLAIS *(traditional/moderate), 19 quai de la Tournelle (5th, M:Maubert-Mutualité), 43.54.17.47.*

Just a couple doors down the quai from the awesome Tour d'Argent with its even more awesome prices, this popular two-room brasserie hums with activity. And for good reason. The food isn't fancy, but it's still no easy trick to make coq au vin as good as this. You can watch the birds being roasted in the adjacent kitchen while you sample one or two of the refreshing Beaujolais on hand. Try a Juliénas or Fleuri. Both are crisp and fruity.

5. AL DAR *(Lebanese/moderate), 8 rue Frederic-Sauton (5th, M:Saint-Michel), 43.25.17.15.*

Marvelous Lebanese. The only way to fly is to order the combinations: 12 different dishes for 440FF, 20 dishes for 730FF, or 26 dishes for 920FF. The quality and quantities are good for the money. And sometimes, if you've really stuffed yourself, they'll bring a bit of baklava at the end for free. If you're hunting for a snack or quick lunch, Al Dar has a takeout deli (some seating) next door.

6. BRASSERIE BALZAR *(traditional/moderate), 49 rue des Ecoles (5th, M:Cluny-Sorbonne), 43.54.13.67.*

A lively brasserie that is as popular with locals as it is with tourists. Daily specials are often best, featuring such simple dishes as sliced leg of lamb, fresh asperagus with a vinaigrette, snails steeped in garlic butter,

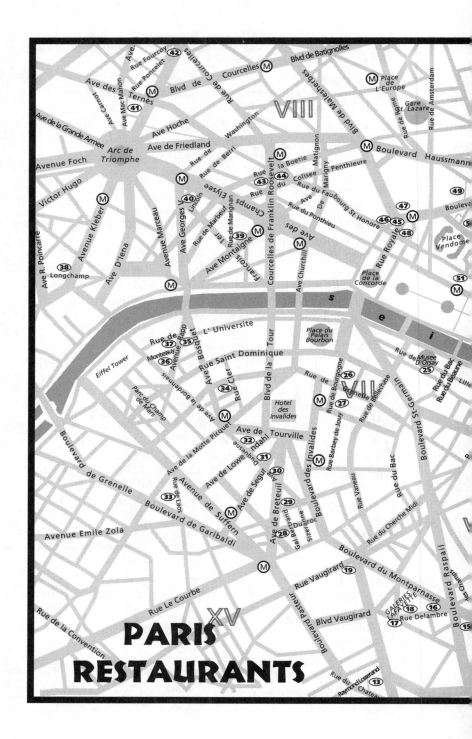

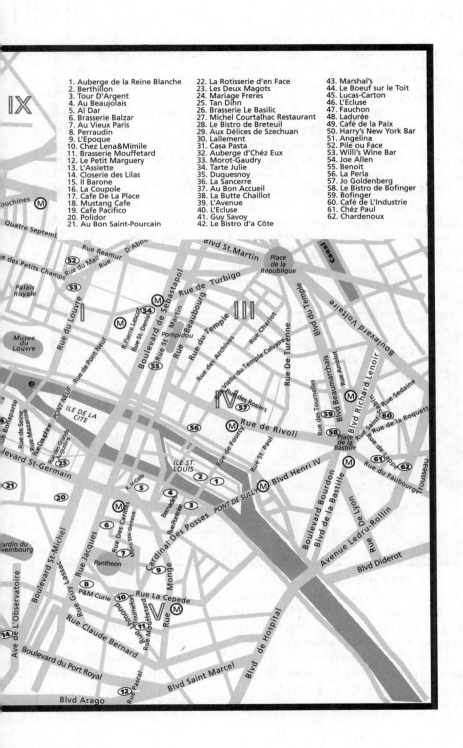

1. Auberge de la Reine Blanche
2. Berthillon
3. Tour D'Argent
4. Au Beaujolais
5. Al Dar
6. Brasserie Balzar
7. Au Vieux Paris
8. Perraudin
9. L'Epoque
10. Chez Lena&Mimile
11. Brasserie Mouffetard
12. Le Petit Marguery
13. L'Assiette
14. Closerie des Lilas
15. Il Barone
16. La Coupole
17. Cafe De La Place
18. Mustang Cafe
19. Cafe Pacifico
20. Polidor
21. Au Bon Saint-Pourcain

22. La Rotisserie d'en Face
23. Les Deux Magots
24. Mariage Freres
25. Tan Dihn
26. Brasserie Le Basilic
27. Michel Courtalhac Restaurant
28. Le Bistro de Breteuil
29. Aux Délices de Szechuan
30. Lallement
31. Casa Pasta
32. Auberge d'Chéz Eux
33. Morot-Gaudry
34. Tarte Julie
35. Duquesnoy
36. La Sancerre
37. Au Bon Accueil
38. La Butte Chaillot
39. L'Avenue
40. L'Ecluse
41. Guy Savoy
42. Le Bistro d'a Côte

43. Marshal's
44. Le Boeuf sur le Toit
45. Lucas-Carton
46. L'Ecluse
47. Fauchon
48. Ladurée
49. Café de la Paix
50. Harry's New York Bar
51. Angelina
52. Pile ou Face
53. Willi's Wine Bar
54. Joe Allen
55. Benoit
56. La Perla
57. Jo Goldenberg
58. Le Bistro de Bofinger
59. Bofinger
60. Café de L'Industrie
61. Chéz Paul
62. Chardenoux

and hot apple tart with crême fraiche. The people-watching here is as good as any floor show. It's the real thing.

7. AU VIEUX PARIS *(traditional/moderate), 2 place du Panthéon (5th, M:Cardinale Lemoine), 43.54.79.22.*

On warm nights, this restaurant sets a few tables outside and opens up the large windows to the interior so that diners can enjoy the view of the majestic Panthéon and the charming Saint-Etienne-du-Mont church. Good standards include the duck breast ("magret de canard"), cooked medium rare with a light red wine sauce.

8. PERRAUDIN *(traditional/inexpensive), 157 rue Saint-Jacques (5th, M:Luxembourg), 46.33.15.75.*

A casual neighborhood bistro with all the basics at a very reasonable price (the salmon and boeuf Bourguignon are among the best picks). Lots of charm and a tight sitting so you'll get to know your neighbors, who are likely to be students or professors at the nearby Sorbonne. No reservations, but if you have to wait in line you'll be treated to a free Kir and some olives.

SEEING STARS

Haute cuisine at its very finest – at least that's what the esteemed Michelin Guide says. These are the five restaurants in Paris that have earned three Michelin stars. (Bring your Platinum credit card.)

L'ABRROISIE, *9 place des Vosges (4th, M:Chemin Vert), 42.78.51.45. Closed Sunday and Monday. Chef Bernard Pacaud's Florentine villa.*

JOEL ROBUCHON, *59 avenue Raymond Poincare (16th, M:Trocadéro), 47.27.12.27. New home for a world famous chef.*

LUCAS-CARTON, *9 place de la Madeleine (8th, M:Madeleine), 42.65.22.90. Closed Sunday. A Belle Epoque belle.*

TAILLEVENT, *15 rue Lamennais (8th, M:George V), 45.63.39.94. Closed Saturday and Sunday. Some say the very best.*

TOUR D'ARGENT, *15 quar de la Tournelle (5th, M:Maubert Mutualite), 43.54.23.31. Closed Monday. Pressed duck and a view of Notre-Dame.*

---

9. L'EPOQUE *(traditional/inexpensive), 81 rue du Cardinale Lemoine (5th, M:Cardinale Lemoine), 46.34.15.84.*

Just off the picturesque Place de la Contrescarpe, this small bistro is an undiscovered gem, serving hearty standards such as pork salé with lentils or roast chicken with tarragon in a casual atmosphere at unParisian low prices. The staff is friendly and willing to explain the menu or just chat about the neighborhood. After dinner, stroll around the corner to the Contrescarpe, sit at one of the cafés, and watch the world go by.

10. CHEZ LENA & MIMILE *(traditional/moderate), 32 rue Tournefort* *(5th, M:Censier-Daubenton), 47.07.72.47.*
A tiny and wonderfully homey bistro tucked away in a corner that most tourists will never find. Good standards are culled from all the wonderfully fresh foods of the open market on the nearby rue Mouffetard. The service is so easygoing you'd think you were a friend of the family, and frequently there will be a piano player and a young songstress singing Edith Piaf classics and rock ballads. A fixed price menu that includes dessert and a half bottle of respectable wine per person.

11. BRASSERIE MOUFFETARD *(traditional/inexpensive), 116 rue Mouffetard (5th, M:Censier-Daubenton), 43.31.42.50. Closed Monday.*
This is the quintessential Left Bank café in the heart of one of Paris's most famous open markets. Locals and workers from the market gather here in the early morning and argue about current events over wine and coffee before setting out to tackle the day's chores. On a sunny day, the café spills out onto the tiny street, where singers, dancers and jugglers add to the carnival atmosphere. Baked-on-the-premises croissants are heavenly. Good for lunch too.

12. LE PETIT MARGUERY *(traditional/moderate), 9 boulevard de Port-Royal (13th, M:Gobelins), 43.31.58.59.*
An absolute favorite, especially during the fall game season, when this well-appointed neighborhood restaurant serves up skillfully prepared game of all kinds — from wild boar to pheasant. Very comfortable and friendly with good service, magnificent food, and an excellent wine list at reasonable prices. And few tourists, because it is just a few blocks further out than most folks like to go. But catch a cab. It's worth it.

SAINT-GERMAIN & MONTPARNASSE
6th & 14th Arrondissements

13. L'ASSIETTE *(traditional/moderate-expensive), 181 rue du Château (14th, M:Gaîté), 43.22.64.86.*
When chef and owner Lucette Rousseau is on her game, this restaurant is truly outstanding. Lucette blends much of the best of traditional and haute cuisine. Plates of marinated salmon or foie gras are enormous. Or start with a lobster salad with garlic, or asparagus with truffles, or smoked duck breast sliced thin and stacked on frisée lettuce. Main dishes are generous as well, with a blanquette of sea scallops, tender and juicy saddle of rabbit, perfectly roasted pigeon, and a petit salé of duck that is sinfully rich and flavorful.

The wine list is as thoughtfully composed as the menu, with lots of Bordeaux and Burgundy from the best of the 1980s (prices are a bit steep). The setting is unspectacular and the neighborhood a bit romoved, but don't let that get in the way of a memorable meal.

14. CLOSERIE DES LILAS *(nouvelle-seafood/moderate), 171 boulevard du Montparnasse (6th, M:Port Royal), 43.26.70.50.*

This onetime country inn, which is now quite stylish, is a sort of monument to the arts and letters community. Former regulars include Baudelaire, Verlaine, Beckett, Joyce, and, of course, Hemingway, who seems to have enjoyed a glass in every conceivable Left Bank café. The bar area even has engraved plaques commemorating some of its past literary glory. Request a table in the garden side of the restaurant, though the bar area has its charm as well.

Dishes include lobster bisque, endive salad with real Roquefort, oysters Florentine, the house steak tartare, and medalions of lamb with fresh herbs in pastry.

15. IL BARONE *(Italian/moderate), 5 rue Léopold Robert (14th, M:Vavin), 43.20.87.14.*

Though this restaurant is unassuming visually, the food is good and the portions generous. Mostly neighborhood folks drop by for starters like marinated sardines, prosciutto di Parma or carpaccio, then follow up with veal scallops with ham and grated parmesan, spagetti with butter and anchovies, or falioline alla carbonara. For dessert, try a plate of profiteroles or a mixed selection of rich gelati. The back room is the lively one.

16. LA COUPOLE *(traditional-seafood/moderate), 102 boulevard Montparnasse (14th, M:Vavin), 43.20.14.20.*

This showplace of a bistro has been fully renovated since it was a haunt to Jean-Paul Sartre and the Americans before him. It is chic, spacious, brightly lit, and noisy – a perfect place to see (be prepared to gawk at the young and beautiful) and be seen . A downstairs ballroom for those who want to kick up their heels to a bit of jazz. The menu offers lots of fresh seafood, as well as filling staples such as a steak and fries. The food is nothing to rave about, but the overall experience is memorable.

17. CAFÉ DE LA PLACE *(traditional/inexpensive), 23 rue d'Odessa (14th, M:Edgar-Quinet), 42.18.01.55.*

Just a block below the often chaotic boulevard de Montparnasse, you'll find this homey little café run by a friendly group of young folks who welcome you as if you were a regular from the neighborhood. The food is very simple. Just salads, omelets, steaks and fries, and that sort of thing. But it's properly prepared and is quite satisfying. And they offer an inexpensive and usually very decent wine du jour. All in all, this warm and woody café with outdoor seating under shady trees is a comfortable little sanctuary where you can refuel in peace and quiet.

18. MUSTANG CAFÉ *(Tex-Mex/moderate), 84 boulevard du Montparnasse (14th, M:Vavin), 43.35.36.12.*

A new hot spot with one of the best Happy Hour deals in town from 4 to 8 p.m. The café draws a young (sometimes very young) French and

American crowd throughout the afternoon and evening. Lots of ogling, nursing beers for hours, smoking, and chattering, all at the same time. The second shift begins at about 8 p.m., when diners arrive for taco combinations, grilled shrimp, barbeque pork ribs, a turkey-bacon club, and Haagën Dazs for dessert.

19. CAFE PACIFICO *(Mexican/inexpensive), 50 boulevard Montparnasse (15th, M:Montparnasse or Duroc), 45.48.63.87.*

Okay, so it's a small chain, with restaurants in London and Amsterdam as well. But the Pacifico is one of the few Mexican restaurants in Paris where you'll find pretty much what you think of as conventional Mexican fare: enchiladas, burritos, and tacos, with lots of refried beans and tangy rice. The prices are right (except for the 300FF pitchers of Margueritas), and there are six tables in a tranquil outdoor patio in back. The bar sizzles at night, when patrons tank up on Dos XX and carbohydrates.

LITERARY LEGACIES

Start with the premise that Hemingway drank everywhere – even places that opened after his death. These are a few of the famous places where the literary giants tanked up on caffeine and entrecote (cheap steak).

CAFÉ LES DEUX-MAGOTS, *170 boulevard Saint-Germain (6th, M:Saint-Germain-des-Prés), 45.48.55.25. The big daddy of them all. Ghosts include: Simone de Beauvoir, Malcolm Cowley, Hart Crane, Gore Vidal, Christopher Isherwood.*

CAFÉ DE FLORE, *172 boulevard Saint-Germain (6th, M:Saint-Germain-des-Prés), 45.48.55.26. Ghosts: everyone who ever stopped at the Deux Magots next door.*

BRASSERIE LIPP, *151 boulevard Saint-Germain (6th, M:Saint-Germain-des-Prés), 45.48.53.91. Waverly Root, Thorton Wilder, Harold Loeb. Did we mention Hemingway?*

LE MONTANA, *28 rue Saint-Benoit (6th, M:Saint-Germain-des-Prés), 45.48.93.08. Jean-Paul Sartre, Simone de Beauvoir, Francois Truffaut.*

LA CLOSERIE DES LILAS, *171 boulevard du Montparnasse (6th, M:Port-Royal), 43.26.70.50. Baudelaire, Verlaine, James Joyce, John Dos Passos, F. Scott Fitgerald, Archibald MacLeish.*

LA COUPOLE, *102 boulevard du Montparnasse (14th, M:Vavin), 43.20.14.20. Henry Miller, Lawrence Durrell, Françoise Sagan, Gabriel Garcia Marquez.*

LE SELECT, *99 boulevard du Montparnasse (6th, M:Vavin), 42.22.65.27. Isadora Duncan, Hart Crane, Harold Stearns. Did we mention Hemingway?*

POLIDOR, *41 rue Monsieur-le-Prince (6th, M:Odéon), 43.26.95.34. James Joyce, Rimbaud, Verlaine, Richard Wright.*

20. POLIDOR *(traditional/inexpensive), 41 rue Monsieur-le-Prince (6th, M:Odéon), 43.26.95.34.*

One of the many former Hemingway haunts, this bustling bistro brings French country cooking to the heart of the Left Bank. Most seating is elbow to elbow at long tables packed with hungry students and tourists trying to choose between rabbit in mustard sauce or veal kidneys. No reservations. Arrive early for a decent seat and be prepared to get to know some perfect strangers.

21. AU BON SAINT-POURCAIN *(traditional/inexpensive to moderate), 10bis rue Servandoni (6th, M:Saint-Sulpice), 43.54.93.63. Closed Sundays. No credit cards.*

This fabulously genuine corner bistro a block from Saint-Sulpice (and from Catherine Deneuve's apartment) has a well-used feel to its faded tile floor, red banquettes, lace curtains, and chalkboard menus. The food is also superb, prepared by chef and owner Daniel Pesle, the tall distinguished looking gentleman who wanders from table to table with a welcoming smile on his face. Dishes are simple and run a bit on the heavy side, so come with a hearty appetite and be ready to dig into escargots, coq au vin, tender beef with olives, blanquette de veau, and the cake or tart of the day. The house Gamay is especially light and refreshing.

22. LA ROTISSERIE D'EN FACE *(nouvelle/moderate-expensive), 2 rue Christine (6th, M:Odéon), 43.26.40.98.*

On a tiny street near the river, this what is known as a "baby bistro," which means it's a place owned by a high rung chef from a pricey nearby restaurant. In this case the chef is Jacques Cagna, whose two-star is "en face," which is to say, across the street. Comfortable contemporary-country setting with lots of imaginative dishes. Though the food was very good, the service was a bit hurried and the prices a tad too high.

23. LES DEUX MAGOTS *(coffee-lunch/moderate), 170 boulevard Saint-Germain (6th, M:Saint-Germain-des-Prés), 45.48.55.25.*

Said to have been one of the favorites for literati before and after World War II, the Deux Magots is directly across from the Saint-Germain-des-Prés cathedral. It is an ideal place to sip espresso or a fine whiskey on a sunny day and watch the beautiful people go by. The food is nothing to write poetry about. And Magots refers to the statues of Chinese merchants that flank the front door, not to bugs.

24. MARIAGE FRÈRES *(a real tea salon/inexpensive), 13 rue des Grands-Augustins (6th, M:Odéon), 40.51.82.50.*

All over Paris you will see what looks like a bistro with an awning that insists that the establishment is a tea salon. Well, that bit of advertising is almost always a complete sham. However, Mariage is the real thing, with a tea shop downstairs where you can choose from a couple hundred teas and purchase all the proper accoutrements (tea balls, pots, cups, etc.).

Upstairs is an airy warm salon with bushy palms, crisp tablecloths, and eight tables where you can sample any of the teas offered on the main floor (hot or iced), and dig into great brunches and salads (who can resist the "Snob Salad" with foie gras, smoked salmon, and artichoke hearts).

The Mariage family, by the way, has been in the tea business for 140 years, and they offer a book filled with family history and recipes.

NEAR THE EIFFEL TOWER
7th Arrondissement

25. TAN DIHN *(Vietnamese/expensive), 60 rue de Verneuil (7th, M:Rue du Bac), 45.44.04.84.*

This smallish restaurant tucked away on an off-the-beaten-track street is a delightful find. The food is extremely good – rich, but delicate, with specialties such as raviolis stuffed with goose, tender strips of marinated lamb and beef, and on and on. The wine list is truly impressive, with one of the largest collections of Pomerol around. And the owners, the Vifians, are ever present, like a roving floor show, commenting on the food, stopping to discuss their strategy for finding fine wines at bargain prices, or just gossiping.

26. BRASSERIE LE BASILIC *(traditional/inexpensive), 2 rue Casimir Perier (7th, M:Solferino), 44.18.94.64. Open daily.*

Tucked behind the picturesque, though little known Sainte-Clotilde church, the Basilic is a warm, welcoming neighborhood brasserie that prides itself on its lamb dishes. Other dishes include cold artichokes, confit de canard, veal chops, medallions of salmon with basil, foot-long eclairs, and the renown Berthillon sorbets. The restaurant has a pleasant patio section, where there is often a refreshing breeze, and a cozy interior of hardwoods and potted palms.

27. MICHEL COURTALHAC RESTAURANT *(traditional/inexpensive to moderate), 47 rue de Bourgogne (7th, M:Varenne), 45.55.15.35. Closed Sunday.*

You can watch Michel cook through the smallish opening into the kitchen from the back section downstairs. This is literally his and his family's tiny restaurant and it is as if you've dropped by a good friend's house for some dinner. It is friendly and very small and fills up quickly with neighborhood residents who've grown to know and love Michel's dedication to fresh ingredients in everything from the salads to the main courses.

The menu is limited to a handful of main dishes, but Michel makes sure that there is true variety in those choices – such as offerings of tender beef stew in Bordeaux, a roast sea bream with corriander, and a salad stacked with preserved duck breast. The selective wine list also includes a recommendation, which is usually a wonderful wine that Michel has recently discovered at a good price and wants to share with his customers.

28. LE BISTRO DE BRETEUIL (*traditional/inexpensive*), *3 place de Breteuil (7th, M:Duroc), 45.67.07.27.*

The neighborhood crowd is drawn here by the dozens every night. The repeat customers, us included, love the reasonable prices, the generous helpings of good food, the friendly service, and the spacious outdoor dining area facing the striking white statue of Louis Pasteur and the colorful garden that occupy the center of the place de Breteuil. A prix fixe at 172FF per person, including a half bottle of wine, the menu offers a tasty salmon tartare, escargots steeped in garlic butter, a goat cheese salad, rack of lamb, veal medallions with blue cheese, and confit de canard. The wines that accompany the meal aren't exactly the finest, but they are quite passable table varieties.

29. AUX DELICES DE SZECHUEN (*Chinese/moderate*), *40 avenue Duquesne (7th, M:Saint-Francois Xavier), 43.06.22.55.*

The first time we ate here, Lauren Bacall came in with her son and a friend and dined at the table next to us. Need we say more. Friendly service and fine food with standard offerings and such specials as grilled ravioli with ginger and smoked duck in tea. Afterward take a refreshing stroll down the striking avenue de Breteuil toward the illuminated dome of Les Invalides.

30. LALLEMENT (*lunch/inexpensive*), *37 avenue Duquesne (7th, M:Ecole Militaire), 47.05.03.87.*

This cheery local bakery, with seating for about twenty people, is one of the rare establishments where you feel instantly at ease and welcome. The menu offers great lunches, with all sorts of salads, quiches and tarts, and hearty daily specials that have yet to disappoint. No wonder the locals crowd in at midday. Check out the chocolates counter if you dare.

31. CASA PASTA (*Italian/moderate*), *avenue Duquesne (7th, M:Ecole Militaire), 45.55.43.43.*

Room enough for twenty people at most, this cozy spot lists a respectable range of dishes, including baked eggplant with parmesan, duck ravioli with capers and truffles, linguine with shellfish, veal scallops doused in lemon and butter – all prepared just seconds before the dishes are served by the owner.

32. AUBERGE D'CHEZ EUX (*southwest French traditional/moderate-expensive*), *4 avenue de Lowendal (7th, M:Ecole Militaire), 47.05.52.55. Closed Sunday.*

No dainty nouvelle portions here. These are massive, country-sized meals. The minute you settle into one of the tables draped with a red-and-white checkered cloth, a waiter brings you Kir poured out of a magnum bottle and slabs of meat cut from one of the dozen or so sausages sticking up like baguettes out of a large woven basket. If you're really hungry, pick the salad cart for your appetiser. They leave the cart in case you want another helping. Or maybe you'd prefer a whole pan of garlic-fried frog legs for an appetiser. Next: main courses of rack of lamb, thick succulent chops, bubbling cassoulet with duck, or the better part of a rabbit bathed in mustard sauce. And finally the dessert cart with fresh fruit, ice cream, custard, chocolate mousse, and more and more and more. Plan a long walk afterward.

33. MOROT-GAUDRY (*haute cuisine/expensive*), *8 rue de la Cavalerie (15th, M:La Motte-Picquet), 45.67.06.85.*

Notable mostly for its eighth-floor view of the Eiffel Tower and its stunning wine list. Many of the big-name wines are here – Haut-Brion, Lafit-Rothschild, Latour. There is even an impressive list of vendage tardives (superior Alsacian wines made from grapes harvested especially late in the season). The ambiance is a bit too hotel-like for our taste and the food is good, but not exceptional. Pigeon surrounded by baby artichokes and the appetiser of rougie and langoustino with avocado and tomato in a saffron sauce are notable.

LEGUME LOVERS

All is not flesh and bone in Parisian cuisine. Venues for vegetarians, all of which are priced very reasonably, include:

AQUARIUS, *54 rue Sainte-Croix de la Bretonnerie (4th, M:Hôtel de Ville), 48.87.48.71. Closed Sunday.*

AQUARIUS, *40 rue de Gergovie (14th, M:Pernety), 45.41.36.88. Closed Sunday.*

AU GRAIN DE FOLIE, *28 rue de La Vieuville (18th, M:Abbesses), 42.58.15.57. Open daily.*

PICCOLO, *6 rue des Ecouffes (4th, M:Saint-Paul), 42.72.17.79. Closed Monday and Tuesday.*

LA TRUFFE, *Restaurant 'Nature,' 31 rue Vieille du Temple (4th, M:Saint-Paul), 42.71.08.39. Open daily. May be the best.*

34. TARTE JULIE (*quiches-tarts/inexpensive*), *28 rue Cler (7th, M:Ecole Militaire), 47.53.91.55.*

The window display alone will drive you crazy. Set in the heart of one of Paris's finest market streets, Tarte Julie creates a fabulous variety of quiches and tarts to munch on right there or take home. Combinations include: salmon with spinach, tomato, feta and basil; tomato, eggplant and red pepper; pineapple, nuts and coconut; pears and chocolate. Julie's also makes a few salads and pizzas.

35. DUQUESNOY (*haute cuisine/expensive*), *6 avenue Bosquet (7th, M:Pont de l'Alma), 47.05.96.78.*

Just a couple of stones' throws from the Eiffel Tower, this newish restaurant in a quiet neighborhood is small, comfortable and chic, with a fine selection of white and red Burgundy wines. Mouth-watering dishes such as a cannelloni stuffed with smoked salmon and scallops, roasted langoustines with wild mushrooms and pepper, pressed pigeon in pastry, and red mullet in a potato crust with parsley and thyme butter.

36. LA SANCERRE *(lunch/inexpensive), 22 avenue Rapp (7th, M:Ecole Militaire), 45.51.75.91.*

Walking into this neighborhood wine bar is like stepping into someone's French country living room. Comfortable, cozy, friendly, and an ideal refuge from the crowds near the Eiffel Tower. Perfect for a light lunch, with good omelets, salads, and dessert tarts. The wine? Sancerre, from the Loire Valley, of course.

37. AU BON ACCUEIL *(traditional/inexpensive), 14 rue de Monttessuy (7th, M:Ecole Militaire), 47.05.46.11.*

After fighting the crowds at the Eiffel Tower, you will welcome this friendly, family-owned restaurant with open arms. It is the perfect place to savor a lovely lunch or intimate dinner, and to gather your wits over a "pot" of Beaujolais or Côtes du Rhône. This tiny restaurant sees relatively few tourists and offers discerning locals healthy portions of reasonably priced and well-prepared meals. Dishes include endive salad topped with chunks of heady Roquefort cheese, tangy oeufs en meurette, magnificent fresh vegetable soups, rabbit fricasée, boudin with roasted apples, roast breast of pigeon, and sinfully rich tiramisu for dessert. Game season brings out the best of the talented young chef. One of our very favorites.

RIGHT BANK

NEAR THE CHAMPS-ELYSEES
8th & 16th Arrondissements

38. LA BUTTE CHAILLOT *(haute cuisine/moderate), 110bis avenue Kléber (16th, M:Boissiäre), 47.27.88.88.*

This lively "baby bistro" belongs to master chef Guy Savoy, whose primary restaurant is located not far from the Chaillot and bears his very marketable name (see number 41 below). The contemporary decor, with sienna painted stucco walls, hardwood floors, and turquoise seating that matches the waiting staff's shirts, would look right at home in Seattle or Sante Fe. Savoy's usual inventive menu, with dishes such as red mullet and sardines marinated in a basil vinaigrette, medallions of lamb with roasted rounds of goat cheese, ravioli with snails and fresh parsley, and a cassis-flavored duck breast. On the down side: the wine list is skimpy and the staff stretched too thin. Americans are often seated in the same corner ghetto, a practice which we absolutely detest.

39. L'AVENUE *(French-Italian/moderate), 41 avenue Montaigne (8th, M:Pont de l'Alma), 40.70.14.91.*

A trendy contemporary restaurant set on an upper crust avenue. The chic crowd is either affluent or just knows how to dress well. The food, with everything from snails to monkfish to pasta, blends French and Italian. A strange mix of genres, though it seems to work. The wine list is adequate, but doesn't go back much further than 1988, thus missing many of the best years of the 1980s. Truth be told: This is one of the most overrated spots in town.

40. L'ECLUSE *(traditional/moderate), 64 rue François-Ier (8th, M:George V), 47.20.77.09.*

This is one of a handful of comfortable wine bars by this name scattered around town. The one across from the Madeleine is our favorite (see number 38 below), but the menu is the same at each and, if you like wine, you would enjoy any of them.

41. GUY SAVOY *(haute cuisine/very expensive), 18 rue Troyon (17th, M:Charles-de-Gaulle), 43.80.40.61. Closed Sunday.*

First class. Newly redecorated in beige fabrics and with modern paintings and African sculptures, this contemporary classic is one of the city's most elegant restaurants. The food is equally stylish and creative, offering such dishes as marinated tuna with caviar, veal kidneys with a mousse of artichokes and mustard, roast veal chops with wild mushrooms, a cream of lentil soup with fresh parsley and langoustines, and chicken breast with spinach and morrel mushrooms in a light cream sauce.

The lengthy wine list is spectacular, with pages of Meursaults and Montrachets, Graves and Pommards, even Champagnes. Ask for the special hand-written list of vintages reaching back to the early 1900s. You'll talk about the food (and the price) for years to come.

42. LE BISTRO D'À CÔTE *(traditional/moderate), 10 rue Gustave-Flaubert (17th, M:Pereire), 42.67.05.81.*

Another "baby bistro," this one belongs to master chef Michel Rostang, whose pricier restaurant is around the corner. This "baby" seats no more than about 30 people and is decorated with Rostang's collection of plates, mugs and other adorable doodads. All in all, the atmosphere is warm and inviting and the food is first-rate, highlighted with daily specials such as pigeon, served pink and juicy, and tender rabbit stew. You're likely to make a new friend here – the manager's tiny poodle, who wanders through periodically to check on your progress.

43. MARSHAL'S *(American/moderate), 63 avenue Franklin D. Roosevelt (8th, M:Franklin-Roosevelt), 45.63.21.22.*

Sort of a cross between contemporary and southwestern decor, Marshal's would be at home in Santa Monica or Phoenix. Nothing fancy, but decent American standards at reasonable prices. Occasionally pass-able live music by the bar area.

44. LE BOEUF SUR LE TOIT *(traditional/moderate), 34 rue du Colisée (8th, M:Franklin-Roosevelt), 43.59.83.80.*

An Art Deco showplace that was remodeled in the mid-1980s, it once drew the likes of Picasso and Coco Chanel. Today, it still attracts an energetic crowd of snappy dressers, hot young professionals, and eager tourists. Try to convince the maitre d' to seat you in the first room, where much of the best people-watching is staged. Just outside you will pass the oyster shuckers who prepare the huge plates of shellfish placed on stands in the middle of so many people's tables. The staff is attentive, but often harried.

45. LUCAS-CARTON, *9 place de la Madeleine (8th, M:Madeleine), 42.65.22.90. Closed Saturday and Sunday.*

This is genuinely elegant dining, set immediately across the avenue from the inspiring Madeleine church. The Belle Epoque decor, especially the remarkable carved wood partitions and paneling, is exquisite. The service, even down to the doorman, is refined and formal and attentive. The wine list is magnficent and the presentations of lamb, pigeon, pheasant, lobster, and various fish are wonderfully imaginative and artistic (desserts are visual masterpieces). On the menu, Chef Alain Senderens notes the perfect wine with each dish, and serves it by the glass so that you can profit from his wisdom. On the downside: The individual wines chosen were not always as good as they should be (inevitable because of the cost of the best wines), and with the money you spend on a single dinner, you could stay in a good hotel, savor a nice dinner somewhere else, and still have money left over for some modest shopping.

46. L'ECLUSE *(traditional/moderate), 15 place de la Madeleine (8th, M:Madeleine), 42.65.34.69.*

Our favorite of the wine bars, and an ideal place for lunch—or, for that matter, for dinner. The ambiance is comfortable and stylish—especially the garden room in the back. The food is limited but satisfying, with carpaccio, smoked salmon, steaks, sausage, foie gras, and potato and watercress salad. And, of course, there is the wine, almost all of which is from the Bordeaux region and much of which is available by the glass, so you can experiment without risking several hundred francs at a throw. Look for the wines that are listed as the "second" wine of one of the premier châteaux. They are often memorable finds.

47. FAUCHON *(everything/moderate), 30 place de la Madeleine (8th, M:Madeleine), 42.66.92.63 for the brasserie and 47.42.56.58 for the restaurant.*

Fauchon is famous as a world-class grocery and take-out deli, with enormous selections of baked goods, fresh vegetables, booze, prepared dishes, candies, canned foods, and anything else you can stuff in your mouth. But the main store also has a brasserie downstairs and a more formal restaurant upstairs. The contemporary brasserie offers reasonable prix fixe lunches and dinners, while the predominantly peach-colored neo-classical restaurant serves a respectable range of traditional dishes with haute cuisine touches. You can order something as simple as sole meunière or filet of beef with Bordelaise sauce, or get a wee bit more complicated with something like filets of red mullet in basil butter with potato purée and olive oil. The grocery is a good place to find a gift for your hungry friends back home.

48. LADURÉE *(tea salon/moderate), 16 rue Royale (8th, M:Madeleine), 42.60.21.79.*

Founded in 1862, and probably one of the more adorable tea salons in town. Busy too, with locals and others who crowd into the tiny tables (often with their puppies by their sides or at their feet) and hold animated conversations over pots of tea, lunch salads, and rich buttery pastries. You'll have to arrive for an early lunch to find a seat in the downstairs section. Gift boxes available here, which you can stuff with pastry or chocolates.

NEAR THE LOUVRE
1st & 2nd Arrondissements
49. CAFE DE LA PAIX *(traditional/moderate), 12 boulevard des Capucines (9th, M:Opéra), 40.07.30.20.*

Gloriously gaudy, this Belle Epoch café's main claim to fame is that it dates back to the opening of the Garnier Opera House, which it faces. Good for people watching over a cold beer on a hot day. Or, even better, sip wine in the evening and watch the smartly dressed crowd arriving at the Opera House. Food is an afterthought.

50. HARRY'S NEW YORK BAR *(ambiance/moderate), 5 rue Daunou (2nd, M:Opéra), 42.61.71.14.*

If it looks like an American bar and smells like an American bar (sour and stale), then ... Well, you know the rest. Harry's claim to fame is: one, that Hemingway drank here regularly; two, that the Bloody Mary was invented here; and three, that a bartender from The Plaza bought the place after World War I and gave it his name. The college pennants on the walls are faded, the hot dogs "served anytime" are not exactly ballpark grade, and the prices are absurd. Visit if you must.

51. ANGELINA *(tea salon/moderate), 226 rue de Rivoli (1st, M:Tuileries), 42.60.82.00. Open daily.*

Hot chocolate like you have never tasted before. So rich and heavy you need to ask for a small pot of steamed milk to thin out the marvelous mixture. This sinful and sumptuous tea salon is decked out in turn-of-the-century marble-topped tables and Empire knock-off chairs and is a civilized retreat from the chaos of the rue de Rivoli. Angelina offers salads, fish dishes, and other light fare, but the real reason for stopping is for the pastries, tea and coffee.

52. PILE OU FACE *(traditional-haute/moderate)*, *52bis rue Notre-Dame-des-Victoires (2nd, M:Bourse), 42.33.64.33. Closed Saturday and Sunday.*

This tiny restaurant, whose name translates as "Heads or Tails," enjoys a bigger and bigger reputation for the warm welcome and the inventive menu. Smartly decorated with burgundy-colored fabric walls, Pile ou Face attracts a trendy crowd, some of whom you will no doubt meet because the space is intimate. Dishes are essentially traditional with clever flourishes, such as the roast quail with braised halves of endives and a sauce laced with foie gras. The white asparagus spears are enormous and the tuna, grilled on one side only and steeped in a tangy caper and olive oil purée, is especially tasty. Their honey-flavored crême brulée is rightly famous.

53. WILLI'S WINE BAR *(nouvelle/moderate)*, *13 rue des Petits-Champs (1st, M:Bourse), 42.61.05.09. Closed Sunday.*

More contemporary, more casual, and less French than we ever imagined. In fact, you'll hear very little French spoken, even by the staff, which, like owner Mark Williamson, is British. Still, the food is quite good, with items such as lobster tail salad, roast pigeon, and hake wrapped around a moist tapenade. The wine list, as you might guess, is a gem. Lots of Bordeaux, Burgundy, and Châteauneuf du Pape from the 1980s, during which there were several good years. A few selections go back to the '50s and '60s. Willi's serves about a dozen relatively recent vintages by the glass.

54. JOE ALLEN *(American/moderate)*, *30 rue Pierre-Lescot (1st, M:Marcel), 42.36.70.13.*

Cut in the mold of the Joe Allen restaurants in New York and London, with essentially the same red, white and blue menu. We're talking burgers, meat loaf with mashed potatos, a T-bone grilled medium rare, Southern fried chicken with corn bread, and apple pie for dessert. Some of the best American food around in a semi-casual brick setting decorated, like the two sister restaurants, with theater posters. Too bad the neighborhood is so seedy.

THE MARAIS & BASTILLE
3rd, 4th & 11th Arrondissements

55. BENOIT *(traditional/moderate-expensive)*, *20 rue Saint-Martin (4th, M:Hôtel de Ville), 42.72.25.76. Closed Saturday and Sunday. No credit cards.*

This classy bistro first opened its doors way back in 1912 just around the corner from the Tour Saint-Jacques. In fact, they have adopted the tower as a part of their logo. This is one of the chic-est bistros in town, with a near-elegant decor of brass light fixtures, cut-glass partitions, and an antiqued paint treatment on the walls. You'll see an unusual number of coats and ties.

The menu is unusually dressy for a bistro as well, with dishes such as artichoke hearts with asperagus and green beans, smoked salmon sprinkled with salmon eggs, a lobster and asperagus salad, chicken in a crust with a ragout of artichokes, mullet and tapenade, sole in spinach leaves – all served on bright new plates with Benoit written on top in a delicate script. Only the wine list is uninspired. Prices are too steep and, remember, no credit cards taken here.

56. LA PERLA (*Mexican/inexpensive*), *26 rue François Miron (4th, M:Saint-Paul), 42.77.59.40.*

A fun corner restaurant with about fifteen tables that are almost always jammed full at dinner time. Lunch is a bit less crowded. Decorated in a Sante Fe prairie pink, La Perla has struck a chord with the young-ish crowd, which can be found yammering at a million miles an hour, sipping beers, and digging into spicy chili and beans, quesadillas with shrimp, onions, cheese and crème fraîche, or burritos with chèvre, spinach, tomato, corn, pineapple and guacamole. For dessert try the brownies or cheese cake. The portions are not the mountains of food you'd find in Lubbock, but the quality makes up the difference.

57. JO GOLDENBERG (*deli/moderate*), *7 rue des Rosiers (4th, M:Saint-Paul), 48.87.20.16.*

A classic Jewish deli that rivals even those in New York. With a jam-packed takeout case up front and often equally jammed restaurant in back, Jo's serves up Hungarian beef goulash, chopped meat balls "grand-mother style," cabbage leaves stuffed with meat and rice, borscht, marinated herring, moussaka, and other wonderfully filling dishes. Photos of Goldenberg with every conceivable local celeb decorate the walls inside and out. A sad sidenote: Six patrons were killed in the summer of 1982 when anti-Semitic terrorists bombed the restaurant.

58. LE BISTRO DE BOFINGER (*traditional/inexpensive*), *6 rue de la Bastille (4th, M:Bastille), 42.72.05.23.*

"The little pleasures of a good bistrot": That's the motto of this newly opened offspring of Bofinger, the Art Nouveau masterpiece of a restaurant directly across the street. Wood paneling, lots of mirrors, red leather banquettes, and a colorful tile floor give this baby bistro a warm and welcoming neighborhood feel to it. The prices are impressively reasonable and, though the menu and wine list are limited, the food is fresh and flavorful. Look for the house steak tartare, grilled andouillette, herring filets and potato salad, chicken fricasée, and claffloutie for dessert.

59. BOFINGER (*traditional-seafood/moderate*), *5 rue de la Bastille (4th, M:Bastille), 42.72.87.82.*

Bofinger claims to be one of the oldest brasseries in town. It is also immaculate and the bursting flower arrangements in the ornate majolica vases give the place a youthful, spring-is-in-the-air atmosphere. Prices for standards such as the steak tartare and escargots are a bit higher than at the Bofinger bistro across the street, though there is a prix fixe menu of about 170FF, including wine. The usual standards and choucroute are available here, but the house specialties tend toward fresh shellfish and other seafood.

60. CAFÉ DE L'INDUSTRIE *(light meals/inexpensive)*, *16 rue Saint-Sabin (11th, M:Bastille), 47.00.13.53.*

A hip neighborhood hangout that would be at home in the San Francisco Tenderloin – hardwood floors, Oriental rugs, paintings by the locals on the walls, young waitresses in black jeans, and a motorcycle or two out on the sidewalk. A great place to nurse a beer, drink too much coffee, or shovel in the house chili.

61. CHEZ PAUL *(traditional/moderate)*, *13 rue de Charonne (11th, M:Bastille), 47.00.34.57.*

Very popular bistro in a neighborhood that has come alive since the completion of the Bastille Opera House in 1989. A bit like a Left Bank restaurant, only more intense as locals cram into every nook until the wee hours, devouring such carefully prepared basics as legs of rabbit with chàvre and mint, steak au poivre flamed in cognac, the house steak tartare, filet of trout, and crême brulée. The bistro's motto: "One drinks, one eats ..." What else is there?

62. CHARDENOUX *(traditional/moderate)*, *1 rue Jules-Vallés (11th, M:Charonne), 43.71.49.52.*

A delightful old-fashioned neighborhood bistro in a still peaceful corner of the 11th arrondissement. This is the way bistros must have been decades ago, with frosted glass partitions, black and white photos on the walls, slightly worn trim (especially on the doors into the kitchen), a bunch of regulars, a neighborly staff, and dishes that stick to your ribs. The oeufs en meurette (poached on small rounds of toast, accompanied by garlic and bacon in a tangy red wine sauce) are excellent, as are the foie gras and green bean salad, and the veal kidney with a mustard sauce.

Other dishes: endive with chunks of Roquefort, gazpacho, veal chops with morel mushrooms, roast saddle of lamb with thyme, chocolate mousse with orange, and vanilla ice cream blanketed with warm caramel. If you lived nearby, this is the kind of place where you'd eat all the time.

FINDS & FAVORITES

Our very favorites, these restaurants have pretty much everything we look for: ambiance, a friendly staff, a good wine list, value for the money, and inventive food made with fresh ingredients.

12. LE PETIT MARGUERY *(traditional-game/moderate)*, *9 boulevard de Port-Royal (13th, M:Gobelins), 43.31.58.59.*

13. L'ASSIETTE *(tradional-haute cuisine/moderate-expensive), 181 rue du ChÉteau (14th, M:GaåtÇ), 43.22.64.86. Closed Monday.*

17. CAFÉ DE LA PLACE *(traditional/inexpensive), 23 rue d'Odessa (14th, M:Edgar-Quinet), 42.18.01.55. For lunch.*

21. AU BON SAINT-POURCAIN *(traditional/inexpensive to moderate), 10bis rue Servandoni (6th, M:Saint-Sulpice), 43.54.93.63. Closed Sundays. No credit cards.*

24. MARIAGE FRÈRES *(a real tea salon/inexpensive to moderate), 13 rue des Grands-Augustins (6th, M:Odéon), 40.51.82.50. Open daily. Best brunch.*

27. MICHEL COURTALHAC RESTAURANT *(traditional/ inexpensive to moderate), 47 rue de Bourgogne (7th, M:Varenne), 45.55.15.35. Closed Sunday.*

28. LE BISTRO DE BRETEUIL *(traditional/inexpensive), 3 place de Breteuil (7th, M:Duroc), 45.67.07.27. Open daily.*

32. AUBERGE D'CHEZ EUX *(southwest French traditional/ moderate-expensive), 4 avenue de Lowendal (7th, M:Ecole Militaire), 47.05.52.55. Closed Sunday.*

37. AU BON ACCEUIL *(traditional/inexpensive), 14 rue de Monttessuy (7th, M:Ecole Militaire), 47.05.46.11.*

42. LE BISTRO D'À CÔTE *(traditional/moderate), 10 rue Gustave-Flaubert (17th, M:Charles-de-Gaulle), 42.67.05.81.*

46. L'ECLUSE *(traditional/moderate), 15 place de la Madeleine (8th, M:Madeleine), 42.65.34.69. For lunch.*

58. LE BISTRO DE BOFINGER *(traditional/inexpensive), 6 rue de la Bastille (4th, M:Bastille), 42.72.05.23.*

62. CHARDENOUX *(traditional/moderate), 1 rue Jules-Vallés (11th, M:Charonne), 43.71.49.52.*

14. SEEING THE SIGHTS IN PARIS

MONUMENTS, MUSEUMS, & PARKS

Notre Dame (4th), the **Eiffel Tower** (7th), and the **Arc de Triomphe** (8th) have become universally familiar symbols of Paris. But these are more than slabs of stone and webs of steel that have been pieced together cleverly. They demonstrate beyond question the strength of the French spirit and the genius of the nation's artisans and builders.

Smaller cases in point are scattered throughout the central section of the city. Taking a simple stroll you are likely to find yourself turning a corner and discovering a magnificent sculpture or an architectural tribute celebrating one of the many heroes or legends of French history.

Paris is equally famous for its museums, the best known of which is the **Louvre** (1st). No question, the Louvre is stunning in its scope and grandeur. Unfortunately, however, the crowds, especially with the opening in late 1993 of the new **Richelieu wing**, are often monstrously large.

In fact, if you are pressed for time, don't lose an entire day by trying to tame the Louvre. There are other fine collections and museums in the city with more charm.

The **Musée D'Orsay** (7th), converted from a dingy railroad station and opened in 1986, is an absolutely beautiful setting for its 19th and early 20th century works. And the **Rodin** (7th) and **Picasso** (3rd) museums are must-sees. They are graceful, welcoming homes and gardens that have been converted into museums. The Rodin especially is unlike any conventional museum you've seen.

In general, museums close one day a week, either Monday or Tuesday, so check in advance. Hours are roughly 10 a.m. to 5 p.m., and admission charges for adults run from about 25 to 45FF, with half price for children and seniors. We have included prices for most museums and monuments, but admission fares have more than tripled in the last eight years and they change constantly. Many museums will also have special exhibits, which cost even more than permanent collections.

A last bit of advice here: pace yourself. Museums are inspiring, but leave time for seeing the city and the people as well.

The parks, too, are a crucial element in the city's personality. There aren't many, and the city has less parkland than most cities its size. Still, there are several well-placed sanctuaries of green that give the city a bit of breathing room in some of its most crowded quarters.

These oases are often decorated with well manicured lawns and spectacularly colorful gardens. And the larger ones offer pony rides and puppet shows for children and tranquil trails where you can daydream in peace.

Fare Cards Save Money

Save yourself time and money by purchasing a **pass** valid for 1, 3 or 5 days (60, 120, and 170FF). The cards are good at almost all museums and monuments, and they allow you to skip the lines at the ticket booth and go directly to the exhibition spaces.

You can find passes at most museums, monuments, Metro stations, and the **Paris Tourist Office** at 127 Champs-Elysées (8th). Helpful phrase: *Je voudrais une carte touristique pour les musées, s'il vous plaît.* This means, "I would like a tourist card for the museums, please."

Touring By Neighborhood

Grouping your sightseeing by neighborhood makes sense if you're pressed for time.

THE ISLANDS

ÎLES DE LA CITÉ & SAINT-LOUIS

Pont Neuf, *near the western end of the Ile de la Cité, connecting the island with both banks (1st, M:Pont Neuf).*

Paris's oldest surviving bridge, begun in 1578 and completed in 1604. It was also the first early Parisian bridge without houses, allowing for a westward view of the city that today takes in the **Louvre** on the Right Bank and the apartment buildings and, if you stretch, the **Musée d'Orsay** on the Left Bank.

The **bronze of Henri IV** astride his steed is an early 19th century copy of the version that was melted down during the Revolution.

Musée de la Conciergerie, *1 quai de l'Horloge (1st, M:Cité,), 43.54.30.06. Open daily. Admission 26FF.*

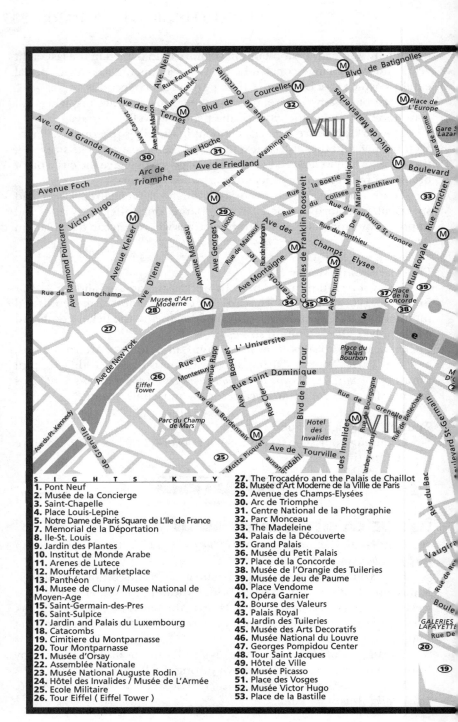

Map labels (as visible):

Blvd de Batignolles · Courcelles · Place de L'Europe · Rue de Courcelles · Blvd de Courcelles · Ave. Neil · Rue Fourcroy · Rue Poncelet · Ave des Ternes · Rue Mac Mahon · Ave Carnot · Gare St Lazar · Rue de Rome · Blvd de Malesherbes · VIII · Ave. de la Grande Armee · Arc de Triomphe · Ave Hoche · Ave de Friedland · Washington · Rue de · Boulevard · Rue Tronchet · Rue Royale · Avenue Foch · Rue la Boetie · Colisee · Matignon · Penthievre · Rue du · Rue de Marigny · Ave De Faubourg St Honore · Avenue Kleber · Victor Hugo · Rue de Franklin Roosevelt · Rue du Ponthieu · Ave des · Champs · Elysee · Rue Georges V · Lincoln · Rue de Marbeuf · Rue de Marignan · Courcelles de Franklin Roosevelt · Ave Churchill · Place de la Concorde · Ave Raymond Poincarre · Rue de Longchamp · Ave D'Iena · Avenue Marceau · Musee d'Art Moderne · Ave Montaigne · François · Place de la Concorde · L' Universite · Place du Palais Bourbon · Ave de New York · Rue de · Rue Rapp · Montessuy · Avenue Rapp · Ave Bosquet · Rue Saint Dominique · Rue de la Tour · Rue de Bourgogne · Rue de Grenelle · Rue de Bellechase · Boulevard St-Germain · Eiffel Tower · Ave de la Bordennais · Ave Cler · Blvd de la Invalides · Hotel des Invalides · VII · Ave du Pt. Kennedy · de Grenelle · Parc du Champ de Mars · Motte Picquet · Ave de Tourville · Taussandall · Ecole Militaire · Tour Eiffel (Eiffel Tower) · Place du Palais Bourbon

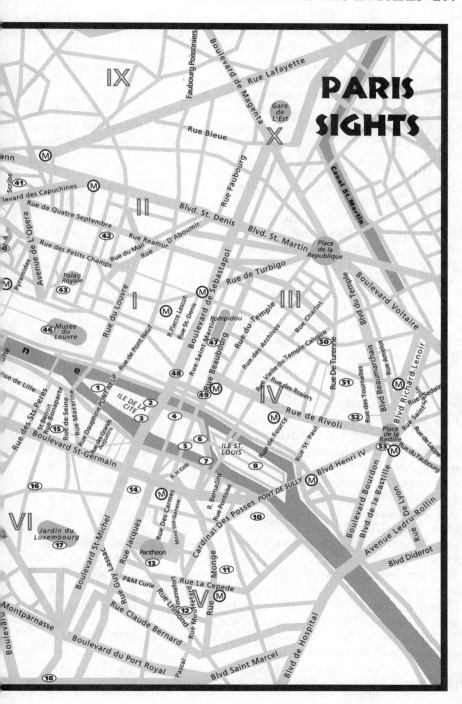

PARIS SIGHTS

A forbidding looking place, to say the least. This 14th-century prison was the last stop for Marie Antoinette and 2,600 others before their heads were lopped off in the name of the Revolution. In an upstairs chamber, you will find a list of 2,780 individuals who were condemned during the Revolution and subsequent Reign of Terror.

Just past the entrance hall is the enormous and impressive **Salle des Gens d'Armes** (Hall of the Men-at-Arms), and beside it a massive kitchen with four fireplaces where meals were prepared for as many as 3,000 at a time.

Also walk the **rue de Paris**, a small, depressing corridor leading to the cells and named after the state's chief executioner, not so fondly referred to as Monsieur de Paris. Further along you will find the **Salle de la Toilette** (where prisoners were prepared for death), a recreation of Marie Antoinette's cell (she was executed October 16, 1793), and a small chapel now named after 22 *Girondins* (members of a liberal party that held power briefly in 1791). The *Girondins* said their last prayers here having been condemned by Danton, who was himself condemned shortly thereafter.

Sainte-Chapelle, *tucked inside the courtyard of the 19th-century Palais de Justice at 4 boulevard du Palais (1st, M:Cité), 43.54.30.09. Admission 26FF.*

Stained glass — lots of it. In fact, there is more stained glass here than in any other church in the world — 6,700 square feet of it, depicting 1,134 Biblical scenes. The scenes run chronologically, beginning with the story of Genesis just to the left inside the entrance. The end, of course, is the Apocalypse.

On a brilliant day, with the sun backlighting the windows, the sight is breathtaking.

Sainte-Chapelle, completed in 1248 after just five years' labor, rises 67 feet into the air without the structural support of flying buttresses (a design considered revolutionary at the time). The cathedral was specifically intended to house various relics, including Christ's crown of thorns and a nail from the Cross. **Louis IX**, who was later canonized (Saint Louis), had purchased the relics for almost three times what it cost for him to build Sainte-Chapelle to house them.

These relics are now found in Notre Dame, and are shown on Good Friday.

Eugene-Emmanuel Viollet-le-Duc, a 19th-century architect who headed the restoration of Notre Dame, also worked on Sainte-Chapelle, repairing damage done to the chapel after the Revolution, when the building was used as a warehouse for the courts.

Place Louis-Lépine, *on the north side of the island, just off of rue de la Cité, which cuts the island in half (4th).*

A lively flower market with an amazing variety of cut flowers and potted plants and trees. On Sundays, bird sellers take over the square, offering thousands of colorful birds, elaborate cages, and various supplies. A great photo.

Notre Dame de Paris *(4th, M:Cité), at the eastern end of the Ile de la Cité, 43.26.07.39. Admission to cathedral, free. Admission to tower, 31FF.*

To stand in the Place du Parvis and to gaze at the western facade of this cathedral is to regain faith in humanity. Sometimes, you realize, the human race can pull off a lasting miracle.

Begun in 1163, during the reign of **Louis VII**, Notre Dame is the acknowledged masterpiece of French Gothic art and architecture. Built on a site where Romans worshiped a thousand years before, Notre Dame took another 182 years and generations of craftsmen, stonecutters, architects and glassworkers to complete. The two towers top off a perfectly balanced facade, and off the northern and southern sides of the cathedral you will find the remarkable flying buttresses that keep this stone marvel on its feet.

Also note the **"Gallery of Kings"** set above the three portals of the western facade, which are dedicated respectively to the Virgin Mary, the Last Judgment, and Sainte-Anne, the Virgin's mother. The gallery is a stunning array of sculptures depicting the 28 kings who are thought by the Catholic Church to be ancestors of Christ.

THE INCOMPARABLE NOTRE DAME DE PARIS

Understandably, Notre Dame has frequently provided the backdrop for French history and literature. It was here where **Henri VI** of England, **Mary Stuart** (made Queen of France by her marriage to François II), and **Napoleon** were crowned. More recently, Requiem masses were held here for **Charles de Gaulle** and **Georges Pompidou**, both popular contemporary French presidents.

Supposedly pushed ahead in part by the huge public popularity of Victor Hugo's classic tale of *The Hunchback of Notre Dame*, the cathedral received a major facelift in the mid-1800s, when an army of artisans marshaled together by architect Eugene-Emmanuel Viollet-le-Duc repaired the roof, reset the doors, and restored the colorful glass windows and small statues that adorn the facade.

For a view of the city and to appreciate the menacing gargoyles that line the western facade, climb the 255 steps leading up the north tower. At times you may think you'll never arrive, but the spiral trek is well worth the workout.

The **Square Jean XXIII**, a small park directly behind Notre Dame, draws lots of visitors, in part because the tour buses for Notre Dame park right behind it. Still, it is a pleasant place to stroll and gaze across the Seine to the apartments that line the Left Bank.

Square de l'Île de France, *also behind Notre Dame at the easternmost tip of the Île de la Cité (4th, M:Cité). Admission free.*

A lovely little park with a dozen or so benches, where you can enjoy the sun, nibble on a sandwich, briefly escape the crush of tourists lined up outside their tour buses just a few yards behind you, and admire the apartments lining the bank of the Ile Saint-Louis just off to your left.

Memorial de la Déportation, *at the easternmost tip of the Ile de la Cité in the Square de l'Île de France behind Notre Dame (4th, M:Cité). Admission free.*

After the Nazi occupation of World War II, more than 30,000 Jewish citizens were rounded up, boarded onto boats at this point, and ferried away to death camps. Designed by **G.H. Pingusson** and finished in 1962, the small, below-ground memorial is somewhat like a tunnel, even though light filters in through narrow windows onto the river. All in all, it is quite disturbing, and, for that, also quite effective.

Île Saint-Louis *(4th, M:Pont Marie).* Until the mid-1600s, there was no such thing as the Ile Saint-Louis. Two smaller islands, the **Île aux Vaches** and the **Île Notre Dame**, were fused together with landfill by real estate speculators, who then sold off lots for residential apartments — most of which are still standing. Tourists flood the main street, **rue Saint-Louis-en-l'Île**, in summertime. There are several fine small shops and galleries, as well as a couple of decent restaurants and hotels.

For such a centrally located place, Saint-Louis's sidestreets and quais are surprisingly quaint and quiet — like an island in the city, you might say.

Some of the apartments are quite grand, though many house artists and others who settle into the more reasonably priced apartments and never leave.

Square Barye, at the eastern end of the island, is a haven of quiet and shade. But beneath its walls, the stone quai and walkway is one of Paris's better known "beaches," where young men and women bare virtually all on a sunny day.

LEFT BANK

THE LATIN QUARTER

5th Arrondissement

Jardin des Plantes, *off of the Quai Saint Bernard, just east of the Jussieu campus of the University of Paris and just west of Gare d'Austerlitz (5th, M:Jussieu). Open daily. Admission charge to the adjacent zoo, 25FF.*

This 350-year-old garden is one of Paris's most pleasant and least overrun gardens. Its long esplanade is planted with brilliant flowers of all kinds, including huge, fragrant roses and marigolds of every possible color. The **Herb Garden** that parallels the main esplanade is a cook's dream come true, the huge greenhouse is bursting with overripe exotica, and the modest zoo provides a pretty and pleasant diversion for the kids.

The **Palaeontological Gallery** along the eastern side of the gardens near the river is home to skeletons of massive prehistoric beasts.

Institut du Monde Arabe, *1 rue des Fosses-Saint-Bernard (5th, M:Jussieu), 40.51.38.38. Closed Monday. Admission to the museum, 25FF.*

On first glance, the **Arab World Institute**, which opened in 1987, resembles a lot of other modern buildings, and seeing modern buildings in a city as rich in history and architectural beauty as Paris always gives us an initial twinge of anxiety. But on closer examination, the award-winning Institute is fascinating — especially the windows.

The 240 windows on the southern facade incorporate what is described as traditional Arab geometry. Each square pane is backed by an ingenious metallic grid of different sized circles surrounding a central portal. When the windows are "closed," lens-like diaphrams fold over part or all of the circles, forming octagons and stars in the process. The guts of the windows, seen from inside the building, resemble the intricate workings of a complex clock. (The shop inside offers wristwatches patterned after the windows.)

The Institute is a treasurehouse of Arab culture and is meant to provide ways to further the West's appreciation of the Arab world. Inside is a massive library, an audio-visual center, a book shop selling jewelry, posters, CDs and, of course, books, and a museum that traces the evolution of Arab culture from a couple hundred years BC to the present. Particularly interesting pieces include a handwritten Koran circa 1400, a series of richly colored Syrian rugs from the 16th century, and hardwood chests with inlaid ivory.

The Institute also boasts a top-floor restaurant and a terrace overlooking the **Seine** at the Ile Saint-Louis. If nothing else, plan a free visit to admire the windows and sip a quick coffee on the terrace.

Arènes de Lutece, *just off of the rue Monge at rue de Navarre (5th, M:Monge). Admission free.*

This Roman arena dating back to the 1st century once seated 15,000 people. It's a bit hard to image, but that's what they say. Today, the arena and small garden along **rue des Arènes** is more like a sanctuary. Even on a sunny day, there will rarely be more than 20 or 30 people, some of them children playing soccer, others adults sitting in the stone stands with a sack lunch or newspaper.

THE FOOD MARKETS

Many Parisians still do their grocery shopping the old-fashioned way: one tiny specialty shop after another. Typical street markets bustle with cheese shops, butchers, bakers, shoe repairs shops, vegetable stands, herb vendors, fish stores with a few watery beasts you may never have seen before, pastry shops, cafés crowded with yammering locals, and newsstands. Take lots of film. And remember that these shops are usually closed all-day Monday, Sunday afternoon, and during lunchtime from about 1 p.m. to 4 p.m.

- **RUE MONTORGEUIL** *(2nd, M:Châtelet).*
- **RUE MOUFFETARD** *(5th, M:Censier-Daubenton).*
- **PLACE MONGE** *(5th, M:Monge), Wednesday, Friday and Sunday mornings only.*
- **BOULEVARD PORT-ROYAL** *(5th, M:Port-Royal), Thursday and Sunday mornings only.*
- **RUE DE BUCI** *(6th, M:Mabillon).*
- **BOULEVARD RASPAIL** *(6th, M:Rennes), Tuesday and Friday mornings only.*
- **RUE CLER** *(7th, M:Ecole-Militaire).*
- **AVENUE DE SAXE** *(7th, M:Ségur), Thursday and Saturday mornings only.*
- **RUE DAGUERRE** *(14th, M:Denfert-Rochereau).*
- **BOULEVARD EDGAR-QUINET** *(14th, M:Edgar-Quinet), Wednesday and Saturday mornings only.*
- **RUE PONCELET** *(17th, M:Ternes).*
- **RUE LEPIC** *(18th, M:Abbesses).*

Mouffetard Marketplace, *rue Mouffetard, southeast of the Panthéon, parallel to the rue Monge in the heart of the Latin Quarter (5th, M:Censier-Daubenton).*

The cobbled **rue Mouffetard**, opened long, long ago as the Roman road to Lyon and beyond, stretches from the **Place de la Contrescarpe**, a picturesque square perfect for a leisurely coffee and a bit of people watching, to the **Place Médard** and the church by the same name. The tiny innocent looking church was the site in the mid-1700s where young women routinely had themselves beaten into what was described as rapturous states of semiconsciousness beside a Jansenist grave that supposedly possessed miraculous powers.

The marketplace near the bottom of Mouffetard, maybe the finest in the city, is a culinary wonderland of cheese shops, vegetable stands, butcher shops, fish shops and bakeries. On weekends, the Mouffetard is transformed into a kind of carnival as theater troupes, dancers, jazz bands, and accordian players serenade the crowd of locals and tourists.

You must stop in the **Brasserie Mouffetard** at the corner of Mouffetard and rue de l'Arbalete. It is the quintessential student, intellectual hang-out, where you're also likely to find a small cluster of elderly local men sipping wine early in the morning and complaining about young people or the government.

Panthéon, *rue Clotilde (5th, M:Cardinal Lemoine). Open daily. Admission 26FF.*

Another favorite of ours. The Panthéon is a bit like the father figure of the Latin Quarter, sitting soberly atop the highest knoll and gazing down on its domaine, almost daring the young residents of the student quarter to misbehave. More literally, this onetime church was ordered built on the "peak" of the Sainte-Geneviève slope in the mid-1700s by a gravely ill **Louis XV**. He had vowed to dedicate a magnificent temple to Sainte-Geneviève if he should survive the sickness. He did and up went the building.

After the Revolution, the Panthéon evolved into a profound burial vault for the heroes of France. **Voltaire**, **Rousseau**, **Émile Zola**, **Victor Hugo**, **Louis Braille** (as in the reading language for the blind) and others repose here. There is legislation pending that would move **Marie Curie's** remains to the Panthéon in honor of her scientific breakthroughs on behalf of Mother France. The view from the top is well worth the climb.

Musée de Cluny, Musée National du Moyen-Age, *6 place Paul-Painleve (5th, M:Cluny), 43.25.62.00. Closed Tuesday. Admission 27FF.*

Even if you're not a medieval history buff, you'd probably be impressed with this museum. This was the site of an enormous Roman bathhouse in the 3rd century and a religious residence beginning in the late 1400s.

The building, which changed hands many times, became a museum in 1844 and now houses an inspiring range of medieval art. Probably the most famous are the tapestries of the *Lady and the Unicorn*, which represent allegories of the senses.

But there are other tapestries that rival that series, including the Life at the Manor series in a bottom floor gallery that places you in the heart of a lovely embroidered garden filled with young lovers, dogs, birds, and blossoms of all description on a blue background. Upstairs, the *Departure of the Prodigal Son*, a huge tapestry from the early 16th century is equally colorful, depicting a young man on his steed with his family and a crowd of friends saying goodbye, and rolling hills in the background.

Downstairs you will also find a gallery of fragments of statues that were ripped from the facade of Notre Dame by the frenzied mob during the Revolution and only rediscovered in 1977. Stained glass, painted wood panels, wood chests, pages from illuminated books, jewelry, and sculpture round out the striking collection.

A personal favorite is in gallery 16: a solid gold rose from 1330, with delicate petals and young buds surrounding it. Truly stunning and absolutely flawless.

SAINT-GERMAIN & MONTPARNASSE
6th and 14th Arrondissements

Saint-Germain-des-Prés, *place Saint-Germain-des-Prés (6th, M:Saint-Germain), 43.25.41.71. Closed Monday mornings. Admission free.*

The 11th century Saint-Germain-des-Pres, the oldest church in Paris, takes its name from **Saint Germanus**, the 6th-century Bishop of Paris, and from the open fields (or *prés*) where the original structure was built. In some ways, it is a shadow of its former self, having only one of its original three towers. The other two towers were victims of the Revolution and subsequent neglect. The church was, in fact, used as a saltpeter factory shortly after the Revolution.

That wasn't all the damage done during the Revolution. Dozens of priests and monks from the church were rounded up and slaughtered in the small square to the south in 1792.

Today, the church and the square in front are focal points for a trendy neighborhood anchored by the well-known **Deux Magots** café across the lane from the entrance to the church. On a nice day, street musicians and artists abound.

Saint-Sulpice, *on the Place Saint-Sulpice between the Luxembourg Gardens and boulevard Saint-Germain (6th, M:Mabillon), 46.33.21.78. Open daily. Free.*

The often peaceful square outside features Visconti's handsome 19th-century fountain adorned with four devotees of the church who were highly regarded at the time, though they never quite made the grade of cardinal.

Work began on the church itself in the mid-1600s and was intended to serve the local peasants. Unfortunately, money, politics, indecision, and several switches in architectural plans delayed completion for more than 130 years. Even now, the church has a not-quite-finished charm (in fact, the tower on the right is incomplete).

Inside you will find one of the most valued organs in Europe, with 6,588 pipes, and, in the first chapel on the right, a series of heroic murals painted in the mid-1800s by Delacroix.

Set into the floor in the transept is a copper strip running north and south. During the winter solstice, sunlight peeps through a small hole in an upper window, strikes and follows the copper band, finally climbing an obelisk on the far wall. In mid-summer the sunlight strikes a copper plaque at the southern end of the copper strip.

Jardin and Palais du Luxembourg, *off of the boulevard Saint-Michel a few blocks south of the boulevard Saint-Germain (6th, M:Luxembourg), 43.29.12.62. Open daily. Admission to gardens, free. Admission charge for Sundays only tour of the palace.*

**CENTRAL POND OF LUXEMBOURG GARDENS,
WITH PANTHÉON IN BACKGROUND**

VISTAS

Because the center of Paris has none of the high rise office buildings we associate with most cities, the views are blissfully unobstructed.

Views from the top of:

NOTRE DAME DE PARIS *(4th, M:Cité), at the eastern end of the Ile de la Cité.*

INSTITUT DU MONDE ARABE, *1 rue des Fosses-Saint-Bernard (5th, M:Jussieu).*

PANTHÉON, *rue Clotilde (5th, M:Cardinal Lemoine).*

TOUR MONTPARNASSE, *33 avenue du Maine (15th, M:Montparnasse).*

EIFFEL TOWER, *Champ-de-Mars (7th, M:Bir-Hakeim).*

ARC DE TRIOMPHE, *place Charles-de-Gaulle (8th, M:Charles-de-Gaulle).*

SAMARITAINE, *19 rue de la Monnaie (1st, M:Pont Neuf). This department store's observation deck also has a small café.*

GEORGE POMPIDOU CENTER, *rue Rambuteau at the corner of rue Saint-Merri (4th, M:Châtelet).*

SACRÉ-COEUR BASILICA, *35 rue du Chevalier-de-la-Barre (18th, M:Anvers).*

LA GRANDE ARCHE, *1 parvis de la Defense, at the end of Metro Line 1.*

The **Luxembourg Gardens** are probably Paris's finest. During season, the beds spill over with incredible mixes of blazing flowers. The lawns are always flawlessly trimmed. The central pool draws hundreds of people, who sit admiring the palace or watching children use long sticks to guide wooden sailboats over the water's surface.

If you want more action, you can reserve an hour on the row of tennis courts or take your children on a pony ride or thump your feet to the bands playing just inside the **Place E. Rostand** gates on the eastern side of the gardens.

And if you tire of the crowds, stroll over to the perimeter enclaves along the garden's south and west sides, where you will find remarkable statues, peaceful glades and lawns, and locals reading a good book while they soak up some sun.

The palace itelf, much more easily admired from the outside than the inside, is currently heavily guarded because it is home to the **French Senate**. Its political legacy goes back to its beginnings in 1612, when Marie de Medici, wife of Henry IV, bought the Duke François de Luxembourg's mansion on the spot and ordered a palace built in a style reminiscent of the Tuscany palace where she was raised.

Her stay in the palace was a short one. She unwisely turned against Richelieu and was banished only five years after having moved in.

Catacombs, *2 place Denfert-Rochereau (14th, M:Denfert-Rochereau), 43.22.47.63. Open 2-4 p.m. Tuesday through Sunday, and 9-11 a.m. weekends. Admission 27FF.*

"Stop! This is the Empire of the Dead," warns a sign to the caves crammed with human remains.

Just as creepy as you would expect. The first trick is to find the entrance. It's the somewhat abused looking green building at the southern rim of the Denfert-Rochereau circle. The big bronze lion in the center of the circle looks right at it. Next, remember to wear old, comfortable shoes. Many passages in the catacombs are slippery and uneven. And take a flashlight, both to see your footing and to better examine "the sights."

The first thing you do on this unguided tour is decend a spiral stone staircase 65 feet straight down. In the first couple of chambers you will learn that in the late 1700s, Parisian cemeteries were bursting at the seams. Local officials decided it was time to do something.

What they did was create the catacombs in old stone quarries and, beginning in 1785, transfer the remains of millions of onetime residents here. Once you reach the ossuary, about a three block walk underground (not a tour for tall people or claustrophobics), various markers will tell you what cemetery the different mounds of bones once occupied. Part of the French underground used the catacombs as a headquarters during World War II. Note that the makers of these piles of bones had an artistic flair, creating patterns such a crosses using skulls fitted into walls of leg and arm bones. Charming.

Cimetière du Montparnasse, *entrances along boulevard Edgar Quinet and rue Froidevaux (14th, M:Edgar Quinet), just off the boulevard Raspail. Admission free.*

Providing a bit of tranquility near the Tour Montparnasse and the bustling boulevard Montparnasse, this cemetery serves as the final resting place of Jean-Paul Sartre and, naturally, his long-time companion and an intellectual great herself, Simone de Beauvoir. Beaudelaire, the master poet, and playwright Samuel Beckett are also tucked away among the hundreds of sculpted tombs here.

Tour Montparnasse, *33 avenue du Maine (15th, M:Montparnasse), 45.38.52.56. Closed Sunday. Admission charge to observation decks, 32 and 40FF.*

Until the late 1960s, Paris had refused to go the way of other world metropolises, who were erecting gigantic towers of steel and glass with total abandon. Why, citizens had said for decades, would we undo the great avenues and open vistas brought to us by Baron Haussmann in the mid-1800s.

Why indeed? Nonetheless, from 1968 to 1970 a massive 688-foot high black glass tower and two lunky black glass wings rose into the sky from a once cozy Left Bank neighborhood near such cultural landmarks as the Select, the Coupole and the Dome restaurants. The tower, besides which is the **Gare Montparnasse**, can be seen from anywhere in the city and dominates everything around it.

Though many highrises were built during the presidency of Gaullist Georges Pompidou (1969-1974), public outrage and political reality put a stop to the construction of any more towers like Montparnasse in the center of the city.

The two tourist draws of the tower are its loftily perched restaurant and the observation deck on the 56th floor, from which you can see literally for miles in all directions.

NEAR THE EIFFEL TOWER
7th Arrondissement

Musée d'Orsay, *1 rue Bellechasse (7th, M:Solférino), 40.49.48.14. or 40.49.48.48. Closed Monday. Admission 36FF.*

Our favorite large museum in Paris. The museum is a wonder not only for the fine collection of 19th century and early 20th century works it houses, but also for its near perfection as an urban renovation project.

This beautiful museum, which opened only eight years ago and was slated to be torn to the ground and replaced with a massive hotel complex, is a recaptured and beautifully refurbished *Belle Epoque* train station. On the outside, it still looks a bit like a trian station. But inside, once past the lines and the ticket booths, you step into the interior under the magnificent barrel dome and look out on a central hall that is as light and lovely as an outdoor courtyard and that is magnificently decked out with sculptures by **Barye**, **Rude**, and others. Overhead, above the entrance, is the incredible massive gold clock that was painstakingly restored at monstrous expense.

The permanent collection of Impressionist paintings by **Manet**, **Degas**, **Renoir**, **Sisley**, **Pissarro**, **Van Gogh**, etc., etc., is largely culled from the works that once hung in the Jeu de Paume at the end of the Tuileries gardens. There is a great deal of fine sculpture from the 1800s, photography by **Stieglitz** and others working around the turn of the century, and a gathering of American works by **James MacNeil Whistler** (yes, a portrait of his mother), **Winslow Homer**, **John Singer Sargent**, and others. Special exhibits are usually quite good and very popular.

The lovely and not horribly pricey museum restaurant is worth a visit for lunch, though arrive early because tables quickly grow scarce. Concerts are also regularly held at the museum.

The down side: lines grow very long in summertime and some people complain that the smaller exhibit rooms off the side of the main hall are a bit dark or that specific works are sometimes a bit hard to find. Special exhibits, often upstairs, wander from one small space to another and, on occasion, from one floor to another so that you feel a bit like a rat in a maze.

Assemblée Nationale, *33 quai d'Orsay (7th, M:Invalides), 40.63.60.00. Closed Sunday.*

Built in 1722 as a home for the **Duchess of Bourbon**, this grand edifice on the opposite side of the Seine from the **Place de la Concorde** now hosts the 577 members of the lower house of the French parliament. Visits are limited to the sessions from the beginning of April to July and from the beginning of October to the week before Christmas. Visits are also limited by space. Some suggest that you write ahead and reserve a spot in the gallery. Write the Affaires Administrative General, 126 rue de l'Universite, 75007 Paris.

Musée National Auguste Rodin, *77 rue de Varenne (7th, M:Varenne), 47.05.01.34. Closed Monday. Admission 27FF.*

A precious jewel of a musuem that blends master works with a setting that would be vibrant and welcoming even without the art. Why aren't there more museums like this one?

Rodin himself did not move into this former manse until about 80 years after it was built in 1730. And he wasn't alone. The mansion had been subdivided into sections, with other tenants over the years including the likes of **Isadora Duncan**, **Henri Matisse**, and **Jean Cocteau**.

Today, the home and large garden surrounding the house belong to Rodin's magnificent work. The garden, aside from being a lovely place to listen to one's own dim muse, provides the setting for masterpieces like *The Thinker*, the troubling *Six Burghers of Calais*, and the even more disturbing *Gates of Hell*.

Inside, some of the smaller, lifelike white marble pieces take on added glow when the sun streams through the windows. Drawings are also on display. And Rodin's famous studies of **Balzac** can be found upstairs. Those powerful works leave one with a sense that Balzac was in total command of all he surveyed.

Hotel des Invalides and **Musée de l'Armee**, *avenue de Tourville (7th, M:Invalides), 45.55.92.30. Open daily. Admission 34FF.*

The magnificent golden dome and 350-foot spire of Invalides is visible from just about anywhere in the 7th arrondissement, as well as from the Right Bank around the Palais de la Découverte and the end of the Jardin des Tuileries.

Most famous now as the resting place of **Napoleon's tomb**, Invalides was begun by **Louis XIV** as a tribute and a home to soldiers wounded during the many wars he sponsored. The original structures were completed after just a few years in 1676. The **Dome Church**, probably the finest specimin of religious architecture from its time, was begun the following year and not finished until 1735.

The vast green esplanade stretching from Invalides's north entrance to the river was also added in the early 1700s. Today, it serves as a green beach for sunworshippers on hot summer days.

Inside Invalides you will find the **Army Museum**, with its enormous collection of swords, muskets, and other weapons dating from the 1700s through to World War II. One hall contains flags and standards from various French armies, as well as some captured from their opponents.

The large, cobbled interior courtyard is lined with cannon adorned with fire-breathing lions.

But the main historical attraction is Napoleon's huge red stone sarcophagus, sunk into a circular crypt directly below the gilded frame and epic murals of the golden dome. Set into the floor around the sarcophagus is a brilliant green garland of laurels and on the walls are frescos paying tribute to French culture, education and industry.

Napoleon actually died on Saint Helena, where he was finally exiled. But his remains were brought to Paris, fulfilling his wish that he rest near "the banks of the Seine among the French people who I truly loved."

Other French heroes are likewise entombed at Invalides. In fact, the most impressive of all may be the tribute to **Marshal Foch**. The bronze sculpture is composed of eight rank-and-file soldiers from *The War to End All Wars*, with their late leader lying on a bed of laurels resting on their shoulders.

Ecole Militaire, *avenue de Motte-Picquet (7th, M:École Militaire), at the southern end of the Champ-de-Mars esplanade behind the Eiffel Tower. Visits by appointment only. Write to: General Direction, 1 place Joffre, 75007.*

Though it was completed in 1772 as a military school and barracks, the school has the architecturally refined and affluent look of a château from the Loire Valley. **Napoleon**, of course, attended, and the school is still active.

Eiffel Tower, *Champ-de-Mars (7th, M:Bir-Hakeim), near the Seine in the northwest corner of the 7th arrondissement, across from the Trocadéro and Chaillot Palace on the Right Bank, 45.50.34.56. Open daily. Admission charge of 20 to 53FF, depending how high in the tower you wish to venture.*

A monstrosity. Well, that's what most people thought way back in 1889 when the tower was topped off. Why on earth, they asked, would the world care to see the guts of a modern building without the grace of its clothes?

Interestingly, this was the same objection made in the 1970s when the George Pompidou Center opened on the Right Bank sporting all the unsightly ductwork and plumbing on the exterior of that contemporary art museum.

Also, like the Pompidou Center, which is now the most visited museum in the city, the Eiffel Tower muffled its critics by quickly becoming the most popular city attraction for turn-of-the-century visitors.

Built for a world's exposition, the tower is 1,051 feet high (that includes the various transmission towers). The antennae are, in fact, a critical part of the tower's history. In 1909 the tower was almost ordered pulled down. But French radio, which relied on the fabulous reception and broadcasting powers of the tower, came to the rescue.

Despite its estimated weight of 7,000 tons of pig iron, the tower's design is so efficient that it presses no more dead weight to the earth per square inch than an average sized man sitting in a chair.

Elevators take visitors seeking a breathtaking panoramic view to any of three levels — 190 feet, 380 feet or 900 feet. Or, if you're looking for a good workout, take the stairs — all 1,652 of them.

If you get tired of the crowds around the tower, stroll down the handsome **Champ-de-Mars** esplanade stretching out southward toward **Ecole Militaire**.

RIGHT BANK

NEAR THE CHAMPS-ELYSÉES
8th and 16th Arrondissements

The **Trocadéro** and the **Palais de Chaillot**, *place du Trocadéro (16th, M:Trocadero)*.

The **Trocadéro** is a fascinating blend of history, art, architecture and gardens directly across the river from the Eiffel Tower. The name, taken from a French victory over Spain in the early 1800s (the conquered Spanish fort was named Trocadero), refers to the neighborhood and not the gigantic palace, as so many visitors think.

The **Palais de Chaillot** is composed primarily of two magnificent wings that span out parallel to the Seine and bracket lovely gardens and a huge pool fed by more than 60 fountains and decorated with several neoclassic and modern sculptures. The palace was built just 57 years ago and replaced a building erected there for the 1878 world fair.

Though Chaillot is home to four museums, its primary draw is as a place to gaze down across the fountains and the river to the **Eiffel Tower**, **École Militaire**, the **Hôtel des Invalides** and much of the rest of the western half of the Left Bank. The spray of the fountains is captivating and the gardens on either side of the long rectangular pool have several peaceful sanctuaries if you want to escape the crowds.

The small roads sloping down on either side of the pool are also gathering places on sunny days for daredevils on rollerskates who wow the crowd with their slaloms and jumps.

One sad note: several low walls are blemished with graffiti, a city-wide problem. The local government has recently increased the penalties to hundreds of thousands of francs, but we'll have to see if the get-tough stance makes a difference.

The four museums housed in Chaillot are:

- **Musée des Monuments Francais**, *44.05.39.10. Closed Tuesday. Admission 21FF.* Striking reproductions and models of famous French monuments and cathedrals.
- **Musée de la Marine**, *45.53.31.70. Closed Tuesday. Admission 45FF.* A must for naval buffs, this museum chronicles the history of the French navy from the 17th century on, with detailed models of galleons that stand five to twelve feet high.
- **Musée de l'Homme**, *44.05.72.72. Closed Tuesday. Admission 25FF.* An anthropology museum whose permanent collection examines early life in the Americas.
- **Musée du Cinéma Henri Langlois**, *45.53.74.39. Closed Monday and Tuesday. Admission 25FF.* Guided tours only. A look at the development of moving pictures from the late 1800s to today. Recently renovated.

Musée d'Art Moderne de la Ville de Paris, *Palais de Tokyo, avenue du President Wilson (16th, M:Iena), 47.23.61.27. Closed Monday. Admission 27FF.*

This is the city's own personal art collection and, sad to say, it's a bit strange. Significant special exhibits of Impressionist work are hosted here, but the permanent collection has mostly minor works. There is a great deal of **Raoul Dufy** (including the striking *La Vie en Rose*), a couple of fine portraits by **Amedeo Modigliani**, and smattering of **Braques**, **Derains**, and others. The best of the contemporary works are **Bernard Rancillac's** 1974 portrait of Diana Ross and **Yan Pei Ming's** 1990 portrait of Mao. Beyond that, there are some pretty silly "artworks" warehoused in these cavernous display rooms.

Avenue des Champs-Elysées, *running east to west from the Place de la Concorde to the Arc de Triomphe (8th).*

At the Place de la Concorde, get out your camera and focus down the length of the **Champs-Elysées** as the sun is setting behind the Arc de Triomphe. What a picture! The other direction, from atop the Arc de Triomphe looking toward the Louvre, is equally awe-inspiring.

But frankly, in between is a forgettable commercial strip clogged with traffic. And there is seemingly constant construction, in large part to create underground parking lots that will allow even more people to flood onto a street that simply does not have a Parisian character anymore.

Fast food, overpriced clothes, mini-malls, car dealers, banks, and huge movie houses showing American films in English dominate the avenue. This is one of the few very public places in the city where we watch our wallets. Bright spots are the **Lido cabaret** and the **Virgin Megastore**, where you can buy just about any CD ever made or happily sip beers in the hip upper-floor café and watch the masses mill around below.

Bottom line: take the awestruck photos and get out.

Arc de Triomphe, *place Charles-de-Gaulle/Etoile (8th, M:Charles-de-Gaulle), at the head of the Champs-Elysées, 43.80.31.31. Open daily. Admission 31FF.*

The arch is a focal point not just of the famed **Champs-Elysées**, but also of French history. Built to memorialize Napoleon's triumphs, it wasn't until 1836 that the arch was finished and 1840 that the emperor's remains were taken by chariot through the arch.

THE ARC DE TRIOMPHE

THE HÔTEL DES INVALIDES

Baron Haussmann, the brilliant city planner under **Napoleon III**, made the circle one of his most important projects. An even dozen avenues spill into the circle (don't try driving around it). **Victor Hugo's** body lay in state beneath the arch in 1885, and victory parades commemorating Allied triumphs in both world wars were staged at the arch.

The arch is also the site of the nation's **Unknown Soldier**.

From pedestrian tunnels beneath the traffic circle, you come up under the arch and can ascend to the top platform 164 feet up for a magnificent view of the **Champs-Elysées** and the **Louvre** to the east and of **La Défense** in the distance to the west.

Centre National de la Photographie, *11 rue Berryer (8th, M:George V), 53.76.12.32. Closed Tuesday. Admission 30FF.*

The photo center only recently moved into the **Hôtel Salomon de Rothschild**, a fabulous onetime mansion on a quiet street in a neighborhood just north of the **Arc de Triomphe**. They'll stay while their wing of the **Palais de Tokyo** is being refitted. Members of the center complain that they have less space, and it's true that the gift shop is inadequate and the exhibition rooms don't follow a nice neat pattern, so you have to double back at times. Still, the shows are usually comprehensive and well lit in handsome rooms. The building itself is also very striking and there is a charming garden in the back where you can critique photographic techniques or just enjoy the afternoon.

Parc Monceau, *bordered on the north by the boulevard de Courcelles and a few blocks northeast on avenue Hoche from the Arc de Triomphe (8th, M:Monceau). Admission free.*

Not too many folks make it this far off the beaten path — aside from the residents of this very pleasant and affluent neighborhood. And it's probably true that the park offers little of huge historical significance, but it's still one of the prettiest parks in the city and is a delightful place to rest your feet.

Tucked away here and there you'll find odd architectural tributes to the pyramid, the windmill, Roman temples, etc. These little pleasantries were part of the original plan designed by the painter **Carmontel** in 1778 for the gardens' owner, the **Duke of Orleans**. The rotunda at the main entrance was once a tollhouse for farmers bringing their wares into the onetime walled city of Paris.

The Madeleine, *place de Madeleine (8th, M:Madeleine), 42.65.52.17. Open daily. Free.*

Not long ago, a friend's young girl passed by the Madeleine and was horrified to find that the immense curtain painted with a church had been taken down and that a huge building stood in its place. "What happened to the painting?" she asked with some disappointment.

The **Saint-Mary Magdalen church**, known as **The Madeleine**, was covered seemingly forever while restorers did their jobs inside and out. Finally, the magnificent windowless church with its fifty-two 66-foot Corinthian columns and exquisite rose marble and gilded interior is open to the public (though repairs are not 100 percent completed).

Up the rue Royal from the Place de la Concorde, the church was begun in 1764. But that and the subsequent structures were torn down before they were finished. The current structure resembling a Greek temple was finally completed in 1842. It remains a church, though it was almost transformed into a railway station and a stock exchange over the years.

Josephine Baker's funeral was held here with great pomp and ceremony in 1975.

Concerts are periodically conducted in the Madeleine. We heard Mozart's *Requiem*. Unbelievable! Tickets are available from FNAC and the Virgin Megastore.

Palais de la Découverte, *avenue Franklin D. Roosevelt a block and a half down from the Champs-Elysées (8th, M:Champs-Elysées), 40.74.81.82. Closed Monday. Admission 22FF.*

This museum is the all-time high school science fair housed in a building connected to and directly behind the **Palais des Beaux Arts**. It's ideal for the kids. Though the exhibits seem a bit out of place set in and off of the magnificent turn-of-the-century rotunda, they are a whole lot of fun. There are glass cages with live bugs of all kinds. There are charts and models and interactive displays of the solar system. There are pulleys and fulcrums and light shows, and a Planetarium with shows every day.

Grand Palais, *3 avenue du Général Eisenhower (8th, M:Champs-Elysées), 44.13.17.30. Closed Tuesday. Admission 45FF.*

Sad to say, the Grand Palais is hurting a bit. Built for the **1900 World Exhibition**, the building is showing its age. The facade still boasts two magnificent equestrian statues at either end of the roof line, but the entrance has been sealed off for repairs for some time.

Things are not much better inside. Once you could see all the way to the massive domed ceiling, but, again because of repairs, much of the inside has been converted into an enclosed maze of exhibition space that never gives you even a peek at the once grand skylights of the ceiling.

Still, the building does occasionally host significant exhibits, such as an expansive appreciation of Swedish arts and a display recounting the beginnings of Impressionism.

Musée du Petit Palais, *avenue Winston-Churchill, just across from the Palais des Beaux Arts (8th, M:Champs-Elysées), 42.65.12.73. Closed Monday. Admission 26FF.*

Like the Palais des Beaux Arts, this building was constructed in 1900 as part of the **World Exhibition**. Today, it is home to a very respectable permanent exhibit of 19th century sculpture and painting (including some massive oils with scenes from the Revolution). Two barrel-shaped wings extend off the main rotunda and look across the street at Beaux Arts. It's a beautifully ornate, but unfortunately somewhat rundown interior.

A highlight is the semi-circular garden in back, surrounded by an arcade with a wonderful mural on the arched ceiling depicting a trellis blanketed with colorful vines and populated by a host of lovers and images of night, day and fertility.

Place de la Concorde, *directly across the Seine from the National Assembly, and between the Jardin des Tuileries and the Champs-Elysées (8th, M:Concorde).*

Chaos. That's one of the first impressions because of the insane traffic swirling around what is probably the most elegant and historic traffic circle in the world. Covering 21 acres, this square came into being in the late 1700s and quickly became soaked with the blood of the bourgeoisie and the innocents who were guillotined in the years just following the Revolution of 1789. **King Louis XVI**, **Marie Antoinette**, and **Robespierre** were just three of thousands who lost their lives here (the location of the guillotine is marked near the statue dedicated to the city of Brest in the northwest part of the square).

At the center stands the **Obelisk of Luxor**, a 220-ton Egyptian obelisk (column) dating back to the 13th century BC and blanketed with hieroglyphics. Found in the ruins of the temple at Luxor, it was given to the French in 1833. Flanking the obelisk are two marvelous statues of horses, the **Chevaux de Marly** and the **Chevaux Ailes**, and surrounding it are eight statues dedicated to prominent French cities.

For a bit of contemporary glitz, step into the **Crillon**, a top-drawer hotel on the north side of the place. This is luxury at its very finest.

The **American Embassy**, on avenue Gabriel, is just across rue Boissy d'Anglais to the west of the Crillon.

NEAR THE LOUVRE

1st and 2nd Arrondissements

Musée de l'Orangerie des Tuileries, *at the western end of the Jardin des Tuileries on the Place de la Concorde (1st, M:Concorde), 42.97.48.16. Closed Tuesday. Admission 27FF.*

A rather homely museum from the outside, this former 19th century greenhouse nonetheless possesses a treasure of Impressionist art. The collection gathered over past decades by Jean Walter and Paul Guillaume includes key works by **Monet**, **Cézanne**, **Picasso**, and **Renoir**. Many of Monet's *Les Nympheas*, water lily murals, are here.

Musée du Jeu de Paume, *place de la Concorde at the rue du Rivoli (1st, M:Concorde), 47.03.12.50. Closed Monday. Admission 35FF.*

Though this museum lost most of its best work to the Musée d'Orsay, it now serves as a very effective showplace for temporary exhibits of major modern artists. Check your *Pariscope* for a description of the current show.

Place Vendome, *between the Garnier Opera House and the Jardin des Tuileries (1st, M:Tuileries).*

This place was first planned in 1680 as a grand square honoring **Louis XIV**, whose statue was to stand proudly in the center of property purchased from a convent and from the **Duke of Vendôme**. However, the equestrian monument erected in 1699 was leveled during the Revolution and replaced during Napoleon's time by a 144-foot column honoring the Little Emperor's triumphs in Germany. In fact, much of the bronze that is wrapped around the stone core of the column was melted down from captured enemy cannon.

Gustav Courbet, the painter, disliked the column so much that he was party to a conspiracy in May 1871 to topple the memorial. He was discovered and ordered to restore the monument at his own expense, which was considerable.The *Place* itself is quietly elegant, almost a bit stuffy. The magnficent **Ritz Hotel** is located here, as are offices for the **Ministry of Justice**. If you are in the market for fine pearls, jewelry, perfume and haute couture, or you just like to drool over luxuries displayed in opulent store windows, you've come to the right place.

Opéra Garnier, *place de l'Opéra (9th, M:Opéra), 40.17.33.33. Open daily. Admission 30FF.*

Unfortunately, "Open daily" is a bit misleading. In fact, the grander-than-grand opera house is going under the knife for a major 350 million franc facelift and much, sometimes all, of the building will be off limits from mid-1994 to early 1996.

"Opera house" is also a bit misleading. Since the opening of the Opéra Bastille in 1989, the Garnier has been dedicated almost solely to dance. Despite the huge stage complex at Garnier, which can in theory accommodate up to 450 artists at a time, it was felt that its 2,200 seats were grossly insufficient for grand (and profitable) opera.

It's really a shame. The exterior of this magnificently ornate art house from the 1870s is just a foreshadowing of what you find inside. Mouths hang wide open at the marble staircases, the ornate gilded reception rooms, the six-ton chandelier, the (seemingly out-of-place) Chagall mural on the interior ceiling, and the rows of red velvet-lined boxes hovering over and around the stage.

Charles Garnier, the state architect who designed this chef d'oeuvre, pulled every imaginable excess out of his hat for this beauty. And really the best way to see this opera house, as with any performance space, is during a performance. Seats, if the theater is open when you come, can be had in the nosebleed section for very reasonable rates — though we suggest you buy a box for the experience.

Bourse des Valeurs, *4 place de la Bourse (2nd, M:Bourse), 42.33.98.83. Closed Saturday and Sunday.*

French capitalism in all its chaotic glory can be watched from the spectators gallery of this Romanesque temple built at Napoleon's order in the early 1800s. It's a spectator sport of a different kind.

Palais Royal, *place Palais-Royal, just north of the Louvre (1st, M:Palais-Royal).*

Though the interior is now closed to the public because it belongs to the very wary **Council of State,** the building and interior gardens are worth a quick visit. The main building was constructed in 1632 for then **First Minister Richelieu,** who willed it to the royal family — thus the name change from the Cardinal's Palace to the Royal Palace.

The buildings surrounding the garden went up in the late 1700s, and now house businesses as well as an arcade of pricey art galleries (**Raymonde Duval** has lovely watercolors) and shops offering haute couture, perfume, rare stamps, and miniature soldiers. Poet **Jean Cocteau** and author **Colette** once lived in the apartments above those shops.

The main garden is really a large esplanade surrounding a central fountain and two gardens brimming over with blooms of all kinds. It's a tranquil place to catch your breath.

And you can't miss, even if you want to, the **Court d'Honneur**, a square just behind the main building in which you will find a grid of black-striped stone columns of heights varying from a few inches to about six feet. This "sculpture" by **Daniel Buren** went up in 1986, causing a stink between the conservatives, who hated the project and fought it in court, and the liberals, who happened at that point to have a stronger than usual voice in government and defended it. (Try to land a coin atop the one column that is set in a below-surface-level niche near the northwest corner of the square. It's not as easy as it looks.)

Jardin des Tuileries, *the huge garden to the west of the Louvre, stretching up to the Place de la Concorde (1st, M:Tuileries).*

The prettiest construction site you'll ever see. Named after the tile *(tuil* in French) factories that once occupied this property and first laid out in the mid-1600s, the Tuileries is a remarkable example of how the French reign in their passionate and sometimes disorganized nature when it comes to gardening. The Tuileries is a picture postcard of meticulous lawns, hedges, trees and flower beds — a lovely place to stroll, or sit and feed the birds.

Unfortunately for the moment, the gardens are undergoing a major overhaul, a complicated and messy process that is scheduled to last through 1996.

Musée des Arts Décoratifs, *107 rue de Rivoli (1st, M:Palais-Royal), 42.60.32.14. Closed Monday. Admission 25FF.*

This museum is pretty much what it sounds like — paintings, furniture, tapestries, table settings and other decorative flourishes from way, way back to new works by the likes of **Philippe Starck**. The museum is very popular, and offers special exhibits on such subjects as the history of fine Delft china.

Musée National du Louvre, *rue de Rivoli (1st, M:Palais-Royal), 40.20.51.51, 40.20.53.17 or 40.20.50.50. Closed Tuesday. Admission 40FF.*

The **Louvre** is considered the mother of all museums. When the first small fortress known as the Louvre was built in 1200 to keep invaders out of the city, **King Philippe-Auguste** could not possibly have imagined it would evolve into the largest palace in Europe and later into probably the best known art museum in the world. And he certainly never would have pictured **I.M. Pei's glass pyramid** that now stands at the heart of the inner courtyard and serves as the main entrance.

The Louvre has just recently rung the bells of critics once again, opening the northern **Richelieu wing** in November, 1993 on the 200th anniversary of the museum. The new wing, which doubled the exhibition space of the Louvre, is roomy, well lit, well organized and maybe the best part of the whole museum. Also, the new shops and cafés of the underground **Carousel area**, which features an upside-down version of

Pei's glass pyramid at its center, is spacious and inviting. There is a particularly great print shop, where you might find a fabulous gift or memento of your trip.

Overall, the addition was a masterstroke because it not only allowed the showing of much more of the Louvre's vast collection, it also improved the image of a museum that was beginning to be perceived as a bit grim, stuffy and confused. (In fact, it's still hard to find some pieces.)

The permanent collection is fat with classics that are household names, such as the *Venus de Milo* and the *Mona Lisa*, and such artists as **Titian, Raphael, Botticelli, Hieronymus Bosch, Breugel, Vermeer**. The list goes on and on. There are epic sculptures, whole chunks of ancient palaces, Egyptian, Roman, and Greek antiquities, paintings reaching back six centuries, graphic arts, and furniture.

Having said all that, we recommend that if you are coming to Paris for the first time and only have a few days, avoid the Louvre or set aside a well-disciplined afternoon at most. The Louvre is awesome, as is the crowd. And as fabulous a museum as it has become again, it would be a mistake to spend all your time in Paris fighting this crowd and not seeing the Paris that is humming with life all around you.

I.M.PEI'S GLASS PYRAMID AT THE ENTRANCE TO THE LOUVRE

THE MARAIS & BASTILLE

3rd, 4th, & 11th Arrondissements

Georges Pompidou Center, *rue Rambuteau at the corner of rue Saint-Merri (4th, M:Châtelet), 44.78.12.33. Closed Tuesday. Varying admission charges to expositions.*

An absolute zoo and, truth be told, an architectural monstrosity. Still, this tribute to the late **Georges Pompidou**, a Gaullist who served as president of France from 1969 to 1974, is The Most Visited Monument in all of Paris.

How can that be? Well, it is a contemporary version of the Eiffel Tower. Its inside-out version of a building, in which ductwork and plumbing are visible and escalators ride up the exterior of the building in large glass tubes was reviled when unveiled in 1977 (as was the Eiffel Tower at the turn of the century). But it was also instantly accepted, especially by the young crowd that was drawn to its extensive library and resource facilities.

The building is a remarkable resource of modern arts and other intellectual endeavors. It houses the fine **Musée National d'Art Moderne**, with many important 20th century works, it hosts significant shows examining modern architecture, it has a video library and regularly screens European film masterpieces, it has a heavily used regular library, and it hosts all sorts of concerts.

A practical note: the interior can be a bit intimidating at first. If you are interested in exhibits or concerts, there is a large information desk and all tickets are purchased at the multi-windowed cashiers offices in the northeast corner of the bottom floor.

If nothing else, ride the escalators to the top floor, where you can enjoy a panoramic view of the city. An outdoor seating area for the top floor café is a perfect place to enjoy the sun.

You should also stop by the fountain on place Stravinsky just to the south of the Pompidou. You've probably seen pictures of this before — the red pouty lips, the playful elephant, the multi-colored coiled snake, and other mechanical gizmos spinning around and spewing water.

Tour Saint-Jacques, *off the rue de Rivoli at the boulevard de Sebastopol (4th, M:Châtelet).*

Turning a corner on the hectic rue de Rivoli or emerging from the Metro, it's a bit startling to see this 171-foot, 16th-century tower standing solo in the middle of a square. What's missing is the medieval Saint-Jacques-la-Boucherie church, which was one of the beginning points for pilgrims who set off regularly to the shrine of Santiago de Compostella in northwestern Spain.

The church was brought down in 1802, but the tower was saved and used in the manufacture of lead pellets for muskets. Today, the Gothic tower serves as part landmark and part weather station.

Hôtel de Ville, *rue de Rivoli at the Place de l'Hôtel de Ville (4th, M:Hôtel de Ville), 42.76.40.40. Guided tours only.*

Home to the city government, currently headed by Jacques Chirac, a conservative who has held power here for years and who wants desperately to be elected president some day. The Hôtel de Ville is also a magnificent structure. The city hall was first built here in the early 17th century, but was largely destroyed in 1871 when the **Paris Commune** took power after Napoleon III's miserable failure in the Franco-Prussian War.

What you see now was rebuilt from the ruins and completed in 1882. Its intricate facade, heavily adorned with statues of national heroes, blends Renaissance elements with the *Belle Epoque.*

Ask about tours of the interior state hall and reception rooms at the information office at 29 rue de Rivoli, where small, free exhibits are held honoring the city's remarkable past.

Musée Picasso, *5 rue de Thorigny (3rd, M:Chemin Vert), 42.71.25.21. Closed Tuesday. Admission 26FF.*

Another gem of a museum. Only nine years old, this tribute to **Picasso** is set in a fabulous renovated mansion built in the 17th century. The collection of paintings, drawings, collages and sculpture walks you chronologically through Picasso's awesome career. There may not be many of the familiar masterpieces, but the collective impact of the exhibit is quite powerful and instructive.

What makes the collection even better is that these pieces came from the master's own collection, donated in part by heirs who couldn't afford the huge inheritance tax slapped on the collection after Picasso's death in 1973. You will also find assorted memorabilia and some works of **Cézanne**, **Braque**, and others who Picasso admired and whose works he collected.

The mansion itself, the **Hôtel Salé** (salt), is named in tribute to the wealth the original owner acquired in the mid-1600s by collecting taxes on salt for the crown.

Place des Vosges, *off of rue des Francs Bourgeois, just north of rue Saint Antoine in the Marais district (4th, M:Saint-Paul).*

The epitome of elegance. Dating back to the very early 1600s, this is the oldest surviving square in Paris. The square is surrounded by 36 houses of red brick and stone, all perfectly balanced and in architectural synch with one another. The large King's Pavilion occupies the southern side, while the Queen's is located at the north.

Along the arcade are a couple of very pleasant bistros and several respected art galleries.

In the center of the square is an equally geometric park, with plenty of shaded spots to catch up on your reading, as well as plenty of open space which is often quickly filled by playing children.

It's hard to picture the decay that came to the square in the 1700s and 1800s. In fact, it was saved finally only in the 1960s, when it was declared an historic district and was pain-stakingly restored.

Musée Victor Hugo, *6 place des Vosges (4th, M:Saint-Paul), 42.72.10.16. Closed Monday. Admission 17FF.*

In the southeastern corner of the elegant **Place des Vosges**, this was home to the literary giant from 1833 to 1848 and claims to have the largest collection anywhere of Hugo memorabilia, including clothes, furnishings, and his sometimes bizarre drawings and doodles.

Place de la Bastille, *at the eastern end of rue Saint-Antoine (4th, M:Bastille).*

A dozen roads converge on this monster of a traffic circle, where the striking 171-foot **July Column** has replaced the dreaded Bastille prison that was torn down 200 years ago. The original layout of the prison is set in the paving stones of the circle.

The prison, of course, was a focal point of the Revolution. In truth, the 400-year-old prison had outlived its usefulness and, a few years before the Revolution arrived, the local government had agreed in principle to demolish the structure. Ultimately the mobs beat them to it, freeing in the process the mere handful of prisoners still held there. Nonetheless, the "storming" was a symbolic victory for the masses, who quickly razed the aged structure.

The area received a very welcome boost on the 200th anniversary of the Revolution when the 3,000-seat **Bastille Opera House** was opened. The neighborhood in the blocks just east of the opera house has since blossomed with trendy restaurants and clubs.

OUTSIDE THE CITY CENTER

The sights listed below are not located in the very heart of Paris, but they are all within easy reach by Metro. They are listed in geographic order, beginning north and moving clockwise to the east, south and then west.

MONTMARTRE
18th Arrondissement

Generally speaking, this area is best known for the striking Sacre-Coeur Basilica, the view of all of Paris below, and the artists who have called this butte home for decades.

Sacré-Coeur Basilica, *35 rue du Chevalier-de-la-Barre (18th, M:Anvers),* *42.51.17.02. Open daily. Admission charge to church dome with panoramic view, 15FF.*

The marvelous white elongated domes of Sacré-Coeur can be seen throughout the city, a stunning monument to a stunning French defeat in Napoleon III's ill-advised Franco-Prussian War of 1870.

The basilica, completed in 1910 after 34 years work, is a Catholic tribute to the 58,000 soldiers who fell in the war, which was a rout. Prayers have been said non-stop for the fallen since the church was consecrated in 1919.

The grounds are as inspiring as the church itself, with seemingly countless steps leading down a steep esplanade to the **Square Willette**. The view of the city is magnificent, the slopes below will be peppered with children feeding the birds, and at the foot of the butte you'll likely run into all manner of artists and musicians, including an ever-present South American group playing haunting melodies on wooden flutes.

For those who'd just as soon ride as walk the 250 steps of the adjacent and much photographed rue Foyatier, there is a small funicular pumping up and down the steep slopes for the price of a Metro ticket.

Rue Foyatier, *just to the west of the slope leading up to Sacré-Coeur (18th, M:Abbesses).*

You'll recognize this street the instant you see it. Steps. Steep steps. Well over 200 steep steps, with an occasional traditional Paris lamppost. Get out your camera.

Espaces Montmartre-Salvador Dali, *9 rue Poulbot-place du Tertre (18th, M:Anvers), 42.64.40.10. Open daily. Admission 25FF.*

Just a few years old, this modernish museum doesn't quite fit the character of the neighborhood. If you're a Dali fan, this is a must-see. There are many familiar and minor prints and reproductions, and quite a few sculptures, like the girl with the neck of a giraffe and various clocks melting over tree limbs. The shop at the end of your tour is first-rate, with Dali postcards, prints, sculptures, puzzles, neckties, watches (you can guess what these look like), T-shirts, and other odds and ends.

Place du Tertre, *just a block or two east of Sacré-Coeur (18th, M:Abbesses).*

How did such an adorable little square in a neighborhood where the likes of Van Gogh and Modigliani toiled become such a silly place? The square itself is a swarm of street artists just dying to paint your portrait (some are much better than others). An outdoor café occupies the central core of the plaza, and cafés surround the square so that people can watch other people having their likenesses immortalized in their choice of oil, pastel or watercolor. The neighborhood here and at the base of the steps to Sacré-Coeur still hosts a few decent art galleries, but much of the shop space has been taken up by vendors hawking T-shirts and other nonsense.

Montmartre Vineyard, *at the corner of rue Saint-Vincent and rue des Saules (18th, M:Lamarck-Caulaincourt).*

That's right, a vineyard. Well, not exactly a vineyard that Château Margaux would be proud of, but it does have the distinction of being the last remaining producing vineyard in Paris proper. You can buy wine from this buccolic little plot in the back of the city hall for the 18th arrondissement (each arrondissement has one) just off the place Jules Joffrin.

Rue du Mont-Cenis, *just a block or two behind Sacré-Coeur (18th, M:Lamarck-Caulaincourt, Jules Joffrin).*

There's not much in the way of famous museums or galleries on this street. It's just a pretty walk that extends from the Saint-Pierre de Montmartre (the city's oldest church, at the top of the butte) down to the place Jules Joffrin and the market street of rue du Poteau. The southern half of the street is mostly a series of steps, scores of them, climbing the northern slope of the butte. It may be a bit of work, but the view is pretty, as are many of the apartment buildings lining Mont-Cenis.

Cimetière de Montmartre, *with the entrance off rue Caulaincourt, just above the boulevard de Clichy (18th, M:Place de Clichy).*

This maze of tombs and markers lined cheek-by-jowl up and down the slopes is a refuge from the unsightly and often disgusting chaos of nearby Clichy and is home to the remains of a few French giants. Degas is here, as is Stendhal and Alexandre Dumas, author of the highly popular and romantic tale of vengeance, *The Count of Monte Cristo*. You're likely to run across a few dozen cats here as well — French cemeteries are very popular with cats.

Place Pigalle, *near the eastern end of the boulevard de Clichy (18th, M:Pigalle).*

Clichy and Pigalle were made famous in part by Henry Miller. But as much as we admire Miller and think of him as one of the truly original American writers of the 20th century, the neighborhood today is a cultural cesspool, with barkers from the sex clubs literally grabbing you as you try to pass by. Remember that no matter what they say and no matter how convincingly they say it, they are lying.

CLIGNANCOURT FLEA MARKET

Take the number 4 Metro line north to the Porte de Clignancourt stop at the very end. When you come up out of the subway, just follow the crowds (and there will be crowds) walking north, past the Periphique beltway and into the suburban neighborhood of Saint-Ouen.

This is probably the most famous of the Parisian flea markets, known in these parts as **Marchés aux Puces** (now you know the French word for fleas). At first you're probably going to wonder why the market is so popular. In the two or three blocks it takes to get to the actual market you will walk a gauntlet of vendors hawking crummy T-shirts, trinkets, used CDs, firecrackers, "American" jeans, and other assorted trash. This is not the flea market you're looking for.

You want the traditional antique dealers wedged in the 'V' formed by avenue Michelet and rue des Rosiers. Here you'll find gilded mirrors and marble-topped tables, shiny sets of silver, ancient armoires, coins, tins, combs and dolls, spurs, stamps, prints, and buttons, turn-of-the-century tabloids ... Well, you get the drift.

Yellow markers on the paths, or *allées*, help you remember where you are and where you saw some special item you've finally decided to go back to buy.

Prices surprised us. They were not too bad. But never, never pay full price or we'll never speak to you again. Bargain. It's part of the party.

In the heart of this little commercial corner is **Chez Louisette's**, a funky brasserie with edible food, reasonable prices, and often a woman who looks like she just walked in off the streets singing her heart out.

Before you bail out, cross Rosiers to the **Marché Dauphine**, which is another set of small antique alleys. In fact, the very best and priciest furnishings are found here. If you like Deco or Empire, you'll spot some truly beautiful pieces.

SAINT-DENIS BASILIQUE

Located at the end of the number 13 Metro line. Open daily. Admission 26FF.

The burial place of kings (literally a couple of dozen), Saint-Denis takes its name from the first bishop of Paris. **Saint Denis** was decapitated in the 3rd century by a jealous regional king who thought Denis was becoming too influential. But, legend has it, Denis retrieved his severed head and marched from Montmartre north to the suburb of Saint-Denis where be was buried by a peasant woman.

Don't be put off by the crummy shopping mall you see when you step out into the village of Saint-Denis. And don't be put off by the exterior of the church, which is just around the corner and is cathedral-like in its majesty, but just a bit sad because it lost one of its towers and is dark with soot.

Don't be put off, especially if you are a history buff, because the tombs of the basilica are astounding. The building has a fascinating history as well, beginning as a Gallo-Roman cemetery, then being reborn in 475 as a small church built at the order of Sainte-Geneviève. Its heyday was under **Abbott Suger** in the 1100s, who decided a grand edifice was in order and set the plans in motion. Still, the cathedral was not completed until the 13th century, and bits and pieces were added, destroyed, rebuilt and destroyed again over the centuries. (Display cases inside give a very good history of the building and the people who shaped it.)

But again, the *raison d'être* for this visit is the tombs and the crypt. The oldest tomb found so far dates back to about 565 and contains the remains of **Aregarde**, wife of Clotaire I, King of Paris. Magnificent tombs in the main hall honor **Henri II** and **Catherine de Medicis**, **François I** and his wife **Claude de France**, **Dagobert I**, and **Louis XII** and his wife **Anne de Bretagne**.

The remains of **Marie Antoinette** and **Louis XVI** lay beneath elegant black marble slabs in the crypt, and a beautiful marble sculpture off the ambulatory honors their tragic deaths. A small sideroom in the crypt lists the burials here of 18 kings dating from Dagobert I in 638 to Henri III in 1589, as well as dozens more queens and various and sundry relatives.

In terms of history, Saint-Denis rivals Notre Dame.

CITÉ DES SCIENCES ET DE L'INDUSTRIE

Located at Parc de la Villette, 30 avenue Corentin-Cariou (19th, M:Porte de la Villette). Closed Monday. Admission 45FF for the basic pass, more if you want to see the Cité and the Géode.

Kids, young or old, who are infatuated with science will find hours of entertainment in this high-IQ theme park in the northeast corner of Paris. Displays bring the science of space exploration and theories of time and matter down to earth for the rest of us. Lots of interactive exhibits — many of which you'll find engulfed by swarms of youngsters.

Also visit the **planetarium**, the **aquarium**, and, most certainly, the **Argonaute submarine**, which you'll find just a few yards from the gleaming spherical **Géode**. Inside the Géode, watch science films on the kind of high-tech screen that sits you down in the center of the action.

CIMETIÈRE PERE-LACHAISE

The main entrance is off the boulevard de Menilmontant (20th, M:Père-Lachaise).

Paris's largest cemetery pitches and rolls over hundreds of acres and is probably best known to Americans as **Jim Morrison's** final resting place. The graffiti besotted tomb of the lead figure of The Doors still draws small crowds of restless neo-hippies, most of whom hadn't been born when the rock band toured in the late '60s. Other "residents" here who are far more deserving of admiration include: **Oscar Wilde**, **Marcel Proust**, **Balzac**, **Modigliani**, **Chopin**, **George Bizet**, and **Colette**. Vandals recently desecrated more than 100 graves, and, once again, former Mayor Chirac had promised to get to the bottom of things.

VINCENNES, THE CHÂTEAU, AND BOIS

Go to the eastern edge of the city, just outside the city proper, at the end of the number 1 Metro line (12th, M:Château de Vincennes).

Step out of the Metro, pivot, and there it is: the gate tower of a medieval castle completed in 1370. Pretty impressive stuff for this modest suburb.

This is the classic castle, complete with moat all around (though it is dry now). Through the gate and into the courtyard, you will find an archaelogical dig where workers with small trowels and brooms are gently bringing to light long forgotten foundations of the earliest castle structures.

Further inside is the towering **Donjon** and the striking **Chapelle Royale**, which was modeled after Sainte-Chapelle and dates back to the 14th century. There are guided tours of the 170-foot-tall Donjon, though, unfortunately, the Chapel is closed to the public.

The **Bois** (meaning woods) is enormous and has what is considered to be Paris's finest zoo, two lakes with islands where you can rent rowboats and putter around, and several sports fields. But in our view, the highlight here is the **Parc Floral de Paris**.

The Parc Floral (10FF admission) is probably the prettiest, most instructive garden in all of Paris. Brilliant tulips spring out of the ground everywhere, there is a small lake in the center bordered by beds of marigolds, petunias, impatens and other flowers, and there is a lily pond populated by ducks and dozens of turtles, who climb the banks on a hot day to sun themselves.

But this isn't just a picture of beauty and tranquility. There are separate gardens carefully seeded around the grounds that contain medicinal plants, aromatic flowers, bonsai, hothouse ferns, bamboo forests, and other manner of flora, all clearly labeled so you can tell your *Syringa micrphylis superba* from your *Poncirus trifoliata*.

What's more, you'll be walking along admiring the plants, turn a corner, and there will be a dazzlingly blue and green peacock standing in your path giving you the once over. A nice restaurant and a crèperie are tucked into unobtrusive corners.

SAINT-CLOUD

Go to the western end of the number 10 Metro line, getting off at Boulogne/ Pont de Saint-Cloud. Then cross the bridge over the Seine and look left for a sign that says "Piètons, Parc Saint-Cloud."

This massive park of 1,100 acres was once the sight of a magnificent château that was Napoleon's favorite residence. This is where he married his second wife, Marie-Louise, after having dumped Josephine. This is also where Henri III was assassinated in 1589 by a young Jacobin monk.

You can glean a bit more history from the **Musée Historique** *near the Grille d'Honneur* (main gate).

But today, Saint-Cloud's attraction is the tranquility of its verdant parkland and the majesty of its fountains. The **Grande Cascade** a couple hundred yards from the entrance is famous for its multi-terraced fountain, with water spewing from the mouths of stone frogs, gargoyles, lions, dogs and all manner of fearsome beasts. The **Grand Jet** just a few yards more to the south shoots water 140 feet into the air. Notice the carp darting around in the waters below. (*Warning*: The fountains are turned on only from May through September, on late Sunday afternoons.)

The terrace which begins above the Grande Cascade was the site of the château (a marble map shows you exactly where it stood) and is now an immaculate lane of greenery and splashy floral beds leading up to the impressive **Rond Point** with its 24 fountains and cozy café.

The **Jardin du Trocadéro**, just up the slope to the north of the terrace where the château stood, is particularly tranquil and inspiring, mixing colorful trees and flowers of all kinds. With a pond at the center, it's a bit like Wonderland. There is a panoramic view of Paris from the southeast corner of this garden.

If you want total privacy, just wander into the forests east of the terrace. Even though there is not much in the way of monuments left here, Saint-Cloud is a very pretty stop.

MUSÉE MARMOTTAN-CLAUDE MONET

Located at 2 rue Louis Boilly (16th, M:Muette), 42.24.07.02. Closed Monday. Admission 35FF.

Facing the quiet Jardin du Ranelagh along the western edge of the 16th arrondissement, the **Marmottan** houses a collection of 65 Monets painted throughout his career and donated to the museum by the painter's son Michel in 1971. Most of the Monets, including well known studies of water lilies, a Japanese bridge, and train stations, line the walls of a basement level gallery that contains a few works by Renoir, Pissarro, and other followers of the Impressionist school.

Monet's *Impression–Sunrise*, one of his most influential pieces, is on view, having been donated to the museum in 1950. It is credited by some with having given the Impressionist movement its name.

The museum was opened in 1934 at the bequest of Paul Marmottan, an art historian who donated his beautiful home as well as his collection of furnishings largely from the Empire and Consular periods.

After visiting the museum, stroll east through the park and up the sloping road to **Dominique Geffroy**, a lovely tea salon *at 8bis rue de la Muette.*

BOIS DE BOULOGNE

Located along the western edge of the 16th arrondissement (16th, M:Porte Maillot, Porte Dauphine, or Porte d'Auteuil).

While the French generally prefer to reign in nature, composing meticulously ordered gardens and parks with crisp lawns, obedient hedges, and sharply delineated beds of flowers arranged by color, the Bois de Boulogne is a virtual wilderness.

The woods themselves, favorites of local dog owners, are ragged and woolly, with paths that meander through the underbrush. In fact, way back in the 1300s, this was a favorite hunting ground, and later it became a trusty hideaway for bad guys who prayed on the rich, then hid in the bushes.

Aside from providing a place of relief for local dogowners and a refuge for young lovers, the 2,200-acre Bois is also home to a great deal of organized activity. To the south end is the famous **Roland Garros** tennis stadium where the **French Open** is played every spring, as well as the **Hippodrome d'Auteuil**, where millions of francs are won and lost daily on the horses (when in season). An even more famous Hippodrome is the **Longchamp**, in the southwestern corner of the park, where the Paris Grand Prix is held in June.

At the northern end of the bois is the **Jardin d'Acclimatation**, with its many amusements for children (see Chapter 18), and the **Musée National des Arts et Traditions Populaires**, with exhibits on agriculture and folklore.

But the biggest draw of the Bois de Boulogne, are the two lakes in the center, the **Inferieur** and **Superieur** lakes, where you can hire a canoe and float around for hours. You can also catch a tiny ferry across to the islands, where you can have a bit of lunch at the café or soak up the sun on the grassy knolls.

The more familiar formal French garden of the **Bagatelle**, where Charles X designed and built a house in three months on a bet with Marie Antoinette, is also worth a peek if you've got time.

LA DÉFENSE & THE GRANDE ARCHE

West of the city at the end of the number 1 Metro line (M:Grande Arche de la Défense), 49.07.27.57. Open daily. Admission 40FF to the observation deck.

To best appreciate this enormous experiment in urban planning and contemporary architecture (with more than 30 office towers), get off at the Esplanade Metro stop and walk the last few hundred yards of the **La Défense** quarter to the **Grande Arche** at the western end. At the eastern base of the esplanade is a large pool with tall masts topped with different colored lights, an artistic theme repeated at the other end, on the other side of the Arche.

The esplanade (no cars allowed) is a brilliantly conceived walkway adorned with gardens, potted plants, sculptures of various kinds, and some "sidewalk" style cafés. On either side, you will gawk up at some truly imaginative office towers (whose indexes read like a Who's Who of international business). It's not exactly a warm and cuddly human space, but students of architecture will be spellbound.

Baron Haussmann himself, the 19th-century designer of the grand avenues of Paris, might even approve of the esplanade, which spills at the foot of the Arche into an enormous plaza ringed by department stores. **Quatre Temps**, **FNAC**, **Habitat**, all the big French stores have an outlet here. Here, you'll no doubt also run into the rollerskaters who seem to be all over the city these days, slaloming between pink pontoons or leaping off ramps.

And finally you will climb the 54 white marble steps that bring you to the underbelly of the Grande Arche, which is quickly becoming another of the universally recognizable Paris sights — this one a monument to the contemporary corporate world. The Arche, designed by architect Johan Otto von Spreckelsen, is referred to as *A Window on the World, A Symbol of Hope for the Future.*

Glass-bubble elevators take you up underneath the arch to the observation platform on top, where you will marvel at the panoramic view. What you see in the distance is the classic Paris. What you see around you is the future.

FINDS & FAVORITES

We simply never grow tired of these remarkable places.

NOTRE DAME DE PARIS *(4th, M:Cité), at the eastern end of the Ile de la Cité, 43.26.07.39.*

MOUFFETARD MARKETPLACE, *rue Mouffetard, southeast of the Panthéon, parallel to the rue Monge in the heart of the Latin Quarter (5th, M:Censier-Daubenton).*

PANTHÉON, *rue Clotilde (5th, M:Cardinal Lemoine).*

JARDIN AND PALAIS DU LUXEMBOURG, *off of the boulevard Saint-Michel a few blocks south of the boulevard Saint-Germain (6th, M:Luxembourg), 43.29.12.62.*

MUSÉE D'ORSAY, *1 rue Bellechasse (7th, M:Solférino), 40.49.48.14. or 40.49.48.48.*

MUSÉE NATIONAL AUGUSTE RODIN, *77 rue de Varenne (7th, M:Varenne), 47.05.01.34..*

OPÉRA GARNIER, *place de l'Opéra (9th, M:Opéra), 40.17.33.33.*

MUSÉE PICASSO, *5 rue de Thorigny (3rd, M:Chemin Vert), 42.71.25.21.*

PLACE DES VOSGES, *off of rue des Francs Bourgeois, just north of rue Saint Antoine in the Marais district (4th, M:Saint-Paul).*

SACRÉ-COEUR BASILICA, *35 rue du Chevalier-de-la-Barre (18th, M:Anvers), 42.51.17.02.*

VINCENNES, *Parc Floral of the Bois de Vincennes (12th, M:Château de Vincennes).*

BOIS DE BOULOGNE, *the islands in the middle of the lakes (16th, M:Porte Maillot).*

15. PARIS - CULTURE

Long-hairs complain that French culture is going through a bit of a slump. They demand to know who's going to replace the Robbe-Grillets of literature, the Genets of theater and the Truffauts of film.

While it may be true that giants are in short supply (and not just in France), there is no shortage of French talent on any cultural front. Local theater is very much alive, as is French film, and internationally renown performers of all stripes include Paris in their itinerary.

And what better way to appreciate such remarkable settings as the **Garnier Opera House** (9th arrondissement) than by attending one of the dance performances there. The five-year-old **Bastille Opera House** (12th arrondissement) should also be on your short list of places where you can enjoy a performance and sightsee from the comfort of your reserved seat.

The **Madeleine** (8th arrondissement), recently reopened after a total facelift, hosts choral and chamber works regularly. There's nothing quite so moving as a piece like Mozart's *Requiem* in such a magnificent setting.

If you are interested in contemporary works — film, theater, dance — pick up a schedule of events from the **Pompidou Center** (4th arrondissement).

DANCE

Though dance holds a beloved place in the French arts and the finest companies in the world routinely schedule stops in Paris, there is not a great deal to see at any given moment. However, Paris is home to one of the most magnficent dance performance halls in the world in the **Garnier Opera House**, opened originally in 1875. It has been devoted entirely to dance since the opening in 1989 of the **Bastille Opera House** across town.

Seating just over 2,000, the Garnier is a masterwork of opulent decor, with massive staircases, ornate reception halls, gilt all around, a six-ton chandelier and, oddly, a Chagall mural on the ceiling.

THE REMARKABLE ÓPERA GARNIER

Prices at various theaters are reasonable by dance standards, often beginning at 40 or 50FF, depending on the company performing.

The Garnier Opera House is located *at the place de l'Opéra (9th, M:Opéra), 47.42.53.71.*

Other halls where dance is performed include:

• **Centre Mandapa**, *6 rue Wurtz (13th, M:Glacière), 45.89.01.60.*

• **Chatelet Theatre Musical de Paris**, *1 place du Châtelet (1st, M:Châtelet), 40.28.28.40.* Primarily an opera house, but some dance.

• **Georges Pompidou Center**, *rue Rambuteau at the corner of rue Saint-Merri (4th, M:Châtelet), 44.78.13.15.* Mostly contemporary.

• **Le Rond-Point-Theatre Renaud-Barrault**, *2bis avenue Franklin-Roosevelt (8th, M:Franklin-Roosevelt), 44.95.98.00.*

• **Théâtre de la Bastille**, *76 rue de la Roquette (11th, M:Bastille), 43.57.42.14.*

• **Théâtre de la Ville**, *2 place du Châtelet (4th, M:Châtelet), 42.74.22.77.* Mostly contemporary works.

FILM

Parisians are consumed with movies, which is not surprising because France has spawned such giants as Truffaut, Rohmer, Godard, Malle and many others.

There are more than 100 cinema houses in Paris proper and more than 250 houses in the metropolitan area, most of which have several screens. About 300 different films are screened each week in Paris.

In fact, one cinema house, **Le Grand Pavois** (*364 rue Lecourbe, in the 15th at the Balard Metro stop; 45.54.46.85*) shows more than 40 different films a week. The Pavois screens everything from first run hits to cult classics like *Blade Runner* — some in French, some in English.

Parisians are so nuts about movies that it is easier in Paris to see American classics on the big screen than it is in almost any American city. On rue des Ecoles (5th arrondissement) in the Latin Quarter there are three houses (the **Action Ecoles**, **Le Champo**, and **Grand Action**, each with multiple screens) where you can watch Hitchcock's best, Audrey Hepburn festivals, musicals like *Guys and Dolls*, even Westerns.

Where Are the Movies?

How do you find them? Simple. Once again, you can't go wrong with *Pariscope*, *L'Officiel*, or the Wednesday *Figaro* supplement. They list every film, with times, prices and descriptions. The films are even cross-referenced so that if you're in the mood for sci-fi, just look under the sci-fi heading to see what's in town.

Though American films often arrive in Paris weeks, sometimes even months, after they have been released in the U.S., there's always a bunch of first-runs to choose from. They are clustered in three primary spots: along the Champs-Elysées (8th arrondissement), along the boulevard Saint-Germain (6th arrondissement), and along avenue Montparnasse (on the border of the 6th and 14th arrondissements).

Listings also note whether the film is being shown 'VF' or 'VO,' meaning the French Version or the Original Version. English films shown VF have been dubbed, and there won't be any English subtitles to help.

Like so many things, movies are a bit pricey. New releases will run you anywhere from 35 to 50FF. There are student and senior discounts, and just about any ID seems acceptable as long as it's presented with confidence. Repertory houses are also somewhat cheaper, with specials running about 25FF.

Helpful phrase: *Deux places pour* (name of movie), *s'il vous plaît,* means "Two tickets for (name of movie), please."

OPÉRA

The enormous new opera house at Bastille dominates the local opera scene. The 3,000-seat main hall, which opened in 1989, hosts all the major production companies, not the least of which are French companies performing such French classics as George Bizet's *Carmen*. The modern complex is worth a visit even if you don't stay for a performance, but combine the two experiences if you can. Prices in the nosebleed section are down to earth at about 60FF.

The **Bastille Opera House** is *located at 120 rue de Lyon (12th, M:Bastille), 44.73.13.00.*

Other houses with opera:

• **Centre Wallonie-Bruxelles**, *46 rue Quincampoix (4th, M:Châtelet), 42.71.26.16.*

• **Châtelet, Theatre Musical de Paris**, *1 place du Châtelet (1st, M:Châtelet), 40.28.28.40.* Also a major house, attempting such difficult works as Wagner's Ring cycle.

• **Opéra Comique**, *5 rue Favart (2nd, M:Richelieu-Drouot), 42.86.88.83.*

• **Peniche-Opéra**, *across from 200 quai de Jemmapes (20th, M:Jaures), 43.49.08.15.*

• **Théâtre des Champs-Elysées**, *15 avenue Montaigne (8th, M:Franklin-Roosevelt), 49.52.50.50.*

SYMPHONY

Classical music can be heard all over town all the time. Literally ten to twenty performances are scheduled every day, with solo artists, choral groups, chamber pieces and full orchestras playing the work of Bach, Mozart, Scarlatti, Schumann, Rossini, Bizet and countless other masters.

Full formal symphonies of world-class orchestras can be heard at the **Bastille Opera House**. But the most fun (and economical) performances are those held in one of the great churches (see the **Madeleine**, **Sainte-Chapelle**, and **Saint-Germain-des-Prés** in Chapter 14, *Seeing the Sights in Paris*). The better conductors make the most of the haunting accoustics, and the combination of eloquent music and grand surroundings can be quite moving.

For a long list of times and places, check your *Pariscope* guide. Also, when you visit museums and churches, odds are that you will find flyers near the entrance announcing a performance or two that week.

THEATER

The Paris theater scene is hugely active with more than 100 productions onstage every single week. Anglophones will spot all sorts of familiar names, from Shakespeare to Oscar Wilde and from Harold Pinter to Woody Allen.

The downside is that there is very little available in English, and unless your French is very, very good, you'd have a rough time trying to keep up with a French production.

But if you're hungry for the stage, scan the *Pariscope* theater listings for the **On Stage Theatre Company**, **Dear Conjunction**, and **Gare Saint-**

Lazare Players, all of which stage English-language productions. Houses that sometimes host English productions include:

• **Théâtre de la Main d'Or Belle de Mai**, *15 passage de la Main d'Or (11th, M:Ledru-Rollin)*, *48.05.67.89.*

• **Théâtre Marie Stuart**, *4 rue Marie Stuart (2nd, M:Etienne-Marcel)*, *45.08.17.80.*

• **Théâtre de Nesle**, *8 rue de Nesle (6th, M:Odéon)*, *46.34.61.04.*

• **Théâtre du Tourtour**, *20 rue Quincampoix (4th, M:Rambuteau)*, *48.87.82.48.*

• **Tremplin Théâtre des Trois Freres**, *39 rue des Trois Frères (18th, M:Abbesses)*, *42.54.91.00.*

WHERE TO FIND TICKETS

All of the theaters and concert halls sell their own tickets, but they are scattered all over town and not always convenient. Some box offices will also annoy you to no end with odd hours and long lunch breaks. Three central clearing houses for tickets to most events can ease your troubles:

*• **FNAC**, 1 rue Pierre Lescot, third level down in the Forum des Halles (1st, M:Châtelet), 40.41.40.00.*

*• **Kiosque Théâtre**, across from 15 place de la Madeleine (9th, M:Madeleine).*

*• **Virgin Megastore**, 52 avenue des Champs-Elysées (8th, M:Franklin-Roosevelt), 40.74.06.48. A second, small Virgin outlet is located at the Carrousel du Louvre (1st, M:Palais Royal), 49.53.52.90.*

16. PARIS - NIGHTLIFE

As you might expect, there is no shortage of nightlife in Paris. Clubs, discos, and cabarets are scattered all over town.

There are three things you should keep in mind before you set out on your nocturnal quest. One, and this is sounding like a broken record, but clubs are very expensive. Don't be surprised if you drop a couple hundred francs in the first hour (if not in the first few minutes).

Two, bands won't strike the first note until about ten or eleven, and discos and other hip and groovy nightspots often don't begin to fill up until midnight or later (though many will sizzle until the sun pushes up into the early morning haze).

Three, the Metro shuts down just after midnight, and cabs are increasingly difficult to find in the wee hours of the morning (except at a few major cab stands, such as the boulevard Saint-Michel). So figure out before hand how you're going to get home.

CABARETS & EXTRAVAGANZAS

There are cabarets and then there are cabarets. The cabaret of yesteryear, which is a kind of old fashioned variety show of singers, dancers, and comedians in a homey theater with too many chairs in too little space, has enjoyed a revival of late. In fact, they abound and they are a blast. But, they are in French and even when you speak the language well, it's not always so easy to get the punchline.

Then there are the big cabarets, the Extravaganzas, which are mostly for tourists, including French tourists from the countryside. They are high-tech, often lavish variety shows with a cast of beautiful dancers, elaborate stages, live orchestras, suave crooners, amazing jugglers, even more amazing magicians, agile acrobats, and the odd elephant or horse threatening to prance right into the audience.

The big cabarets are expensive — 130 to 700FF, depending on the show and whether you have dinner too. Our advice is to have a nice dinner somewhere else and enjoy a nightcap at the cabaret for dessert. These shows have an unfair reputation for being an emporium for T&A. The better shows are actually good clean fun. Our most straight-laced friends have taken their young daughters to the Lido, and the kids described the show as an elaborate circus — which, in fact, is exactly what it is.

Old-Style Cabarets

- **L'Ane Rouge**, *3 rue Laugier (17th, M:Ternes)*, *45.62.52.42*. Mostly comedy and a fair amount of gags that draw the audience in. All in French at this typically cozy traditional cabaret.
- **Au Lapin Agile**, *22 rue des Saules (18th, M:Lamarck)*, *46.06.85.87*. Lots of singing, comedy and even poetry. Poetry? Hey, why not.
- **Chez Michou**, *80 rue des Martyrs (18th, M:Pigalle)*, *46.06.16.04*. A parody of the big shows, in drag.

Extravaganzas

- **Crazy Horse Saloon**, *12 avenue George V (8th, M:George V)*, *47.23.32.32*. *Open nightly. Admission for revue starts at 290FF*. If the dancers weren't all about the same age, you'd think they were sisters. The classy Crazy Horse set in an even classier neighborhood selects a very particular look, then enhances the physical similarity by dressing the dancers (with names like City Nebula and Funky Coconut) in identical wigs and costumes. Stage numbers make the most of contemporary light shows, and the magicians are wild.
- **Folies-Bergere**, *32 rue Richer (9th, M:Cadet)*, *44.79.98.98. Closed Monday. Admission for revue-only: 150-700FF*. An immense hall seats 1,600 for this classic revue that was resurrected from the dead only a year or so ago.
- **Lido de Paris**, *116bis avenue des Champs-Elysées (8th, M:George V); 40.76.56.10, Fax 45.61.19.41. Open nightly. Admission: 465-670FF*. The biggest and brightest of the big bright shows, with a stunning cast of dozens of men and women who clearly get more than adequate exercise. Elaborate shows feature a frenzy of lights, a live band, jugglers doing the impossible, wacky skits, and fountains, ice rinks, and a submarine that emerge from the floor. How do they do that?
- **Moulin-Rouge**, *place Blanche (9th, M:Blanche)*, *46.06.00.19. Open nightly. Admission for revue only, 465FF*. This is supposedly where the can-can was kicked off. They still perform it with style. But there's a lot more to this show, which boasts 100 performers, 1,000 costumes (with headdresses towering to the ceiling), and a pool of crocodiles.
- **Paradis Latin**, *28 rue du Cardinal-Lemoine (5th, M:Cardinal-Lemoine), 43.25.28.28. Admission: 465-670FF*. Who'd have guessed that such an unassuming student neighborhood would play host to such a dazzling and popular Extravaganza. This is a favorite stop for bus tours.

LIVE MUSIC

If you're in the mood for a trashy garage band, no problem. If you want some funk, you got it. Or if you're feeling cool and would like to sit in a corner booth and soak in some jazz, Paris has that too. Jazz is still particularly popular here and there seem always to be a few big names in town. The Madonnas pass through regularly as well, playing to thousands in the newish Bercy sports palace on the Right Bank a few blocks east of the Gare de Lyon.

For the big concerts and popular clubs, stop by the **Virgin Megastore** or **FNAC** (see *Paris-Shopping* chapter), check out the posted listings, and buy your tickets there. For more intimate settings, buy *Pariscope* or pick up a free copy of *FUSAC, Paris Voice, Paris City Magazine* or the *Time Out Guide*, all of which are distributed widely and have current music listings.

Once again, be prepared to spend. Even at the smaller clubs there is likely to be a cover charge, or you will be charged a premium rate for your first (and mandatory) drink. Play it safe and reserve ahead.

A few live music clubs:

- **Bataclan**, *50 boulevard Voltaire (11th, M:Oberkampf), 48.06.21.11.* A jazz club that pulls in lots of visiting artists and some big names, like Wynton Marsalis.
- **Bilboquet**, *13 rue Saint-Benoît (6th, M:Saint-Germain-des-Prés), 45,48,81.84.* Jazz nightly, with mostly local talent in a real party neighborhood.
- **La Cigale**, *120 boulevard de Rochechouart (18th, M:Pigalle), 42.23.15.15.* Fans call it a magical club.
- **La Coupole**, *102 boulevard du Montparnasse (14th, M:Vavin), 43.20.14.20.* Have a hearty meal upstairs, then head downstairs for a mambo combo or two.
- **Duc des Lombards**, *42 rue des Lombards (1st, M:Châtelet), 42.33.22.88.* Local and imported jazz talents.
- **Elysee Montmartre**, *72 boulevard Rochechouart (18th, M:Anvers), 42.52.25.15.* A mixed menu, from hard rock to country in another popular party neighborhood.
- **Front Page**, *56 rue Saint-Denis (1st, M:Etienne-Marcel), 42.36.98.69.* A rocking spot for traditional blues, jamming, even an occasional Hendrix tribute. Funky neighborhood at night, with lots of streetwalkers. Not for everyone.
- **Hot Brass**, *Parc de la Villette, 211 avenue Jean-Jaures (19th, M:Porte de Pantin), 42.00.14.14.* A bit of Latin with a dash of jazz. Talents like Les McCann and Abbey Lincoln grace this club.
- **Lattitudes Paris Saint-Germain**, *7 rue Saint-Benoît (6th, M:Saint-Germain-des-Prés), 42.61.53.53.* Another jazz *boite* in a neighborhood where it's easy to club hop.

• **Meridien, the Lionel Hampton jazz club**, *81 boulevard Gouvion-Saint-Cyr (17th, M:Porte Maillot), 40.68.30.42.* Lots of solid and often young talent. Mostly imported to this very classy house that Lionel, the jazz giant, built.
• **Montana**, *28 rue Saint-Benoît (6th, M:Saint-Germain-des-Prés), 45.48.93.08.* Among the most famous of the Saint-Germain jazz clubs.
• **New Morning**, *7 rue des Petites-Ecuries (10th, M:Château-d'Eau), 45.23.51.41.* Contemplative jazz the likes of Cedar Walton.
• **Olympia**, *28 boulevard des Capucines (9th, M:Opéra), 47.42.82.45.* French rap and rebuilt bands like the Velvet Underground.
• **La Villa**, *29 rue Jacob (6th, M:Saint-Germain-des-Prés), 43.26.60.00.* Lots of quality mid-range jazz talents playing interpretations of classics in a basement *boite*.

NIGHTCLUBS & DISCOS

After the spring and fall fashion shows, the models inevitably cruise uptown to **Les Bains** for a party with likewise beautiful people. Though it is certainly one of the most popular clubs, it can be one of the most frustrating too. Doors open around midnight and the bouncers will give you a good looking over before they let you in or tell you to get lost. Fortunately there are lots of other options.

Check the *Pariscope* listings for one nighters that feature the hot DJs. They will also draw the most interesting crowds — and they can get pretty interesting if you like loud costume parties.

Women often get in free (gee, why is that?). And things get going late. Real late.

Some nightclubs:
• **L'Arc**, *12 rue de Presbourg (16th, M:Charles de Gaulle-Étoile), 45.00.45.00.* A relatively upscale crowd in a plush setting featuring a garden looking out on the Arc de Triomphe.
• **Les Bains**, *7 rue du Bourg-l'Abbe (3rd, M:Etienne-Marcel), 48.87.01.80.* You wish.
• **Blue-Billard**, *111 rue Saint-Maur (11th, M:Saint-Maur), 43.55.87.21.* Not much for dancing, but ideal if you want to shoot some pool, play a bit of backgammon and listen to the blues.
• **Castel's Princess**, *15 rue Princess (6th, M:Mabillon), 43.26.90.22.* If you can get into this famous club you can count yourself among the select.
• **La Locomotive**, *90 boulevard de Clichy (18th, M:Blanche), 42.57.37.37.* Monster club.
• **Queen**, *102 avenue des Champs-Elysées (8th, M:George V), 42.89.31.32.* Big new night spot. Very popular with the gay crowd, but everyone is invited.

• **Le Rex Club**, *5 boulevard Poissonière (2nd, M:Bonne Nouvelle), 42.36.83.98.* Grunge, they say.
• **Le Tabou**, *33 rue Dauphine (6th, M:Odéon), 43.25.66.33.* Party time in a party neighborhood.
• **La Scala**, *188bis rue de Rivoli (1st, M:Palais Royal), 42.61.64.00.* Like a movie version of a disco.
• **O'Brasil**, *10 rue Guénégaud (6th, M:Odéon), 43.54.98.56.* A disco with a, you guessed it, Brazilian pulse.

IRISH PUBS

Feeling a bit o' that Irish yearning, are ye? Need a nice warm Guinness to pick up your spirits? Maybe want to toss a dart or two with a few good fellas? Well, you're not in sweet Dublin, but put your mind and body at ease. The Irish are everywhere.

• ***Carr's**, rue du Mont Thabor (1st, M:Concorde), 42.60.60.26*
• ***Connolly's Corner**, 12 rue de Mirbel (5th, M:Censier-Daubenton), 43.31.94.22. A personal favorite.*
• ***Au Gobelet d'Argent**, 11 rue du Cygne (1st, M:Etienne-Marcel), 42.33.29.82*
• ***James Joyce Pub**, 71 boulevard Gouvion-Saint-Cyr (17th, M:Porte Maillot)*
• ***Kitty O'Shea's**, 10 rue des Capucines (2nd, M:Opéra), 40.15.08.08*
• ***Molly Malone's**, 21 rue Godot-de-Mauroy (9th, M:Madeleine), 47.42.07.77*
• ***The Quiet Man**, 5 rue des Haudriettes (3rd, M:Rambuteau), 48.04.02.77*

ABSOLUTELY ADULT

Paris has a reputation for being the free love capital of the world. The French are not nearly as promiscuous as Americans would like to believe and, as we've said so many times by now, virtually nothing is free.

Still, there are plenty of opportunities to satisfy carnal interests in bookstores concentrated around the **Place Pigalle** (9th) and **rue Saint-Denis** (1st) on the Right Bank, and along **rue de la Gaîté** (14th), just below the boulevard du Montparnasse on the Left Bank. The area around Place Pigales also has oodles of strip joints eager to serve you crummy drinks and separate you from as much money as they can — probably without showing you a thing.

Live sex shows, or *Spectacles Érotiques*, are sprinkled around town. Some are listed in *Pariscope*. Costs range from 200 to 400FF.Clubs known as American Bars, also listed in Pariscope and elsewhere, thrive on bad champagne and hostesses looking for a "date."

Keep these thoughts in mind: One, streetwalking is legal in France (the rue Saint-Denis is lined with perfectly legal but largely unattractive ladies of the evening), but pimping and prostitution initiated in clubs are not. And two, France has a frighteningly high AIDS rate and only a knucklehead would tempt such an awful fate.

Helpful phrase: *Je voudrais des préservatifs, s'il vous plaît.* Translation: "I'd like some condoms, please."

17. PARIS - SHOPPING

INTRODUCTION

To shop or not to shop? For many of us, given the sky-high prices here, that *is* the big question.

No matter where in the U.S. you live, you're bound to come to the same conclusion. We came to France from fifteen years in New York and Washington, DC — two of America's most expensive cities — and with ample warnings about the prices, and we were still stunned.

So what's a dedicated shopper on a limited budget to do? Give up? Never! Instead, strategize!

You can have more fun window shopping in Paris than spending real money in most places. Paris has some of the most lushly appointed shop windows (*vitrines*) in the world. You can soak up enough fashion to flesh out a million fantasies. And don't be shy about stepping inside to admire the *bibelots* and other *objets* even if you have no intention of opening your wallet. Why deprive yourself?

If you plan to return home with gifts, look around before you buy. On past trips, we'd browse for a few days, then set aside some time on the last day to return to the places with the best values.

THE TAX MAN

Every time you feel your taxes are too high in the States, come to France. Their combination of income, social security and property taxes equal more than 50 percent of the average worker's earnings (though to be fair, their social safety net is unbelievable).

That won't concern you, of course. But the **VAT** will. VAT (the French acronym is **TVA**) stands for value-added tax — a whopping 18.6 percent sales tax that is already included in the price you see on the tag.

The bad news is that you have to pay that tax on virtually everything you buy. The relative good news is that if you buy more than 2,000FF worth of merchandise in any one store and you're taking it all back to the

States you can arrange to be reimbursed for up to 18.6 percent on the purchase price.

The refund is called a *détaxe*. All reputable store owners and managers will have the proper paperwork. If they don't volunteer it, speak up.

All you need is your passport. You'll be asked whether you want the refund mailed to you in a French-franc check (it's a hassle) or have it credited to one of your credit cards (it's fast, easy and the money is in dollars).

When you leave France, give the *detaxe* paperwork to the Customs officials for stamping. Do this before you hand over your bags or go through customs or passport control. When you get home, mail the documents to the store, and *Voila!* It's a done deal.

Don't forget your own Tax Man.

As we write this, you can bring back per person $400 worth of merchandise purchased overseas duty free. After that, there will be a 10 perent tax on the next $1,000 worth of items. Beyond $1,400, each item is assessed an individual duty and the rates vary wildly.

TYPES OF STORES

bijouterie - *jewelry shop*
bricolage - *repair and home improvement*
coiffeur - *hairdresser*
cordonnerie - *shoe and leather repair*
drogerie - *small hardware store*
encadrement - *frame shop*
esthétiques - *beauty aids*
homéopathie - *pharmacies specializing in natural remedies*
horlogerie - *clocks and watches*
librarie - *bookstore*
parfumerie - *perfume shop*
pharmacie - *pharmacy*
pressing - *dry cleaners*
tabac - *tobacco, stamps, Metro tickets, phone cards*

SHOPPING TIPS

Hours

Many small shops close for one or two hours at lunch and all day Sunday and Monday. Most stores close at 7 p.m. The department stores stay open later one night a week, though each store stays open a different evening. Exceptions include T-shirt, post card, and similar stores in the most touristy neighborhoods.

Sales

Although there are almost always some sales racks in department stores, smaller retailers have sales (*soldes*) twice a year. Period. Winter merchandise goes on sale in January (sales sometimes extend into early February), and summer merchandise is available at reduced prices in July and sometimes August.

The sales are not always much to boast about. We've seen signs announcing all of "10 percent off." We've also seen signs that say "one for 50FF, two for 100FF." Go figure.

Cashiers

When you are ready to pay, look for a sign that reads *Caisse*. Sometimes, you will be asked to go to the *caisse*, pay and return to retrieve your purchase after showing your receipt.

SIZES

To paraphrase the alleged exchange between Fitzgerald and Hemingway (this is Paris, after all), French women's bodies are different from yours and mine. Yes, they have no hips.

Be prepared to take several sizes into the fitting room. Beware of buying clothes as gifts. Even two items marked with the same size aren't always really the same.

Women's Suits and Dresses

American	6	8	10	12	14	16	18	20
French	36	38	38	40	42	44	46	48

Women's Stockings

American	8	9	9	10	10
French	1	2	3	4	5

Women's Shoes

American	4	4	5	5	6	7	8	9	9	10
French	35	36	36	37	37	38	39	40	41	41

Men's Suits

American	35	36	37	38	39	40	42
French	36	38	40	42	44	46	48

Men's Shirts

American	14	14	15	15	16	16	17	17	18
French	36	37	38	39	40	41	42	43	45

Men's Shoes

American	6	7	7	8	9	9	10	11
French	39	40	41	42	43	44	44	45

Courtesy

It's customary in small shops for the sales person to greet the customer with a *Bonjour Madame/Monsieur,* and for the customer to respond in kind. When you leave, regardless of whether you've made a purchase, saying *Merci, Au revoir,* is also customary.

Dressing Rooms

These are called *cabines.*

Credit Cards

Virtually all stores take major credit cards. In fact, using them may make more economic sense than you realize. For one, you won't have to carry as much cash or as many travelers checks, and, secondly, credit card companies give you the exchange rate that's valid the day the purchase goes through with no fee for conversion.

Returns

Not in this lifetime. Except for the high end shops, be sure, be sorry or be prepared to do battle.

DEPARTMENT STORES

The *grands magasins* are huge, and hugely popular, department stores — not at all unlike the big city counterparts in the States.

The *grand magasin* with something completely different is **La Samaritaine** because its rooftop is an observation deck (and restaurant) with a view that should not be missed.

- **Bazar de l'Hôtel de Ville**, *52-64 rue de Rivoli, (4th, M: Hôtel-de-Ville), 42.74.90.00.* Known mostly by its initials, BHV, this mammoth store has a basement hardware department that would make any do-it-yourselfer think he or she had died and gone to heaven.
- **Au Bon Marché**, *38 rue de Sèvres (7th, M:Sevres-Babylone), 42.60.33.45.* The name means bargain in French, but most Parisians will tell you that Au Bon Marché is the most expensive of the grands magasins. It does, however, have a huge supermarket (yes, food), and the enormous prepared food section can be fun to stroll through.
- **Galeries Lafayette**, *40 boulevard Haussmann (9th, M:Chausée d'Antin), 42.82.34.56.* This prestigious store (now in the U.S. too) hosts fashion shows every Wednesday, also Fridays from April through October, in the Salon Opera. For reservations, call 48.74.02.30.
- **Marks & Spencer**, *35 boulevard Haussman (9th, M:Chausée d'Antin), 47.42.42.90.* The big British chain comes to Paris. The place to shop for your favorite British-made products if you didn't include London on your itinerary.

• **Au Printemps**, *64 boulevard Haussmann (9th, M:Chausée d'Antin), 42.85.22.22.*
• **La Samaritaine**, *75 rue de Rivoli (1st, M:Pont-Neuf), 45.08.33.33.*
• **Aux Trois Quartiers**, *17 boulevard de la Madeleine (1st, M: Madeleine), 42.60.39.30.* Many call this mall the chicest in all of Paris.

FASHION

The big names in fashion, whether you want to buy or just gawk.
• **Armani**: *6 place Vendôme (1st, M:Opéra), 42.61.55.09.*
• **Céline**: *26 rue Cambon (1st, M:Concorde), 42.61.34.45; 58 rue de Rennes (6th, M:Saint-Sulpice), 45.48.58.55; in Au Bon Marché department store, 38 rue de Sèvres (7th, M:Sèvres-Babylone); 24 rue François-Ier (8th, M:George V), 47.20.14.33; men only, 38 avenue Montaigne (8th, M:Franklin-Roosevelt), 49.52.08.79; 3 avenue Victor-Hugo (16th, M:Victor-Hugo), 45.01.80.01.*
• **Cerruti**: For women, *15 place de la Madeleine (8th, M:Madeleine), 47.42.10.78; 42 rue de Grenelle (7th, M:Sävres-Babylone), 42.22.92.28; 17 avenue Victor-Hugo (16th, M:Victor-Hugo), 45.01.66.12.* For men, *27 rue Royale (8th, M:Madeleine), 42.65.68.72; 48 rue Pierre Charron (8th, M:Franklin-Roosevelt), 40.70.18.81;*
• **Chanel**: *29 rue Cambon (1st, M:Concorde), 42.86.28.00; 42 avenue Montaigne (8th, M:Franklin-Roosevelt), 47.23.74.12.*
• **Christian Dior**: *11 rue François-Ier (8th, M:Franklin-Roosevelt), 40.73.54.44; 30 avenue Montaigne (8th, M:Franklin-Roosevelt), 40.73.54.44.*
• **Christian Lacroix**: *26 avenue Montaigne (8th, M:Franklin-Roosevelt), 47.20.64.92.*
• **Courrèges**: *40 rue François-Ier (8th, M:Franklin-Roosevelt), 47.20.70.44; 46 rue du Faubourg Saint-Honoré (8th, M:Madeleine), 42.65.37.75.*
• **Emanuel Ungaro**: *2 avenue Montaigne (8th, M:Franklin-Roosevelt), 47.23.61.94.*
• **Giani Versace**: *62 rue du Faubourg Saint-Honoré (8th, M:Madeleine), 47.42.88.02; 41 rue François-Ier (8th, M; Franklin-Roosevelt), 47.23.88.30.*
• **Givenchy**: *3 avenue George V (8th, M: George V), 44.31.50.06;* for women, *8 avenue George V (8th, M:George V), 47.20.81.31; 28 rue du Faubourg Saint-Honoré (8th, M:Madeleine), 42.65.54.54;* for men, *56 rue François-Ier (8th, M:Madeleine), 40.76.00.21.*
• **Guy Laroche**: *22 rue de la Trémoille (8th, M:Alma-Marceau), 40.69.68.00; 29 avenue Montaigne (8th, M:Franklin-Roosevelt), 40.69.69.50.*
• **Hermés**: *24 rue du Faubourg Saint-Honoré (8th, M:Madeleine), 40.17.47.17; 42 avenue George V (8th, M:George V), 47.20.48.51.*
• **Kenzo**: *3 place des Victoires (1st, M:Bourse), 40.39.72.03; 23 boulevard de la Madeleine (1st, M:Madeleine), 42.61.04.14; 60 rue de Rennes (6th, M:Saint Sulpice), 45.44.27.88; 16 boulevard Raspail (7th, M:Rennes),*

42.22.09.38; 18 avenue George V (8th, M:Georges V), 47.23.33.49; 99 rue de Passy (16th, M:La Muette).
- **Lanvin**: for women, *22 rue du Faubourg Saint-Honoré (8th, M:Madeleine), 44.71.33.33*; for men, *15 rue du Faubourg Saint-Honoré (8th, M:Madeleine), 44.71.33.33.*
- **Nina Ricci**: *17 rue François-Ier (8th, M:Franklin-Roosevelt), 49.52.56.00.*
- **Paco Rabanne**: for men, *7 rue de Cherche Midi (6th, M:Saint-Sulpice), 42.22.87.80.*
- **Yves Saint Laurent**: For women, *6 place Saint-Sulpice (6th, M:Saint-Sulpice), 43.29.43.00; 38 rue du Faubourg Saint-Honoré (8th, M:Madeleine), 42.65.74.59; 12 Rond-Point Champs-Elysées (8th, M:Champs-Elysées), 45.62.00.23; 19 avenue Victor-Hugo (16th, M:Victor-Hugo), 45.00.64.64.* For men, *12 place Saint-Sulpice (6th, M:Saint-Sulpice), 43.26.84.40.*

WINE

- **L'Amour du Vin**, *48 avenue de la Bourdonnais (7th, M:Ecole Militaire), 45.55.68.63. Also, 94 rue Saint-Dominique (7th, M:Ecole Militaire), 45.56.12.94.* Very good wines at shockingly good prices chosen by owner Patrick Dussert-Gerber, author of "Le Guide Dussert-Gerber des Vins de France." Currently our favorite stores.
- **CCA**, *128 rue Vieille du Temple (3rd, M:Saint-Sébastien), 48.87.55.67; 84 rue Monge (5th, M:Monge), 45.35.71.93; 37 boulevard Malesherbes (8th, M:Saint-Augustin); 51 avenue La Motte Picquet (15th, M:La Motte Picquet), 43.06.26.65.* A small chain that offers a variety of smart recent vintage wines at reasonable prices. Look for several of the "second" wines produced by the major Bordeaux châteaux.
- **Caves Estève**, *10 rue de la Cerisaie (4th, M:Bastille), 42.72.33.05; 292 rue Saint-Jacques (5th, M:Port Royal), 46.34.69.78; 32 avenue Félix Faure (15th, M:Lourmel), 44.26.33.05).* A very good small chain that offers regular tastings and stocks lots of reasonably priced, carefully selected alternatives to the obvious Grand Crus. Popular with the locals.
- **Cave Jean-Baptiste Besse**, *48 rue de la Montagne Sainte-Geneviève (5th, M:Maubert-Mutualité), 43.25.35.80.* A trusty neighborhood wine shop for more than 60 years.
- **Les Caves Taillevent**, *199 rue du Faubourg Saint-Honoré (8th, M:Saint-Philippe-du-Roule), 45.61.14.09.* Though only open since 1987, this shop profits from its association with the famous restaurant by the same name.
- **Nicolas**. A large chain with shops everywhere. Popular, though we've never been terribly impressed with their selection.
- **Au Verger de la Madeleine**, *4 boulevard Malesherbes (8th, M:Madeleine), 42.65.51.99.* A family-run enterprise since 1937, with a large selection of rare wines.

ANTIQUES

Rather than list individual shops, we note several antique shopping districts and centers which house hundreds of dealers, scores of which are top-notch.

- **Carré d'Or**, *46 avenue George V (8th, M:George V)*. Several shops dealing primarily in jewelry.
- **Carré Rive Gauche** *(7th, M:Rue du Bac)*. An area of usually high quality independent dealers just east of the Musée d'Orsay, bounded on the river by the Quai Voltaire, the east by rue des Saints-Pères, the south by rue de l'Université, and the west by rue du Bac.
- **Cour des Antiquaires**, *54 rue du Faubourg Saint-Honoré (8th, M:Concorde)*, *42.66.38.60*. Twenty dealers mostly showing artworks.
- **Louvres des Antiquaires**, *2 place du Palais Royal (1st, M:Palais Royal)*, *42.97.27.00*. More than 200 dealers in high-end antiques and art.
- **Marché aux Puces**, *Porte de Clignancourt (18th, M:Porte de Clignancourt)*. *Open Saturday through Monday*. Paris's largest flea market with very good sections and very bad sections.
- **Puces de Vanves**, *avenue Georges-Lafenestre (14th, M:Malakoff)*. *Open-air flea market on weekends only*.
- **Saint-Paul** *(4th, M:Saint-Paul)*. An area of often quirky dealers in an area between the rue Charlemagne and the quai des Célestins.
- **Village Suisse**, *78 avenue de Suffren (15th, M:La Motte Picquet)*. *Open Thursdays through Sundays*. Well over 100 high end dealers.

GLASS & CRYSTAL

- **Baccarat**: *11 place de la Madeleine (8th, M:Madeleine)*, *42.65.36.26*.
- **Lalique**: *Galerie Carrousel du Louvre (1st, M:Louvre)*, *42.86.01.51; and 11 rue Royale (8th, M:Concorde)*, *42.66.52.40*.

ENGLISH LANGUAGE BOOK STORES

In case you've run out of things to read on the plane going home:

- **Abbey Bookshop**, *29 rue Parcheminerie (5th, M:Saint-Michel)*, *46.33.16.24*. This small shop specializes in the works of Canadian authors.
- **Attica**, *23 rue Jean de Beauvais (5th, M:Maubert-Mutualité)*, *46.34.62.03*.
- **Brentano's**, *37 avenue de l'Opéra (2nd, M:Pyramides)*, *42.61.52.50*. This is the biggest of them all.
- **FNAC**, *Forum des Halles (1st, M:Les Halles)*, *42.61.81.18, or 136 rue de Rennes (6th, M:Saint-Placide)*, *45.55.39.12, or 26 avenue de Wagram (8th, M:Wagram)*, *47.66.52.50*. Not, strictly speaking, English language bookstores, but they are enormous and have some English language books and magazines.
- **Galignani**, *224 rue de Rivoli (1st, M:Tuileries)*, *42.60.76.07*.

- **Le Nouveau Quartier Latin**, *78 boulevard Saint-Michel (6th, M:Sorbonne)*, *43.26.42.70.*
- **Shakespeare and Company**, *37 rue de la Boucherie (5th, M:Saint-Michel)*. Once the loving brainchild of Sylvia Beach, this is the most famous.
- **W.H. Smith & Son**, *248 rue de Rivoli (1st, M:Tuileries)*, *42.60.37.97.*
- **Tea and Tattered Pages**, *24 rue Mayet (6th, M:Duroc)*, *40.65.94.35.* Mostly used books, good prices. Also a tea shop with American-style baked goods.
- **Village Voice**, *6 rue Princesse (6th, M:Mabillon)*, *46.33.36.47.*

OPEN MARKETS
Plants, Birds, Stamps, & Stuff

Generally speaking, most of the open markets (*marchés*) listed below are worth a visit just because they are so different from anything in the average American's shopping experience. They're informal, wide-open and there's absolutely no pressure to buy.

The main open-air markets are:

- **Plant and Pet Market**, *quai de la Mégisserie (1st, M:Pont-Neuf)*. *Daily, 9 a.m. to 6 p.m.* Noisy and sometimes a bit smelly.
- **Marché aux Fleurs** (flowers), *place Louis-Lépine, Ile de la Cité (4th, M:Cité)*. *Monday through Saturday, 8 a.m. to 4 p.m.* Beautiful. And smells great!
- **Marché aux Oiseaux** (birds), *place Louis-Lépine, Ile de la Cité (4th, M:Cité)*. *Sunday only, 9 a.m. to 7 p.m.* Interesting, even for those who prefer warm-blooded pets.
- **Marché aux Timbres** (stamps), *Rond-Point des Champs-Elysées (8th, M:Champs-Elysées)*. *Open Thursday, Saturday and Sunday, 10 a.m. to 7 p.m.* Did you see the classic film *Charade*? The crucial scene takes place here. Echoes of Cary Grant and Audrey Hepburn can still be heard by film buffs.
- **Marché aux Puces** (flea market), *by Porte de Clignancourt, (18th, M:Porte de Clignancourt)*. *Open Saturday through Monday, 9:30 a.m. to 6:30 p.m.* Alledgedly the largest flea market in France. Don't be put off by the initial offerings of junk. Keep going and you will come to scores of tiny stalls filled with everything from vintage posters, silver thimbles, and glass doorknobs to dining tables and armoires that would have made William Randolph Hearst proud.

SHOPPING NEIGHBORHOODS

If department stores aren't your style, there are several well-known retail neighborhoods where you can feast your eyes on products of all kinds.

LEFT BANK

BOULEVARD SAINT-GERMAIN

6th Arrondissement

Though **Saint-Germain** is a grand boulevard that cuts through the trendy 6th arrondissement, here we're really using the name as a point of departure. And what we'll really be talking about is the **Saint-Germain-des-Prés area** between the boulevard Saint-Germain and the Seine — a quarter that is defined by style, sidewalk cafés, and narrow twisting streets that are home to charming boutiques and restaurants galore.

You'll find lots of the biggest names in chic French and international fashion and home furnishings, including Issey Miyake, Sonya Rykiel, Yves Saint Laurent, and half a dozen Roche Bobois stores. There are also a number of smaller shops to explore.

Below you'll find selected shops worth a visit.

Debauve & Gallais (chocolate), *30 rue des Saints-Pères (6th, M:Saint-Germain-des-Prés), 45.48.54.67.*

A real find! If you love chocolate, these are the people for you. Founded in 1800, Debauve & Gallais bill themselves as the oldest chocolate store in Paris. It seems that Monsieur Debauve, while serving as the pharmacist to Louis XVI, discovered the curative powers of chocolate and capitalized on the idea. There are 40 types of bite-sized confections (*bouchées*) and bars (*tablettes*) to choose from. French chocolate is generally darker and less sweet than its Swiss and Belgian counterparts. Indeed, Debauve & Gallais sell a tablette that purports to be 99 percent cacao. Ask about the perfect replicas of golf balls. Great gifts for the folks back home.

Atelier d'Anais (needlepoint), *23 rue Jacob (6th, M:Saint-Germain-des-Prés), 43.26.68.00.*

For those who do needlepoint or cross-stitch. Also a selection of tassles, as well as scissors and other tools of the art that are perfect as souvenirs or gifts.

La Maison Ivre (pottery), *38 rue Jacob (6th, M:Saint-Germain-des-Prés), 42.60.01.85.*

A find! You can bring sunshine into the darkest winter with the handmade pottery sold at this warm and welcoming shop. The bright colors that one associates with the South of France are here in abundance and the store's friendly staff is glad to pack it up so it won't break on your trip home. Although you could spend a fortune here, there are also plenty of small items such as egg cups, salt shakers and candlesticks with prices that fit any budget.

Demons et Merveilles (exotic gifts), *45 rue Jacob (6th, M:Saint-Germain-des-Prés), 42.96.26.11.*
Arts and crafts, costumes, jewelry and furniture from Eastern Europe, Afghanistan, Tibet, and India. A treasure trove for people who enjoy mementos from off the beaten path.

L'Ile du Demon (exotic gifts), *13 rue Bonaparte (6th, M:Saint-Germain-des-Prés or Mabillion), 43.26.92.53.*
Similar to, but different from, Demons et Merveilles, this somewhat larger shop sells everything from jewelry (necklaces of African stones start at 50FF) to very large items such as the gilded sculpture of the Indian god Shiva-Bhiraba (a mere 200,000FF). Also dozens of different African masks and other pieces of tribal art.

Patrick Frey (fabric), *2, rue de Furstemberg (6th, M:Saint-Germain-des-Prés or Mabillion), 46.33.73.00.*
Parisians love to decorate with fabric and they adore to be comforted by fine linens. Here they are.

Au Fond de la Cour (antiques), *49 rue de Seine (6th, M:Mabillion or Odéon), 43.25.81.89.*
What first drew us into the aptly-named Au Fond de la Cour was its setting at the back of a courtyard visible through open wooden doors from the sidewalk. The courtyard is set up as if a small garden party is about to take place. With the exception of some rattan furniture and a fine collection of elegant bird cages, this shop is dedicated to majolica, including an entire fireplace with beautiful white lilies tinged with lavendar and flowing gracefully into long green stems.

Galerie Documents (posters), *53 rue de Seine (6th, M:Mabillion), 43.54.50.68.*
Magnificent authentic period posters from theaters, fairs, arts exhitions, etc.

RUE D'ALÉSIA
14th Arrondissement
This street has many affordable shops.
If your closet is crammed with things from Filene's bargain basement or factory outlet stores, then you won't want to miss **rue d'Alésia** in the 14th arrondissement.
A Paris avenue of average charm and grace, rue d'Alésia is lined on both sides by off-price retailers, factory outlets and multi-maker close-out stores. The street is a bit out of the way and you won't find many tourists here, but there's absolutely no reason to fear you'll come into harm's way.
Take the No. 4 Metro line in the direction of Porte d'Orleans and get off at Alesia, the second to the last stop.

The bulk of the stores are concentrated between **Stock and Sold** *(56 rue d'Alésia)* and the **Chevignon** outlet *(122 rue d'Alésia)*. In between you will find clothing styles to match virtually any taste. There's lots for men and kids to choose from, but the largest selection is in women's casual clothes.

It's possible at most of the stores to buy last year's styles for as much as 60 percent off their original price. And many stores have super discount racks with even greater savings. Offerings from the current season are readily available in the 20 percent off category.

Keep in mind that it usually takes a year or two for Paris styles to reach America's most fashion-conscious cities, so you can buy last year's merchandise at low, low prices and still be ahead of the style curve when you get back home.

Try to avoid shopping on Saturdays when the sharp Parisians with their even sharper elbows will be out in force. Although very little English is spoken along here, prices are clearly marked so there shouldn't be a problem. Take lots of cash if you are a serious shopper because not every place takes credit cards. And be sure to ask about the détaxe (see page 153) if you buy more than 2,000FF worth at any one store.

Below is a partial list of stores offering better-known brands. Not every store on the street is a discounter; the key words to look for are *Stock* or *Dégriffé*. The words *Solde* and *Promotion* mean additional markdowns. Hours tend to be 10 a.m. to 7 p.m. (although some of the smaller shops will close for one to two hours for lunch).

Stock and Sold, *56 and 85 rue d'Alésia (14th, M:d'Alésia), 43.27.04.31.* Two shops across the street from each other. Pierre Cardin and other brands. Women's clothing only. Good selection.

Evolutif, *72 rue d'Alésia (14th, M:Alésia), 45.45.34.34.* Mostly menswear. Brands include Kenzo, Yves Saint Laurent (YSL), Cerrutti.

Diapositive, *74 rue d'Alésia (14th, M:Alésia), 45.39.97.27.* Womenswear from this one maker. Good markdowns. One of the best bargain racks.

Pret-A-Porter STOCK 2, *92 rue d'Alésia (14th, M:Alésia), 45.41.65.57.* A real find! This Daniel Hechter outlet is the largest of all the stores we vistited and, not surprisingly, offered the best range. You can find men's and women's clothes in casual and professional styles, as well as outerwear and kids' clothes. The large staff means there's always someone to help, but the ability to speak English doesn't seem to be a condition of employment. Discounts go as high as 40 percent.

Stock Saint Clair, *110-112 rue d'Alésia (14th, M:Alésia), 45.43.80.86.* Forty percent off last season's clothes for men and women. Lots of outerwear. Great prices in men's sports jackets. Well-lit and spacious.

Kookai, *111bis rue d'Alésia (14th, M:Alésia), 45.42.33.66.* An outlet for one of France's most ubiquitous brands of play clothes. Great for juniors.

Compagnie Scandinave de Fourrures, *113 rue d'Alésia (14th, M:Alésia)*, *40.44.94.44*. Another find! Furs and leather goods at discount prices. In mid-winter it seemed that every woman in Paris was wearing a mink. Now we know where many shopped. We're not experts, but we saw nice three-quarter length dark mink jackets for 7,900FF (roughly $1,400). If you take advantage of the *détaxe* that will bring the price down another $260. Not bad for being able to say for 20 years that you bought your mink in Paris. If your politics and your purse permit it, worth a stop.

Cacharel Stock, *114 rue d'Alésia (14th, M:Alésia), 45.42.53.04*. Men's, women's, and children's clothes in casual and dressy styles from the well-known maker. Up to 48 percent off clothes from last year.

Majestic S.A. Chevignon, *122 rue d'Alésia (14th, M:Alésia), 45.43.40.25*. Chevignon is one of the trendiest brands for the young in Paris and those in the know in the States. Other outlets for this brand are located at 82 rue du Commerce in the 15th and 42 rue de Levis in the 17th.

RIGHT BANK

RUE SAINT-HONORÉ
1st & 8th Arrondissements

The richest, most glamorous people in the world shop here. Why shouldn't you? The primest of this prime real estate runs from **avenue Matignon** in the 8th arrondissement to **rue de Castiglione** in the 1st arrondissement.

The giants of the postwar international elegance industry include Yves Saint Laurent, Lanvin, Hermés, Valentino, Cartier, Givenchy, Armani, Chanel, Mikimoto, Gucci and many more. They're all here and easy to find just by strolling along.

Selected shops worth a visit:

Hermés (scarves and clothing), *24 rue du Faubourg Saint-Honoré (8th, M:Madeleine), 40.17.47.17*.

Many of the stores are on the small side and the sales people can seem intimidating, especially if you have no intention of buying. One notable exception is Hermés. It's more like a small department store, and the staff is enormous. Indeed, you can have your own personal escort who can converse in the language of your choice. Or you can walk around unbothered to check out the suede T-shirts ($1,000) and handmade shoes.

Kenneth Jay Lane (jewelry), *249 rue Saint-Honoré (1st, M:Concorde), 42.60.06.27; and 14 rue de Castiglione (1st, M:Tuileries), 42.60.69.56*.

If you're shopping for that special woman in your life, whether she's a girlfriend or your mother, you will want to know the name Kenneth Jay Lane. An American, he built his reputation back in the '60s on high quality reproductions of some of the world's most elegant jewelry. Another advantage to shopping at Kenneth Jay Lane's is that you can exchange a piece at one of his shops in the States.

Swann's (American-style drug store), *6 rue de Castiglione (1st, M:Tuileries), 42.60.72.96.*

If you forgot your prescription medicine at home, don't panic. Marylene Rocher, the *docteur en pharmacie*, speaks excellent English and is equipped to fill virtually any American prescription. Also, if you forget your over-the-counter American remedies (Sudafed, Maalox, Listerine, etc.), Swann's is one of the rare places in Paris that might have them.

Parfumerie Catherine (perfume), *6 rue de Castiglione (1st, M:Tuileries), 47.44.02.15.*

Next door to Swann's is this tiny but well-stocked cosmetics and perfume boutique that swears it takes all the taxes off the price of your purchases right at the register (even if the total is less than 2,000FF). Very friendly mother, father and daughter team who run the store.

THE GOLDEN TRIANGLE

8th Arrondissement

The rue Saint-Honoré is hardly Paris's only elegant and expensive shopping playground. The quarter known by some as the **Golden Triangle** (bounded by the **Champs-Elysées** to the north, **avenue George V** to the west, and **avenue Montaigne** to the east) offers a stunning variety of luxury shopping experiences and out-of-this-world prices.

The avenue des Champs-Elysées may very well be one of most famous streets in the world, but, as we've said before, its days of deserved glory are past. Today, it's primarily movie theaters, fast food restaurants, airline ticket offices, and a construction project (underground parking) that many believe will never end.

If you can't resist shopping there, check out boutiques in the dozens of galleries that snake off the main thoroughfare. And don't say we didn't warn you if you pay too much for something you probably could have found at home.

Now, if you're looking for a memorable shopping experience, leave the Champs-Elysées behind and walk south a couple of blocks to rue François Ier or avenue Montaigne. Flanked by many of the world's most famous designers, these streets offer window shopping at its best.

Selected shops worth a visit:
• **Cartier**, *51 rue François 1 (8th, M:George V), 40.74.61.84.*
• **Christian Dior**, *30 avenue Montaigne (8th, M:Franklin-Roosevelt), 40.73.55.14.*
• **Hermés**, *42 avenue George V (8th, M:George V), 47.20.48.51.*

• **Ines de la Fressange**, *14 avenue Montaigne (8th, M:Champs-Elysées)*, *47.23.08.94.*

• **Louis Vuitton**, *54 avenue Montaigne, (8th, M:Champs-Elysées), 45.62.47.00.*

• **Virgin Megastore**, *52 avenue des Champs-Elysées (8th, M: George V), 40.74.06.48.* The prices for CDs and books are way too high, but, as the store's own PR promises, "from its creation in October 1988, the store has revealed itself to be a phenomenon of society." With 15,000 to 20,000 visitors a day, you know there's something going on. It's hip, it's cool and it's open until midnight every day and on Sundays, which in France is about as radical as you can get.

18. PARIS - CHILD'S PLAY

Just because children don't have a taste for fine wines and Empire period furnishings doesn't mean they can't have a good time in Paris.

There are circuses, pony rides, carousels, science museums and puppet shows galore to keep the kids entertained. Most organized activities are scheduled for weekends and Wednesdays, when Parisian children are off from school.

A word about food for kids: They are likely to be disappointed by the local hamburgers and hot dogs, and they are only marginally welcome in many restaurants, where the local clientele wants to savor dinner without childish interruption. But children's eyes light up when they see all the pastries in bakery windows.

BABYSITTING SERVICES

Some of the top-rung hotels can arrange babysitting. An alternative is one of the city's many au pair services, some of which can provide a babysitter for a night or two, or refer you to a service that can. Babysitting and au pair services include:

- **Alpha Baby**, *43.65.16.16.* Babysitting seven days a week. Also party arrangements with clowns, magic, etc.
- **Au Pair International**, *44.49.04.98 or 34.93.00.26.*
- **Inter-Service Parents**, *43.48.28.28.* A free advisory service for parents looking for help.
- **Nannies Incorporated**, *45.74.62.74.*

AND IF YOU FORGET THOSE BABY NECESSITIES ...

EuroBaby, a service "For Babies Who Like to Travel," renting prams, car seats, and other doodads necessary for taking care of small children. Call 43.44.23.04.

CIRCUSES, ZOOS, & ANIMAL PARKS

The French (adults as well as kids) are crazy about animals and circuses. And fortunately, neither presents language problems.

Circuses are seasonal, so be sure to call in advance. Prices range wildly, from as little as 45FF to well over 200FF. Check *Pariscope* for current listings and prices. Circuses and zoos usually offer special prices for children.

Circuses

Circuses come and go, but there is always at least one, and as many as five, going on at any given time of the year. Often there is one being staged in the children's section of the **Jardin d'Acclimatation** *in the Bois de Boulogne (16th, M:Sablons).*

But most are presented in the nearby suburbs, such as **Saint-Cloud** or **Nanterre**. Prices range wildly, from as little as 45FF to well over 200FF, with special deals for children. Check *Pariscope* for current listings.

Zoos

• **Ménagerie du Jardin des Plantes**, *57 rue Cuvier (5th, M:Jussieu), 40.79.37.94. Admission 25FF.*
• **Parc Zoologique de Paris**, *53 avenue de Saint-Maurice (12th, M:Porte Dorée), 44.75.20.10. Admission 40FF.*

Animal Parks

Parc Zoologique de Thoiry. From the safety of your car or a touring trolley, watch elephants, giraffes, hippos and 800 of their closest friends cavort freely in this beautiful wooded park. The park also features a 16th-century château, known as the Château du Soleil for the way its architectural layout is patterned after the path of the sun.

To reach the park, which is 25 miles west of Paris, take a SNCF train from Gare Montparnasse to the Montfort l'Amaury station. There, you can hop on a Thoiry shuttle bus the rest of the way. If you have a car, take the A13 autoroute to the A12 toward Versailles and Dreux, exiting at D11 to Thoiry. *Admission 92FF for adults, 75FF for children. For information in English, phone 34.87.45.90, or Fax 34.87.54.12.*

Saint-Vrain. This recreation of a prehistoric world also boasts wild animals and a boat safari ride. By car, take the A6 autoroute south to the Viry-Chatillon exit, toward Bretigny-sur-Orge and look for signs reading Saint-Vrain. *Admission 75FF for adults, 65FF for children under 10. For information, phone 64.56.10.80.*

CLASSES FOR KIDS

• Drawing and painting, for lessons at home or in your hotel room. *45.24.58.27.*
• Language lessons, arts and crafts, storytelling and other activities at the **Lennen Bilingual School of the American Church**. *47.05.66.55.*
• Swimming instruction, for ages 3 and above, at **La Piscine Pontoise**, *19 rue de Pontoise (5th, M:Maubert-Mutualité), 43.54.82.45.*
• Theater workshop, for ages 8 through 13, at the **Théâtre Marie Stuart**, *4 rue Marie-Stuart (2nd, M:Etienne-Marcel), 45.48.24.13 or 45.08.17.80.*

PUPPET SHOWS

Puppets are another traditional passion of French children. Language could be problem here, though many foreign children still enjoy the universal slapstick humor. Once again, *Pariscope* will help with times and prices, listing puppet shows under "Marionnettes."

Shows in the major city parks are usually scheduled for about an hour in the midafternoon on Wednesdays, Saturdays and Sundays. Prices range from 10 to 20FF.

• **Marionnettes du Champ-de-Mars**, *on Champ-de-Mars (7th, M:École Militaire), 48.56.01.44.*
• **Marionnettes des Champs-Elysées**, *Rond point des Champs-Elysées (8th, M:Champs-Elysées), 42.57.43.34.*
• **Marionnettes du Luxembourg**, *in the Jardin du Luxembourg (6th, M:Vavin), 43.26.46.47.*
• **Théâtre de la Petite Ourse**, *in the Jardin des Tuileries (8th, M:Concorde), 42.64.05.19.*

MISCELLANEOUS FUN STUFF

American Library

The **American Library**, *10 rue du General Camou (7th, M:École Militaire), 45.51.46.82. Admission free.* A children's section with storytelling and other activities every Wednesday afternoon.

Aquaboulevard de Paris

Located at 4 rue Louis-Armand (15th, M:Balard), 40.60.10.00. Admission varies from 49 to 55FF for kids, and 68 to 75FF for adults. A paradise for children (and adults), where they can swim, play tennis, bowl, putt their way around two miniature golf courses, or just fool around.

Also located here is **Gymborée**, which offers a variety of exercises and games for parents and their infants and very small children.

Parc Asterix

Parc Asterix, *in the northern suburb of Plailly off the A1 autoroute at the Parc Asterix exit (or take the B line RER to Roissy Charles-de-Gaulle, where you can catch a shuttle bus the rest of the way),* *44.62.31.31, 44.60.60.00 or 36.68.30.10. Admission, 150FF for adults and 105FF for children.* A theme park park that takes its name from the famous cartoon character and recreates the world of the Gauls.

EuroDisney

Did you really come all the way to France to see Mickie and Minnie? If you did (or even if you didn't but your kids insist anyway), see pages 278-279 for more information.

Jardin d'Acclimatation

The **Children's Amusement Park**, *located in the northern section of the Bois de Boulogne (16th, M:Sablons). Admission charge depends on activities, but the total charge per child shouldn't be much more than 20FF.* A small zoo, an art museum where youngsters can experiment in a workshop, a miniature railroad, and a giant doll's house.

Musée Grevin

This is the **Wax Museum**, *10 boulevard Montmartre (9th, M:Rue Montmartre), 42.46.13.26. Admission 48FF for adults, 34FF for children.* A century-old wax museum with more than 400 characters from history and films. Also demonstrations and "fantasy shows."

Palais de la Découverte

Located at the avenue Franklin D. Roosevelt (8th, M:Franklin-Roosevelt), 40.74.81.82 or 40.74.80.00. Admission 22FF for adults, 11FF for children, free for children under 7. A paradise of hands-on science-fair projects that teach kids about everything from bugs to supernovas.

Pony Rides

Available at the Luxembourg Gardens (5th, M:Luxembourg) and the Champ de Mars (7th, M:École Militaire), on weekends. Fees vary. Also children can rent small wooden sailboats for the huge pool just behind the Luxembourg palace.

19. PARIS - SPORTS & RECREATION

Paris is not exactly swarming with joggers on a chilly dewy morning, and Parisian athletic clubs often hype their in-house cafés as much as their Nautilus equipment. Still, health and fitness are of increasing concern to the French. Even smoking levels are down a bit — except for teenagers, who seem to do little else.

If walking several miles a day sightseeing isn't enough exercise, there are several pools and clubs in town that offer single day rates. As always, it's a good idea to call ahead (or have the concierge of your hotel phone for you) to see what the rules and rates are. Some facilities, especially pools, are seasonal and won't be open at all.

AEROBICS & WEIGHTS

- **Aquaboulevard**, *4 rue Louis-Armand (15th, M:Balard), 40.60.10.00.* See also "Bowling" and "Swimming Pools" below).
- **Body Gym**, *157 rue Faubourg Saint-Antoine (11th, M:Faidherbe-Chaligny), 43.42.42.33.*
- **Club Quarter Latin** (see Piscine Pontoise below).
- **Espace Vit'Halles**, *48 rue Rambuteau (3rd, M:Rambuteau), 42.77.21.71.* Major fitness center with all the latest gizmos and dance steps.
- **Gym Club Opera**, *2 rue Scribe (9th, M:Opéra), 40.07.31.03.*
- **Gymnase Club**, *147 bis rue Saint-Honoré (1st, M:Palais-Royal), 40.20.03.03; 26 rue de Berri (8th, M:Georges V), 43.59.04.58; 10 rue de la Victoire (9th, M:Le Pelletier), 48.74.58.49; 9 rue de Malte (11th, M:République), 47.00.80.95; 28 avenue Général-Leclerc (14th, M:Denfert-Rochereau), 45.42.50.57; and 24 rue de Chazelles (17th, M:Courcelles), 43.80.66.14.* As you can see, a chain with several locations.
- **Sportive du Printemps**, *28 rue Joubert (9th, M:Chausée-D'Antin), 48.74.56.42.*

BOWLING

- **Aquaboulevard**, *4 rue Louis-Armand (15th, M:Balard)*, *40.60.10.00*. (See "Aerobics and Weights" and "Swimming Pools" — get the idea of the scope of this place?).
- **Bowling Champerret**, *2 rue Corporal-Peugeot (17th, M:Champerret)*, *43.80.24.64*.
- **Bowling International Stadium**, *66 avenue d'Ivry (13th, M:Porte d'Ivry)*, *45.86.55.52*.
- **Bowling Montparnasse**, *25 rue Commandant Rene Mouchotte (14th, M:Gaîté)*, *43.21.61.81*.
- **Bowling Mouffetard**, *73 rue Mouffetard, in back and underground (5th, M:Monge)*, *43.31.09.35*.
- **Bowling de Paris**, *Jardin d'Acclimatation in the Bois de Boulogne (16th, M:Porte Dauphine)*, *40.67.94.00*.

SWIMMING POOLS

- **Aquaboulevard**, *4 rue Louis-Armand (15th, M:Balard)*, *40.60.10.00*. The big daddy of them all, with huge indoor and outdoor pools, water slides, wave machines, tennis, everything.
- **Piscine Emile-Anthoine**, *9 rue Jean-Rey (15th, M:Bir-Hakeim)*, *45.67.10.20*. A pool and gym near the Eiffel Tower.
- **Piscine Hebert**, *2 rue des Fillettes (18th, M:Marx-Dormoy)*, *46.07.60.01*. Newly renovated.
- **Piscine Henry-de-Montherlant**, *32 boulevard Lannes (16th, M:Porte-Dauphine)*, *45.03.03.28*. Large new pool with an accompanying gym and tennis courts.
- **Piscine du Marche Saint-Germain**, *7 rue Clément (6th, M:Mabillon)*, *43.29.08.15*. An underground pool in an old covered market.
- **Piscine Pontoise**, *19 rue de Pontoise (5th, M:Maubert-Mutualité)*, *43.54.06.23*. Large below street-level pool with health club facilities upstairs.
- **Piscine Suzanne-Berlioux**, *10 place de la Rotonde (1st, M:Châtelet)*, *42.36.98.44*. Underground in the Forum des Halles complex. Said to be young and trendy.

TENNIS & SQUASH

- **Action Tennis**, *145 rue Vaugirard (15th, M:Falguière)*, *47.34.36.36*.
- **Forest Hill**, a chain with several locations for squash and tennis, though all are in the suburbs except the one at Aquaboulevard (see above).
- **Le Parisien Tennis Club**, *7 rue des Petites-Ecuries (10th, M:Château-d'Eau)*, *48.24.16.96*.
- **Squash Club Quartier Latin** (see Piscine Pontoise above).

- **Squash Montmartre**, *14 rue Achille Martinet (18th, M:Lamarck)*, *42.55.38.30.*
- **Squash Rennes Raspail**, *149 rue de Rennes (6th, M:Montparnasse)*, *45.44.24.35.*
- **Stadium Squash Club**, *66 avenue d'Ivry (13th, M:Porte d'Ivry), 45.85.39.06.*

20. ILE-DE-FRANCE

INTRODUCTION

If you've gotten to the point where the big city is getting to you, even though it's Paris and one of the most comfortable big cities in the world, it's time to get out of Dodge for a couple of days.

Fortunately, you don't have to go far to find a bit of relative peace and, more importantly, a treasure chest of majestic castles, sumptuous gardens, mysterious forests, and villages steeped in history.

Paris is surrounded by four small *départements* (the rough equivalent of counties) that make up what is called the **Ile-de-France**. Taken as a whole, the Ile-de-France resembles something you might see in a Rorschach test – a misshapen blotch. But inside that cartographer's nightmare is a wealth of easy-to-reach getaways.

The Ile-de-France is home to the magnificent castle at **Versailles**, the expansive rock-strewn forests of **Fontainbleau**, Monet's inspirational lily ponds, and even Mickey Mouse's European headquarters.

We've chosen just a few of the more spectacular sights of the Ile-de-France, all of which are within an hour from Paris. That means you can visit for an afternoon and still make it back to Paris for dinner. Or you can find yourself a colorful local inn, soak up a hearty supper, and settle in for a night or two.

Almost all the stops we note can be reached by using the RER commuter train service that branches out of Paris in all directions and is reasonably priced.

If you want to cut the logistical strain of an out-of-town afternoon to a minimum, you might consider a tour bus. Companies such as Paris Vision visit every destination we've listed below, sometimes combining two or three sights in a single long day (see the *Paris – Basics* chapter).

In at least a couple of instances, we've ignored our own warning against the hazards and hassles of renting a car. There are times that such a luxury would be welcome, allowing you the flexibility to explore as many country lanes as you like.

The list below is arranged geographically, beginning to the north of Paris and moving clockwise to the east, the south and, finally, the west.

FINDS & FAVORITES

- *Chantilly*
- *Vaux-le-Vicomte*
- *Abbaye des Vaux de Cernay (see Chartres)*

CHANTILLY

Rolling green hills, dense forests rustling with birds of all kinds, a picturesque village, a magnificent racecourse, and a castle surrounded by a moat and expansive gardens.

Wait, there's more: **Chantilly**, *about 45 kilometers (28 miles) north of Paris*, is far enough away from the city that most tourists forgo this masterpiece, allowing you plenty of room to gawk at the castle and grounds.

What more could you ask?

The most famous legend associated with Chantilly goes back to 1671, when the owner, Louis de Bourbon, invited Louis XIV and several hundred of his court to dinner. Vatel, the most renowned chef of the era, was to do the culinary honors. Unhappily, the fish course was late and, overcome with humiliation, Vatel took his own life.

Much of the original château was dismantled by the mobs during the Revolution. What you see now can be credited largely to Henri d'Orléans, who was the duc d'Aumale and a Bourbon himself. The duke helped restore the castle in the 19th century and then bequeathed the château and grounds to the Institute of France.

The interior is now largely given to the **Conde Museum**, a rich collection of tapestries, portraits, miniature paintings, silver, books, and other items. A favorite for us was the **Galerie des Cerfs**, a huge dining hall in the center of which stands a 30-foot-long table.

The dining hall is decorated with tapestries glorifying the hunt, the skins of two lions felled by a nobleman, stags' horns, and wonderful candlestick holders in the shape of men's arms protruding from the walls. Over one doorway there is also an unusually seductive painting of Diana of the hunt, lolling about in a forest clearing with a weary cherub and a stag by her side.

Two sections of the museum are open only to guided tours in groups of 10, which can be a bit annoying if you want to see much of the antique furnishings.

When you're ready for a break, there is a pleasant little café in the château cellar. Other nearby cafés can be found across from the stables. Or bring a picnic lunch and set yourself down on the racecourse grounds.

PARIS AREA EXCURSIONS

Giverny• •Chantilly
•Euro Disney
Versailles• •PARIS • Vaux-le-Vicomte
Chartres• •Barbizon
•Fontainebleu

(DISTANCES FROM PARIS)
•Barbizon **65 km**
•Chantilly **45 km**
•Chartres **60 km**
•Euro Disney **35 km**
•Fontainebleu **35 km**
•Giverny **50 km**
•Vaux-le-Vicomte **60 km**
•Versailles **20 km**

Germany

Atlantic
Ocean

Spain

Mediterranean Sea

N

Horses never had it so good as with the **Grand Ecuries**– the Chantilly stables, which are a couple of hundred yards from the château (this is a separate entrance fee). The massive, 610-foot-long structure with soaring interior arches once sheltered 240 horses and as many dogs.

Today, there are probably fewer than 20 horses and not a dog in sight. Still, you can meet (but not touch) Petit Blond, a playful Palomino born in 1988; Fresco, a regal grey Portuguese with gorgious long tresses; and six or seven other noble beasts. A performance showcasing the horses and their skills is staged in a central ring three times daily.

The remainder of the stables are given over to a comprehensive museum tracing the evolution of horseshoes, harnesses, saddles, and just about anything else you might associate with horses.

Getting to Chantilly

Several trains leave the Gare du Nord daily for Chantilly and beyond. Fares are 76FF roundtrip and the trip is about 30 minutes each way. Or take the D line of the RER, which you can catch at Gare du Nord or Châtelet and which takes about 45 minutes. The bigger bus tour companies also offer half-day trips to Chantilly for about 300FF.

Cabs and local buses will take you from the station to the château, which is about a mile. Or, on a nice day, you can stroll to the château. Just walk straight out from the station into the woods a block away. After a brief walk down the open path you'll emerge at the famous Diane racecourse, pass by the awesome stables (you may at first mistake them for the château) and, finally, arrive at the moat surrounding the castle.

For information, write Château de Chantilly, B.P. 243, 60631 Chantilly Cedex, or phone 44.57.08.00. Closed Tuesday. Admission is 37FF to the château and 45FF to the stables and the Living Museum of the Horse.

WHERE TO STAY

CHÂTEAU DE LA TOUR, *Chemin de la Chaussée, 60270 Gouvieux; 44.57.07.39, Fax 44.57.31.97. Rooms: 41. Double: 490-890FF. Restaurant.*

Located just west of Chantilly. A lovely almost Tudor-looking residence from the turn of the century with an enormous park, its own small forest, a tennis court and pool, and good dining.

CHÂTEAU D'ERMENONVILLE, *60950 Ermenonville; 44.54.00.26, Fax 44.54.04.32. Rooms: 60. Double: 390-990FF. Restaurant.*

Located 22 kilometers (14 miles) southeast of Chantilly off the N330. A large, muscular castle where the philosopher Jean-Jacques Rousseau is said to have spent his last days. The castle with its soaring turrets is protected by a large moat and stands of trees.

LE PRIEURÉ, *60950 Ermenonville; 44.54.00.44, Fax 44.54.02.21. Rooms: 11. Double: 450-500FF. No restaurant.*

Located 22 kilometers (14 miles) southeast of Chantilly off the N330. Le Prieuré is a small but loveable inn in the village of Ermenonville. It's warm and comfortable, with antique furnishings with enchanting gardens.

EURODISNEY

EuroDisneyland, approaching the end of its third year, has seen more print on the Business pages of newspapers in recent months than in the Entertainment sections. Having brought in 20 million visitors in its first two years, it ranks as the top tourist draw in Europe. Still, during its second fiscal year, it lost $930 million. Yikes, as Mickey would say.

We feel ambivalent about recommending you visit EuroDisney. If you've come all this way, why not see France instead. Having said that, if you enjoy Disneyland and you don't mind spending a bit more than you would for the same rides back home, you'll no doubt have a blast, and that's the point of going on vacation.

EuroDisney is exactly what it sounds like– all the rides, shops and parades you'd find at any Disney theme park. There are the familiar five sections to the park – **Main Street**, **Fantasyland**, **Frontierland**, **Adventureland** and **Discoveryland**.

Attractions include the Pirates of the Caribbean, Sleeping Beauty's castle, the Mad Hatter's Teacups, the Dumbo flying carrousel– in short, all the fun stuff that made Disneyland such a hit in the first place.

The latest ride to open is quickly becoming one of the most popular– **Indiana Jones's Temple du Peril**, said to be the first Disney rollercoaster to pull full-throttle, upside-down, stomach-in-your-throat loop-the-loops.

Despite the pricy extra ticket for entrance, **Buffalo Bill's Wild West** show, with elaborately staged shoot-'em-up cowboy and Indian skits, is ever popular– further evidence of the French fascination with the myths of the American West.

You'll find lots of familiar food. Among the more notable establishments is Annette's Diner, with roller-skating waitresses zipping around with trays of burgers and fries. And the park's Manhattan Jazz Club pulls in some top performers.

Six hotels offer a range of prices and themes, from the fancy **HOTEL NEW YORK** to the almost too adorably Southwestern **HOTEL SANTE FE**. *For information and prices, phone 49.41.49.10 or, in the States, call 1-800-WDISNEY.*

Getting to EuroDisneyland

A station for France's TGV trains has just opened at Marne-la-Vallée to serve EuroDisney. Still, it's just as easy to catch the A4 line of the RER going 35 kilometers (22 miles) east to the Marne-la-Vallée/Chessy stop (about a 30-minute trip for 70FF roundtrip). If you have a car, catch the A4 autoroute east toward Nancy and Metz and watch for signs.

Admission charges have been all over the map as Disney tries to shore up consumer interest and compete with French theme parks such as Asterix (it's the battle of the cartoon giants in a country that is obsessed with children's and adult comics). Recently, entrance fees that covered all rides was 225FF for adults, and 150FF for children. Prices also vary according to season.

For information, write EuroDisneyland Resort, B.P. 100, 77777 Marne-la-Vallée, Cedex 4, France, or phone 64.74.30.00.

WHERE TO STAY

LE MANOIR, *D402, 77610 Fontenay-Trésigny; 64.25.91.17, Fax 64.25.95.49. Rooms: 15. Double: 790-950FF. Restaurant.*

Located 25 kilometers (16 miles) south of EuroDisney off the N4. A stunning former hunting lodge surrounded by 40 acres of parkland, and featuring marvelous dining.

WHERE TO EAT

AUBERGE DE CONDÉ, *1 avenue de Montmirail, 77260 La Ferté-sous-Jouarre; 60.22.00.07, Fax 60.22.30.60.*

Located 22 kilometers (14 miles) east of EuroDisneyland off D407. Gourmet dining not far from EuroDisney, featuring lamb, lobster, magnificent desserts, and a lengthy list of Champagnes.

VAUX-LE-VICOMTE

Said by some to be the château that comes closest to perfection, **Vaux-le-Vicomte** is a symbol of symmetry, artistic success, and royal treachery.

This is the home that Nicolas Fouquet built. He was appointed financial minister to France in 1653, served under Cardinal Mazarin and Louis XIV, and is said to have used all his genius in a mere eight years to successfully restore the royal treasury after its utter collapse.

Fouquet employed that same genius, an astute appreciation for the arts, and an acquaintance with the finest talents of the day to build this glorious château and its expansive gardens leading past several fountains to a lovely canal and sculpted grotto beyond. So proud was he of his home, he invited the young Louix XIV and his court to what was to be one of the most lavish balls of French history.

Legend has it that Louis XIV was insanely jealous of his host's grand home and had Fouquet arrested 19 days after the gala and imprisoned for the rest of his days. Indeed, Louis XIV absconded not only with many of Fouquet's art treasures, he also took charge of Fouquet's architect, garden designer, and decorator, ordering them to Versailles to build a château of unparalleled grandeur.

Political intrigue was as much the catalyst of Louis's actions as jealousy, but whatever the true cause, Fouquet died years later in prison while Versailles arose to the west of Paris as a tribute to Louis XIV. Versailles may be more awe-inspiring in its regal excess, but we feel that Vaux-le-Vicomte is the more refined and graceful of the two châteaux.

Several of the current small rooms at Vaux-le-Vicomte are now given over to some rather plain engravings, but there is plenty of greatness in the mansion. Note the marvelous tapestries depicting various months of the year in Fouquet's bedroom, the magnificent billiard table and ornamented rafters of **The Square Room**, the vibrant and sensuous painted ceiling of the **Salon des Muses**, and the trompe l'oeil everywhere in the **Hercules Salon**.

The latter part of the unguided tour walks you through several rooms on the main floor and the basement, recounting with the help of elaborately dressed mannequins and taped voices the unjust destruction of Fouquet's world at the hands of the young king.

In the gardens, be sure to walk to the end of the main terrace, where you will find a glorious view back toward the château, as well as a perfect vantage point overlooking the canal and, across the canal, the magnificent grotto. Up on the hillside above the grotto stands Hercules himself, surveying Fouquet's domain.

Getting to Vaux-le-Vicomte

About the only unpleasant aspect of Vaux-le-Vicomte is that it's tough to get to, requiring you to rent a car or join a guided bus tour. About 60 kilometers (38 miles) southeast of the heart of Paris, Vaux-le-Vicomte is due east of the town of Melun. Take the N6 highway toward Melun, turning east just on the outskirts of Melun on N105 toward Meaux. The N105 is not adequately marked, but look for signs leading you to Meaux. Before long you'll see signs guiding you to the château.

Admission to the château and gardens, 56FF. There is also a café with a modest menu but a pleasant outdoor terrace. For information, write Domaine de Vaux-le-Vicomte, 77950 Maincy, or phone 60.66.97.09.

WHERE TO STAY

LE MANOIR. *Located 25 kilometers north of Vaux-le-Vicomte. (See "EuroDisney, Where to Stay" above.)*

FONTAINEBLEAU

If you're looking for opulence on a massive scale and would willingly spend a bit more time on transportation if it meant you could avoid a tortuous crowd scene, **Fontainebleau** will suit your tastes better than Versailles.

Unlike Versailles, which was built largely under the rule of a single king (Louis XIV), Fontainebleau is a marvelous conglomeration of wings, courtyards, and gardens that were added and substracted over the centuries according to the whims and decrees of several regal owners–François I (where you see an 'F' adorning an architectural element, the 'F' stands for François, not Fontainebleau), Henri IV, Louis XV, Napoleon and others.

The gardens, though designed by Le Notre, the same man who laid out the gardens at Vaux-le-Vicomte and Versailles, are not quite as magnificent as those at the other two châteaux. Still, they are well worth a stroll or a quick sandwich on a bench. Also, pass by the **Etang des Carpes** pond, where you will see some of the largest carps on the planet, having been well fed by the locals and tourists.

As with Versailles, the tour of the castle interior begins in chambers dedicated to portraits and landscapes that document the history of the château. Here, too, you will find a remarkable collection of painted plates, set into the walls and recounting the castle's past glories.

Next, the chapel, as in Versailles, is an absolute gem of artistic excess, with sumptuous allegorical murals, and multi-colored marble and generous giltwork throughout.

A little further on, a stairwell sculpted in the 16th century for a favorite love of François I resembles a boudoir, having been dedicated to the beauty of the human body, with frescos and sculptures of numerous voluptuous maidens being watched over by attentive cherubs.

The **Ballroom** is a triumph dating back to Henri II's time and rivaling even the Hall of Mirrors at Versailles for its splendor and elegance. It boasts one of the most impressive coffered ceilings we've ever seen. And the gilt-laden **Throne Room**, though a royal bedchamber until Napoleon had it transformed, exudes Raw Power.

There is more than enough here to keep you very busy for a very long time.

Getting to Fontainebleau

About 70 kilometers (44 miles) southeast of Paris, Fontainebleau can be reached by a combination of train (from the Gare de Lyon) and local bus from the Fontainebleau station. If you have a car (allowing you also to visit the remarkable forests that surround the village), take the N6 or N7 highways south and you will see signs leading you to this town of 16,000 people. Another option is a tour bus. Various companies offer day and half-day trips to the château and the surrounding area.

Closed Tuesday, and for lunch every day. Basic admission, 31FF. Guided tours of the gardens 25FF. For information, write Château de Fontainebleau, 77300 Fontainebleau, or phone 64.22.27.40.

BARBIZON

This tiny hamlet of 1,400 residents a few kilometers northwest of Fontainebleau is known as the village of painters for having served as a homebase in the mid-1800s for Rousseau, Corot, Diaz, Daubigny, Barye, and other pre-Impressionists who were fond of wandering into the woods and setting up their easels in front of bucollic landscapes.

Several houses bear plaques claiming that so-and-so was once a resident in the house. Rousseau's and Jean-François Millet's former homes are now museums dedicated to the town and the artists.

Barbizon is still an art colony, though the quality of the pieces you'll see in the many small galleries will probably never grace the walls of the Musée d'Orsay. Still, the village is a pleasant stop and there are a couple of small cafés in garden courtyards that would be ideal for lunch. If you're in the mood for something grander, the **Bas-Bréau** in the center of town has a Michelin one-star restaurant.

And if you're itching for a nature walk, Barbizon is set in the massive and, at times, spectacular Fontainebleau forest, which is home to several lovely glades, as well as dramatic outcroppings of rock and deep gorges.

Getting to Barbizon

Take the N7 highway out of the west end of Fontainebleau and turn northwest toward Paris. Before long you'll see signs to Barbizon. Some bus tours include Barbizon in their Fontainebleau itinerary.

For information, write Office de Tourisme, Grande Rue, 77630 Barbizon, or phone 60.66.41.87.

WHERE TO STAY

HÔTELERIE DU BAS-BRÉAU, *22 rue Grande, 77630 Barbizon; 60.66.40.05, Fax 60.69.22.89. Rooms: 12. Double: 900-1,500FF. Restaurant.*

Right in the heart of town, this rustic former hunting lodge has been transformed into the lap of luxury with a magnificent garden and grand dining.

HOSTELLERIE LES PLÉIADES, *21 rue Grande, 77630 Barbizon; 60.66.40.25, Fax 60.66.41.68. Rooms: 23. Double: 320-550FF. Restaurant.*

Also in the center of town, this very comfortable hotel offers very good cuisine and a warm atmosphere.

HOSTELLERIE DE LA CLÉ D'OR, *73 rue Grande, 77630 Barbizon; 60.66.40.96, Fax 60.66.42.71. Rooms: 16. Double: 420FF. Restaurant.*

On the edge of the village, as well as the forest, this is a quaint onetime coach inn with antique-bedecked rooms and fine dining that won't cost you an arm and a leg.

LOIRE VALLEY

This is Château Country, where, in the 15th and 16th centuries, royal families and the vulgar rich built hundreds of castles, each trying to outdo the other.

The result of this opulent game is quite remarkable – so remarkable that we dedicate an entire chapter to the region later in this guide. We include it here because many visitors to Paris try to squeeze in a day or two in the Loire area.

The **Loire Valley** is home to the epic castle of Chambord, with more than 200 rooms and a double-helix stone staircase rising up its center.

There is **Cheverny**, still owned by the marquis de Vibraye, with its sophisticated architectural balance, prized tapestries, and pen of handsome hunting hounds. There is **Chenonceaux**, with its meticulous gardens and massive stone wing spanning the Cher river in five graceful bounds.

The Loire also traverses two wine regions. Just to the west of Orléans, you enter the area where Vouvray and Chinon are produced. Much further west, near the coast, is Muscadet country, where the wine and the fresh seafood complement one another perfectly.

In short, the Loire is a vast and marvelous region. Too vast in our opinion for a frantic day-trip.

Our recommendation is to save the Loire for a separate trip, when you have a car for several days and can wander through the river valley at will, sightseeing at the château of your choice, exploring the countryside by tiny sideroads, or dallying at a vineyard for a tasting of the local wines. And there's nothing quite like bedding down in one of the elegant châteaux that have been converted into hotels – there are many.

Getting to the Loire Valley

Having said that, if you're determined to get a feel for the Château Country, our second recommendation is to take a day-tour by bus. (See the Basics chapter of the Paris section of this guide.)

Prices run 800FF and up for a single day-tour, but that includes hassle-free transportation, admission charges and lunch. Tours leave at about 7 a.m. and don't get back until just before dinner.

WHERE TO STAY

(See *Loire Valley* chapter.)

CHARTRES

It's just like they've been saying for centuries: As you're hustling down the highway, looking out over the broad fields of this fertile plain south of Paris, suddenly in the distance you spot two spires. As you approach, the muscular **Notre-Dame de Chartres** cathedral, whose history reaches back more than 1,000 years, appears to rise out of the plains– practically floating on air.

It's an impressive sight.

As is so often the case with such truly ancient landmarks, the history of this cathedral is a bit murky. Early texts claim that a cathedral here was razed by the angry Duke of Aquitaine in the 740s. Another cathedral here was supposedly burned to the ground by a Viking conqueror 100 years later.

In 876, a third cathedral was consecrated here and presented with a strip of cloth said to have been worn by Mary when she gave birth to Christ. That relic, a modest swathe of plain cloth still held in the cathedral treasury, is what first lured visitors to this hamlet by the thousands.

Though **Chartres** itself, a town of 40,000 is charming, the cathedral and its holdings are still what draw visitors here from all over the world. The cathedral you see now is yet another incarnation, having been dedicated in 1037 after the previous building was destroyed by fire.

There are many highlights, beginning with the three doorways of the **Royal Portal**, dating from the mid-12th century and adorned with sculpted portrayals of the kings and queens of Judah and other Old Testament patriarchs. Inside, standing beneath ceiling vaults that soar 120 feet high, you will find yourself gawking at the three massive circular stained-glass windows, or staring at the Jesse window (from about 1150) and wondering how the colors of the family tree that springs from a reclining Jesse's crotch can remain so brilliant.

Chartres is said, in fact, to have more than 150 stained-glass windows dating back to the 12th and 13th centuries, making it the preeminent showcase of this captivating medieval craft.

Inside, also note the remarkable stone choir screen. Wrapping around the choir, the 41 sculpted scenes depicting various moments in Christ's life took two centuries to complete, beginning in the early 1500s. The high altar, executed in the 1770s, is also quite stunning, with its representation of Mary's ascent to heaven.

Behind the altar and up a stone staircase you will find a vault with a small, though dazzling, collection of embroidered ceremonial robes and golden chalices.

And be sure to walk around the outside of the cathedral to admire its buttresses and the steeples (the one on the right dates back to the 12th century, while the more elaborate Gothic version on the left was built in the 16th century). Also, stroll around to the very back of the church and enjoy the view of the town and the Eure River below.

Getting to Chartres

Chartres can be reached by train from the Gare Montparnasse in Paris. Bus tours also offer half day trips. If you're driving, take the A11 or N10 highways southwest about 80 kilometers (50 miles).

For information, write the Office de Tourisme, B.P. 289, Place de la Cathedrale, 28005 Chartres, or phone 37.21.50.00.

WHERE TO STAY

ABBAYE DES VAUX DE CERNAY, *78720 Cernay-la-Ville; 34.85.23.00, Fax 34.85.20.95. Rooms: 60. Double: 390-1,050FF. Restaurant.*

Located about midway between Versailles and Chartres, just east of Rambouillet off the N306. Remarkable 12th-century abbey with the arched arcades bordering the central lawn, and 160 acres of parkland, fishing, a pool, tennis, a fitness center, everything. This stunning hotel was first renovated by the Baron de Rothschild.

CHÂTEAU D'ESCLIMONT, *Saint-Symphorien-le-Château, 28700 Auneau; 37.31.15.15, Fax 37.31.57.91. Rooms: 48. Double: 650-1,850FF. Restaurant.*

Located 22 kilometers (14 miles) west of Chartres off the N10 and A11. A visually imposing 16th-century castle complete with moat and manicured grounds. There is even a tiny "pitch-and-putt" golf area. First-rate in every regard.

VERSAILLES

Versailles is nothing less than a magnificent monument to opulence, excess, and ego.

Louis XIV, the Sun King, was supposedly so incenced by the elegance of the château at Vaux-Le-Vicomte owned by his finance minister Fouquet that he stole away Fouquet's architect, decorator, and master garden designer and ordered them to come up with something to top Vaux-Le-Vicomte. (There was more to it than that, but jealousy was indeed a factor in the king's treachery.)

Many still believe Fouquet's glorious home is the more perfect of the two, but none question the splendor that is Versailles. It's difficult even to select what is the most impressive because there is so much that dazzles.

There are the epic murals of the chapel ceiling, the many-hued masses of sculpted marble framing the windows of the **Hercules Salon**, and the trompe l'oeil porticos in the **Venus Salon** that are so real you feel as if you could step right into the walls they cover.

There are the brilliant golden cherubs guarding the corners of the **Mars Salon**, the luxurious floral fabrics that decorate the Queen's bedchamber (and that Laura Ashley would die for), and the massive 40-foot canvases of the **Coronation Room** that glorify Napoleon's rise to power.

And, of course, there is the **Hall of Mirrors**, a dizzying collection of chandeliers, mirrors, and murals looking out on the fountains below.

When you arrive at Versailles, stop at one of the small information booths and pick up a schedule that explains the various visiting options you have. Depending whether you are alone or in a group, and depending whether you want to see things for yourself or take a guided tour, you will be directed to specific entrances of the château.

A brief warning: Once you are inside and making the rounds, the press of human flesh will make it impossible to turn back.

While you look around with your mouth hanging open, remember that Versailles, made the seat of government by Louis XIV, was largely abandoned after the mobs came for Louis XVI and Marie-Antoinette and beheaded them in the name of the Revolution. The magnificence you see now is a credit to a hugely expensive restoration that began after World War II and was fueled by a great deal of American, as well as French, wealth.

And don't forget to leave time for the gardens. Some visitors even prefer the gardens to the château (and not just because they're free). Walk past the twin pools of the upper **Water Terrace** beside the château, down the green lawn to the **Apollo Basin** and the **Grand Canal**, where you can rent a rowboat or grab a bite to eat at the café.

If you want to get away from the crowds and were wise enough to bring a small bottle of water and a sack lunch, the **King's Garden** is a bucolic sanctuary. The gardens around the **Grand Trianon**, a small pink-marble mansion where the King dallied with sweet young ladies (not his wife) are also pretty and quiet.

You will no doubt notice that few if any fountains are on. The fountains are turned on most Sunday afternoons during the summer. The schedule is a bit wacky.

For information about the full show, with fountains ablaze with light and actors playing past royalty, write to the Office de Tourisme, 7 rue des Réservoirs, Versailles, or call 39.50.36.22. There are four "Grandes Fâtes de Nuit," with admission charges of 60 to 185FF. Mini-trains will ferry you around the Versailles gardens for 27FF for the day. You can get on and off whenever you like.

Getting to Versailles

To reach Versailles, catch the C line of the RER at any of the stops in Paris, such as the Gare d'Austerlitz or Invalides, and go to Versailles-Rive Gauche (25FF roundtrip for about a 30-minute trip). The château is a short walk from the train station. (Beware: Do not catch the RER train going to Versailles-Chantiers, which is often abbreviated as "Versailles-Ch.")

For information, write Château de Versailles, 123 avenue de Villiers, 75017 Paris, or phone 30.84.74.00 or, for a recording, 30.84.76.76. Closed Monday. Basic admission 40FF.

WHERE TO STAY

LA FORESTIÈRE, *1 avenue Kennedy, 78100 Saint-Germain-en-Laye; 34.51.93.80, Fax 39.73.73.88. Rooms: 25. Double: 850FF. Restaurant.*

Located about 10 kilometers (6 miles) north of Versailles in the town of Saint-Germain-en-Laye, which is home to the château where Louis XIV was born. La Forestiäre is a lovely country-style estate with a generous garden, roaring fireplace, stylish rooms, and fine cuisine.

GIVERNY

In *The Masterpiece*, one of the best and certainly the most autobiographical of Emile Zola's remarkable Rougon-Macquart series capturing French life in the 1800s, the main character is one of the founders of Impressionism and wanders off for several years to the French countryside, where he is inspired by the dazzling beauty of nature itself.

Of course, that calls to mind Claude Monet, and intentionally so. Zola's Claude Lantier was a composite of Impressionists, and Monet was a prominent ingredient in the mix. Fortunately, Monet, who lived in **Giverny** from 1883 to his death in 1926, had a somewhat happier ending than did Zola's fictional character.

Giverny is a must, if you're traveling midsummer to early fall, when the magnificent gardens are ripe with colors and scents potent enough to inspire the artist in even the most curmudgeonly tourist.

Here you will see firsthand one of Monet's most common and captivating subjects: the lily pads floating on the ponds beneath the Japanese bridge. Breathtaking. And the experience will give you an even greater feel for the *Nymphéas*, or *Water Lilies* works on view at the Orangerie and Marmottan-Claude Monet Museums in Paris. (See *"The Sights"* chapter of the Paris section.)

You can also visit the lovely green-shuttered house where Monet lived and which is now a museum with reproductions of his paintings and photographs taken of him and his colleagues.

Getting to Giverny

Giverny, about 48 kilometers (30 miles) northwest of Paris, can be reached by train from the Saint-Lazare station. Buy a ticket to Vernon, then catch a bus to Giverny, which is a couple miles from the station. If you have a car, take the A13 and exit at Bonniäres and look for signs to Giverny.

Bus tour groups offer half-day trips. *For information, write La Fondation Claude Monet, 27620 Giverny, France, or phone 32.51.28.21.*

WHERE TO STAY

CHÂTEAU DE LA CORNICHE, *5 route de la Corniche, 78270 Rolleboise; 30.93.21.24, Fax 30.42.27.44. Rooms: 38. Double: 250-750FF. Restaurant.*

Located 12 kilometers (8 miles) east from Giverney off the N13. This former home to Belgium's king Leopold II sits high above the Seine.

21. NORMANDY

INTRODUCTION

Rarely will you find a battleground as captivating as **Normandy**. It's quite amazing, in fact, how well this lush province has held up considering the violence it's witnessed.

The **Vikings**, or Northmen, vanquished this land in the 9th century and bequeathed the region their name. The last successful conqueror of England, **William the Conqueror**, cut his militaristic teeth on battles throughout his Normandy homeland in the 11th century. The region was pounded during the Hundred Years War with England in the 1300s and 1400s (**Jeanne d'Arc** was burned at the stake here as a result of that conflict). And, of course, the miraculous **D-Day landings** were staged along this coastline and changed the course of World War II.

The hostilities have been epic-sized with grim consequences evident in the partially felled castles and the countless cemeteries where thousands upon thousands of French, British, Canadian and American soldiers are buried.

But for all that (and for its sometimes wicked weather blowing in from the English Channel), Normandy is a picturesque paradise with a boundlessly fertile landscape of rocky coasts, green valleys, broad rivers, apple orchards, and interior ranges so dramatic they're referred to (a bit too enthusiastically) as the Switzerland of Normandy.

This is also home to Monet's beloved **Rouen cathedral**, the bustling port of **Le Havre** where the Seine meets the sea, the picturesque old fishing port of **Honfleur**, the posh beach resorts of **Deauville** and **Trouville**, the horse farms of **Calvados**, the birthplace of William the Conqueror, châteaux of all shapes and sizes, and, of course, the **church of Mont Saint-Michel**, one of the most dramatic monuments to human determination you're ever likely to find.

The poet **Malherbe** was born in Caen, and the great 17th-century playwright **Pierre Corneille** and the 19th-century novelest **Gustave Flaubert** were reared in Rouen. Flaubert dreamed up a bucolic Normandy village for his heroine, Madame Bovary. **Guy de Maupassant** was another giant who gave literary life to his Norman surroundings.

The cuisine of Normandy isn't lacking either. **Camembert** and **Pont L'Evêque** cheeses are just two of the famed Norman dairy products. Calvados apple brandy and Benedictine distilled from more than 20 herbs are natives of Normandy, as are fish of all kinds, quality beef, cream sauces, and sinful desserts.

A last advantage to Normandy, one which makes the region one of the most visited in France, is its size and location. Essentially centered between Paris and London, it can be toured from either city with ease in three to six days.

FINDS & FAVORITES

• *Cathédrale Notre-Dame in Rouen. It's no wonder Monet was obsessed with this beauty. (See Rouen)*

• *Palais Benedictine. The castle-distillery where that wonderful brew is made, in Fécamp. (See Upper Normandy)*

• *Ferme Saint-Siméon. Hotels don't get any better than this. Luxury, charm, beauty, and fine cuisine. (See Honfleur)*

• *American Cemetary at Omaha Beach. Rows upon rows of those who helped turn around World War II. (See Bayeux and the D-Day Beaches)*

• *Manoir de la Drime. A tiny family-owned restaurant in the village of Balleroy. (See Bayeux and the D-Day Beaches)*

• *Mont Saint-Michel. Deservedly one of the world's most famous religious monuments. (See Mont Saint-Michel)*

ROUEN

Most tours of Normandy begin in **Rouen**, home to the cathedral that Monet captured in every conceivable light of day and home to the site where Jeanne d'Arc spent her last horrible moments engulfed in flame.

Just 140 kilometers (90 miles) northwest of Paris, this busy city of 103,000 people on the northern bank of the Seine is worth a stop even if you're no great fan of cities. In fact, you'll want to avoid all but the city center. (Getting to the city center through all the road work will be your first aggravation, but patiently follow signs reading **Centre Ville**.)

ARRIVALS & DEPARTURES

The first order of business is to dump the car because most of what you will want to see is within easy walking distance. There is a roomy underground lot right on the Place du Général de Gaulle opposite the

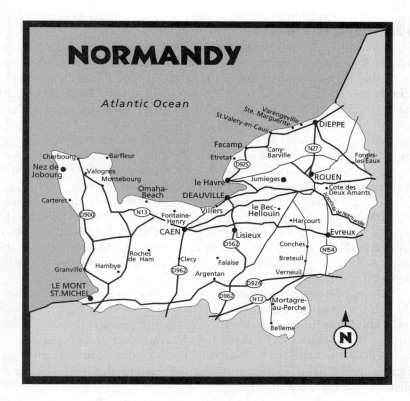

Hôtel de Ville and the Saint-Ouen Abbey. Follow the signs leading to Hôtel de Ville, then look for the big blue 'P' sign. That's your lot.

WHERE TO STAY

PULLMAN ALBANE, *rue Croix de Fer, Rouen; 35.52.69.52, Fax 35.89.41.46. Rooms: 125. Double: 550-680FF. Restaurant.*
Centrally located and comfortable.

HÔTEL DE LA CATHÉDRALE, *12 rue Saint-Romain, Rouen; 35.71.57.95, Fax 35.70.15.54. Rooms: 24. Double: 180-330FF. No restaurant.*
Cozy and modest just off cathedral square.

WHERE TO EAT

GILL, *9 quai Bourse, Rouen; 35.71.16.14, Fax 35.71.96.91.*
Pricey but respected riverside restaurant.

LES NYMPHÉAS, *9 rue Pie, Rouen; 35.89.26.69.*
Named after Monet's water lilies, just off the square with the modern church of Jeanne d'Arc.

SEEING THE SIGHTS

Rouen is like most Normandy cities that took a beating during World War II. Its core is a patchwork of the ancient and the modern. Once out of the lot, turn west down **rue de l'Hôpital** and you'll find all manner of trendy new shops selling fabrics, clothes and pastries. There is even the neon-lit **Consolation Bar** for a quick beer if the drive in was particularly awful.

Make a left down rue Beauvoisine and in a few blocks you will clear the shops and find yourself standing in the **Place de la Cathédrale**, gazing up at the western facade of the Gothic **Cathédrale Notre-Dame** that mesmerized Claude Monet a century ago. It is, indeed, pretty as a painting. (The Tourist Info office will be right behind you on the square.)

The church is a fascinating amalgam of styles resulting from the length of time and the number of political administrations it took to complete. Fires, hurricanes, and bombings did their damage over the years as well. Begun in the 11th century, it was another five centuries before it was finished.

The ages are easy to see in the structure. For instance, the two towers, the Saint-Romain on the left and the Butter Tower on the right, are vastly different. Saint-Romain is an early 12th-century structure with a sober Gothic base, while the 250-foot Butter Tower, so named because its construction was funded by local merchants who bought the right from church authorities to eat butter during Lent, is an elaborate 16th-century structure with a 56-bell peal.

Behind, at the opposite end of the church, you will see the intricate, almost delicate spire soaring into the sky. Inside you'll note that few of the windows have the original stained glass – a shortcoming largely due to the violence of World War II.

Turn your back on the cathedral and wander due west on the **rue du Gros Horloge**. No doubt the most visited medieval lane in the city, the Gros Horloge is a shopping street that takes its name from the marvelous Renaissance clock tower that straddles the street about two blocks down.

Walking down the ancient street, we wished the city elders had worked a little harder to keep out the bargain shops and their largely unattractive wares. Even McDonald's is here. But we did give points to the proprietors of the small public house beneath the Gros Horloge – called **The Big Ben Pub**.

A few blocks down you will emerge onto the old **marketplace**. You can't miss it, with vendors hawking flowers, fish, vegetables, cheeses and everything else that graces a good Normandy kitchen.

You may at first be puzzled by the strange church in the center, with its steeply peaked roofline and its pagoda-like arches. What you're looking at is the contemporary **Église de Jeanne d'Arc**, marking the spot where the warrior and visionary met her horrible death at the stake on May 30, 1431.

Windowshop along a couple of sidestreets or sip coffee at one of the cafés bordering the market square before you double back and loop around the northern side of the cathedral along the narrow **rue Saint-Romain** (named after the adjacent cathedral tower) toward the Renaissance **Église Saint-Maclou** a block and a half behind.

There are a few inviting cafés alongside the Saint-Maclou on **rue Martainville**, where you will also find the entrance *at 186 rue Martainville* to the **Aitre Saint-Maclou** – an art school with a grim past.

Stroll down the walk to the entrance to the inner courtyard of this 16th-century building, step inside and you'll find yourself in the heart of a onetime infirmary where the dead and near dead were taken during The Plague. Carved into the dark wooden beams are such lovely reminders of that time as skulls, crossbones, and shovels.

Other Sights
- **Église Saint-Ouen**, *on the square with the city hall.*
- **Jeanne d'Arc Tower**, *rue du Donjon*. The ominous-looking tower in the northwest corner of the city center was where Jeanne d'Arc was held before execution.
- **Musée des Beaux-Arts**, *Square Verdrel, three blocks west of the Place du Général de Gaulle, 35.71.28.40. Closed Tuesday.* A collection of works by such French masters as Monet, Renoir, Delacroix, and Rouen-born Théodore Gericault.
- **Musée de Céramique**, *Hôtel d'Hocqueville, 1 rue Faucon, 35.07.31.74. Closed Tuesday.* Ceramics from Rouen and Normandy.

BUS TOURS OF ROUEN AND NORMANDY
- *Cars Perier Voyages, 130 rue Martainville, Rouen; 35.98.59.00.*
- *Michel-Voyages, 5 rue Saint-Etienne-des-Tonneliers, Rouen; 35.08.18.10, Fax 35.70.82.10.*
- *Normandy Tourisme, 78 rue Jeanne d'Arc, Rouen; 35.71.23.59, Fax 35.70.36.27.*

PRACTICAL INFORMATION
- **Rouen Office de Tourisme**, *25 place de la Cathédrale, B.P. 666, 76008, 35.71.41.77.*

UPPER NORMANDY

A quick drive northwest from Rouen, along Normandy's **Alabaster Coast**, are two must-sees: the **Palais Benedictine** in Fécamp and the white chalk cliffs flanking the tiny town of **Etretat**.

WHERE TO STAY

PLAGE, *87 rue Plage, Fécamp; 35.29.76.51, Fax 35.28.68.30. Rooms: 22. Double: 210-330FF. No restaurant.*
A block off the beach.
DORMY HOUSE, *route du Havre, Etretat; 35.27.07.88, Fax 35.29.86.19. Rooms: 51. Double: 440-560FF.*
A modest hotel, but with a view of the cliffs and the ocean.

WHERE TO EAT

LE VIKING, *63 boulevard Albert 1er, Fécamp; 35.29.22.92.*
One side upstairs is a restaurant with a respectable menu and a view. The other side is for quick casual snack food.
GALION, *boulevard René Coty, Etretat; 35.29.48.74.*
A block off the beach.

SEEING THE SIGHTS

Fécamp, a town of 21,000 people *40 kilometers (25 miles) north of Le Havre*, is a bustling little port (fishing, canning, and timber) that served for centuries as the region's spiritual center. A convent was established there in the 7th century and, four centuries later, a powerful monastery took control until the Revolution. Evidence of its influence is the impressive **Holy Trinity Church**, built in an early Gothic style in the 1200s.

But the gem of the town is the **Palais Benedictine**, where the *Benedictine* liqueur invented 400 years ago is fermented to this very profitable day. (The city tourist office is across the small park facing the entrance to the palais.)

The world-famous spicy liqueur is a credit to the very imaginative Brother Bernado Vincelli, a 16th-century Venetian monk and pharmacist who got the bright idea of distilling some of the more than 20 varieties of local herbs in a blend of Cognac and Armegnac. Tea, thyme, coriander, nutmeg – he threw it all in, and the results were, well, heavenly.

Unfortunately, the recipe was lost and lived only in legend until it was rediscovered by Alexandre Le Grand in the 19th century. In honor of the monks who first brewed the elixer, he affixed the letters DOM to the label, meaning *Deo Optimo Maximo*, or "To God, the Best and Greatest."

The current **distillery**, built by Le Grand with his handsome profits, is located in a stunning 19th-century Renaissance-style building *on 110 rue Alexandre Le Grand, 76400, 35.10.26.00. Open daily.*

The price of admission is well worth it. The first rooms show off his collection of art and artifacts, including coins dating back to Charles V, a thousand volumes of hand-copied manuscripts fashioned by the monks, collections of keys and ornate doorknobs, and, naturally, a fine gathering of silver goblets from which to sip the brew.

You can't miss the stained glass window that portrays *The Founder*, Le Grand himself, addressing an angel carrying a bottle of Le Grand's best Benedictine. It's probably the most stunning advertising billboard you'll ever see.

Downstairs, you'll watch how they make the brew, with all the caskets and computers and bins of raw herbs. And last but not least, you'll come upon the tasting room, where you can sip a B&B or a Benedictine with orange juice in a lovely glass-enclosed atrium.

About 13 kilometers (8 miles) back toward Le Havre you'll find **Etretat**, a tiny town of fewer than 2,000, whose main claim to fame is the landscape that surrounds it. Find your way to the seaside parking lot and take a look at the massive chalk cliffs that rise up on either side of this small bay.

Atop one cliff is a steep walk leading to **Notre-Dame de la Garge** chapel (an irresistable photo op). On the other side, in the distance, is the **Manneporte**, a gnarled stone archway into the sea carved out by fierce winds and heavy tides over the milennia. From atop the south cliff you can also see the **Aiguille d'Etretat**, the famed **Etretat Needle** of stone that juts out of the sea.

The cliffs, which inevitably recall the cliffs of Dover just opposite the English Channel, are the best argument yet for the geological theory that continents broke up eons ago and drifted apart from one another.

Other Sights

• **La Musée Centre-des-Arts**, *21 rue Alexandre-Legros, Fécamp; 35.28.31.99.* Nineteenth-century paintings, ceramics, arms, and other regional arts.

PRACTICAL INFORMATION

• **Maison du Tourisme de Fécamp**, *113 rue Alexandre Le Grand, B.P. 112, 76400 Fécamp; 35.28.51.01, Fax 35.27.07.77.*
• **Office de Tourisme**, *Place Maurice Guillard, B.P. 3, 76790 Etretat; 35.27.05.21.*

HONFLEUR & DEAUVILLE

The eastern half of the **Calvados Coast** is a study in contrasts. The old harbor of **Honfleur**, a village of 10,000 *about 32 kilometers (20 miles) north of Lisieux*, is as quaint as quaint can be with its colorful old fishing boats (and spanking new sail boats) and its slate-roofed shops so old that they seem to lean over with the crusty weight of age.

Down the road, *a few kilometers to the west*, is **Deauville**, a hip and trendy beach resort where rich folks race their favorite horses, invoke Lady Luck at the gaming tables of the casinos, attend the famous spring American film festival, and soak up the sun and huge quantities of vintage Calvados.

WHERE TO STAY

FERME SAINT-SIMÉON, *rue Adolphe-Marais, 14600 Honfleur; 31.89.23.61, Fax 31.89.48.48. Rooms: 29. Double: 990-5,100FF. Restaurant.* Wow! Elegant converted farm with a stunning view of the sea, plush rooms and suites, a lavish enclosed pool, a sauna, vibrant garden, and handsome dining room just to the west of Honfleur. Such luxury doesn't come cheap. But what a memory you'll have. If nothing else, try to have lunch here.

HOSTERLERIE LECHAT, *place Sainte-Catherine, Honfleur; 31.89.23.85, Fax 31.89.28.61. Rooms: 23. Double: 350-550FF.*

Not elegant, but a passable timbered hotel on the main square overlooking the wooden church.

NORMANDY, *38 rue J. Mermoz, Deauville; 31.98.66.22; Fax 31.98.66.23. Rooms: 294. Double: 1,800FF and up.*

Rooms of this grande dame overlook a small park, the beach, and the ocean beyond.

WHERE TO EAT

FERME SAINT-SIMÉON (see *Where to Stay* above). Scallops with truffle oil and artichokes; grilled salmon in balsamic vinegar; ravioli of camembert, walnut oil and pork breast; French toast with vanilla pods and raspberries. Massive, brilliant wine list.

L'ASSIETTE GOURMANDE, *8 place Sainte-Catherine, Honfleur; 31.89.24.88.*

Waterside neo-Deco restaurant looking out on the port, with fixed menus from 150 to 380FF. Lobster salad with endive, apples and grated nuts; grilled scallops with asparagus and orange; and roast lamb with anchovy and olives.

L'ALBATROSS, *on the western side of the Old Port, Honfleur.*

A hole in the wall that attracts the locals, who sip Pastis, play backgammon, and contemplate the seagulls. Friendly.

BRASSERIE DE LA MER, *on the boardwalk next to the much respected Ciro's restaurant, Deauville.*

A perfect sand-side spot to lap up some cider and fish soup, or maybe a potato and herring salad, and watch the beautiful people. Service on the beach on nice days.

SEEING THE SIGHTS

Get your camera and walking shoes ready because **Honfleur** is a lovely little village. It owes its existence over the centuries to ship building, cod fishing, and art.

In the early 1500s, explorers such as Jean Denis departed for the New World from Honfleur. In the 1800s, local native Eugene Boudin, a fine painter in his own right, gathered Monet, Dufy, and other artists here, establishing a colony that mulled over the priniciples of color and light that would ultimately take hold in the Impressionist movement.

Even today, art plays an enormous role in Honfleur's culture and economy. Park the car in one of the public lots, then take a leisurely stroll through the tiny streets and you'll find shops and galleries everywhere with surprisingly good work–oils, watercolors, prints, etc.

For a more formal examination of Boudin's work and the formative Impressionist period, visit the **Eugène-Boudin Museum** *on the narrow rue de l'Homme de Bois (31.89.54.00)*. The 20-year-old museum, which is closed Tuesdays, is a bit stark in its modernism, but the works are instructive.

Honfleur has two lovely squares, the **Place Sainte-Catherine** and the **Place Arthur Boudin**, both of which are transformed Saturday mornings into a full blown bazaar of regional food, lace, and ceramics (and some junk). The Place Sainte-Catherine faces the 16th-century wooden church by the same name, which was erected by local shipbuilders after the Hundred Years War, which explains why the naves resemble the hulls of ships.

For an out-of-body experience, leave Honfleur behind and visit one of the casinos in Deauville or Trouville (the latter is directly across the Touques river from Deauville and was the preferred social hot spot decades ago).

The **Lousiane Follies** is a great peach whale of a casino *on the Trouville beach*, humming with the sound of slot machines, clinking glasses, water cascading down the paddlewheels that flank the door, and the curses and squeals of losers and winners.

The place is truly very strange. Flaubert, said to be a frequent visitor of Trouville long before the Lousiane Follies arrived, surely would have disapproved. (Still, we couldn't resist trying our luck.)

Deauville, nicknamed the 21st arrondissement of Paris for all its Parisian visitors (there is even a local publication called *21st Arrondissement, Magazine of the Elite*), is home to an internationally famous annual film festival and is impressively chic, with handsome mansions, a busy boardwalk, and a wide beach that's ideal for sunbathing, windsurfing, or body gawking. The architectural design of newer buildings was carefully planned to blend in with the Tudor-like style of the aging manses.

Don't forget this is where the horsey set gets crazed as well. Major races are held at the **Hippodromes de Deauville** throughout July and August. Riding and lessons are available in the area as well.

Auctions are another great local sport, though the stakes are extremely high. The items up for sale are yearlings, great wines, and fine art. It's entertaining if you can find a way to get in for free.

Other Sights
- **Musée du Vieux Honfleur**, *on the quai Saint Etienne in the former church of Saint-Stephen on the Old Harbor, Honfleur.* A collection of maritime historic objects from past centuries.
- **Musée d'Ethnographie et d'Art Populaire**, *on rue de la Prison, Honfleur.* Objects of Norman life and popular art, including recreations of 12 representative rooms.

PRACTICAL INFORMATION
- **Office de Tourisme**, *Place Arthur-Boudin, B.P. 137, 14602 Honfleur; 31.89.23.30, Fax 31.89.31.82.*
- **Office de Tourisme**, *32 boulevard F. Moureaux, alongside the river in Trouville; 31.88.36.19.*
- **Office de Tourisme**, *place Mairie, Deauville; 31.88.21.43.*

BAYEUX & D-DAY BEACHES
A picturesque village of 15,000 people *30 kilometers (18 miles) northwest of the city of Caen,* **Bayeux** is famous for its association with epic wars. During the D-Day invasion, Bayeux was the first town to be liberated and was one of very few to survive the fierce battles virtually unscathed.

WHERE TO STAY
LION D'OR, *71 rue Saint-Jean, 14400 Bayeux; 31.92.06.90, Fax 31.22.15.64. Rooms:28. Double: 400-750FF. Restaurant.*

In an old post office, comfortable rooms, pleasant sitting room and bar, and a well reviewed restaurant that is good, despite annoying lapses in service. Do not choose the demi-pension because it can be more expensive than just paying for the room and eating a la carte.

CHÂTEAU DE BELLEFONTAINE, *49 rue de Bellefontaine, 14400 Bayeux; 31.22.00.10, Fax 31.22.19.09. Rooms: 15. Double: 450-650FF. No restaurant.*

Very friendly staff in a handsome and quiet converted château on the edge of town.

Bed & Breakfasts: If you're looking for something more homey – literally in a home – contact the local tourist office or write to **Gîtes de France**, *Service Réservation: Chambre d'Agriculture, promenade de Mme. de Seigne, 14050 Caen; 31.82.71.65.*

WHERE TO EAT
MANOIR DE LA DROME, *on the single main road of Balleroy, a couple hundred yards below the marvelous Château, about 15 minutes west of Bayeux off D572, 31.21.60.94. Closed Mondays.*

Sounds complicated to get to, but it's not. And it's well worth the drive. The Leclercs set a beautiful table and push Norman cuisine to the limits – frog legs in a cream sauce in pastry, fricasée of sole with foie gras and pasta, Brittany lobster in pastry with coriander and leeks, cabbage and turbot with cream and seaweed, wedges of Pont l'Evêque cheese marinated in balsamic vinegar with arugala.

SEEING THE SIGHTS

Bayeux was the town where Charles de Gaulle first addressed the French people on his return from exile in England. A monument in **Charles de Gaulle Square** a couple of blocks west of the inspiring 11th-century **Notre-Dame Cathedral** commemorates his first official words and his promise of liberty for France.

Bayeux is also keeper of the famous **Bayeux Tapestry**, a remarkable 230-foot-long linen scroll that recounts William the Conqueror's triumph over England in 1066.

The first room of the **Tapestry Museum** is a recreation of the cloth with contemporary interpretations of each of the 58 cartoon-like panels. But because of the crowds, the going here can get pretty tough. A much more accessible English-language narrative is given in film form in the comfortable theater upstairs. (The narrator is supposedly Odo, who was the bishop of Bayeux and William's half brother. It was Odo who commissioned the tapestry.)

The museum also displays a reproduction of the Domesday Book, the official accounting leger from 1086 in which William's vast properties were itemized. He didn't do too badly for himself. He triumphed over the stain of illigitimacy to become Duke of Normandy, then King of England. He also introduced Normandy to the first codes that defined and enforced property rights and legal redress.

About 24 kilometers (15 miles) outside town to the southwest is the **Château de Balleroy**, a wonderful hilltop castle in the village by the same name. The majestic early 17th-century mansion was said to be one of the first efforts by François Mansart, future master architect under Louis XIII.

Approach the house through the lovely garden and past the museum honoring the hot air balloon. Inside are richly-decorated interiors with a huge library and a gallery of portraits by Mignard. Back on the main road from Bayeux, you might stop for lunch at the **Relais de la Forêt**, a crossroads café with lots of locals wolfing down good home cooking.

The D-Day Beaches

The five D-Day beaches are a few minutes north of Bayeux, stretching from **Sword Beach** *at Ouistreham on the east* to **Utah Beach** *at Sainte-Marie-du-Mont in the west.* It's a long haul from one end to the other, but there are two beaches you must try to visit: **Gold Beach** *at Arromanches,* where British troops braved the shore, and **Omaha Beach** *near Colleville sur Mer,* where thousands of Americans fought desperately for their lives – and ours – during what became known as "The Longest Day."

Find a parking spot in Arromanches (no easy task) and walk down to the waterfront where you will find a small semi-circular viewpoint with a four-foot metal box. Switch the dial on the box to English, drop in your five francs and gaze out at the dozens of huge misshapen metal hulks that form an arch a mile out to sea.

The voice in the box will tell you that the arch is what's left of the miraculous harbor that was prefabricated in England and floated across the English Channel beginning in the wee, wee hours of the morning June 6, 1944 – better known as **D-Day.** First, the box explains, 18 ships were scuttled to help calm the waters, and within days a seven-mile waterbreak and 4,000-foot piers were in place where Allies unloaded 56,000 vehicles, 326,000 men, and 110,000 tons of supplies.

Even with today's technology, such a task seems impossible. In fact, it's hard to imagine that anyone dared pitch the harebrained scheme to the generals, much less that the execution of the plan would mark a turning point in World War II.

The **Musée du Débarquement,** or **D-Day Landing Museum,** on the harborfront goes into great detail about the invasion, though you are likely to find it overwhelmed with visitors. *The museum phone is 31.33.34.31, and Fax 31.92.68.83. Open daily.*

A prefab harbor was also used in the landing at Omaha, several miles west, though a wicked storm wiped it out not long after it was set in place. Today, the cliffs overlooking Omaha Beach are home to the **American Cemetery,** set on 172 vibrant green acres with 10,000 white stone crosses and stars of David set in rows reminiscent of the Arlington National Cemetery in Virginia. The remains of about 14,000 other men who had been buried in this area were shipped to the States at the request of families.

At the central memorial you will find enormous maps recounting the Normandy campaign and the ultimate defeat of Nazi Germany.

Omaha is a quiet place. Even children are hushed by the sense of history and the immaculate formality of the cemetery. And, whereas in Arromanches you are likely to stumble across a couple of veterans rehashing their memories, at Omaha people tend to walk with arms folded, stopping only to gaze down at the beach and out to sea.

Other Sights
• **Baron-Gérard Museum,** *place des Tribunaux, just to the north of the Cathédrale Notre-Dame, 14400 Bayeux; 31.92.14.21. Open daily.* In

honor of Franáois Gérard, a painter in the early 1800s, and Henri-Alexandre Gérard, a curator in the late 1800s, this museum houses a fascinating collection of 19th-century pre-Impressionist and Impressionist paintings, fabulous 19th-century ceramics from a local company founded by Joachim Langlois, and a display demonstrating just what a pain it is to make lace, with more than 30 bobbins to fashion a piece of trim no more than an inch wide.

• **Cathédrale Notre-Dame**, *rue du Bienvenue, 14400 Bayeux*, with 11th-century towers rising 250 feet into the sky.

• **Conservatoire de la Dentelle de Bayeux**, *Hôtel du Doyen, 6 rue Lambert-Leforestier, 14400 Bayeux; 31.92.73.80*. Created to safeguard the traditional way of making Normandy lace, with demonstrations and finished pieces for sale.

• **Memorial du Général de Gaulle**, *10 rue de Bourbesneur, 14400 Bayeux; 31.92.45.55. Open daily*.

• **The Museum for Peace**, *Esplanade Dwight-David-Eisenhower, B.P. 6261, 14066 Caen; 31.06.06.44, Fax 31.06.06.70*. A history of the 20th century with a great deal about World War II and a gallery dedicated to Nobel Peace Prize winners.

PRACTICAL INFORMATION

• **Office de Tourisme**, *at the corner of the rue Saint-Martin and rue des Cuisiniers, B.P. 343, 14403 Bayeux; 31.92.16.26, Fax 31.92.01.79*.

• **American Battle Monuments Commission**, *68 rue du 19-Janvier, 92380 Garches; 47.01.19.76*.

• **Comité Départemental du Tourisme du Calvados**, *Place du Canada, 14000 Caen; 31.86.53.30, Fax 31.79.39.41*.

MONT SAINT-MICHEL

Located on the cusp of Normandy and Brittany, **Mont Saint-Michel** (the **rock** and the **Abbey**, which blend one into the other) is one of the best known religious monuments in the world. And with good reason. You will never forget your first sighting as you approach by car, then drive the long raised road crossing the mudflats to this rocky promintory.

A quick word about the mudflats: Don't fool around here. They can be treacherous. There is quicksand and very sudden tides can catch you off guard.

WHERE TO STAY

MANOIR DE LA ROCHE TORIN, *50220 Courtils, a tiny village just six miles from Mont Saint-Michel; 33.70.96.55, Fax 33.48.35.20. Rooms: 12. Double: 400-600FF. Restaurant*.

Handsome quiet château with horse riding, walking trails, and a restaurant boasting seafood and an exquisite lamb raised on salt marsh grasses.

HÔTEL DU CHÂTEAU D'AGNEAUX, *50180 Agneaux, near Saint-Lo, a few miles away; 33.57.65.88, Fax 33.56.59.21. Rooms: 12. Double: 380-850FF. Restaurant.*

Very woodsy setting for this 13th-century castle. Friendly staff and good cuisine.

A word of warning: The highly-rated **CHÂTEAU DE LA SALLE**, *outside Coutances en route to Mont Saint-Michel*, is truly isolated, somewhat grim, and run by one of the rudest, most unpleasant women we've ever encountered.

SEEING THE SIGHTS

Legend has it that the 280-foot high rock on which the Abbey sits was once surrounded by forest, but that the trees were claimed in 709 by a vicious tidal wave. After this disaster Saint Michael, patron saint of Normandy, appeared to the local bishop and ordered that a small chapel be built on the rock.

The beginnings of this place of sanctuary and prayer date back to the 9th century, though several additions were made over the centuries as the Abbey grew in power. What you see now is an amalgam of efforts that spanned time from the 11th to the 19th centuries.

The lowpoint of this glorious work rising out of stone was touched during the Revolution, when the grand Abbey was transformed into a grim prison. It remained a prison until 1863. Today, it is well cared for and, in fact, the magnificent edifice is still occupied by a handful of monks.

Take the full tour so that you can fully appreciate the imposing 13th-century guardroom, the crypts where you will see the huge stone support pillars, Sainte-Mary Magdalene's chapel, the enchanting cloisters in the 'Marvel,' and the wonderful Lace Stairway.

One disappointment: the trinket shops inside the main gate. Odd to see something so tacky in the presence of such magnificence.

PRACTICAL INFORMATION

• **Office de Tourisme**, *Corps de Garde des Bourgeois, 50116 Manche; 33.60.14.30.*

THE COUNTRYSIDE

There are a couple of country roads worth touring if you've got the time (the Normandy tour office claims there are 21 car-tours posted in the region, including tours of cider country, iron country, granite country, and even the Neufchatel cheese country). Just wander and burn up some gasoline.

One tour follows route D562 south from Caen into what is called **Swiss Normandy**. The hilly landscape isn't quite as dramatic as the name would lead you to believe, but the stretch along the **Orne river** from **Thury-Harcourt**, *32 kilometers (20 miles) south of Caen*, to the **Roche d'Oetre**, *another 32 kilometers (20 miles) south and east off route D511* is a real beauty.

Enter **Clécy**, *just off 562 south of Thury-Harcourt*, and you'll see signs for the **Route Touristique**. This two-laner will wander along the river, up the hills, and past recreation areas that are popular for fishing and kayaking. The massive ridge you'll see with the green and yellow foliage clinging to its steep sides is the **Pain de Sucre**, on top of which you will find a stunning view.

Clécy is also home to the **Musée du Chemin de Fer Miniature**, or the museum of miniature trains. The French are ga-ga over miniatures, but this could really wow the kids, with more than 200 locomotives whizzing by villages with more than 600 houses. *Just follow the signs, or call 31.69.07.13.*

Just south of **Pont-d'Ouilly**, another adorable village, you'll find signs for the **Roche d'Oetre**, which will give you another scenic view of the countryside. The nearby **Gorges de Saint-Aubert** can be seen a little further down the river, *off D21 and D239 near Rabodanges*.

Return north from this voyage to the underrated and absolutely charming town of **Falaise**, said to be William the Conqueror's birthplace and site of a storybook castle that dates back to 1127. Quite a place.

The second country route follows D579 into the **Auge region** *south of Lisieux, which is east of Caen*. This region is best known for its cheese and ciders. Again, the order of the day is just to wander at will.

About 40 kilometers (25 miles) south of Lisieux is the tiny village of **Camembert** with a statue of Marie Harel, the farmwoman who was said to have invented the cheese by the same name. You've got to love a country that builds monuments to inventors of cheese.

Livarot, *midway between Lisieux and Camembert*, is also a big producer of cheese, as is **Pont L'Evàque** *just north of Lisieux*.

All along the route, you will see signs inviting you to pull off to sample the famed Normandy apples and apple brandies (or Calvados) made by the locals. It's worth a stop.

Calvados, named after this general region of Normandy, has been brewed since the 12th century. You may have heard the phrase *trou normand*, or Norman hole, referring to a long stretch in the middle of an even longer dinner during where guests quaff lots of Calvados – theoretically to make room for more food.

This is also château country. Among the best is **Saint-Germain-de-Livet**, 6 *kilometers (4 miles) south of Lisieux off D579 on D268.* Begun in the 12th century as a fortress, it was refurbished and enlarged in the late 1400s. It was enlarged again in the late 1500s. The cylindrical turrents and main walls are a checkerboard pattern of stone and green-glazed brick. Tours are available.

22. BRITTANY

INTRODUCTION

Bet you didn't know this:

Sainte-Anne, the patron saint of **Brittany**, hailed from a royal family that lived on the rugged Cornouaille peninsula at the far southwestern end of Brittany. Despite her lofty station in life, Anne's existence was not a happy one. Her brutish husband regularly fell into fits of rage and beat her.

Angels, witnessing the abuse, took pity on Anne and whisked her away to sanctuary in Nazareth. There she lived in peace, giving birth to a serene baby girl who would later become revered as the Virgin Mary.

After some time had passed, Anne returned to her native Brittany to spend her last days. But before she died, Anne was visited by her grandson, Christ, who, during his brief stay, called up from the earth the sacred spring of Sainte-Anne-la-Palud.

It wasn't long after that visit that Joseph of Arimathea, a disciple of Christ, voyaged to Brittany with a cup containing drops of the Savior's blood. It is said that he lived a reclusive existence in the Paimpont forest just a few kilometers west of modern-day Rennes. Six centuries later, King Arthur, accompanied by 50 knights, arrived and searched in vain for that Holy Grail.

Merlin, the magnificent magician, came along with King Arthur during that venture. Deep in the forest one day, the sorcerer met a fairy and fell in love. He lived out his life in those woods in blissful isolation.

You wouldn't have to look far to find experts able to shoot enormous holes in these accounts, but what would be the fun of that? Brittany, known as **Bretagne** to the natives, is a land of gnarled coves, crashing waves, soulful searches for spiritual truth, and extravagant legends.

The people's obsession with the mysteries of the universe dates back thousands of years, long before historians began to keep track of things.

Near **Carnac**, along Brittany's south-central coastline, you will find the world's largest gathering of stone menhirs and megaliths lined up in rows following various astronomical pathways (similar to Stonehenge, but on a larger scale). Experts speculate that these early civilizations worshipped the sun and the moon.

Later on, when Christianity arrived, the locals took the faith to heart, recognizing literally hundreds of saints, whose job it was to protect villages, crops, fishing fleets–really, just about anything worth protecting.

Pardons, or small pilgrimages, were routinely staged to appeal to these saints. Some pardons are still held today, and they are quite a scene, with local residents decked out in traditional Breton dress, including high starched lace bonnets for the women.

Independent Spirits

Legends also reveal that the Breton people are enormously independent, in part reflecting the area's geographic isolation.

The **Brittany peninsula**, with more than 1,200 kilometers (750 miles) of craggy coastline juts like an elbow out of the northwest corner of France just below Normandy. Even today, though the ports are busy and small highways connect virtually all the larger towns, Brittany is not a particularly convenient place to visit.

France's superhighways skirt only the very eastern edge of Brittany, and the peninsula's countless inlets make coastal trips, though visually spectacular, slow-going.

This means that if you're planning a visit, you should set aside at least five to seven days–all of them with a car.

The Breton independence also has political origins. Though the lands bordering Brittany's eastern flank became part of France in the early 1200s, Brittany itself was not formally absorbed into the realm until 1532.

First known as Armor, meaning "country of the sea," this land was occupied by the Gauls, then the Roman conquerors. But the Brittany which emerged from the Roman times was shaped primarily by Celts, who were driven out of Britain in the 5th, 6th and 7th centuries. They were the ones who renamed the peninsula Little Britain, which later evolved into Brittany.

United under various counts who behaved more like independent kings, Brittany did fierce battle over the centuries with all comers – the French, the Normans, the British, the Germans, and even one another.

Then came Duchess Anne of Brittany (not to be confused with Sainte-Anne), the last ruler of a truly autonomous Brittany. Her marriage in 1491 to Charles VIII bound her land to the crown in a peaceful alliance.

Anne's daughter, Claude, violated her promise to her mother to keep Brittany independent when she ceded the duchy to her husband, François I. Finally and forever, despite even the occasional contemporary campaign for secession, Brittany became a part of France.

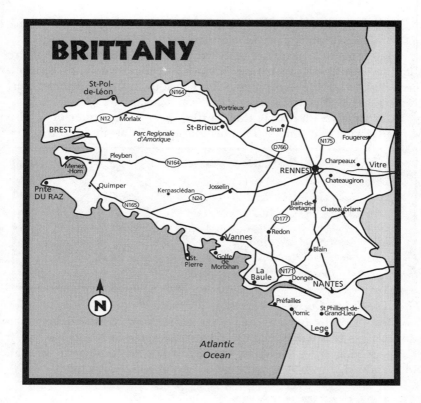

Predictably, the union has slowly eroded the distinctive Breton culture. There are valiant efforts today to preserve the very difficult Breton language (the teaching of which was banned for years by the national government) and the region's cultural traditions, such as the pardons.

But realistically, most of these cultural relics will find their fate in university libraries and museum display cases.

BRETON CUISINE

Despite all the battles that were fought here and despite a relatively meager economy based on fishing and agriculture, Brittany is a beautiful region. It is a land of picturesque fishing villages, walled cities, beach resorts, rolling hills, and ancient treasures.

And when you've had your fill of sightseeing, you'll find plenty of hearty food to fill your belly. The seafood and shellfish are fabulously varied and fresh (the lobsters from **Camaret** are spectacular, as are oysters from **Cancale**). You'll find lots of pork and lamb dishes as well.

Artichokes and strawberries are specialties in the region. And be sure to sit yourself down at a crèperie or two.

The **crèpes** of Brittany are deservedly renown. Lists of ingredients are lengthy, both for the lunchtime buckwheat galettes made plump with mixtures of Gruyere cheese, eggs, and various meats, and the dessert crèpes filled with chocolate, jams, fruits and sugar.

And you can wash it all down with a hearty local cider or a crisp Muscadet wine that is made in enormous quantity around Nantes.

FINDS & FAVORITES

- *The walled city of* **Saint-Malo**
- **La Reine Hortense hotel** *in Dinard*
- *The fishing village of* **Camaret**
- **La Plage hotel** *in Sainte-Anne-la-Palud*
- *The menhirs near* **Carnac**
- **La Domaine de Rochevilaine hotel** *in Pointe de Pen-Lan*
- *The rocky shoreline just about anywhere*

The Northern Coast

Most trips to Brittany begin either at **Mont Saint-Michel**, as a continuation of a visit to the southwestern stretch of Normandy, or, if you're coming from Paris, in **Rennes**. If you're coming in through Normandy, then you've already got a car and you're all set.

RENNES & ENVIRONS

Rennes, with just over 200,000 people, is the capital of Brittany and *lies about 350 kilometers (215 miles) west of Paris.*

Rennes is a perfectly decent city, though many say it is so modern and industrial that it doesn't possess the genuine Breton character. We would agree that you wouldn't want to settle in for any length of time because that would take away from your tour through the coastal towns, which are much more enchanting.

ARRIVALS & DEPARTURES

From Paris, take the A11 autoroute to Le Mans, then the A81/N157 to Rennes. It's a three - or four - hour drive, depending on traffic out of Paris and around Le Mans.

Another option is to catch a train from the Gare Montparnasse in Paris to Rennes, where you can arrange for a rental car to be waiting. From Rennes, you follow the N175 to Mont Saint-Michel or the N137 to Saint-Malo. Both distances are around 65 kilometers (40 miles).

WHERE TO STAY

HÔTEL D'AVAUGOUR, *1 place du Champ-Clos, 22100 Dinan; 96.39.07.49, Fax 96.85.43.04. Rooms: 27. Double: 420-480FF. Restaurant.*

Overlooking the ramparts in the center of town with a homey atmosphere and very decent re*staurant.*

CHÂTEAU DE LA MOTTE BEAUMANOIR, *35720 Pleugeuneuc; 99.69.46.01, Fax 99.69.42.49. Rooms: 8. Double: 700-900FF. Restaurant.*

This 15th-century converted Château boasts an elegant decor, large rooms, beautiful wooded grounds, a central lake, boating, fishing, a heated pool, and fine dining.

LA VILLEFROMOY, *7 boulevard Hébert, 35400 Saint-Malo; 99.40.92.20, Fax 99.56.79.49. Rooms: 20. Double: 450-650FF. No restaurant.*

In a residential seaside neighborhood on the northwestern section of the city, this mid-19th century onetime residence is very comfortable and is a stone's throw from the beach.

LA REINE HORTENSE, *19 rue Malouine, 35800 Dinard; 99.46.54.31, Fax 99.88.15.88. Rooms: 10. Double: 750-1,300FF. No restaurant.*

A gem of a hotel that was once home to a royal Russian family, which built this magnificent home-away-from-home just prior to the Russian Revolution. The very stylish hotel overlooks the beach, the bay, and Saint-Malo in the distance. Ask for one of the rooms on the top floor that share a large terrace.

DOMAINE DU VAL, *22400 Planguenoual; 96.32.75.40, Fax 96.32.71.50. Rooms: 35. Double: 400-950FF. Restaurant.*

Fax for directions to this lovely deluxe hideaway about 30 kilometers west of Dinard, near Saint-Brieuc. Delightful grounds sloping down to the sea, a Renaissance-style main house, with small stone cottages, a covered swimming pool, tennis and squash courts, and a pricey but very good restaurant.

WHERE TO EAT

RESTAURANT DE BRICOURT, *rue Duguesclin, 35260 Cancale; 99.89.64.76, Fax 99.89.88.47.*

A Michelin two-star that specializes in oyster dishes (naturally, given the location).

LE BINIOU, *in the tiny village of Pen-Guen just before you reach Saint-Cast-le-Guildo; 96.41.94.53.*

Seafood with a great view.

LA COTRIADE, *au port de Piegu, near Pléneuf-Val-André, 22370 Pléneuf-Val-André; 96.72.20.26.*

Sample grilled lobster while you gaze at the sea.

SEEING THE SIGHTS

For our purposes here, we're going to skip any discussion of Mont Saint-Michel because it is technically a part of Normandy and we have included it in that section of this guide. So we'll assume your visit begins in Rennes.

If you stop for a bite and a brief tour, find your way to **Le Vieux Rennes**, a north-central section of the city that escaped the devastation of a massive fire in 1720. Here, you'll discover narrow, half-timbered shops and homes, the **Cathedrale Saint-Pierre**, and the **Palais de Justice**.

The ceilings of the 19th-century cathedral and the Grand Chambre of the 17th-century Palais are sumptuously decorated with murals and gold leaf. The Grand Chambre also features some fine Gobelins tapestries.

Another stop you might consider is the **Musée de Brittany** in the **Palais des Musée** *on Quai Emile Zola in the center of the city*. It will give you a good sense of the peninsula's colorful history.

But, as we said before, you should head for the Emerald Coast to the north with all due dispatch because that's where you will drag your chin across the ground in awe.

En route to the coast you'll see signs for **Dinan** *on D794 then N176*. If you've got time for a drive-by, this is a lovely village of 12,000 entered by way of an ancient viaduct that crosses the Rance River.

Above you, on the plateau where this once-strategic town sits, you will see the medieval ramparts that almost completely encircle the heart of the city and that protected the town for centuries against its many enemies.

As in Rennes, a walking tour is in order if you can find a spot to leave the car near **Vieille Ville (Old Town)** and the **Tour de l'Horloge** (the **Clock Tower**). In fact, you can get a splendid view of the town from atop the 15th-century Clock Tower. Take time to visit the Romanesque church of **Saint-Sauveur** and the **Château** with its huge 14th-century tower known as the Dungeon of Duchess Anne. Tour boats can also take you down the **Rance River** all the way to the sea. It's a lovely river, but the tour requires the better part of a day.

The stretch of coastline just north of Dinan is the cream of the Northern Coast. To the east is **Mont Saint-Michel**, then follows **Cancale** (famous for its oysters), then the walled city of **Saint-Malo**, then the resort of Dinard, and, finally, the rugged **Cap Fréhel** (with its fabulous view of the sea) and the **Côte d'Emeraude (Emerald Coast)**, which has several lovely beach villages.

Somewhere along here you should plan on bedding down for a night or two. There are several nice towns, hotels, and restaurants, some of which we've recommended (see above, *Where to Stay* and *Where to Eat*).

Begin your tour at the tiny port of **Cancale**, with only 5,000 residents, almost all of whom have something to do with the thriving oyster trade in the broad bay beneath the town. These mudflats, exposed for hundreds of yards during low tides, are home to some of the most productive oyster beds in all of France.

Part of the credit for the oysters' fine taste is theoretically due to the type of plankton found in these waters. You'll be surprised at the taste. Unlike oysters that have been washed (as in American restaurants), these still carry the tangy piquancy of the sea. Don't you dare smother the taste with cocktail sauce (a little vinegar maybe, but no sauce).

The finest oysters are the *Cancales* and *Belons*, though *Claire* and *Papillons* are also tasty. Try to arrange a dinner at the **Restaurant de Bricourt**, mentioned above.

Your next stop is **Saint-Malo**, a magnificent walled city, much of which has been carefully rebuilt after destruction rained down on it during World War II. The walled portion occupies what was once an island located on the northwestern tip of the city. The ramparts themselves were begun in the 12th-century and were expanded up through the 18th-century.

In fact, after you've parked the car outside the walled city and poked through the **Porte Saint-Vincent**, hang a right and climb the stairs to the ramparts. From here, you can walk the entire perimeter of the city, admiring the shops and residences that line the narrow lanes inside the walls and gazing out over the broad beaches toward the sea.

It was from this port that Jacques Cartier, a local hero, sailed in 1534 looking for the New World. What he found was the mouth of the Saint-Lawrence River.

If you have time, visit the **Château**, begun in 1395, and the **Saint-Malo Museum**, which traces the history of the city and its various heroes (and pirates).

Also walk across the waters to the **Ile Grand Bé** and the **Fort National**, both of which are few hundred yards off of Saint-Malo's ramparts, giving you a fabulous view of the city and the Emerald Coast.

The tomb of François-René de Châteaubriand, the great French author and statesman born in Saint-Malo in 1768, is located on the Ile Grand Bé. The fortress was built in 1689 by Vauban, a famous general under Louis XIV, to protect the city.

Dinard, *a few kilometers west of Saint-Malo*, is a delightful resort with a broad arching beach protected by the rocky **Pointe du Moulinet** that juts out into the bay. The town's population of 10,000 swells during tourist season with mostly well-heeled visitors who want to enjoy its **Grande Plage**, the centrally-located casino, the view, and nearby haute cuisine.

Be sure to stroll along the flower-bedecked **Promenade du Clair de Lune**, *on the eastern side of the Pointe du Moulinet* and which has a captivating view into the estuary of the Rance River.

Continue west through Dinard on D786 for a visit to the wilder end of this Emerald Coast. The trip is slow going, but it's well worth the time. The coastline dips, and skips, and bends, and soars past a landscape of scenic points and romantic coves.

Stop by the tiny resort of **Saint-Lunaire** and visit the broad beach and the **Grotte des Sirénes (Sirens' Cave)** on the ragged **Pointe du Décollé**. Further on, you'll cross the dramatic **Frémur River bridge**, dip through the beach village of **Lancieux**, and stop to visit the castle ruins at **Le Guildo**, where the poet Gilles de Bretagne was smothered to death by his brother in the 15th century.

Keep plugging along and you'll come to **Saint-Cast-le-Guildo**, **Fort la Latte**, **Cap Fréhel**, **Cap d'Erquy**, and **le Val-André** – all of which are well worth a stop (especially the dramatic Cap Fréhel).

Further west along the coast, past le Val-André and the western end of the Emerald Coast, you will reach the **Côte de Granit Rose** (the **Coast of Pink Granite**). This shoreline is also jagged and dramatic, though fewer visitors make it this far because they are worn down by the difficult coastal driving.

The most distinctive feature of the Côte de Granit Rose is, as you have already guessed, the granite. As the sun moves across the sky, the granite takes on a rainbow of colors ranging from brilliant orange to flamingo pink.

Worthy stopping points are **Perros-Guirec** (a resort with a pleasure-boat harbor and beaches), **Ploumanach** (a fishing port with a lovely lighthouse), **Trégastel-Plage** (a tiny resort peninsula with enormous rock formations, caves, and a beach guarded by islands) and **Trébeurden** (another adorable beach resort).

PRACTICAL INFORMATION
• **Dinan Office de Tourisme**, *6 rue Horloge, 22100 Dinan; 96.39.75.40.*
• **Saint-Malo Office de Tourisme**, *esplanade Saint-Vincent, 35400 Saint-Malo; 99.56.64.48.*
• **Dinard Office de Tourisme**, *2 boulevard Féart, 35800 Dinard; 99.46.94.12.*

Inland Toward the Western Coast
While hearty souls with lots of time can continue along the rugged northern coast all the way to the end, we recommend that you angle inland somewhere around **Saint-Brieuc**. *At Saint-Brieuc itself you can catch the N12, leaving the coastline and heading due west.*

How much time you want to spend in the Brittany interior (known in ancient times as the **Argoat**, meaning "wooded country") will determine when you turn off of N12. Whatever you do, you should plan to tour the pretty mountain country between **Morlaix** (*on N12*) and **Pleyben** *about 50 kilometers (30 miles) south of Morlaix on the N164.*

This area is also famous for its **Parish Closes**. A *close* is really a collection of religious structures at the center of which is usually a cemetery.

Surrounding the cemetery are the church itself, an ornamented triumphal arch that symbolizes the entrance into the afterlife, a charnel house (where the bones of the long-dead are stored, thus making room in the cemetery for the more recent dead), and a *calvalry*. The calvalry is usually a granite sculpture with a grouping of crosses emerging from a platform on which dozens of small figures form Biblical scenes.

The calvalries are often the most interesting element of a close. For instance, the calvalry at the famous close in Pleyben was built in the mid-16th century, then reworked in the mid-1700s. It depicts the Last Supper, the washing of the disciples' feet by Christ, the adoration of the shepherds, and other scenes.

Other famous closes in the area just southwest of Morlaix can be found at **Saint-Thégonnec**, **Guimiliau**, and **Lampaul-Guimiliau**. Visits to any of these spots put you in perfect position to explore the **Arrée Mountains**, *which are about 20 kilometers (12 miles) south of Morlaix.*

Though the Breton mountain ranges (both the Arrée and the Noires, a bit further south) are nothing so dramatic as the Alps, they are still quite captivating. The slopes are often gradual, rising to a top elevation of only 1,200 feet, and they have very little in the way of trees. They are blanketed by a rugged green and golden heath reminiscent of some parts of southern England, and needles of granite poke up through the surface, especially along the crests.

And the view (especially from the **Roc Trévezel**, the highest peak of all) reaches out forever, overlooking forbidding bogs, isolated stands of trees, a patchwork of plowed fields, and the odd village here and there.

The **Montaigne Saint-Michel**, *about 8 kilometers (5 miles) south of Trévezel,* is also picturesque with its tiny chapel near the peak. These hills are also popular with hang gliders, in case you're in the mood to take your life into your hands.

THE WESTERN COASTLINE

Heading toward the dramatic **Crozon Peninsula** you will see the **Menez-Hom**, an 1,100-foot high peak, which is actually the western-most peak of the **Noires Mountains**. From atop the peak on a good day, you can see almost to the end of the Crozon Peninsula.

Take the D887 toward Camaret, and be ready to swing off onto tiny sideroads so you can take advantage of spectacular views. The huge, saw-toothed Crozon Peninsula juts wildly 40 kilometers (24 miles) into the sea. It's a natural wonder of precipitous sandstone cliffs and thundering waves.

WHERE TO STAY

LA PLAGE, *29127 Sainte-Anne-La-Palud; 98.92.50.12, Fax 98.92.56.54. Rooms: 26. Double: 550-900FF. Restaurant.*

A fabulous hotel located on a long beach, with a first-rate dining room overlooking the sea. Most rooms look out on the bay, whose waters recede hundreds of yards at low tide.

MANOIR DE MOËLLIEN, *29550 Plonévez-Porzay; 98.92.50.40, Fax 98.92.55.21. Rooms: 10. Double: 320-340FF. Restaurant.*

Located off D107, just south of Plonévez-Porzay. A lovely stone, 17th-century manor and outbuildings in the countryside not far from a sandy beach.

MANOIR DE KERHUEL, *29720 Plonéour-Lanvern; 98.82.60.57, Fax 98.82.61.79. Rooms: 26. Double: 550-600FF. Restaurant.*

Located 10 kilometers (6 miles) southwest of Quimper off D156. A stunning 18th-century manor on 15 acres of wooded property, with a lovely pool, sloping lawns, and 16th-century stone outbuildings.

MANOIR DU STANG, *29940 La Forêt-Fouesnant; 98.56.97.37. Rooms: 26. Double: 590-860FF. Restaurant (residents only, and by reservation only).*

Located 12 kilometers (7 miles) southeast of Quimper off D783. This stately stone 16th-century former residence sits on 100 acres of woods, formal gardens, lakes and fields. It's really quite special and could serve visitors to either the western or southern coasts.

WHERE TO EAT

Many of the best restaurants are located in hotels like those above. In addition, try:

LE CAPUCIN GOURMAND, *29 rue Réguaires, 29000 Quimper; 98.95.43.12.*

A pricey, but (as the name suggests) gourmet restaurant just a block or so east of the magnificent Cathedral in the heart of Quimper.

SEEING THE SIGHTS

The **Pointe de Penhir,** with its stark monument to the **Bretons of Free France,** is the most well-known of the promontories, but the **Cap de la Chévre** and the **Pointe de Dinan** are dramatic as well. Visitors tend to gape in awe, their hair blown back and the occasional mist of a broken wave sweeping up into their faces. There are also a handful of pretty beaches along here, where you can settle in with some sunblock and a sandwich.

You must also be sure to visit the tiny fishing port of **Camaret.** It's worth half a roll of film, with its colorful boats and tiny bayside shops and homes. It has survived as much on tourism in recent years as on its lobster catch. The chapel at the end of the dyke was built in the mid-1600s.

Leaving Camaret, *swing north on the D355 to the Pointe des Espagnols*, from which you can see the bustling modern city of **Brest**. In our opinion, the military and commercial port, beaten up badly during World War II, is best seen from a distance.

Just south of the Crozon Peninsula, *on the Douarnenez Bay*, is a tiny village called **Sainte-Anne-la-Palud**, site of a fabulous hotel called La Plage (noted below), and, more importantly, home to one of the finest *Pardons* in all of Brittany.

On the last Sunday of August, pilgrims in full Breton dress, with the high starched women's hats and richly embroidered dresses and aprons, carry crosses and statues of the Virgin along the shore, and stop at the 19th-century chapel with its granite statue of Sainte-Anne (the patron saint of Brittany) that dates back to 1548.

Other Sights
- **Quimper**, a town of 60,000, *whose city center is located right near the juncture of the Odet and Steir rivers*. The Odet runs right through the heart of the town and right past the Gothic cathedral which was built from the 13th through the 15th centuries (the two intricate ornamented steeples went up in the mid-1800s). The **Musée des Beaux Arts**, very close to the cathedral, is one of the best in Brittany, with a solid gathering of Dutch and Flemish works from the 16th and 17th centuries.
- **Pointe du Raz**, maybe Brittany's most impressive finger of misshapen land stabbing into the sea. *Raz Point is at the western end of the Cornouaille Peninsula west of Quimper*. The rough stone point soars more than 200 feet above the deafening sea, and a lighthouse warns weary sailors to steer clear.

PRACTICAL INFORMATION
- **Brest Office de Tourisme**, *1 place Liberté, 29200 Brest; 98.44.24.96.*
- **Camaret-sur-Mer Syndicat d'Initiative**, *quai Toudouze; 29570 Camaret-sur-Mer; 98.27.93.60.*
- **Quimper Office de Tourisme**, *place de la Résistance, 29000 Quimper; 98.53.04.05.*

THE SOUTHERN COAST

This part of Brittany has the more busy ports than the northern coast, but it is also home to plenty of beaches and boating for holiday travelers. This is where you will also find the famous *menhirs* and *megaliths* – great stones that were set on end and laid out in astrological patterns by primitive cultures.

WHERE TO STAY

PONT-AVEN, *11 quai Théodore-Botrel, 29930 Pont-Aven; 98.06.13.06, Fax 98.06.03.89. Rooms: 15. Double: 300-600FF. Restaurant.*

Right in the heart of the tiny village of Pont-Aven, said to be one of Gaugin's favorite towns, this adorable hotel is partially fashioned out of a 18th-century thatched cottage.

LES MOULINS DU DUC, *29350 Moëlan-sur-Mer; 98.39.60.73, Fax 98.39.75.56. Rooms: 27. Double: 650-1,350FF. Restaurant.*

Located about 12 kilometers (7 miles) southeast of Pont-Aven, outside the little village of Moëlan-sur-Mer (watch closely for signs). Absolutely charming, especially if you can talk your way into one of the independent stone cottages at the far end of the property. The main building is a former 16th-century mill sitting beside a large pond. Fine dining, with a roaring fireplace when it's cold.

LES GRANDES ROCHES, *Route des Grandes-Roches, 29910 Tregunc; 98.97.62.97. Rooms: 22. Double: 280-360FF. Restaurant.*

Located just a few kilometers southeast of Concarneau off D783. Rooms are located in lovely renovated thatched cottages that surround this old farmhouse.

DOMAINE DE ROCHEVILAINE, *Pointe de Pen-Lan, 56190 Billiers; 97.41.61.61, Fax 97.41.44.85. Rooms: 25. Double: 580-950FF.*

Located at the end of D5 going south from the N165 at Muzillac. A magnificent gathering of 15th- and 16th-century stone manors set on the rocks overlooking the sea. The better rooms are wonderfully large and also feature views of the sea and the seaside, salt-water pool. First-class service and cuisine. A new addition with an indoor pool should be finished by 1995.

HÔTEL DU GOLF DE LA BRETESCHE, *44780 Missillac; 40.88.30.05, Fax 40.66.99.47. Rooms: 27. Double: 430-640FF. Restaurant.*

Located 8 kilometers northeast (5 miles) of Pontchâteau off the N165. For golf lovers and gourmets, this hotel is housed in the outbuildings of a 14th-century castle on a lake and golf course.

WHERE TO EAT

LE GALION, *15 rue Saint-Guénolé, 29900 Concarneau; 98.97.30.16.*

A tranquil hideaway with gourmet food on the walled inner city island.

LANN ROZ, *12 avenue Poste, 56340 Carnac; 97.52.10.48.*

Reasonable seafood with a lovely garden.

LE RELAX, *27 boulevard Castero à la plage de Kermorvan, 56170 Quiberon; 97.50.12.84.*

Away from the central port overlooking the Port Haliguen on the northeast side of the town.

SEEING THE SIGHTS

Our tour of this coast begins in the west with **Concarneau**, which seems bigger than its population of 20,000 would suggest. It is said to be the third largest fishing port in all of France, but it's most interesting feature for you is its walled island (**Ville Close**) in the very center of the city. The ramparts that surround the inner village were begun in the 14th century and not finished for another 300 years.

On the last Sunday in August, Concarneau's annual **Fillets Bleus Festival** (**Blue Nets Festival**) showcases the traditional Breton clothing with the high starched lace bonnets and embroidered dresses and jackets. The festival began in 1902, when it was a charity event to help needy fisherman and their families during what was called the sardine crisis.

Another 14 kilometers (8 miles) along the coast on D783 will bring you to the tiny mill town of **Pont-Aven** (the name means Aven bridge, and indeed, the town straddles the gurgling Aven River).

Pont-Aven is a romantic little spot and, over the years, has captured the imagination of many artists, the most famous of which was Gaugin, who settled here for a time in the late 1800s. The town's **Musée de Pont-Aven** routinely displays works from artists who painted local scenes during Gaugin's era.

But *la pièce de la résistance* along this coastline is around **Carnac** and the **Quiberon Peninsula**, *70 kilometers (43 miles) further east.* Here, there are more than 3,000 great stones upended and set in the ground so that they point skyward. Some weigh more than 300 tons, which makes it all the more remarkable that they were arranged by a primitive race that lived here well over 2,000 years before Christ.

The experts say that the patterns predict the paths of the sun and other heavenly orbs – and with great accuracy. Their suggestion is that the early civilization responsible for arranging the stones worshipped the sun or the moon, or both.

Some of the better known menhir patterns can be found just north of Carnac, where the stones form what is called the **Alignements du Ménec** (**Ménec Lines**). Another interesting site is the nearby **Saint-Michel Tumulus**, a mound 400 feet long and 40 feet high housing several ancient burial chambers. The Tumulus is just outside the northeastern corner of the village.

The **J. Miln and Le Rouzic Museum** in Carnac is also worth a peek if you are interested in prehistoric tools, jewelry and other artifacts.

The **Quiberon peninsula**, connected to the mainland by a mere thread of sand, descends 14 kilometers (8 miles) straight into the sea. The peninsula's rugged western coast (the **Côte Sauvage**) is as wild looking as its name suggests.

Quiberon itself is a lovely little fishing port (sardines are the big catch) with a great beach. It is also the point where you can catch the ferry for a quick visit to **Belle-Ile**, which is the largest of the Breton Islands and is very popular.

Nearing the end of our Brittany visit, we come to the **Morbihan Gulf** and yet another kind of watery wonderland. This enormous gulf, *south of the city of Vannes*, is peppered with 30 islands, most of them small wooded mysteries (though some have homes on them). The gulf, 12 miles wide and 9 miles across, was supposedly formed when the interior lands, already eroded by rivers, settled further and further down, finally allowing the sea to creep in over it.

Caesar himself (with the help of Brutus) is said to have overseen the conquest of the tribes who occupied the gulf and the surrounding villages.

A variety of boats tours, some lasting a few hours and others lasting all day, are available from several spots along the gulf.

Other Sights

• **Josselin**, *which is about 50 kilometers (30 miles) inland above Vannes off the N24 highway.* This is a possible stop if you're going back to Rennes to catch a train to Paris. Josselin is just a tiny village tucked in the woods on the **Oust River**, but it has a fabulous **castle** that was begun in the 1300s. The Château's main facade, with three giant turrets, faces the river. Up a lane of half-timbered houses is the **Basilica of Notre-Dame-du-Roncier**, whose origin (at least in legend) dates back to the 9th century, when a peasant found a statuette of the Virgin in some bushes. He took the statuette home, only to discover later that it had magically returned to the spot where he found it. That spot is where the church now stands.

PRACTICAL INFORMATION

• **Concarneau Office de Tourisme**, *quai d'Aiguillon, 29900 Concarneau; 98.97.01.44.*
• **Carnac Office de Tourisme**, *avenue Druides, 56340 Carnac; 97.52.13.52.*
• **Quiberon Office de Tourisme**, *7 rue Verdun, 56170 Quiberon; 97.50.07.84.*

NANTES

Glancing at a map, **Nantes**, a large city of more than 260,000, would appear to be part of the Loire Valley. True enough, the Loire feeds right through the southern section of the city before it reaches the sea. However, Nantes was historically part of the Breton land and, in fact, was its capital for some time.

Nantes was also considered the greatest, most powerful and prosperous of all French ports in the close of the 18th century. Sad to say, but the slave trade accounted for a great deal of that prosperity.

During the Revolution, Nantes was site to some of the most infamous sort of "justice." A representative of the Revolutionary Council ordered that thousands of people thought to be loyal to the crown be executed by loading them onto barges and sinking the barges in the Loire.

The **Edict of Nantes** was signed here by Henri IV in 1598 in hopes that it would ease the vicious hostilities between Protestants and Catholics (it didn't, of course). And among the French champions born here are Anne of Brittany (who, by chance, was twice crowned Queen of France – first to Charles VIII in 1491, then to Louis XII in 1499) and Jules Verne, whose imaginative works are internationally famous.

WHERE TO STAY

ABBAYE DE LA VILLENEUVE, *Route des Sable-d'Olonne, 44840 Les Soriniéres; 40.04.40.25, Fax 40.31.28.45. Rooms: 20. Double: 515-890FF. Restaurant.*

Just south of Nantes off N137. A stately hotel that was an 18th-century abbey, with stone fireplaces in the lounge and timbered ceilings in the bedrooms.

CHÂTEAU DE LA COLAISSIÉRE, *49270 Saint-Sauveur-de-Landemont; 40.98.75.04, Fax 40.98.74.15. Rooms: 13. Double: 800-1,700FF. Restaurant.*

Located 25 kilometers (15 miles) east of Nantes. Take the N23, turning south at Oudon and crossing the Loire River into Champtoceaux. Drive out the southern end of the village on D153 toward Saint-Sauveur-de-Landemont. Yes, it's kind of in the middle of nowhere, but it's quite elegant. Once owned by the Dukes of Brittany and Anjou, the building's two main wings date back to the 1200s and the 1500s and are decorated in antiques. Riding and boating available.

HÔTEL DE LA GARE, *place Gare, 44190 Clisson; 40.36.16.55. Rooms: 36. Double: 110-290FF. Restaurant.*

Absolutely plain, but the staff is very pleasant and everything is clean and neat. (Besides, for once, you can save a few francs.)

WHERE TO EAT

AUBERGE DU CHÂTEAU, *5 place Duchesse Anne, 44000 Nantes; 40.74.05.51.*

Call ahead for a table at this reasonably priced restaurant facing the Château des Ducs.

TORIGAÏ, *Ile de Versailles, 44000 Nantes; 40.37.06.37.*

On a tiny island in the Erdre River just a wee bit north in the city from the cathedral. With a view and outdoor dining.

L'ESQUINADE, *7 rue Saint-Denis, 44000 Nantes; 40.48.17.22.*
Just a block west of the cathedral.
BONNE AUBERGE, *1 rue O. de Clisson, 44190 Clisson; 40.54.01.90, Fax 40.54.08.48.*
Contemporary surroundings, but classic French cuisine with lots of fish, as well as lamb and pigeon.

SEEING THE SIGHTS

Obviously then, Nantes is an historic stop. The inner old quarter is also quite charming. Dump your car and walk through the narrow lanes, browsing at shops and stopping for cider and crêpes.

After lunch, stroll around the **Château des Ducs**, built at the order of Duc François II in 1460 to replace an older castle that had occupied the site. Anne of Brittany, his daughter, saw to it that the castle, with its broad moat and impregnable walls, was completed. Today, the fortified walls are surrounded by a tranquil park.

Turn north up the hill (*rue Henri IV and the Cours Saint-Pierre*) until you reach the magnificent **Cathédrale Saint-Pierre** on your left. Its splendid western facade, built in the 15th century, features impressive and highly detailed portals. Inside is the tomb of Duc François II.

Other Sights

• **Musée des Beaux Arts**, *Quartier Jardin des Plantes, 10 rue Georges Clemenceau; 40.41.65.65.*
• **Musée Jules Verne**, *3 rue de l'Hermitage; 40.69.72.52.* A history of Verne (1828-1905) who brought you *Journey to the Center of the Earth* and *Around the World in 80 Days.*
• **Clisson**, *a tiny village about 35 kilometers (21 miles) southeast of Nantes along N149.* It's absolutely charming, with the ruins of an impressive 13th-century castle where Duc François II spent a great deal of time. Unfortunately much of the castle was destroyed by Kléber during the Revolution. Still, the village and castle overlooking the **Sévre Nantaise River** is a delight and there is gourmet food to be eaten (see *Where to Eat*).

PRACTICAL INFORMATION

• **Nantes Office de Tourisme**, *place Commerce, 44000 Nantes; 40.47.04.51.*
• **Clisson Office de Tourisme**, *6 place Trinité, 44190 Clisson; 40.54.02.95.*

23. LOIRE VALLEY

INTRODUCTION

Not even Cinderella – for that matter, not even Michael Jackson – could imagine a more picturesque fairyland than the **Loire Valley**, with its mighty river, fertile plains, dense forests and, most importantly, elegant castles surrounded by protective moats and meticulously sculpted gardens.

The Loire Valley, known both as the Garden of France and the Valley of Kings, is hugely popular with tourists and the French alike. Parisians, who never met a holiday they didn't like, take full advantage of innumerable long weekends during the spring and fall to race down to play in the Loire Valley less than 150 kilometers (90 miles) south.

They gawk at the river, explore new châteaux, and indulge their favorite pastimes of eating cholesterol-rich meals and sampling as many regional wines as they can, while leaving enough active brain cells to guide them to their rooms. (And still, Parisians complain incessantly, moaning *La vie parisienne, c'est très stressée*, which means, "Parisian life is very stressful." Yeah, right.)

The French love affair with its own Loire Valley goes back long before France was really France. The **Loire River** is the longest in all of France, beginning just west of **Lyon** and threading its way north toward **Orleans** before detouring west through **Tours**, past **Anger** and **Nantes**, and into the Atlantic Ocean. In all, it covers more than 950 kilometers (600 miles).

It's no surprise, then, that it was the major trade route ferrying goods west to east and south to north. And given the fertile fields, the rich variety of tasty table wines, and woods chock-full of game, it's also no wonder that the Loire Valley became a playground for the vastly rich lords and ladies who dominated the nation from the 15th century right up to the revolution of 1789.

During that period as many as 1,000 châteaux were constructed (counts vary), some of them fortresses to protect duchies, but most of them sheer pleasure palaces. The more famous are located in the subregion known as the **Tourain**, which stretches about 160 kilometers

(100 miles) along the southern banks of the river from Orléans west to Tours and Saumur.

ARRIVALS & DEPARTURES

The principle highways connecting the endpoints are the A10 autoroute, the major N152 highway, and the much smaller route D951. We recommend that you steer clear of the A10 and the N152 and stay on the south side of the river, where you will frequently detour off the D951 to admire the châteaux.

This means, of course, that you must have a car. Yes, there are Paris-based bus tours that visit the Loire Valley, but the region is enormous and the landscape and villages that are tucked away in the rolling hills will forever remain a mystery unless you leave the principle highways behind and cruise the small roads that criss-cross the countryside.

FOOD & WINE

Besides, seeing the châteaux is only one *raison d'être* for this excursion. A visit to the Loire Valley is yet another excuse to pamper yourself. Dozens of smaller castles have been converted by cash-hungry former royal families into stunning, yet still affordable, hotels.

And the Loire is yet another French home to *haute cuisine* — though there are a couple of regional standards that make our stomachs go bumpety-bump. One is *andouillette*, a sausage filled with pig's small intestines, and *rillette*, a stringy potted pork concoction that we have a hard time getting down.

Fortunately, there is a lot of fine food to sample, including goat cheeses (*chèvres*), rabbit, veal stews, pork and prune *fricassée* (better than it might sound), and shellfish of all kinds (especially at the western end of the Loire). Dishes at finer hotels should measure up almost to Paris standards.

Another reason for visiting the Loire: It is one of France's most productive winemakers. Most of the wines have neither the endurance nor the body nor the cachet of the bolder wines of Bordeaux, Burgundy, and the Côte du Rhône, but they are well worth a try.

The *Muscadets* from around Nantes, the *Savennières* from the Angers area, the *Vouvrays* from Touraine, and the *Sancerres* from the east end of the Loire are all fine white wines that are perfectly suited to the local cuisine. For reds, the *Chinon* and *Bourgueil* from the Touraine are generally best.

In fact, no trip to the Loire would be complete without a visit or two to one of the countless regional cellars where you can wet your whistle and lighten your pocketbook.

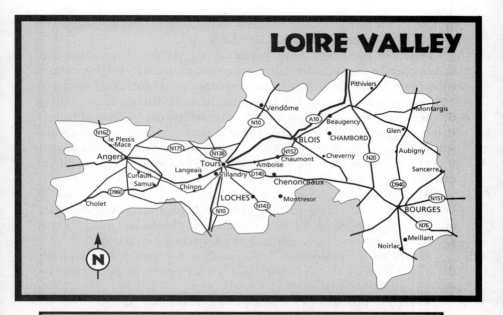

FINDS & FAVORITES

- *Chenonceau (see Châteaux)*
- *Cheverny (see Châteaux)*
- *Chinon (see Châteaux)*
- *Domaine de la Tortinière (see Châteaux/Where to Stay)*
- *Château des Reaux (see Châteaux/Where to Stay)*

THE CHÂTEAUX

The **châteaux** that dot the Loire Valley fall into two categories. One, the early medieval fortresses behind whose turrets and ramparts regional dukes ruled their lands, and, two, the elegant residences that sprang up after the English were finally driven from the area in the late 1400s at the culmination of the Hundred Years War.

What had once been military encampments gave way to Renaissance residences neatly turned out with ornamented dormer windows, detailed balustrades, and liberal use of exterior and interior moldings.

Part of the architectural shift can be credited to François I, who ruled from 1515 to 1547. He was completely charmed by the Italian Renaissance, so much so that he brought Leonardo and other Italian masters to France to help design and expand several châteaux.

The heavily ornamented Renaissance style preferred by François later gave way to a Classical period. During the 17th and 18th centuries, architects strove for a stately, almost stuffy air achieved through rigid symmetry and a taste for cornices and columns.

Probably the single best demonstration of the three dominant architectural periods can be found in the château at Blois, which has three wings, one each from the medieval, Renaissance, and classical eras.

During your visits, you will find some châteaux virtually empty, others that serve largely as museums for tapestries and paintings, and still others that are decorated as furnished homes in period pieces. Still others are still at least partially occupied by the owning family. Tourists are charged for the privilege of roaming the bottom floors or a wing so that the family can better afford its tax bill.

All châteaux charge an admission fee, though the price ranges wildly because some are state-owned and others are held privately. Guided tours are offered at most of the larger châteaux, though we find it more satisfying to grab the literature and wander around on our own.

Many châteaux close down or drastically reduce visiting hours during the winter months, so call ahead if you're touring the area off-season or during national holidays.

There are dozens of châteaux to visit, and it would take an equal number of trips to see them all. So we concentrate here on the major châteaux stretching west of Orleans to Saumur. We have ordered them here geographically moving from east to west.

WHERE TO STAY/WHERE TO EAT

Why even consider a stuffy hotel in a city when there are converted manors and castles seeded throughout the countryside, many of which have superb dining to complement their elegant settings and wealth of creature comforts. In fact, all of the châteaux we mention below are first-rate and almost all offer gourmet dining.

Like the castles listed in the following section, we have ordered these converted châteaux geographically, starting with those closest to Orléans and moving west toward Angers.

MANOIR DE CLENORD, *Route de Clenord, 41250 Mont-pres-Chambord; 54.70.41.62, Fax 54.70.33.99. Rooms: 4. Double: 700-900FF. Restaurant. Located 8 kilometers (5 miles) southeast of Blois on route D765.*

Remote and not as grand as some, still this 18th-century manor house is quite striking and intimate. Pool, tennis, horseriding, canoeing, walks through the nearby woods, and, of course, dining.

RELAIS DES LANDES, *Ouchamps, 41120 Les Montils; 54.44.03.33, Fax 54.44.03.89. Rooms: 28. Double: 495-725FF. Restaurant. Located 15 kilometers (9 miles) south of Blois off D7.*

This large 17th-century manor house, with two main buildings and a couple of smaller wings, sits on a 25-acre park. Just step right into the woods or hire a bicycle. The Landes touts its gourmet cuisine.

CHÂTEAU DE CHISSAY, *Route de Pierrefitte-sur-Sauldre, 41400 Chissy-en-Touraine; 54.32.32.01, Fax 54.32.43.80. Rooms: 31. Double: 550-1,500FF. Restaurant. Located 40 kilometers (25 miles) east of Tours off D76.*

The look and feel of a real castle, the Château de Chissay has, in fact, hosted a couple of kings as well as de Gaulle himself. Rooms in the striking turrets are especially nice, the dining is excellent, and the grounds offer a pool and lovely walks through the gardens and adjacent woods.

HÔTEL DU BON LABOUREUR ET DU CHÂTEAU, *6 rue du Dr. Bretonneau; 47.23.90.02, Fax 47.23.82.01. Rooms: 36. Double: 280-600FF. Restaurant. Located 35 kilometers (22 miles) east of Tours off D40, very near Chenonceau castle.*

Okay, this isn't a manor house or a castle, but it is a wonderful hotel with extremely good dining and is only a short stroll from the magnificent Chenonceau château. The hotel has three very cozy sitting rooms where you can daydream or enjoy a cocktail before dinner.

CHÂTEAU DE PRAY, *RD751, B.P. 146, 37400 Amboise Cedex; 47.57.23.67, Fax 47.57.32.50. Rooms: 17. Double: 550-870FF. Restaurant. Located 25 kilometers (15 miles) east of Tours off D751.*

This handsome manor house complete with turrets dates back to the 1200s, when it was a fortress. Today, with its white-shuttered windows, it appears anything but threatening. The owner boasts about his own cooking, which includes dishes such as lobster cannelloni and hare fixed the way the kings liked it.

CHÂTEAU DE LA BOURDAISIÈRE, *25 rue de la Bourdaisière, 37270 Montlouis-sur-Loire; 47.45.16.31, Fax 47.45.09.11. Rooms: 7. Double: 450-950FF. No restaurant. Located 11 kilometers (6 miles) east of Tours off N152.*

Incredible castle whose origins date back to the 14th century and which was presented as a gift from king François I to his mistress, Marie Gaudin. The large rooms, all of which are named after famous French women, are richly decorated in period furnishings. The extensive grounds include various formal gardens and an arboretum. Also, there is a pool, tennis, and riding.

DOMAINE DE LA TORTINIÈRE, *Les Gués de Veigné, 37250 Montbazon; 47.26.00.19, Fax 47.65.95.70. Rooms: 21. Double: 455-1,160FF. Restaurant. Located 15 kilometers (9 miles) due south of Tours just off N10.*

An absolutely superb Second Empire manor house on 30 acres overlooking the Indre River and various villages below. Incredible dining (lobster ravioli, for instance), a very good wine list, and a pool set in the grassy slopes beneath the white turreted château.

CHÂTEAU DES RÉAUX, *le Port-Boulet, 37140 Bourgueil; 47.95.14.40, Fax 47.95.18.34. Rooms: 17. Double: 450-950FF. Restaurant. Located just on the edge of Bourgueil north across the river from Chinon.*

This 15th-century historic monument is an absolute jewel, with its checkerboard-tiled turrets and the wonderfully warm reception. Dine with other guests at long tables (group dining like this is called "table d'hote," meaning table of the host), then sip after-dinner cordials with the very elegant and genial Madame Goupil de Bouillé.

CHÂTEAU DE NOIRIEUX, *26 route du Moulin, 49125 Briollay; 41.42.50.05, Fax 41.37.91.00. Rooms: 19. Double: 550-1,160FF. Restaurant. Located a few kilometers northeast of Angers.*

A stunning property with château, a 16th-century chapel dedicated to Saint-Joseph, a conservatory, and a 15th-century manor house. Rooms decorated in Louis XIII, Louis XV, Regency, and Art Deco styles. A pool, jacuzzi, tennis court, and excellent dining.

CHAMBORD

Chambord is the largest and most architecturally monumental of all the châteaux in the valley. Though built as a hunting lodge by François I in the early 1500s, it is immense and became a favorite playground for several kings up until the Revolution.

To give you a sense of its size: the Cosson River was diverted to form the broad moat, the estate occupies more than 13,000 acres (most of it blanketed with heavy forests), and the château itself boasts 440 rooms and 365 chimneys. You'll have a tough time backing up far enough to get the entire 420-foot facade into the viewfinder of your camera.

François I was said to have brought parties so large that 12,000 horses were needed to ferry his guests around. Molière staged two productions here, including *Le Bourgeois Gentilhomme*, for Louis XIV's court. The Marechal de Saxe, who was presented the castle by Louis XV in thanks for the marshal's victories, kept two full regiments of calvalry at the château and regularly staged massive military exercises.

From the front, you will immediately see the masterful symmetry of the castle, the design of which some historians credit to Leonardo, who was brought to France in 1516 by François I. At either end are massive corner towers. In the center, you'll see even broader towers that shape the facade of the central keep and above which you will see the riot of dormers and chimneys.

The château is actually a huge rectangle entered from the rear. Once through the gates, you step into a courtyard and see ahead of you the central keep.

The two most famous features of the château are the central staircase of the keep and the rooftop terrace. The stone staircase is actually two spirals that twist around one another never meeting as they rise. From the terrace you can get a closer look at the forest of chimneys, spires, turrets, and capitals.

Located 18 kilometers (11 miles) east of Blois off of D33 or D122. Off-season: Open daily from 9:30 a.m. to 4:45 p.m., with breaks for lunch from noon to 2 p.m. During summer months: Open daily from 9:30 a.m. through 5:45 p.m. with no breaks. Admission: 31FF. Information: Château de Chambord, 41250 Loir-et-Cher; 54.50.40.18, Fax 54.20.34.69.

CHEVERNY

This elegant classical castle has remained in the Hurault family since its doors were opened in 1634. That's pretty impressive staying power. (The family is able to occupy some quarters here thanks to you and other tourists who pay to browse through their lovely home.)

The architect, Boyer de Blois, who also directed the building of Blois and Chambord, chose to construct this impressive estate of Bourre stone, a local stone which grows harder and whiter as it ages. You'll recognize the stone in several châteaux in the valley.

Inside Cheverny are lots of treats. The dining room is decorated with leather wallcovering and 34 painted panels from the 1600s depicting Don Quixote's adventures. The chandelier, dating from the end of the 18th century, is said to weigh more than 200 pounds.

On the first landing of the Louis XIII style staircase are antlers dating back thousands of years. The guard room, the largest room in the house, contains an interesting collection of 15th- and 16th-century weaponry and armor.

The coffered ceiling of the king's bedroom was painted by Jean Mosnier, the decorator of Chambord. Striking tapestries from the early 1600s depict the tale of Ulysses. You'll get a good sense of the Hurault family history through the portraits hung in the large drawing room and the gallery.

Outside, be sure to stroll down to the kennels, where you'll see dozens of handsome hounds ready to bound off after the nearest fox. We found the trophy room, which is celebrated for its wall to wall antlers, a bit grizzly. Nearly 2,000 stags gave their lives to the decor. It's not exactly a House & Garden kind of look.

Located about 15 kilometers (9 miles) southeast of Blois off of D765. Off-season: Open daily from 9:30 a.m. to 5 p.m., with a two-hour midday lunch break. During summer months: Open daily from 9:15 a.m. to 6:45 p.m. Admission: 30FF. Information: Château de Cheverny, 41700 Loir-et-Cher; 54.79.96.29, Fax 54.79.25.38.

BLOIS

The majestic château at **Blois** is a masterful blend of different châteaux arranged in a sort of collapsed 'U.'

The enormous castle was begun in earnest in the early 13th century by various Counts of Blois. All that remains of the original medieval structure are the towers and stairways of the **Foix Tower** and the **Chamber of the States General**.

Louis XII, who had been the Count of Blois, came along at the very end of the 1400s, building an ornate Renaissance-style wing with spire-adorned dormers, generous windows, and patterned exterior walls. In 1508, he ordered a chapel to be built at the opening of the 'U'-shaped courtyard. This would become his palace and the seat of government during his relatively brief reign.

Only 15 years later, François I, who seems to have touched every significant châteaux in the land, built another new wing, this one even more heavily ornamented in design and featuring galleries overlooking the town below and, on the courtyard side, a magnificent octagonal stone staircase (heavily decorated with images of salamanders, François I's royal symbol).

It was in the François I wing that Henri, Duc de Guise, was murdered as part of a plot organized by Henri III in 1588. The Duc had become head of the Catholic League during the Wars of Religion pitting Catholic against Protestant. In retaliation for the killing, a fanatical monk assassinated Henri III the following year.

The last wing was added by Gaston d'Orléans in the 1630s. Designed by François Mansart, probably the most famous French architect in history, the new wing is a study in classicism, employing balance, restraint, elegant lines, and columns to make its forceful statement.

Located 50 kilometers (30 miles) southwest of Orléans on the Loire River by way of A10, N152 or D951. Off-season: Open daily except for Christmas from 9 a.m. to 4:45 p.m., with a two-hour lunch break. During summer months: Open daily from 9 a.m. to 5:45 p.m. Admission: 30FF. Information: Château de Blois, 41000 Loir-et-Cher; 54.78.06.62, Fax 54.56.08.59.

CHENONCEAU

Chenonceau is one of the most famous châteaux, largely thanks to Catherine de Medicis, whose idea it was in the mid-1500s to add a two-story wing off of the main building onto a bridge that crosses the **Cher River** in five graceful arches. She also expanded the stunning symmetrical gardens just to the west. She may have played hardball in the political arena, but she also had an eye for grace and beauty.

Catherine de Medicis, Diane de Poitiers (who was given the château by Henri II), and four other women played such an important role in the development of the castle and its cultural status that Chenonceau is also known as *The Château of Six Women.*

CHENONCEAU

The château, begun in 1513 by a local farmer whose fortune shrank to nothing in his efforts to erect a grand castle in his own honor, is just off the quiet village of the same name up a lengthy dirt avenue through a small forest (though the village, with an 'x' at the end, is spelled slightly differently).

There is plenty to see inside the château. Beginning in the guard room, you will find some beautiful 16th-century Flemish tapestries depicting life at the château. Similar tapestries can also be found in Diane de Poitier's room.

The 65-yard-long gallery spanning the river gives you an ideal view of the Cher coursing below. During World War I, this gallery was sometimes used as a hospital, and in World War II, it is said that though the entrance to the castle lay in a military zone occupied by the Germans, the south door to the gallery was located in a free zone.

The **Vendôme** room and the **bedroom of Catherine de Medicis** are both regally decorated in reds and gold, and are a tribute to the restoration work that has been undertaken over the years at Chenonceau.

Probably the most interesting stop in your tour will be **Louis de Lorraine's bed chamber**. After her husband, Henri III, was assassinated by a monk during the wars between the Catholics and Protestants, she retired to Chenonceau where, dressed in the white of royal mourners, she prayed virtually from dawn to dusk. The dark colors and the symbols of death decorating the ceiling are quite eerie.

Located about 35 kilometers (22 miles) east of Tours off D176 or N76. Off-season: Open daily from 9 a.m. to 4:30 p.m. During summer months: Open daily from 9 a.m. to 7 p.m. Admission: 40FF. Information: Syndicat d'Initiative, rue Château, 37150 Chenonceaux; 47.23.90.07, Fax 47.23.80.88.

VILLANDRY

Villandry, built in 1536 and considered the last of the great Renaissance châteaux constructed along the Loire, is unusual in that it is far better known for its gardens than for the castle itself.

In fact, the interior of the château, which was built by Jean Breton, a secretary of state to François I, has been completely redone by its true savior, Dr. Joachim Carvallo, a Spaniard who purchased the estate in 1906 just as others were mulling over the idea of tearing it down. True to his personal tastes, many of the current interior decorations are more Spanish than French, including a painted and gilded ceiling brought from Toledo in Spain.

But again, the gardens are what draw the crowds here. Carvallo deserves credit for that as well. Though no renderings of the original gardens survived, he ordered the garden redone in a manner consistent with era during which the château was built.

What you see today is probably the perfect example of a French formal garden, which couldn't be more at odds with the British notion of letting nature take its shaggy course. Here, every twig and bloom is strictly disciplined in tight geometric patterns, with each of the many squares in this puzzle dedicated to nature featuring a different design.

Walk to the uppermost level and gaze down for the best perspective. And don't forget your camera.

Located about 15 kilometers (9 miles) due west of Tours on D7. Off-season: The castle, closed from Nov. 12 through Feb. 14, is open daily from 9 a.m. to 5 p.m., and the gardens are open daily from 9 a.m. to 6 p.m. During summer months: The castle is open daily from 9 a.m. to 6 p.m., and the gardens are open daily from 8:30 a.m. to 8 p.m. Admission: 40FF to the castle, 26FF to the gardens. Information: Château de Villandry, 37510 Villandry; 47.50.02.09, Fax 47.50.12.85.

AZAY-LE-RIDEAU

Considered by many (though not us) to be the closest thing to a perfect château, **Azay-le-Rideau** is another hugely costly bauble serving no purpose when it was finished in 1529 other than to serve as the party house of a royal economist under François I.

Unfortunately for the financier, Gilles Berthelot, politics and scandal drove him from the country shortly after the château was finished (though some accounts say he was executed). In either case, François I took possession of the property, then presented it as a gift to his Captain of the Guard. (You will note that above the entrance is a salamander, symbol of François I.)

The château is set down a tree-lined avenue on what is essentially an island in the Indre river, which itself has been trained to circle the château as a natural moat. The reflection in the water adds a bit of splendor to an already striking château with delicate spire-topped corner towers and ornamented dormers. The feminine grace and fine hand are credited to Berthelot's wife, Philippe Lesbahy, who oversaw construction.

The interior of the L-shaped castle is sparsely furnished and less interesting than other châteaux along the route. Still, if you have a chance, steal a peek at the grand stone staircase and the huge ceiling beams of the Grande Salle.

Located 28 kilometers (17 miles) southwest of Tours on D751. Off-season: Open daily from 9:30 a.m. to 5 p.m., with a two-hour lunch break. During summer months: Open daily from 9 a.m. to 6:30 p.m. Admission: 31FF. Information: Château d'Azay-le-Rideau, 37190 Indre-et-Loire; 47.45.42.04, Fax 47.45.26.61.

CHINON

Get out those cameras again because **Chinon** is a picture waiting to happen.

Before climbing around the ruins atop the hill overlooking the village of Chinon below, drive down to the riverfront and cross the bridge so you can look back and get the whole view. We stood for twenty minutes with our mouths open and our shutters snapping.

Your mission at Chinon is two-pronged. You'll want to spend time in the village and touring the ruins. The village is a web of tiny streets lined with shops, bistros, 16th-century mansions with corner turrets, and history. Richard the Lion-Hearted died here in 1199. Rabelais was born nearby in 1494.

The hamlet's most important event took place in 1429 when a young woman named Jeanne d'Arc rode into town looking for the Dauphin, who would become Charles VII when the French finally booted the English from this territory during the Hundred Years War. She came to say she'd had a vision and that God instructed her to battle the British. Charles VII, who later made the castle at Chinon the seat of his reign, was convinced and Joan was equipped with troops.

The castle is truly a fortress, the first walls having gone up in the latter half of the 10th century. It was expanded during the reign of Henri II, who ruled England and most of France. Historians also report that he died here in 1189.

Unfortunately, the castle, which consists of parts of three intersecting châteaux, was largely abandoned in the 1500s. Parts of it, in fact, were dismantled so that the stone could be used to build another château at Richelieu more than 20 kilometers (12 miles) away.

THE LOVELY VILLAGE OF CHINON

Little is left but ramparts, a few towers, and a chunk of the royal lodgings. Still, it's well worth a tour and the views of the village and river below are inspiring.

Located 46 kilometers (28 miles) southwest of Tours on D751 right on the Vienne River. Off-season: Open daily from 9 a.m. to 5 p.m., with a two-hour lunch break. During summer months: Open daily from 9 a.m. to 7 p.m. Admission: 23FF. Information: Château de Chinon, 37500 Indre-et-Loire; 47.93.13.45.

Other Sights

• **Le Château de Valenáay**, *58 kilometers (36 miles) south of Blois on D956.* Begun in the first half of the 16th century, it took another couple of centuries to complete. Noted for its handsome domed towers and its Musée de l'Automobile, with more than 80 antique cars.

• **Le Château de Chaumont-sur-Loire**, *18 kilometers (11 miles) southwest of Blois on D751 right on the river.* This 15th-century château occupies a pretty park on a hill overlooking the river and the valley below. Once more of a fortress than a home, it was restored and refitted with central heating in recent times. Best known as the château that Catherine de Medicis gave Diane de Poitiers after forcing her to leave Chenonceau.

• **Amboise**, *25 kilometers (15 miles) east of Tours on D751 on the Loire.* The château is a shadow of its former self. In 1492, at the order of Charles VIII, who had been born in Amboise, work began on what was conceived of as a magnificent royal residence. After a military victory over Italy, Charles brought back several Italian artists and architects to further glorify his new home. Unfortunately, he was felled passing through a low doorway and died (what a way to go). Much of the glory brought to Amboise by Charles and then François I was dismantled over time by war and bad judgments shown by the owners. Still worth a visit.

PRACTICAL INFORMATION

• For a copy of *Château Accueil*, a guide to château hotels around France, write *Holding Presse International, 68bis boulevard Pereire, 75017 Paris; 42.74.19.60, Fax 42.74.51.15. Or contact the French Tourist Office, 8 avenue de l'Opéra, 75001 Paris; 1.42.96.10.23.*
• **Comité Regional de Tourisme**, *10 rue du Colombier, 45023 Orléans Cedex.* For written requests of château hours, etc.
• **Blois Office du Tourisme**, *Pavillon Anne-de-Bretagne, 3 avenue Jean-Laigret, 41000 Blois; 54.74.06.49.*
• **Tours Office du Tourisme**, *boulevard Heurteloup, 37000 Tours; 47.05.58.08.*
• **Chinon Office du Tourisme**, *12 rue Voltaire, 37500 Chinon; 47.93.17.85.*

ORLÉANS & TOURS

Frankly, neither city does much for us, but we mention them because they've played key roles in the region's history and development. In fact, no sooner we were in them that we wanted out and, with traffic and misleading traffic signs, escape was no easy task.

Orléans was creamed during World War II. No two ways about it. There's not much left to see. However, the city of 106,000 does boast an impressive history.

Orléans was once the capital of France. Long, long ago, in 996, Robert the Pious, king of France, was crowned in the cathedral at Orléans.

A geographical turning point in the Loire River, Orléans also marks a political turning point for the nation. Jeanne d'Arc was said to have liberated Orléans in 1429, stealing away a key holding of the English forces that then controled a great deal of France.

The victory was said to have turned the tide against the British in the seemingly endless Hundred Years War that actually endured from 1337 to 1475. You'll find that the residents of Orléans cling to this great triumph, naming streets, squares and just about everything else in honor of Jeanne d'Arc.

Tours, a city of 130,000 *which straddles the Loire and Cher Rivers about 75 miles west of Orléans*, is far more interesting than Orléans, even though it too took its lumps during the Allied bombings of World War II. Though few question the Allied tactics, it's often sad to see the level of destruction that was necessary to drive the well-entrenched German army out of the French countryside.

WHERE TO STAY

Find yourself a converted château in the countryside. (See *Where to Stay* in the Châteaux section.)

WHERE TO EAT

Again, a lot of the good food in the Loire Valley is what's served at the converted châteaux. (See *Where to Stay* in the Châteaux section.)

LES ANTIQUAIRES, *2 rue au Lin, 45000 Orléans; 38.53.52.35.*

Just off the river near the center of town with gourmet food at digestible prices.

L'HERMITAGE, *9 rue Sept Dormants, 45000 Orléans; 38.62.15.61.*

Right in the heart of the old part of the city.

LA RÔTISSERIE TOURANGELLE, *23 rue Commerce, 37000 Tours; 47.05.71.21.*

Near the Saint-Martin ruins, with outdoor service.

LA ROCHE LE ROY, *55 route Saint-Avertin, 37000 Tours; 47.27.22.00.*

Just off the A10, just below the Cher River in a park with outdoor service.

Tours

Your first test is to follow the **Centre Ville** signs and find your way to the central part of the city's oldest quarter near the ruins of the 13th-century Basilica of Saint-Martin. The core of the old town area, which was restored over the past decade, is off limits to cars, so find one of the car parks as quickly as you can and tour the city core on foot.

At the center of the Touraine region (as is obvious by the name), Tours established itself as a market town for crops and wines going back even before the Romans took charge. Though it has had its ups and down, having been targeted by various tyrants over the centuries, Tours is still recognized as a bustling business center and university town. (Thanks in part to the university, whose origins reach back to medieval days, the city offers a reasonable selection of cultural events, fairs, and nightclubs).

Sights include ruins of the first **Basilica of Saint-Martin**, named after a native Hungarian who was sent on military duty to the Loire region, and who performed various miracles, and was subsequently named the city's first bishop in 372. Little is left today of the basilica other than the clock tower and the **Tour Charlemagne** with its 11th-century frescoes.

Overlapping the floor plan of the original basilica stands a new church, which was completed in 1924. The shrine of Saint-Martin, in the crypt of the new basilica, occupies the exact place it did in the original building.

Also visit the colorful **Place Plumereau**, with its 15th-century timbered buildings, and, a few blocks east, the **Saint-Gatien Cathedral**, which was begun in the 13th century but took well over 200 years to complete. The recently restored Gothic facade is brilliant with delicate detailing, and the dazzling stained glass windows date back to the 13th to 15th centuries.

PRACTICAL INFORMATION

• **Orléans Office du Tourisme**, *place Albert 1er, 45000 Orléans; 38.53.05.95.*
• **Tours Office du Tourisme**, *boulevard Heurteloup, 37000 Tours; 47.05.58.08.*

WINETASTINGS

It's true that most Loire Valley wines are simple and are meant to be drunk quite young. Still, there is an immense variety and many of the wines are quite good. Besides, it's always fun to do a tasting at one of the cellars, where you can relax, compare and often buy at reasonable prices. Call before hand because hours vary wildly. Watch for road signs leading you to the cellars ("caves").

• La Cave Touristique de la Dive Bouteille, 37140 Bourgueil; 47.97.72.01. Wines from the Bourgueil area, most of which are reds from the Cabernet Franc grape.

• Cave Coopérative des Producteurs des Grands Vins de Vouvray, 38 La Vallée Coquette, 37210 Vouvray; 47.52.75.03. Represents a few dozen growers. Vouvrays are whites made from the Chenin Blanc grape.

• Cave Touristique du Montlouis, place Abraham Courtemanche, 37270 Montlouis; 47.50.82.26. Opposite the Loire from Vouvray, representing another group of whites made from the Chenin Blanc.

• Couly-Dutheil Père et Fils, 12 rue Diderot, 37500 Chinon; 47.93.05.84. Red wines from the Chinon area made mostly from the Cabernet Franc grape.

• Musée des Vins de Touraine, Celliers Saint-Julien, 16 rue Nationale, 37000 Tours; 47.61.07.93. A wine museum describing the winemaking process and wine's role in history.

24. ALSACE

INTRODUCTION

We had just pulled over to snap a picture of the stone gateway to the tiny wine village of Wangen when Eugene Kratz lurched out of the brush and onto the narrow road atop a tractor even more weathered than his tattered cap.

Spying our camera, Kratz knew he had a couple of live ones. He dismounted from his perch, took us in tow to his property across the road, and swept his arm toward the vineyards blanketing the nearby hills. Wine is the very soul of Alsace, he declared, adding with a wink and a broad smile, "And I made some of the very best."

Kratz, 82, shuffled into his house, retrieving a half dozen brightly colored labels for Riesling, Tokay, Gerwurztraminer, and other wines bottled under his name before he retired from winemaking in 1985.

"The men tend to prefer the Tokay or Riesling, which have a finer, more subtle taste," said the native Alsatian, who began tending vines in the late 1920s. "The women like the Gerwurztraminer, which has a strong, beautiful bouquet."

But rest assured, he said in his heavy Germanic-accented French, there is a wine for every taste – except, Kratz added, scrunching up his nose, "young people today choose the Coca Cola."

Alsace has produced fine white wines for centuries – which is no easy feat, considering that, like so many French regions, the countryside here has been periodically threatened with annihilation by some world-class tyrants.

Julius Caesar's crowd was the first to subjugate the tribal farmers who occupied this narrow valley, which is 190 kilometers (120 miles) long and a bit more than 45 kilometers (30 miles) wide. No doubt the Romans were smitten with the fertile plains and foothills, the dazzling waters of the Rhine River along Alsace's eastern flank, and the sandstone and granite peaks of the Vosges Mountains bordering the region to the west.

After an era of relative peace under the Roman watch, Alsace became victim to a continental, centuries-long tug of war. No less than Attila the

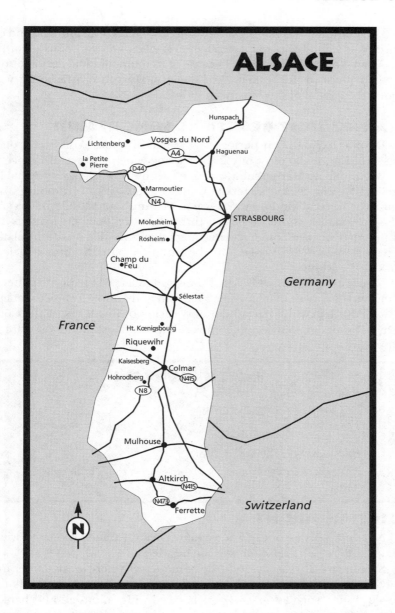

Hun, the Holy Roman Empire, Louis XIV, the Kaiser, and Hitler himself have pounded on Alsace and claimed it for themselves.

It wasn't until 1648 that Alsace officially became part of the French nation (Strasbourg was not annexed until 1681), and even then, the region was lost to the Germans after the disastrous Franco-Prussian War of 1870. France would not regain sovereignty over Alsace until the end of World War I, and they lost it again for several years during World War II.

After World War II, in part because of its multi-national heritage and in part tribute to the resiliency of the Alsatian spirit, Strasbourg was named the capital of the European union.

FRANCE'S MOST BEAUTIFUL WINE REGION

Despite having been periodically scarred by war, Alsace is widely considered to be the most physically stirring wine province of France.

Beginning at **Marlenheim**, a stone's throw from Kratz's vegetable patch and about 24 kilometers (15 miles) due west of Strasbourg, the regional wine road winds its way down to **Thann** about 120 kilometers (75 miles) south. En route, it passes through more than 60 hamlets of geramium-bedecked homes and bustling squares nestled on the dramatic eastern slopes of the **Vosges**. In the distance, past the broad plains, sparkles the **Rhine**.

Nearly everywhere are fields of vines and cellars where proud vinters, young and old, insist that you take a load off and sample a choice vintage or two. Alsace may not have the snooty cachet of Bordeaux or the Côte d'Or, but the region produces some of France's finest (and most affordable) white wines.

FINDS & FAVORITES

- *Hôtel Les Violettes (see Route du Vin)*
- *Le Clou restaurant (see Strasbourg)*
- *The astronomical clock of the great pink angel of Strasbourg (see Strasbourg)*
- *Kaysersberg (see Route du Vin)*
- *1983 Gewurztraminer, by Lorenz in the village of Bergheim (see "A Bit About Alsatian Wines," below)*

ALSATIAN CUISINE

Not only is Alsace one of France's most beautiful and productive wine makers, the region is also among the best fed.

Stop at virtually any *winstub* (the homey cafés where locals gather for food, drink, and gossip – not necessarily in that order) and you will find age-old dishes, such as *tarte à l'oignon*, laced with onions and bechamel sauce, and *tarte flambée*, which consists of a thin crust topped with fromage blanc, cream, lardons and onions, all fired over a hot flame.

Really hungry? Try *choucroute*, with sausages, ham, and bacon heaped like firewood on a bed of sauerkraut that has been steeped in wine. Or set aside an hour or two to gnaw on a bowl of *baeckhoffa*, a generous helping of lamb, beef, and pork atop a stew of potatoes, carrots, onions, and herbs.

For more delicate tastes, Alsace kitchens are also home to escargots and foie gras. And gourmets can dine on dishes as refined as sole meuniäre or as glamorous as duck à l'orange, both of which can be found at the many first-rate restaurants scattered throughout the region.

No wonder so many families, even in the face of vicious wars, refused to leave such a wondrous place behind.

STRASBOURG

Most tours of Alsace begin with **Strasbourg**, a handsome ancient city near the Rhine that has survived the wrath of some of the world's most notorious tyrants. Today, a thriving city and symbol of the post-war alliance between Germany and France, Strasbourg is the seat of the European Parliament.

At the northern end of the Alsatian **Route du Vin**, Strasbourg is about 480 kilometers (300 miles) east of Paris.

ARRIVALS & DEPARTURES

Trains leave several times a day from the Gare de l'Est in Paris, the most direct taking about four hours to reach Strasbourg. Fares run about $100 roundtrip per person for second class, which is quite comfortable.

You can also fly, catching one of a handful of **Air Inter** flights that leave daily for Strasbourg from the Orly airport just south of Paris. The cheapest fares, requiring a Saturday night stay, also run about $100 roundtrip per person. But bottom line, you need a car to get the feel of the region and its people.

It's a six-hour journey by car from Paris to Strasbourg and, in the first hour after you arrive, you may wish you'd never sat behind the wheel. Several of the main thoroughfares in the ancient inner-city have been torn up by construction (maybe work will be complete by the time you visit). But steel yourself and ultimately you will find your way to the Place Gutenberg in the heart of the city, under which is an enormous garage a block from the great cathedral of Strasbourg.

WHERE TO STAY

HÔTEL DES ROHAN, *17 rue Maroquin, 67000 Strasbourg; 88.32.85.11, Fax 88.75.65.37. Rooms: 36. Double: 300-600FF. No restaurant.*

Comfortable and smartly decorated. Most importantly, the hotel is only a few yards from the cathedral square, so it's within easy walking distance to every corner of Strasbourg's ancient city core.

HÔTEL MAISON ROUGE, *4 rue Francs-Bourgeois, 67000 Strasbourg; 88.32.08.60, Fax 88.22.43.73. Rooms: 140. Double: 400-580FF.*

A striking old hotel near the center of the old city.

WHERE TO EAT

LE CLOU, *3 rue Chaudron, 67000 Strasbourg; 88.32.11.67.*
Family style dining with regional classics.
CHEZ YVONNE, *10 rue Sanglier, 67000 Strasbourg; 88.32.84,15.*
One of the better known winstubs.
MAISON DES TANNEURS, *42 rue Bain aux Plantes, 67000 Strasbourg; 88.32.79.70.*
Probably the city's most famous restaurant.
BUEREHIESEL, *in the park by l'Orangerie near the Palais de Europe, 67000 Strasbourg; 88.61.62.24.*
A former Alsatian home, now with gourmet (and expensive) cuisine.
MAISON KAMMERZELL, *16 place Cathedrale, 67000 Strasbourg; 88.32.42.14.*
A famous Alsatian house from the 16th century right on the square facing the cathedral.

SEEING THE SIGHTS

The must-sees, and your vacation, begin upstairs from where you've left the car if you're driving (see *Arrivals & Departures*).

The **Place Gutenberg**, as is obvious by its name, is dedicated to the inventor who perfected the printing press in Strasbourg in the mid-1400s. Like Strasbourg's nearby Place Kléber, a memorial to the famous general who died during Napoleon's campaign through Egypt, the Place Gutenberg is bordered by shops and outdoor cafÉs where you can while away hours sipping golden French and German beers.

The bronze statue of Gutenberg that stands in the center of what was a vegetable market until the late 1700s is immediate evidence of the city's bicultural personality. Composed by the famous French sculptor, David d'Anger, the bronze celebrates a famous German inventor.

That theme is echoed a hundred yards away in the square facing the magnificent Gothic cathedral. In that plaza, opposite the cathedral entrance, is the **Pharmacie du Cerf**, one of France's oldest pharmacies, which claims as its most famous customer the somewhat intimidating German author, Johann Wolfgang von Goethe.

The **cathedral** itself, commonly known as "the great pink angel" because of its reddish stone, was begun in earnest about 1000 A.D. and was finished when the 465-foot spire was topped in 1439. The figurines and fragile looking stone spines of the facade, the breathtaking 15th-century pulpit, the inspired stained-glass windows, and the magnificent organ are all worth seeing. But the highlight is an **astronomical clock**, begun in 1547.

Clock hands tipped with tiny globes mark the movement of the planets around a face adorned with signs of the Zodiac. Allegorical figures representing the Four Ages of Man strike the quarter hours, and representations of various blessed and damned pilgrims pass solemnly before statuettes of Christ and Death.

Continue your tour by strolling a couple of blocks southeast to the banks of the **Ill River** and the elegant **Château Rohan**. Built in 1742 as a residence for Strasbourg's bishops, the classically symmetrical Château is now home to three museums – the **Musée des Beaux-Arts** (fine arts), the **Musée Archéologique** (archeology), and the **Musée des Arts Décoratifs** (decorative arts).

A few blocks to the west of the cathedral, you'll find **La Petite France**, a small charming neighborhood laced with canals beside which tanners and millers once toiled. The quarter, which dates back to the 1200s, is now home to some of the city's most famous restaurants, including **Maison des Tanneurs**, legendary for its monstrous portions of *choucroute*.

The **Place Broglie**, a handful of blocks northwest of the cathedral, is home Wednesdays and Fridays to one of the city's finest open markets, where merchants sell fresh vegetables, fruits from Europe and Africa, herbs, cheeses, and fish – in short, just about anything you'd care to eat, as well as kitchenware and lots of trinkets.

Set aside some time to wander aimlessly down the narrow roads and alleys that branch out through the old section of the city. You'll find countless timbered shops and tiny bistros serving regional specialties. And make sure you walk along the eastern and southern banks of the River Ill, which encircles the inner city and is criss-crossed by flower-laden bridges.

And then, of course, leave several hours free for sampling food and wine. If you've found a restaurant during your walk through the city, or if you choose one of our suggestions, be sure to book dinner in advance so you don't have to settle for some dive (and there are several). Nothing's more leaden than bad Alsatian food prepared by some clueless chef.

Try the **Winstub Le Clou** on the block-long rue Chaudron. It's a couple doors down from a tiny shop that sells nothing but *foie gras* and caviar, which you should take as a sign that this tiny lane is dedicated to fine food.

Le Clou, a homey wood-paneled dining room decorated with copper pans and floral-patterned plates, offers first-rate choucroute on a bed of cabbage steamed in Riesling. The sheer volume can be overwhelming, though you'll very likely see a 70-year-old local at an adjacent table fly through mountainous portions in minutes. The Alsatians have a stunning capacity for food.

We would also recommend that you accompany your meal at Le Clou with a bottle of 1987 *Cuvée Frédéric Emile Riesling*, produced by F.E. Trimbach of Ribeauvillé, located at about the midway point on the Route du Vin. F.E. Trimbach has been producing wines since 1626, and this is a fine example of the family's wares and good omen for the wine road you'll travel on the rest of your visit to Alsace.

Other Sights
• **Palais de l'Europe**, *avenue de Europe, about a half mile northeast of the cathedral on the opposite side of the River Ill.* This modern complex houses the European Parliament, which came into existence after World War II in an effort to heal Europe's wounds and prevent future conflict. Members from the various countries have been popularly elected only since 1979.

PRACTICAL INFORMATION
• **Strasbourg Office du Tourisme**, *10 Place Gutenberg, 67000 Strasbourg; 88.32.57.07.*
• For bus tours of the nearby wine region, at about 200FF a head, phone **Tourisme Fleury** *at 88.84.62.60.*

THE ROUTE DU VIN
A Bit About Alsatian Wines
Before embarking on the wine route, it helps to study up a bit on the wines that you will find at the countless wine cellars (*caves*) that line the road, offering free samples (*degustations*) and often cut-rate prices on bottles.

Ask just about any winemaker in Alsace and you will hear that their wines are among the most misunderstood, especially by the American consumer.

"There is a big confusion between our wine and the German wines, which are really very sweet," complained George Lorenz, 31, whose family has been making wine in the village of Bergheim for six generations. By comparison, he explained, the Alsatian wines are often fruity, but quite dry.

And though many are meant to be drunk young to complement a meal, Alsace has cultivated sophisticated wines meant to be savored after 10 and even 20 years, Lorenz said. Examples: the *cuvées*, which are made with special care by the best vineyards, and the *vendage tardives*, which are made from grapes harvested especially late in the season.

As proof, Lorenz or one of his crew will be happy to set out several *Gewürztraminers* for a tasting. For us, he poured a recent vintage *cuvée*, an award winning cuvée, a 1983 vintage, and a 1989 *vendage tardive*. Though the first two were flavorful, they were a bit fruity by our standards. However, the 1983 was remarkably soft and dry. The tardive was full-bodied, but still somewhat heavy, Lorenz explained, because it is years from its peak.

Unlike wine from other regions, which take their names from the place where they are produced (such as Bordeaux or Champagne), Alsatian wines take their names from the grapes.

There are seven primary varieties grown in Alsace – **Sylvaner**, **Pinot Blanc**, **Muscat**, **Tokay** (or **Pinot Gris**), **Riesling**, **Gewürztraminer**, and **Pinot Noir**. All are white wines but the Pinot Noir. When grown in the Côte d'Or, the Pinot Noir grape is the foundation of hearty Burgundies. But plucked from the Alsatian soil and microclimates, it often produces a light and much less interesting wine more akin to rosé.

Alsace has also become known for its *Crémant*, a sparking wine similar to champagne, its marc, a potent distillate made from grape skins, and its eaux-de-vie after-dinner *degustifs* distilled from pears, raspberries, plums, and more than 20 other fruits.

WHERE TO STAY

The **Route du Vin** has some world-class hotels and restaurants. Some of the finest we've described in more detail in the *Touring the Wine Route* section below.

HÔTEL LE SCHOENENBOURG, *rue Piscine, 68340 Riquewihr; 89.49.01.11, Fax 89.47.95.88. Rooms: 43. Double: 350-500FF.*

Only a few years old, but quite comfortable, reasonably priced, and just a hundred yards from the gates to the old village.

LE MARÉCHAL, *4 place des Six Montagnes Noires, 68000 Colmar; 89.41.60.32, Fax 89.24.59.40. Rooms: 38. Double: 650-1,400FF.*

Classy and colorful, with first-rate dining right on the canals of Colmar.

LES VIOLETTES, *in Thierenbach-Jungholtz, 68500 Guebwiller; 89.76.91.19, Fax 89.74.29.12. Rooms: 24. Double: 520-710FF.*

One of the most enjoyable places we have ever stayed anywhere. See description starting on page 347.

Visitors can also stay on working farms (*fermes auberges*). For information about accommodations in the northern half of the route, *write to the Relais Départemental des Gites Ruraux De France, 7 Place des Meuniers, 67000 Strasbourg; 88.75.56.50.* For rooms in the southern section, *write the Association Départementale du Tourisme du Haut-Rhin, Hôtel du Département, BP 371, Colmar 68007; 89.23.21.11.*

WHERE TO EAT

Along the wine route, hotels tend to have the best dining.

HÔTEL-RESTAURANT ARNOLD, *67140 Itterswiller; 88.85.50.58, Fax 88.85.55.54.*

Specialties of baeckhoffa and Coq au Riesling.

LES VOSGES, *2 Grand Rue, 68150 Ribeauvillé; 89.73.61.39, Fax 89.73.34.21.*

Gourmet dining in one of the larger villages of the wine route.

AUBERGE LE SHOENENBOURG, *rue Piscine, 68340 Riquewihr; 89.47.92.28, Fax 89.47.89.84.*

Chef François Kiener, a local who studied in Burgundy and San Francisco, strays from the traditional heavy Alsatian dishes in favor of inventive nouvelle combinations.

CHAMBARD, *in the Hôtel Résidence Chambard, 68240 Kaysersberg; 89.47.10.17, Fax 89.47.35.03.*

Fine food in a wonderful inn with 20 rooms, ranging from 550-800FF.

FER ROUGE, *52 Grand Rue, 68000 Colmar; 89.41.37.24.*

A 17th-century converted Alsatian home with gourmet dining.

MAISON DES TÊTES, *19 rue des Tetes, 68000 Colmar; 89.24.43.43.*

Colmar's most famous and colorful winstub.

LE MARÉCHAL (see *Where to Stay*).

LES VIOLETTES (see *Where to Stay*).

TOURING THE WINE ROAD

Alsace and its wine region are divided into two subregions, the **Bas-Rhin** and the **Haut-Rhin**. Despite what you might think, Bas-Rhin refers to the upper half, and Haut-Rhin to the lower. If you're beginning your Alsatian trip in Strasbourg, you will visit the Bas-Rhin first.

Leaving Strasbourg, look for the N4 highway leading due west about 24 kilometers (15 miles) to Marlenheim, the first village on the Route du Vin and, if you need a wine road map, your first stop. Though brochures and books insist that the Route du Vin is well marked, it is not. Small signs are tacked onto the bottom of some road markings, and sometimes there are no signs at all. You must have a map and you can find them at the miniscule tourist offices along the route or even at some of the larger winemakers.

Because the wine road is only 120 kilometers (75 miles) long, you could travel it in a single mind-numbing day of dips and curves and sudden bends in the road. But that would defeat the purpose, which is to mosey on down the road, stopping to admire the vast vineyards stretching up the slopes of the Vosges, taking snaps of tiny villages generously decked out with planters spilling over with dazzling geraniums, and, most importantly of all, sitting down to eat and drink.

In short, think of the route as a moveable feast that will last anywhere from two to five days, depending on your appetite. Not long after you set out on the wine road, you'll find yourself in **Traenheim**. Stop for a quick prelunch tasting at **Charles Muller et Fils**. You'll probably be met by Jean Jacques Muller, one of the sons, who can explain the subtle variations between various Rieslings.

Muller also has another warehouse down the road a mile or so where he can also show you how *Crémants* are stored upside down in capped bottles to filter sediment into the neck. The bottles are then made so cold that the carbonation is inhibited while they are opened to drain the sediment and then corked for storage and ultimately consumption.

Back on the road, you should find the stretch from Barr to Nothalten particularly inspiring – in part because several of those villages are far up the slopes of the Vosges, which are blanketed in dense forests.

In that same stretch, stop at the deservedly renowned **Hôtel Arnold** *in Itterswiller*, poised on a cliff overlooking the vineyards, for a hearty lunch of *baeckhoffa* and *Coq au Riesling*, a variation on *Coq au vin*. Though their *baeckhoffa* is billed as their specialty, the *Coq au Riesling* is even better. And you can wash down the massive portions of food with plenty of 1990 Riesling made locally by Arnold-Simon – the same Arnold as of the hotel.

A few miles down the road, detour off the Route du Vin to admire the **Haut-Koenigsberg castle** *atop the mountains above the villages of Saint-Hippolyte and Ribeauvillé*. The first stone structures of the castle were erected in the 12th century and, over the years, nations and noble families fought and bargained for the majestic edifice that towers more than 2,300 feet above the Alsatian plain.

The castle was renovated in the early 1900s, and a few rooms are no longer truly medieval in character or architecture. But the sidetrip is well worth the drive and 30FF entry per person to wander through the maze of dining halls and trophy rooms replete with stags' horns and boars' heads. And the views of the valleys and plains stretching to the Rhine are exhilarating.

In fact, Haut-Koenigsbourg is so interesting, you're probably better off bedding down in some nearby village (Ribeauvillé, Riquewihr or Kaysersberg) and doubling back to the castle in the morning when you're fresh and the crowds are more manageable.

Rejoining the wine route below the castle, turn south again and quickly find **Riquewihr**, one of the most famous of the Alsatian villages. It's still a lovely spot. But, sad to say, though the walled hamlet was spared the devastation that was visited on nearby towns during the world wars and its residents have carefully maintained its heritage and kept up its enchanting homes, it appears to have lost its battle against crowds of tourists and merchants hawking crummy souvenirs at virtually every corner.

Kaysersberg, *about six villages down the road*, is virtually the historic equal of Riquewihr, offers more variety in restaurants and shops, and has the ambiance of a real town, not a theme park.

Kaysersberg is set back in a valley shaped by the Weiss river that gurgles through the edge of town. It's watched over by the remains of an ancient castle on the hillside, as well as by several families of storks who've made their homes on rooftops around the village. The stork is the symbol of Alsace and is said to have arrived in numbers from North Africa in the 13th century.

But there is one crucial element in Riquewihr's bag of tricks that Kayserberg does not enjoy: François Kiener, the chef at the **Auberge Le Schoenenbourg**. Though young, he is a master, preparing plates blanketed with carpaccio of foie gras sprinkled with tarragon, fennel and other herbs, ravioli with prawns, and sea bass with a tomato and basil confit. Kiener offers an intelligent regional wine list as well, including a Riesling-Schoenenbourg, grand cru 1990, made by the Raymond Berschy family whose office is 100 feet down a narrow road from the restaurant.

Kiener, who routinely makes the rounds of the diners' tables, was trained in Burgundy and San Francisco and acknowledged that his was not the traditional Alsatian cuisine. Nonetheless, he is the genuine article, having been raised in Riquewihr and spent time as a youth trimming vines and picking grapes in the hot autumn sun.

After a quick visit to the walled inner city of **Turckheim**, where, if your timing is right (mid-August), you'll find a city fair boasting booths devoted to wine and garlic-laden frog legs, you should head for **Colmar**, the business capital of the wine region.

Colmar

Colmar, with a population of more than 63,000, is a smaller version of Strasbourg. It too boasts a fine cathedral, the **Collegiate Church of Saint-Martin**, dating back to the 13th and 14th centuries. There are also several worthy museums, including the **Unterlinden**, which houses a variety of religious paintings and artifacts.

In the south central quarter of the city, explore the narrow streets and canals of what is known as **Petite Venise**. One of the city's better known and more captivating hotels is located there: the **Hostellerie Le Maréchal**, a whimsical conglomeration of four 16th-century homes that have been joined in recent years into a distinguished four-star hotel overseen by the ever-energetic Madame Ingeborg Bomo, her husband, Gilbert, and her Great Dane, Ferro.

Rooms named after various composers (Wagner was the most expensive at 1,400FF a night) are elegantly decorated, many have air conditioning, and some feature a whirlpool tub for the road-weary traveler. Though many visitors to Colmar are inclined to eat at the famous **Maison des Têtes** – so named because of the busts and sculptures adorning the facade – Madame Bomo and an appetizer of carpaccio of lamb and wild

**THE FAMOUS MAISON DES TÊTES RESTAURANT,
TYPICAL OF ALSATIAN ARCHITECTURE**

mushrooms might convince you to consider the Maréchal's open dining terrace alongside one of the canals.

Madame Bomo will be more than happy to share her scrapbook with you, showing off the signatures of Yehudi Menuhin and other notable musicians who have performed at Colmar's annual classical music festival and have stayed at the hotel.

Her and her husband's love of classical music was what gave rise to their decision to name rooms after composers. "It's so much better than just a number," she said. "It makes a good memory."

Back on the Route du Vin

Resuming the wine route, *stop off to visit the stone towers perched on the hills above Husseren.* The crumbling walls exude a mysterious historic presence, and the view is spectacular. *Back on the road toward Thann and the end of the wine route,* you will pass through another string of charming villages with timbered homes dripping in boxes of geraniums. In fact, you may be villaged-out. If so, there is an ideal remedy. Turn to the mountains you have skirted for so many days.

There are several small roads that lumber up and down the mountainside – and quite a few good hotels as well. None are so welcoming as the **Résidence Les Violettes** *in Thierenbach, just up the mountain slopes from Guebwiller on the wine road.*

Les Violettes is set in an exquisite valley with a view from virtually every room of the adjacent forested slopes and the onion-shaped bell tower of Notre-Dame de Thierenbach. The rooms are modest in size, but very comfortable and reasonably priced. And the dining is fabulous.

Make sure to take lunch on the enclosed terrace. The view of the valley below is magnificent and the table settings are especially elegant, with crystal goblets, fine china, and bursting displays of roses and geraniums. It's like stepping into a cover shot from Gourmet Magazine.

The food is inspiring as well, with a menu that includes veal medallions blanketed with morel mushrooms, and a collection of fish fillets with salmon, bass, and other delights. With it, order one of the more full-bodied Pinot Noirs, such as a 1990 from *Dorpf & Irion*, a vintner based in Riquewihr. The dinner menu is even more mouth-watering, with dishes such as frog legs and duck breast *à l'orange*, followed by an assortment of mousses and ices doused with raspberry sauce. Given a wine list generous with fine Burgundies and Bordeaux, you might even be tempted to stray from the Alsatian varieties for a night.

To make room for all this fine dining, ask about the many paths that lead into the forest behind the hotel. The staff will show you an extensive map of the terrain with instructions simple enough that it's virtually impossible to get lost if you pay attention to the markings on the paths.

After a hike, relax on the outdoor patio set off a few yards from the main house, where a young waiter will greet you and take your orders for afternoon cocktails.

Credit for the setting and the wanton gluttony goes to Jean Pierre Munsch, the owner, chef, and main attraction of Les Violettes. If your French is up to the task, it is well worth asking him to show off his 21 vintage cars, which are tucked away in a well-camouflaged garage under the outdoor patio.

The first acquisition in Monsieur Munsch's collection is a blue 1925 Citroen B12 coupe with leather seats. "My parents had one of those when I was young," said Munsch, now 65. "When I saw one, I bought it and repaired it." But his favorite: a six-cylinder 1931 Citroen Roadster, painted a sky blue, with deep-water blue detailing and a leather canopy that folds back so passengers can enjoy the open air.

During our visit, he climbed in, pushed a button, fretted with the choke, and vrooom! *Ça marche*, he exclaimed, punching the accelerator to emphasize his point.

Other Sights
• Even if it is only for a half hour walk, take advantage of the **Vosges** mountains. They are beautiful and accessible, with walking and ski trails everywhere. Just drive up into the mountains.

- Town festivals featuring local wines, food, music, and crafts spring up everywhere in late summer and fall – especially during harvest season. Some are free and some charge a few francs. Signs are sprinkled everywhere announcing dates and times.
- Wine lovers might want to visit the **Musée du Vignoble et du Vin d'Alsace** *in Kientzheim*, where the Confrerie Saint-Etienne wine association holds an extensive (though private) annual tasting of the year's best wines. *Open only in the summer and fall. For information, phone 89.78.21.36.*
- The **Ecomusée d'Alsace** *just east of Guebwiller off the lower half of the wine route* is a living recreation of life as it was in Alsace centuries ago, complete with ox cart rides. *For information, phone 89.74.44.54.*
- The **Musée National de l'Automobile** (the **National Automobile Museum**) *in Mulhouse*, just southeast of the wine route, features 500 cars dating back to the 1870s.
- The **Musée Français du Chemin de Fer** (**French Railroad Museum**) *in Mulhouse* houses train cars going back to the days of the steam engine.
- **Munster**, home of the cheese by the same name, *is a short detour about 24 kilometers (15 miles) west of Colmar on D417.*
- **Colmar** hosts an annual classical music festival, usually in July, that lasts several days and draws international talents.

WINETASTINGS

Among the many, many places you can stop to sip a little wine (times and admission charges vary from vineyard to vineyard and season to season):

- *Cave Vinicole de Traenheim, RN422, 67310 Traenheim; 88.50.67.27.*
- *André and Remy Gresser, 2 rue de l'Ecole, 67140 Andlau; 88.08.95.88.*
- *Gustave Lorentz, 35 Grande Rue, 68750 Bergheim; 89.73.63.08.*
- *Cave Coopérative de Ribeauvillé, 2 route de Colmar, 68150 Ribeauvillé; 89.73.61.80.*
- *Dopff & Irion, Château de Riquewihr, 68340 Riquewihr; 89.47.92.51.*
- *Maison Leon Beyer, 2 rue de la 1ere ArmÉe, 68420 Eguisheim; 89.41.41.05.*
- *Kuentz-Bas, 14 Route du Vin, 68420 Husseren-les-Châteaux; 89.49.30.24.*

PRACTICAL INFORMATION

• Colmar Office du Tourisme, *4 rue Unterlinden, 68000 Colmar; 89.41.02.29.*
• The Comité Interprofessionnel des Vins d'Alsace, *8 Place de Lattre-de-Tassigny, 68000 Colmar; 89.41.06.21.* For information about regional wines.

25. BURGUNDY

INTRODUCTION

Colette, probably the most famous 20th-century author to come from the massive **Burgundy** region of France, had this to say about her native turf: "Burgundy is like a pig: Some parts are more memorable than others, but every bit of it is edible."

Not exactly poetic (and you may not agree that all pig parts are edible), but you get the drift. Colette is saying that Burgundy, known to the locals as **Bourgogne**, is fabulously varied. Virtually no matter where you turn, you will find something pleasing.

It might be sites of epic battles fought eons ago, or gurgling rivers snaking through deep forests, or storybook villages perched on verdant knolls, or gourmet kitchens humming with activity, or fields of limestone-rich soil blanketed with vines that yield worldclass wine.

HISTORY

In between meals and wine tastings, you'll want to see a few sights so you can work up an appetite.

There's plenty of history to learn, especially in the hill country of northwestern Burgundy, a landscape of sunflower fields, rolling hills, rushing streams, and captivating villages. Here, at Alise-Sainte-Reine, is where Caesar himself did battle with the great Celtic king and warrior, Vercingétorix. For centuries afterward, Burgundy remained under Roman rule.

Attila the Hun swept through in the early 400s, about the same time that groups of Germanic tribes fled parts of contemporary Germany and took refuge in Burgundy. In fact, the name Burgundy evolved from the name of those tribes, the Burgondiones.

Centuries later, during the 1300 and 1400s, Burgundy enjoyed a golden era. The famous Valois dukes of the era established a court whose political power extended into Flanders and whose cultural and artistic presence was the most influential in all of France.

Ultimately, they too fell and the area was claimed by the Holy Roman Empire.

Swiss and German armies attacked Dijon in 1513 as part of the Empire's effort to secure their claim. Several more times over the centuries, including during the Franco-Prussian war and the two world wars, German troops plowed through Burgundy.

Though periodically distracted by war and earthly politics, Burgundy had a powerful spiritual side as well. It was a powerful center for the Christian faith from the 9th through the 16th centuries.

For instance, the cathedral at Cluny, established in 910, was the largest religious edifice in Christendom until Saint-Peter's was erected in Rome hundreds of years later. The exquisite Madeleine church in Vézely, said at one time to house the relics of Mary Magdalene, was built in the late 11th century and quickly became a major meeting place for Christian pilgrims.

Richard the Lion-Hearted and Thomas à Becket sought religious inspiration and refuge at Vézelay and Sens in Burgundy. And Saint-Bernard walked from Burgundian village to Burgundian village in the 1100s, preaching the Christian faith and expanding the Benedictine order's already impressive reach by founding scores of new abbeys.

As is so often the case, winemaking and history (especially spiritual history) are closely linked in Burgundy. For evidence, one need look back no further than Chanoine Kir, the former priest and mayor of Dijon who in the mid-1900s brought fame to the apéritif that blended white Burgundy with a splash of Crème de Cassis and white Burgundy. The result, Kir, bears his name.

Searching for just the right soil that would nourish vineyards, the Cistercian monks of the 11th century settled in the region near where Savigny-lès-Beaune is now produced. The rapid growth of the order and their dedicated work in the fields was said to be crucial to the beginnings of serious viniculture in the region.

The marriage of winemaking and spiritual aid is nowhere more apparent than in Beaune, where the charitable Hospices de Beaune has been producing and selling fine wines for more than five centuries, then using the money to help meet the medical and religious needs of the region's sick and aged.

BURGUNDY CUISINE

Burgundians are passionate about food and wine, and will be sorely disappointed if you don't share their obsession.

Even the most snobbish international gourmands tout Burgundy cuisine. And why not? Burdundy is home to *escargots*, the snails that are cultivated en masse and then transformed from slimy garden pests into rich delicacies served bubbling hot in pools of butter suffused with parsley or garlic, or both.

Coq au vin, usually a range-bred chicken steeped in a broth heavy with red Burgundy wine, is another classic local dish. The same with *boeuf Bourguignon* – cubes of beef marinated for hours, then stewed in red wine, bacon, and onions. Trout is available in abundance in the hill country of the northern section of Burgundy. And game, including venison, wild boar, and all manner of bird, graces just about any decent menu in the mid- to-late fall.

And you must try *oeufs en meurette*, which is a luscious concoction of poached eggs sitting atop tiny rounds of toasted garlic bread and drenched in a sauce of red wine, bacon, garlic, shallots, bay, rosemary, and other herbs. If it's made correctly, your cholesterol count should soar.

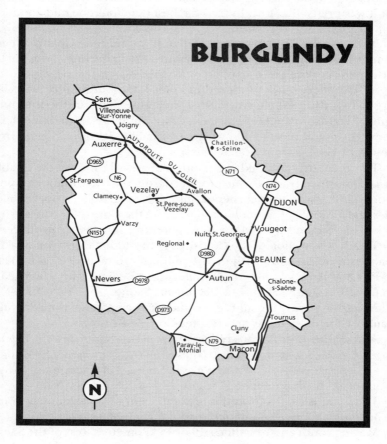

BURGUNDY WINE

The magnificent dishes are matched by equally wonderful local wines. Obviously, wine is an economic mainstay of this region, and tourists are drawn by the thousands to poke around the fields, tour wine cellars, and stop for an hour or two for a *degustation* (a tasting at one of the dozens of cellars and shops that line the roads crisscrossing the foothills).

Burgundies are sometimes underestimated by Americans, which is not difficult to understand. Long ago when we were students, we would occasionally invite friends over to share a couple of jugs of cheap California wine. According to the labels, the red was a Burgundy and the white was a Chablis.

But even by our incredibly low standards in those days, we recognized that it was pretty vile stuff. In fact, the best that could be said about the swill was that it was dirt cheap.

It was years later that we learned that Burgundy and Chablis are not crummy California wines. Instead, they are among the finest wines in the world, and they are not cheap.

As with most wines produced in France, the Burgundies are called Burgundy for the simple reason that they were made in the Burgundy region. Likewise, a *Chablis*, which is a white Burgundy, is the wine that is produced in and around the village of Chablis. *Pommards* come from Pommard, *Volnays* from Volnay, etc.

The vines are cultivated in a handful of areas in Burgundy. Chablis, a crisp almost steely white wine produced from the Chardonnay grape, is made near the northwest corner of Burgundy in an isolated pocket many miles and a couple of mountain ranges from the **Côte d'Or** (the western bank of the Saône River, where most good Burdungies are produced).

The richest section of the Côte d'Or, Burgundy's finest winemaking area, begins just south of **Dijon** (the political capital of the region) and extends about 74 kilometers (46 miles) past **Beaune** (the winemaking capital of Burgundy) almost to **Chalon-sur-Saône**.

Along the way are the subregions and microclimates of **Côte de Nuits**, **Beaune**, **Côte de Beaune**, and **Hautes-Côte-de-Beaune**.

Among the most famous red wines from this region are the *Beaune, Côte de Beaune, Pommard, Volnay, Nuits-Saint-Georges, Chambolle-Musigny, Gevrey-Chambertin, Vosne-Romanée, Vougeot, Santenay,* and *Savigny-läs-Beaune.* All are made from the Pinot Noir grape.

The famous whites from this area (all from the Chardonnay grape) are *Meursault, Chassagne-Montrachet,* and *Puligny-Montrachet.*

Moving south and remaining 10-or-so kilometers west of the Saône, the last major Burgundy wine regions are the **Côte Chalonnaise** (near Chalon-sur-Saône) and **Mâconnais** (surrounding Mâcon). Well-known

Chalonnaise wines are the red and white *Rullys* and the red *Mercureys*. *Mâcon Blanc, Mâcon Villages,* and *Pouilly-Fuissé*, all whites, are probably the best known of the Mâconnais wines.

The last subregion along this stretch is **Beaujolais**. Located between Mâcon and Lyon, it is not technically included in the political départements which make up the Burgundy region. Nonetheless, Beaujolais wines are routinely mentioned in the same breath as Burgundies.

Good Beaujolais wines include *Fleurie, Juliénas, Regnié, Brouilly, Morgon, Moulin-à-Vent,* and *Saint-Amour*. All the Beaujolais are made from the Gamay grape and take their names from tiny villages where the light fruity wine is made.

FINDS & FAVORITES

- *The village of* **Beaune** *(see The Côte d'Or)*
- *Dinner at* **Bernard Mabillon** *in Beaune (see The Côte d'Or)*
- *Demeure Saint-Martin winetasting in Beaune (see The Côte d'Or)*
- *Abbaye de Fontenay (see The Yonne and Hill Country)*
- *Dinner at* **Chez Camille** *hotel in Arnay-le-Duc (see The Yonne and Hill Country)*
- *The village of* **Semur-en-Auxois** *(see The Yonne and Hill Country)*
- *Hostellerie de Bellecroix hotel (see The Côte d'Or)*
- *Lunch at* **Hostellerie des Clos** *in Chablis (see The Yonne and Hill Country)*
- *Coq au Vin restaurant in Juliénas (see The Côte d'Or)*

ARRIVALS & DEPARTURES

By Car

Of course, to profit by all this richesse, you're going to need a car. There is just too much ground to cover to handle the trip any other way.

This enormous region stretches from Sens, about 125 kilometers (77 miles) southeast of Paris, to Mâcon, an additional 350 kilometers (220 miles). Four governmental *départements* (somewhat like states) are included in Burgundy: the Yonne in the northwest, the Côte-d'Or in the northeast, the Niävre in the southwest, and Saône-et-Loire to the southeast.

The Seine and Yonne rivers, which merge just east of Fontainebleau, have their sources in the Burgundy hills. The Loire and Saône rivers bracket the region on the west and east. And navigable canals crisscross the region.

By Barge & Bicycle

All this water offers you your one attractive alternative to the car – that is, the barge. Barge tours are growing more and more popular. You can join a group or rent your own boat. Bicycles are standard on the boats so that when you dock at a small village, you've got easy transportation. For information, write to the Dijon tourist office mentioned below.

THE YONNE & HILL COUNTRY

We start our tour in the **Yonne** département, which occupies the northwest quadrant of the Burgundy region and would be your point of arrival if coming from Paris. Much of the rich religious history of Burgundy is set in the Yonne River valley and the hills and forests on either side.

WHERE TO STAY

HOSTELERIE DES CLOS, *89800 Chablis; 86.42.10.63, Fax 86.42.17.11. Rooms: 26. Double: 230-560FF. Restaurant.*

Very pleasant inn right in the village, with very fine food and an excellent wine list.

HOSTELERIE DE LA POSTE, *13 place Vauban, 89200 Avallon; 86.34.06.12, Fax 86.34.47.11. Rooms: 23. Double: 400-1,100FF. Restaurant.*

Located just outside the ramparts that surround the center of this lovely village just 13 kilometers (8 miles) east of Vézelay. Built in a former 18th-century post office, with a colorful garden.

POSTE ET LION D'OR, *89450 Vézelay; 86.33.21.23, Fax 86.32.30.92. Rooms: 48. Double: 230-580FF. Restaurant.*

Very comfortable largish hotel right at the foot of the cobbled lane leading up to the basilica. Decent, reasonably-priced dining, and a friendly staff.

L'ESPÉRANCE, *89450 Saint-Päre; 86.33.20.45, Fax 86.33.26.15. Rooms: 33. Double: 350-1,300FF. Restaurant.*

Right in the heart of the village. Gourmet dining said to be world-class, with occasional lapses by rude waiters.

CHEZ CAMILLE, *1 place Edouard-Herriot, 21230 Arnay-le-Duc; 80.90.01.38, Fax 80.90.04.64. Rooms: 14. Double: 395-800FF. Restaurant.*

Located in Arnay-le-Duc about 35 kilometers (22 miles) northwest of Beaune. Right in the center of town, with a modern annex that is very cheap. The food's the thing here, with gourmet dining in a bright and cheery garden room off the more formal main lobby.

HOSTELLERIE DU VAL-SUZON, *Route N71, 21121 Val-Suzon; 80.35.60.15, Fax 80.35.61.36. Rooms: 17. Doubles: 400-500FF. Restaurant.*

Located just 17 kilometers northwest of Dijon off N71. This is good staging point for planning your assault on Dijon the next morning. Very tranquil grounds with two buildings and a simple but pleasant dining room where you can enjoy a good meal.

WHERE TO EAT

JARDIN GOURMAND, *56 boulevard Vauban, 89000 Auxerre; 86.51.53.52.*

Pleasant outdoor dining terrace and very good food for reasonable prices at the northwest edge of the center of town.

HOSTELERIE DES CLOS, *Chablis.* See *Where to Stay.*

L'ESPÉRANCE, *Saint-Päre.* See *Where to Stay.*

CHEZ CAMILLE, *Arnay-le-Duc.* See *Where to Stay.*

GOURMETS, *rue Varenne, 21140 Semur-en-Auxois; 80.97.09.41.*

A homey inn with two dining rooms serving good country cooking at reasonable prices. Lots of freshwater fish.

AUXERRE

Just north of **Auxerre**, a town of about 40,000 people *170 kilometers (105 miles) southeast of Paris*, you will see a turnoff from the A6 autoroute leading you to the city's northern entrance. It's the most direct route, but if you were to continue just a wee bit further on A6 to the N65 turnoff toward Auxerre, your first glimpse of the city would be from opposite the Yonne River, and it would be a memorable sight.

You know you've arrived in Auxerre when you spot the towers of the **Abbaye-de-Saint-Germain**, the **Saint-Etienne cathedral**, the **Saint-Pierre-en-Vallée church**, and, from some views, the **Tour l'Horloge (Clock Tower)** in the center of town. You can find parking very near the Tour l'Horloge and cathedral. Just look for the 'P' signs.

The **abbey** is the most important historical stop in this busy river-port town. It was dedicated to Saint-Germanus, who became the first bishop of Auxerre in the 400s. Not to be confused with Saint-Germain of Saint-Germain-des-Prés in Paris, this bishop is remembered in Paris by the Saint-Germain-l'Auxerrois cathedral just a block east of the Louvre.

Saint-Germanus tackled the tough task of converting regional tribes to Christianity. The abbey's impressive crypt is still said to contain his remains, as well as some remarkable frescoes painted in the late 800s depicting the death of Saint-Etienne.

The 14th-century **Saint-Etienne** cathedral, with its single tower and heavily ornamented portals, is also well worth a visit. Its vast crypt, which contains surprisingly fresh looking frescoes and a chapel, dates back to the early 11th century. The church also guards a treasure vault containing Saint-Germain's tunic and various other pieces dating to the 13th century. A plaque outside the cathedral and a statue inside near the altar commemorate a visit paid to the cathedral by Jeanne d'Arc on February 27, 1429.

Just up the narrow sloping road from the cathedral (past the Army Surplus store with display windows featuring such anomolies as cowboy boots and Georgetown University baseball caps) you will run across a large shopping and parking plaza, off of which is a market street leading to the **Tour l'Horloge.**

The rose-colored clock face is brightened by a brilliant golden sun radiating from the center. The clock also boasts four hands – two for telling the time, and a third and fourth for following the positions of the sun and moon.

The rather odd statue near the tower of a woman who resembles a somewhat weary Mary Poppins is a likeness of Marie-Noél, a 20th-century poet who lived in virtual solitude in Auxerre. (Would she really approve of this cartoonlike figure in the midst of clothing and shoe stores?)

CHABLIS

If you head for **Chablis** from Auxerre – a perfectly natural thing to do, especially if you haven't had lunch yet – be prepared to pitch a fit for about 10 minutes. The road signs, as is too often the case, get you started in one direction, then vanish just as you arrive at a tricky fork in the road. The only solution is to persevere, *moving slowly east and keeping an eye out for anything that reads N65, then D965 toward Tonnerre, a town several kilometers past Chablis.*

Once you're on course, life will improve immeasurably. Leaving the river behind, you climb into the hill country, weaving in and out of various valleys which, before long, are blanketed in vineyards.

Chablis, *16 kilometers (10 miles) due east of Auxerre*, is by far the most isolated of the Burgundy wine regions. The town was founded in 867 by the monks of Saint-Martin-de-Tours, who nurtured the Chardonnay vines for what would one day become a famous wine.

With only 2,600 residents, Chablis is an admittedly tiny place. Still, it is quite charming, with several outdoor cafés and a few good restaurants. The **Hostellerie des Clos**, an inn with 26 rooms, has a peaceful dining room overlooking a small garden and rose-covered trellis.

Their gourmet menu includes such things as an entire selection of lobster preparations, including a lobster salad with artichokes, lobster in a crust with baby vegetables, roast lobster with mushrooms, etc. Several sauces, like those for the freshwater pike, use Chablis as their base. The wine list is, as it should be, heavy with Chablis, with an inspiring selection of Grand and Premier Crus.

Any visit to Chablis would be incomplete without a quick stop in one of the local cellars to sample the distinctively crisp, almost green-tasting wine that is so good with just about any kind of fish. (See *Winetastings* box below.)

VÉZELAY

Vézelay, *50 kilometers (31 miles) south of Auxerre*, is one of the most famous and historic villages in all of Burgundy. *Approaching from the north on the N6 and then the D951 that hugs the Cure River*, you will see down the valley in the distance what appears to be a magical castle perched atop the highest hill. The main tower you see is the single bell tower of the **Basilique Sainte-Madeleine**, said at one time to contain the relics of Mary Magdalene.

Vézelay has a remarkable history, having supposedly received the relics in the mid-11th century and become a crucial stopover for Christian pilgrims en route from the north to the holy city of Santiago di Compostela in northwest Spain. Saint-Bernard, responsible for opening scores of Benedictine abbeys in Burgundy, is said to have come to Vézelay on Easter in 1146 and to have spiritually bolstered warriors embarked on the Second Crusade.

Richard the Lioned-Hearted passed through Vézelay during the Third Crusade and Louis IX (Saint-Louis) worshipped here before continuing on in the Seventh Crusade in 1248.

The town's reputation and influence suffered mightily in the 13th century, when the true relics of Mary Magdalene were supposedly discovered in Provence, and then again during the religious wars in the 1500s when horrible battles broke out all over France between Catholics and Protestants.

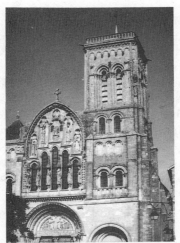

BASILIQUE SAINTE-MADELEINE, VÉZELAY

Truth be told, though the church is impressive and the village of 600 residents, with its narrow cobbled lanes lined with shops and small bistros, is attractive, Vézelay is a bit disappointing. It is crowded with tourists and the shops clearly exist primarily to separate those tourists from their money.

And there is little here but a spectacular view of the valley below and the basilica, which was completed in 1104. The building has a stark, though harmonious beauty, which may fail to satisfy visitors who prefer brilliant stained-glass windows and heavy interior ornamentation.

The basilica's most striking architectural features are its capitals ⸳rning the pillars. They capture various religious scenes very cleverly, ⸳to the scenes over the enormous interior portals.

A nearby attraction is the tiny village of **Saint-Père** at the foot of the hill occupied by Vézelay. Here, you will find **L'Espérance**, the famous three-star restaurant and inn with its pricy menu and lovely garden.

SEMUR-EN-AUXOIS

Another 85 kilometers (53 miles) down the A6 autoroute, you'll find the D980 turnoff to **Semur-en-Auxois***, which is all of 7 kilometers (4 miles) north. Get your camera ready.*

Though coming into town from the east on D954, Semur is a pretty dull looking spot, but when you arrive by D980 to the south, you navigate a bend and then boom, there across a stone bridge arching over the **Armançon River** is one of the prettiest little villages you can imagine. Four bulky stone turrets rise from the town's riverfront and behind are the red-roofed homes and the bell towers of the delicate-looking 11th-century Notre-Dame church.

This storybook place, whose old section sits on a kind of peninsula surrounded by the Armançon River, was one of the toughest fortresses around in the 14th and 15th centuries, when there were 18 stone towers spaced long the ramparts.

Today, Semur is a tranquil collection of half-timbered buildings, cobbled lanes, shops, and cafés. Just dump the car somewhere and wander at will, stopping in the church to admire the *Mise au Tombeau*, a striking medieval sculpture depicting Christ's followers lowering his body into a tomb.

Also take time to peek into shop windows. There are several antique shops and merchants who traffic in rare books (though most the tomes are in French, of course).

ONE OF THE MAIN BRIDGES INTO SEMUR-EN-AUXOIS

FONTENAY

The **Abbaye at Fontenay**, *20 kilometers (12 miles) north of Semur-en-Auxois, just past Montbard on D980*, is another must-see in this region.

Set in a wooded valley with a playful creek, the bucolic abbey for Cistercian monks was established in 1118 by Saint-Bernard, whose intelligence and religious determination was a powerful influence throughout the northern Burgundy region. Fontenay grew quickly and prospered during up through the 15th century.

The monks' religious tranquility began to come unglued in the 16th century, in large part because of the national religious strife caused by the battles between Catholics and Protestants. After the Revolution of 1789, the grounds lost even more of their blissful air of solitude when the buildings were converted into a papermill.

The property is currently owned by the Aynard family, a branch of the Montgolfier clan, whose historic claim to fame is its early fascination with and promotion of hot-air ballooning. The Aynards, who bought the property in 1906 and still live on the grounds, have made an enormous effort to restore it to its original glory.

Today, a private tour (at 38FF per person) will guide you through the grounds, beginning at the 15th-century gatehouse. Highlights include the dirt-floored church built between 1139 and 1147. It is, in fact, the country's oldest standing Cistercian church.

The dormitory, 182 feet long and with magnificent hand-hewn ceiling beams of Spanish chesnut, is also quite impressive. The monks were said to sleep here on straw mats with no heating even during the coldest of the cold snaps.

The cloister, a picture of serenity, offers several inspiring camera angles. It is surrounded on all sides by four arcades featuring well-worn columned arches. In the center of the small lawn is an herb garden bursting with rosemary, thyme, and lots and lots of sage – all of which were believed to have medicinal as well as culinary applications.

MONT FOUILLES D'ALÉSIA

Just 14 kilometers (9 miles) southeast of the Abbaye de Fontenay on D905, is another must for history buffs. This itty bitty hillside village was the battle ground for two huge figures in French history: **Vercingétorix** and **Julius Caesar**.

You obviously know who Caesar was, but have probably never heard of Vercingétorix and his tonque-twister of a name. Vercingétorix, an awesome warrior, was effectively the king and general of the Celtic tribes who ruled a wide stretch of Burgundy in 52 BC.

Though Caesar described these Celts to his leaders in Rome as a particularly rich and barbaric tribe, many historians say that they were relatively peaceful and brought such civilized inventions to France as the wooden barrel and salted meat. Nonetheless, Caesar wanted the land for himself and he wanted Vercingétorix's hide. Inevitably, Caesar's superior numbers and battle strategies paid off.

The town, the region, and Vercingétorix were conquered. He was taken to Rome, where he was said to have been paraded through the streets, then strangled to death at the foot of the Roman Capitol.

Today you will find the hilltop ruins of a Gallic-Roman town, with the foundations and a few pillars of what were once homes, a theater, and other public structures. On a nearby promontory (you'll see signs) is a 40-foot statue of Vercingétorix placed there in the 1800s by order of Napoleon III. The monument overlooks the great Gaul's former domain (unfortunately, part of the view is of **Venarey-les-Laumes**, a charmless town dominated by tacky apartment buildings, warehouses, and a rail yard).

Other Sights
• **Tanlay Château**. *Located 10 kilometers (6 miles) east of Tonnerre, or 44 kilometers (27 miles) east of Auxerre off route D965*, this 17th-century Renaissance-style Château was actually begun by Francois de Coligny, a Protestant leader during the religious wars of the 1500s. Its handsome and symmetrical design features a moat, rounded turrets

with bell-shaped domes on either end of the facade, and ribbed columns fronting a stately gatehouse. Stroll around gardens and park as well. Several furnished rooms of this privately owned home are accessible.

- **Ancy-le-Franc Château**. *Located 15 kilometers (9 miles) southeast of Tanlay just off of D905*, the castle is an Italian work designed by architect Sebastiano Serlio of Bologna. The regal, though almost too symmetrical Château has four square towers at its four corners and four entrances that give access to the inner courtyard. Inside, there are several fine frescos.

- **Bussy-Rabutin Château**. *Located 25 kilometers (15 miles) southeast of the Abbaye de Fontenay and just 6 kilometers (4 miles) northeast of Mont Fouilles d'Alésia on D954*. This is certainly the Burgundian Château with the most colorful history in that its original owner, Roger de Rabutin, the Count of Bussy, was banished here after he wrote a tongue-in-cheek treatise poking fun at Louis XIV and his lovers. Not to be deprived even in exile of his lusty youth, Rabutin transformed this handsome castle into a personal playground said to be frequented by soldiers and lovely women. Judging by historical accounts and the smirk on his oval portrait in the Hall of Uniforms, he was quite a scoundrel.

- **Source of the Seine River**. This little spot, *off a tiny road off of N71 8 kilometers (5 miles) northwest of Saint-Seine-l'Abbaye*, is not exactly en route to anywhere and may not be worth a special trip. The first challenge is just finding it. Going northwest out of Saint-Seine, watch carefully for the little white signs that will finally lead you left off the highway and into the countryside of plowed fields and scattered stands of trees. This once holy Roman site, where pilgrims bathed in what they believed were curative waters and offered gifts to the goddess Sequana, there is now some artist's conception of a grotto occupied by a plump water nymph. Somehow, it just doesn't work.

- **Saint-Seine-l'Abbaye**. Tucked into a small valley, this tiny village founded by Saint-Seine (Sequanus) in the 6th century is practically dwarfed by its 14th-century Saint-Seine Benedictine abbey. There are two altar screens with frescos dating back to the 16th century. In some spots, the paint seems just barely to be holding on and in others there appears to have been some pretty rough retouching. Still, you can decipher enough to follow the story of Saint-Seine, who meets both Christ and the Virgin in the course of spreading the faith.

PRACTICAL INFORMATION

- **Auxerre Office de Tourisme**, *1 quai de République, 89000 Auxerre;* *86.52.06.19.*

- **Vézelay Syndicat d'Initiative**, *rue Saint-Pierre, 89450 Vézelay; 86.33.23.69.*
- **Semur Maison du Tourisme**, *2 place Gaveau, 21140 Semur-en-Auxois; 80.97.05.96.*
- **Abbaye de Fontenay**, *21500 Montbard.*

DIJON

If you've spent a day or two meandering through the western Burgundian hills or wine country of the Côte d'Or, **Dijon** can seem intimidating at first. *Located 311 kilometers (192 miles) southeast of Paris*, it seems a bit larger than its 148,000 population would suggest.

Still, once you've suffered through the confusing signs leading you to a parking lot and have dumped the car somewhere near the **Place de la Libération** (the town's Ground Zero), you'll realize that the most interesting sights are all within easy walking distance and that Dijon is really a very manageable place.

Dijon is probably best known to Americans for its mustard. Dijon businesses produce the lion's share of mustard exported from France. But what you didn't know is that the Dijon mustard industry imports the bulk of seeds used to make its mustards. In fact, a good chunk of the seeds come from the United States.

We have to add right here that the much-touted **Dijon mustard shop** *on rue de la Liberté a couple of blocks west of the Palais des Ducs* was a huge disappointment. They had very few flavors. Not even garlic mustard! Can you imagine!? And most of what they display are the types of mustard and cornichons that you can find at your local Safeway.

Dijon History

Obviously Dijon, the political capital of Burgundy, is noted for a great deal more than its condiments. Dijon was home to the much heralded succession of Valois Dukes, who put the Burgundian court on the map in the 1300 and 1400s.

The first was Philip, named duke in 1364 by his father, King John II (John the Good). Philip (the Bold) married Margaret of Flanders in 1369, thus expanding his political sway well beyond today's French borders. He also took the opportunity to invite the gifted Flemish artists and architects of the time to Dijon to adorn his palace and the city.

John the Fearless became duke in 1404. He showed remarkable political prowess and laid a covetous eye on the national throne – that is until the day in 1419 when he was assassinated en route to a meeting to discuss the future with those close to the increasingly insane King Charles VI.

Next followed Philip the Good, who reigned for 48 years. During that time, the Hundred Years War was raging and Burgundy profited by a brief alliance with England. In effect, the Duke had grown more powerful and ruled a greater kingdom than the king himself. Ultimately, the agreement with England was dissolved and Philip chose the more popular alliance with the French crown.

The last of the epic Dukes, under whose leadership Burgundy had flourished politically and artistically, was Charles the Bold. He died in a battle at Nancy in 1477, the same year his daughter wed Maximilian, the emperor of the Holy Roman Empire. Off and on for the next 400-plus years, German leaders invaded or claimed rights to pieces of Burgundy.

WHERE TO STAY

CHAPEAU ROUGE, *5 rue Michelet, 21000 Dijon; 80.30.28.10, Fax 80.30.33.89. Rooms: 30. Double: 450-850FF. Restaurant.*

Located a stone's throw from the Saint-Bénigne and Saint-Philibert churches near the center of town, with what is said to be the best hotel kitchen in Dijon.

PULLMAN LA CLOCHE, *14 place Darcy, 21000 Dijon; 80.30.12.32, Fax 80.30.04.15. Rooms: 76. Double: 510-600FF. Restaurant.*

Right by the arch at the western end of the rue de la Liberté, this is a large, but comfortable hotel that gives you easy access to the city center.

WHERE TO EAT

LE PRÉ-AUX-CLERCS ET TROIS-FAISANS, *11 place de la Liberté, 21000 Dijon; 80.67.11.33.*

Right on the place with a view of the dukes' palace from some tables and two or three menus to suit your budget. A decent wine list. Probably better for lunch than for dinner.

LA DAME D'AQUITAINE, *23 place Bossuet, 21000 Dijon; 80.30.36.23.*

A good restaurant with hearty fare and an intriguing space shaped out of a 13th-century crypt.

SEEING THE SIGHTS

There's lots to keep you busy here, but before you get started you're going to need a map.

The **tourist offices** *on place Darcy near the commanding arch at the western end of rue de la Liberté and on rue des Forges directly behind the Palais des Ducs* have handy layouts (free) of the downtown area with a numbering system that guides you counterclockwise from stop to stop.

If you arrive in town on a Tuesday, Friday or Saturday morning and you park in the huge underground lot *near Trémouille* (watch for signs), your first stop is going to be the enormous **open market**. It's one of the largest and busiest we've seen. Part of it is contained in a massive central warehouse-style building *on rue Bannelier*, inside of which you'll find every imaginable type of vegetable, fruit, meat, cheese, and baked good.

Lining the streets around the quarter are vendors selling clothes (a seemingly unnatural volume of underwear), shoes, kitchenware, and all manner of just-plain-stuff. The buzz of activity borders on outright chaos, but it's fun to nose around, stopping occasionally to sample some food or sip a coffee at one of the cafés.

The **ducal palace** is another must, including its very good **Musée des Beaux Arts** and the **Guard Room**. The museum houses several master-pieces by Flemish artists brought here during the Dukes' finest hours in the 1400s. The guard room is the resting place of two exquisite tombs, one of Philip the Bold and the second of John the Fearless and his wife, Margaret of Bavaria. Their feet rest on lions and angels sit at their heads.

Other Sights

• The **Porte Guillaume**, *the arch at the western end of the shop-lined rue de la Liberté*, named after Guillaume de Volpiano, who designed the Benedictine Abbey of Saint-BÇnigne in the 11th century.

• **Saint-Bénigne**, the gothic cathedral *two blocks south of the Porte Guillaume*, with a crypt dating back to 1007.

• The fine Renaissance-style **Saint-Michel cathedral** *at the eastern end of the rue de la Liberté*.

• **Notre-Dame church**, *just a block north of the Palais des Ducs*, with completely crazed gargoyles jutting out of the main facade and with a *chouette*, a lucky charm in the shape of an owl, on the northern exterior of the church. It's supposed to bring good fortune when stroked, and you can tell by its sheen that it gets plenty of rubbing.

PRACTICAL INFORMATION

• **Dijon Office de Tourisme**, *Place Darcy, 21000 Dijon; 80.44.11.44. Or: rue des Forges, 21000 Dijon; 80.44.11.44.*

THE COTE D'OR

As we've said, the region just south of Dijon is the premier winemaking area of Burgundy, almost all of which lies along the fields and foothills *about 10 to 20 kilometers (6 to 12 miles) west of the Saône River.*

There are villages along the way that are so adorable you'll wish you could pack them up and take them home with you. And, of course, you will see umpteen signs tempting you to stop at this or that cellar (*cave*) or château for a tasting of the local wines.

CÔTE DE NUITS

The first leg of this area's *route de vin* is the **Côte de Nuits**, *beginning just south of Dijon near the village of Chenôve and continuing 20 kilometers (12 miles) to the village of Corgoloin just short of Beaune. For the full effect, leave Dijon and find the tiny D122 highway parallel and just to the west of the N74.*

The D122 will lead you through several interesting spots: **Fixin**, with François Rude's ethereal sculpture of *Napoleon's Awakening*; **Brochon** and its fanciful castle; **Gevrey-Chambertin**, site of what was said to be some of Napoleon's favorite winemakers; and the famous **Clos de Vougeot**, where Cistercian monks began fermenting fine wines centuries ago.

The **Clos**, the most historically important stop along the Côte de Nuits, is currently home to the prestigious **Confrérie des Chevaliers du Tastevin**, the wine brotherhood that conducts an annual tasting of all the local wares and acknowledges the best wines with their *Tastevinage* medallion. The medallion will appear on wine labels and is an excellent guide when you're shopping for bottles of the best Côte de Nuits.

After Clos-de-Vougeot, the D122 rejoins the N74, taking you through **Nuits-Saint-Georges** (a delightful stop, where you can find lots of cafés and shops) and such tiny hamlets as **Vosne-Romanée**, where seven Grands Cru Burgundies are made.

CÔTE DE BEAUNE

The **Côte de Beaune** *extends another 20 kilometers (12 miles) south along N74 from Ladoix-Serrigny to Cheilly-lès-Maranges just past Santenay.* The Hautes-Côtes de Beaune, a subregion you will find identified on wine labels, refers to the vineyards laid out on the hilly slopes directly to the west of the Côte de Beaune.

Plan on bedding down in this area for at least a night or two so that you can dedicate yourself to some serious winetasting. Here you will find flavorful, but never overpowering reds: *Pommard, Volnay, Savigny-lès-Beaune,* and *Beaune.* There are also rich elegant whites: *Meursault* (the largest of the Beaune villages), *Puligny-Montrachet,* and *Chassagne-Montrachet.*

Stops such as **Château Meursault** are heady experiences in that you get to visit a world famous château and sip as many as a dozen wines. However, the tasting is not cheap and they don't always put out the best of the recent vintages. The tasting at Meursault (with the tasting cup, which you obviously need) is a whopping 90FF per person, and the bottles available for sale are no cheaper than you would find in Paris wine shops.

The moral to this story is that you should also pop into some tiny cellars in more obscure villages, where you are more likely to be invited to imbibe for free and to find reasonably priced bottles to take back to your hotel.

BEAUNE

This busy little town of 22,000, with its ancient central quarter surrounded by ramparts and a narrow park, is the prized jewel of the Côte d'Or and probably our favorite place in all of Burgundy. It is, in fact, the wine capital of Burgundy, so noted for several reasons, not the least of which is that many of Burgundy's best wines are produced in and around Beaune.

Amateur oenophiles (winelovers to you and me) while away untold hours sipping and philosophizing in Beaune's first-rate cellars and wine shops. You should be able to find no end of *Côte de Beaune, Nuits-Saint-Georges, Meursault, Montrachet, Pommard, Volnay,* and other vintage wines available for tasting.

But all is not hedonistic pleasure here. Serious business is conducted inside these city walls. In late November, a massive annual charity auction that hails back to the mid-1800s is hosted by the **Hospices de Beaune**, an organization that provides care for the elderly (see below, *Seeing the Sights,* for more detail).

WHERE TO STAY

LE CEP, *27 rue Maufoux, 21200 Beaune; 80.22.35.48, Fax 80.22.76.80. Rooms: 49. Doubles: 550-1,000FF.*

Next door to the exquisite Bernard Morillon restaurant. Stylish, comfortable, and located right near the Hôtel-Dieu.

BELENA, *12 boulevard Foch, 21200 Beaune; 80.24.01.01. Fax 80.24.09.90. Rooms: 34. Doubles: 500-900FF.*

Next door to the very good Jacques Lainé restaurant. Contemporary, almost more like Italian decor. Good sized rooms. All the amenities right on the edge of the central part of the town.

HOSTELLERIE DU CHÂTEAU DE BELLECROIX, *6 route Nationale, 71150 Chagny; 85.87.13.86, Fax 85.91.28.62. Rooms: 21. Double: 500-950FF. Restaurant.*

Truly lovely converted château with distinctive pointy-rooved turrets on either flank of the facade. A pool and very good food.

HÔTEL DE BOURGOGNE, *place Abbaye, 71250 Cluny; 85.59.00.58, Fax 85.59.03.73. Rooms: 15. Double: 500-1,000FF. Restaurant.*

The perfect spot facing the famous abbey. You can visit the village with ease and enjoy the hotel's fine cuisine.

CHÂTEAU DE PIZAY, *Route de Ville Morgon, 69220 Saint-Jean-d'Ardières; 74.66.51.41, Fax 74.69.65.63. Rooms: 62. Double: 625-980FF. Restaurant.*

A large but interesting wine-producing château in the center of Beaujolais country. Huge outdoor dining terrace.

WHERE TO EAT

BERNARD MORILLON, *31 rue Maufoux, 21200 Beaune; 80.24.12.06, Fax 80.22.66.22.*

One of the best meals we have ever eaten, with a superb wine list. Lots of game during mid-to-late fall. Dishes include starters of scallops and pigeon liver on a bed of watercress and a finely sliced wild duck breast and foie gras (the real thing) with truffles. Among the list of main courses were roast partridge and tender medallions of venison, both surrounded by a mix of cooked chesnuts, grapes, apples, and red current jelly. Try a sampling of regional cheeses and the dessert of grapefruit, caramel, and vanilla sorbets.

Gustav, Madame Morillon's tiny Yorkshire, will drop by the table periodically to check on your progress.

HÔTEL COQ AU VIN, *place du Marché, 69840 JuliÇnas; 74.04.41.98.*

Reasonably priced and you just can't miss with the coq au vin and a chilled house Juliénas in this charming restaurant decorated with roosters everywhere.

DANIEL ROBIN, *Les Deschamps, 69840 Chénas; 85.36.72.67.*

Another spot in the heart of Beaujolais country, with a lovely dining terrace and hearty regional menu.

SEEING THE SIGHTS

The November **charity auction**, mentioned above, is a frenzied affair, live theater at its best (too bad it's a private affair). Wine produced in local fields, donated over the centuries to the Hospices, is up for sale. About 750 barrels, each containing the equivalent of 300 bottles of wine, are sold annually. The proceeds after expenses go to three nearby homes for the aged. The auction, though a charity, also sets the tone for the commerical pricing of each year's crop.

Whether or not you attend the auction and the public three-day bacchanalian bash preceeding it, the **Hôtel-Dieu** founded by the Hospices is well worth a visit. Built in 1443 as a hospital for the poor, *the Hôtel-Dieu is just off the town's central Place Carnot.* Its dreary exterior gives no hint of the expansive inner courtyard surrounded by hospital quarters topped with cheery multi-colored tile roofs.

Inside the infirmary, rows of canopied sick beds are lined up opposite a partial wall from the chapel – the proximity to the altar allowing even the dying to practice their faith. And the pharmacy still houses shelf after shelf of labeled jars containing the best known cures of long ago.

The Hôtel-Dieu, which ceased functioning as a hospital in 1971, also has a wonderful collection of tapestries and a dazzling polyptych painted by Roger van der Weyden in 1443 depicting the Last Judgment. The colors, guarded from the sun in a darkened room, are unbelievably radiant.

Other must-sees in town include the nearby golden-hued **Église de Notre-Dame** and the enormous **wine museum**, where you will gape at huge wooden presses, vats, and odd contraptions dating back to the 16th century. And shoppers hunting for crystal decanters, silver tasting cups, and original art will find plenty of enticing display windows throughout the town center.

While visitors often stop to sip wines at the Hospices headquarters, we much preferred the tour and tasting at the **Demeure Saint-Martin** *on the edge of the central village* (see *Winetastings*, below). The former residence belonged to the first magistrate of Beaune, Jacques-Philibert, Marquis de Santenay. A captain in Louis XV's army, he was an avowed bachelor and unrepentant scoudrel.

"He had a terrible personality. Fought with everybody," said Gale Le Goff, our charming Canadian-born guide, who moved to Beaune years ago with her French husband. The three-story château just outside the ramparts had fallen into miserable disrepair until it was purchased in 1985 by Andre Boisseaux, a prominent local vintner who regularly buys a third of the wine sold at the Hospices auction.

He restored much of the Château as a showplace of the Louis XV period and has stocked the sizable cellar with more than 100,000 bottles of regional wine, some dating back to the 1920s and many for sale to visitors (10-page catalogues are available). Madame Le Goff can tell you practically to the knoll where the grapes for each are grown.

Any visit to Beaune should also include a meal at the **Restaurant Bernard Morillon** *adjacent to the Hôtel Le Cep* (see *Where to Eat,* above). The restaurant, run by Bernard and his charming wife, Martine (who, with her artistic makeup and expansive gestures, resembles a diva), is set in two large rooms with muscular timbered ceilings set off by soft peach-colored fabrics on the walls and dining tables topped with pink roses.

Other Sights

- **Chalon-sur-Saône**, a town of 55,000 *on the Saône River located just a few kilometers east of the large Chalonnaise winegrowing region beneath the Côte de Beaune.* Chalon prospered early on as a major north-south trade route trafficking in lumber, textiles, and, of course, wine. It's a busy town, but with a charming old quarter near the Saint-Vincent cathedral where you'll find narrow streets, half-timbered buildings, shops, and some pretty good eating.
- **Tournus,** *on the Saône 30 kilometers (18 miles) south of Chalon-sur-Saône,* boasts the Abbaye de Saint-Philibert, where pilgrims gathered en masse from the 11th through the 15th century.

- **Cluny**, *37 kilometers (23 miles) southwest of Tournus on D980*, is clustered around an abbey that was the largest in the world when it was consecrated in 1095 by Pope Urban II. Referred to by some as the "Second Rome," Cluny was the religious power base that controlled 3,000 monasteries scattered around Europe. From afar, you will see the abbey's octagonal **Tower of the Blessed Water** rise into the sky.
- **Beaujolais country** *at the very southern end of Burgundy* actually falls partially outside the region's political boundaries. There is a string of lovely villages beginning just to the southwest of the city of **Mâcon**. You will find plenty of tasting cellars and good food.

PRACTICAL INFORMATION

- **Beaune Office de Tourisme**, *place de la Halle en face de l'Hôtel-Dieu, 21200 Beaune; 80.22.24.51.*
- **Comité Interprofessionnel de la Côte d'Or et de l'Yonne pour les Vins AOC Bourgogne**, *rue Henri Dunant, 21200 Beaune; 80.22.21.35.*
- **Mâcon Office de Tourisme**, *187 rue Carnot, 71000 Mâcon; 85.39.71.37.*

WINETASTINGS

CHABLIS

• *La Chablisienne*, 8 boulevard Pasteur, 89800 Chablis; 86.42.11.24. Represents more than 200 growers from most of the principle villages that produce Chablis.

• *Simonnet-Febvre et Fils*, 9 avenue d'Oberwesel, route de Tonnerre, 89800 Chablis; 86.42.11.73. The Simonnet family produces a variety of good Chablis.

CÔTE D'OR

• *La Grande Cave*, 21640 Vougeot; 80.61.11.23. Perfect follow-up to a tour of the Clos-de-Vougeot.

• *Château de Savigny*, 21420 Savigny-lès-Beaune; 80.21.55.03.

• *Marche aux Vins*, rue Nicolas-Rolin, 21200 Beaune; 80.22.27.69. Just opposite the Hôtel-Dieu in Beaune with a few dozen regional wines, including those sold at the Hospices de Beaune auctions.

• *Demeure Saint-Martin*, 4 boulevard Maréchal Foch, 21200 Beaune; 80.22.38.00. Tour the lovely Château and taste a dozen wines.

• *Les Caves des Hautes-Côtes*, route de Pommard, 21200 Beaune; 80.24.63.12. A modern cooperative representing the products of more than 100 winemakers.

• *Château de Pommard*, 21630 Pommard; 80.22.07.99. The largest privately-owned wine property along the Côte d'Or.

• *Château de Meursault*, 21190 Mersault; 80.21.22.98. Cellars that wander underground seemingly forever under old farm buildings beside an elegant château.

• *Caveau Municipal de Chassagne-Montrachet*, Chassagne-Montrachet, 21190 Meursault; 80.21.38.13. The products of more than 20 winemakers, with reds as well as the famous whites.

CÔTE CHALONNAISE & MÂCONNAIS

• *Caveau Union des Producteurs de Pouilly-Fuissé*, 71960 Solutré; 85.37.80.06. Another collective, with 250 members and a focus on the tart Pouilly-Fuissé white wine.

• *Domaine du Château de Fuissé*, 71960 Fuissé; 85.35.61.44. A 15th-century Château with wines produced by the Jean-Jacques Vincent.

BEAUJOLAIS

• *Cave Coopérative des Grand Vins*, Château du Bois de la Salle; 69840 Juliénas; 74.04.42.61. Tasting of several of the major refreshing Beaujolais wines.

• *Château des Jacques*, 71570 Romanèche-Thorins; 85.35.51.64. Highlighting the Moulin-à-Vent AOC made by the Thorin clan.

• *Georges Duboeuf*, Gare de Romanèche-Thorins, 71570 Romanèche-Thorins; 85.35.22.22, Fax 85.35.21.18. Georges Duboeuf owns a major chunk of just about every significant vineyard in Beaujolais and produces much of the best wine.

26. BORDEAUX

INTRODUCTION

Bordeaux. Everyone has heard the name and most people have tasted the wine, but not so many have visited the city. It's a lovely area and parts of the city are quite nice, but, aside from the draw of the famous vineyards,Bordeaux just can't compete with many of France's more seductive regions.

With more than 200,000 residents, Bordeaux is one of France's largest cities. It is also one of the nation's busiest ports and most lucrative centers of commerce. In fact, if you visit the city, the first thing you will notice as you cross the **Garonne River** into town is the industrialized and lagely unattractive river bank.

Two factors have played lead roles in local prosperity over the centuries. One is Bordeaux's location, right on the Garonne River just a few kilometers northwest, the mighty **Gironde**, fed by both the Garonne and the **Dordogne**, empties into the Atlantic.

In short, its easy access to the Atlantic connects Bordeaux to the world, while the Garonne and Dordogne rivers extend Bordeaux's reach well into the heart of southern France. The result: trade, lots of it.

The other factor that shaped the fate of Bordeaux is, of course, the wine. The region all around Bordeaux has been prodcuing wine since vines were first imported by the Greeks before the Christian era took root.

Whenver you hear the British discuss their infatuation with claret, they are really talking about Bordeaux wines. This region was dominated by the British for almost 300 years, beginning in the 12th century when Elanor of Aquitane inherited the lands from her father and later married Henri Plantagenêt.

By birthright dating back to William the Conqueror, Henri was later crowned Henri II of England. Thus began the British occupation of Bordeaux that would not be settled until the end of the Hundred Years War in 1453. The Bordeaux region was, in fact, one of the last strongholds of the Britsh rulers as they were finally driven from French soil.

But you can be sure that no matter how vicious the battles nor how close the British came to defeat, a division or two of soldiers remained behind the front lines in Bordeaux with strict orders to maintain the steady flow of fine wine to the homeland.

THE BORDEAUX WINES

Whether you're familiar or not with the history of Bordeaux, you are surely acquainted with the wine. This, too, can be attributed to two primary factors. One, the prestigous châteaux such as Margaux, Latour, Lafite-Rothschild and Mouton-Rothschild have been producing exquisite winse for so long that they have become the standards by which most other wines are measured.

Second, the Bordeaux area exports a sea of table wines – a half billion bottles of reds and whites and dessert wines. If you have sampled even the most modest variety of wines over the years, you cannot have escaped Bordeaux.

And it is largely for the wines and the wine culture that visitors come to Bordeaux. First on their itinerary, inevitably, are the **Haut Médoc** and **Médoc** subregions *just north of the city of Bordeaux along D2*. The villages of **Margaux**, **Saint-Julien**, **Pauillac**, **Saint-Estèphe** and others line the route that snakes along parallel to the river.

There are tasting opportunities galore for all but the top-rung châteaux. For the finest, you must make reservations for tours and *dégustations* (tastings). Sad to say, but some of the most famous properties don't make it a priority to entertain gusts.

Just south of the Bordeaux is the **Graves** region, whose most famous château is **Haut Brion**. Fine red and whites are produced here. A bit further south along the Garonne toward the city of Langon, you run into *Sauternes* country, where rich, supple dessert wines are fashioned with great care.

To the southeast, occupying the delta between the Garonne and Dordogne rivers is the aptly-named **Entre-Deux—Mers** (Between Two Seas) region. Some delightful and inexpensive whites are grown here. And to the east, across the Dordogne are the regions where the famous *Pomeroi*, *Saint-Emilion*, and *Fronsac* wines are made, among a host of others. Here, you are likely to meet with a more agreeable producer, who will sit down and talk shop for hours while sipping one wine after the other.

For detailed information about the wines and the wine makers, stop by one of the *Maisons du Vin* (see sidebar below), where youcan pick up literature, schedule tastings and tours, and sometimes sample or buy a wine or two.

Most of the hotels we note below will also help you schedule tours and tastings. Still, for the big, big names, you should phone well in advance of your arrival if you want any hope of getting in.

WHERE TO STAY

NORMANDIE, *7 cours 30 Juillet, 33000Bordeaux; 56.52.16.80, Fax 56.51.68.91. Rooms: 100. Double: 300-550FF. No restaurant.*
A bit funky, but reasonbly priced and located near the Grand Théâtre, the Esplanade des Quinconces and the Place des Grands Hommes.

LE SAINT-JAMES, *3 place Camille-Hostein, 33270 Bouliac; 56.20.52.19, Fax 56.20.92.58. Rooms: 15. Double: 850FF. Gourmet restaurant.*
On the opposite side of the Garonne from the city of Bordeaux, this remarkable hotel has a view of Bordeaux, a stunning contemporary decor and some truly fine cuisine. A favorite with gourmets.

HOSTELLERIE DES CRIQUETS, *130 avenue 11 Novembre, 33290 Blanquefort; 56.35.09.24, Fax 56.57.13.83. Rooms: 22 Double: 300-370FF. Restaurant.*
This adorable little inn with spacious rooms and an outdoor dining terrace is just outside the northern city limits of Bordeaux. One of the more welcoming and affordable small inns, especially given the first-rate menu.

LA RÉSERVE, *74 avenue de Bourgailh, 33600 Pessac; 56.07.13.28, Fax 56.36.31.02. Rooms: 18. Double: 560-800FF. Restaurant.*
Another spot that is just on the outskirts of Bordeaux, this time to the wouthwest. Despite its proximity to the big city, the Réserve occupies the center of its own large and tranquil park. The food is first-rate, the pinkish hotel lovely and the staff will be happy to help you arrange tours of the vineyards.

RELAIS DE MARGAUX, *Chemin Ile-Vincent, B.P. 5, 33460 Margaux; 56.88.38.30, Fax 56.88.31.73. Rooms: 26. Double: 875-1,215FF. Restaurant.*
Surrounded by a lovely park and located in the heart of one of the world's most famous wine-producing areas, this is a favorite stop for wine and food lovers. It combines elegant surroundings with fine cuisine.

CHÂTEAU DE CORDEILLAN-BAGES, *Route des Châteaux, 33250 Pauillac; 56.59.24.24, Fax 56.59.01.89. Rooms: 21. Double: 800-870FF. Restaurant.*
An ideal base for exploring the finest of the Médoc wines, this converted 17th-century château also hosts wine tasting courses and tours of the local countryside. The interior is richly and cheerfully adorned and the food is marvelous, with all sorts of lamb, pigeon, and other delights.

CHÂTEAU DE VALMONT, *Domaine de Valmont, 33720 Barsac; 56.76.28.24, Fax 56.27.17.53. Rooms: 10. Double: 295-595FF. Restaurant.*

About 30 kilometers (19 miles) southeast of Bordeaux off the N113, Barsaac is a quaint village in the Sauternes region. In fact, each room of this comfortable and welcoming manor is named after an esteemed Sauternes wine château.

CHÂTEAU DE COMMARQUE, *33210 Sauternes; 56.76.65.94, Fax 56.76.64.30. Rooms: 10 Double: 180-275FF. Restaurant.*

Set on the edge of the Sauternes vineyards about 50 kilometers (30 miles) south of Bordeaux, this is sort of an antique version of a courtyard motel, transformed from a one-time working farm. Decor is simple, the two-level bedrooms are comfortable, and the food is hearty.

CHÂTEAU DU PARC, *33580 Saint-Ferme; 56.61.69.18, Fax 56.61.69.23. Rooms: 4. Double: 450-560FF. Restaurant.*

About 60 kilometers (37 miles) southeast of Bordeaux, due west a few kilometers from Sauveterre-de-Guyenne on D127. This is actually a home in which the owners have opened a few rooms. They also set a memorable table. The distinguished manor house was once a residence for the Saint Ferme abbots. This is an ideal spot from which to visit the Entre-Deux-Mers wine producers.

LE MOULIN DE L'ABBAYE, *1 route de Bourdeilles, 24310 Brantôme; 53.05.80.22, Fax 53.05.75.27. Rooms: 17. Double: 650-950FF. Restaurant.*

A bit west of the Bordeaux country, this lovely former abbey is set on the wooded banks of the Dronne River. In fact, you can dine on the terrace by the river, admiring both the waters and the vine-bedecked residence, parts of which date back 700 years.

WHERE TO EAT

Much of the best cuisine can be found in the finer hotels, some of which are noted above, *Where to Stay.*

LE CHAPON FIN, *5 rue Montesquieu, 33000 Bordeaux; 56.79.10.10, Fax 56.79.09.10.*

Pricey but gourmet. Seafood specialties and turn-of-the-century decor.

PAVILLON DES BOULEVARDS, *120 rue Croix de Seguey, 33000 Bordeaux; 56.81.51.02, Fax 56.51.14.58.*

Lovely outdoor dining on a pleasant night. Gourmet cuisine with lots of seafood and, naturally, a brilliant wine list.

LE VIEUX BORDEAUX, *27 rue Buhan, 33000 Bordeaux; 56.52. 94.36.*

Just a few blocks toward the river from the Cathédrale Saint-André, the Vieux Bordeaux serves a magnificent menu of regional specialties at digestible prices. And the wine list, well, you won't have much trouble finding something satisfying to sip on.

SEEING THE SIGHTS

While you're in the area, you should clearly stop in the **old quarter** in the city of Bordeaux. There are a few nice larger hotels and some very good restaurants, all of which are close to the most worthy sights.

The **Place de la Comédie** is considered the historic center of town, and with good reason. The **Grand Théâtre**, in all its 18th-century grandeur, *occupies the better part of the eastern face of the plaza.* Its neoclassical design, finished in 1780, features a grand facade of cloumns supporting a balcony lined with statues.

The enormous **Esplanade des Quinconces**, said to cover 1.37 million square feet, *is just a couple of blocks north.* The grassy expanse is home to statues of Montaigne, Montesquieu, and the Girondins, the locally-based politicians who briefly assumed the leadership of the Revolution in 1791 before being toppled and sentenced to death.

The **Cours de l'Intendance** *extending west from the Place de la Comédie and the Rue Sainte-Catherine radiating due south* are lined with chic shops offering the latest in *haute couture* and jewels. The **Cathédrale Saint-André** *several blocks southwest of the Place de la Comédie* is well worth a visit. Said to be the most magnificent in the Bordeaux region, it is only slightly smaller than the Notre Dame in Paris. Begun in the 11th century, construction of various facets continued into the 18th century. The **Porte Royale** and **Portail Nord**, with stunning sculpted details of the life of Christ, are especially impressive.

MAISONS DU VIN

A **Maison du Vin**, *or House of Wine, can help you locate various producers and explain the wine varieties. Some will book tours for you and some well offer a sample of wine, along with the opportunity to purchase a bottle or three.*

• **Maison du Vin de Bordeaux**, *1 cours du 30 Juillet, 33000 Bordeaux; 56.52.82.82. Info about all the Bordeaux varieties.*

• **Maison du Vin Margaux**, *place la Trémoille, 33460 Margaux; 56.88.70.82. Info about Margaux wines.*

• **Maison du Vin de Pauillac**, *19 rue de Maréchal Juin, 33250 Pauillac; 56.59.02.92. Wines from Pauillac.*

• **Maison du Vin de Graves**, *rue François Mauriac, 33720 Podensac; 56.27.09.25. Wines from the Graves area.*

• **Maison du Vin de Saint-Emilion**, *place Pierre-Meyrat, 33330 Saint-Emilion; 57.74.42.42. Saint-Emilion wines.*

• **Maison du Sauternes**, *place de la Mairie, 33210 Sauternes; 56.63.60.37. Sauternes wines.*

For a remendous view of the city, mount the 200-plus steps up the **Tour Saint-Michel** to the visitor's platform, which is only halfway up the 370-foot tower. In the cellar beneath the tower, you will find 70 human mummies, exhumed in the 18th century from the local cemetery. As you can imagine, it's a bit creepy.

The **Musée des Arts Décoratifs** houses a fine collection of 16th to 18th century furniture, glass, and ceramics. And the **Musée des Beaux-Arts** is home to an enormous variety of works stretching over almost 500 years and including pieces from masters ranging from Titian to Rodin.

WINETASTINGS

There will be umpteen opportunities to pull over and sample the local wines. But for the big names, phone or write well in advance of your arrival to reserve a spot on a tour. Some of the larger producers:

- **Château Margaux**, *33460 Margaux; 56.88.70.28*
- **Château Beychevelle**, *Saint-Julien Beychevelle, 33520 Pauillac; 56.59.23.00*
- **Château Mouton-Rothschild**, *33250 Pauillac; 56.59.22.22*
- **Château Lafite-Rothschild**, *33250 Pauillac; 42.56.33.50*
- **Château Haut-Bailly**, *33850 Léognan; 56.21.75.11*
- **Domaine Château Millet**, *33640 Portets; 56.67.18.16*
- **Château Cheval Blanc**, *33330 Saint-Emilion; 57.24.70.70*
- **Château Troplong-Mondot**, *33330 Saint-Emilion; 57.24.70.72*

Other Sights

- **Saint-Emilion**, *about 65 kilometers (40 miles) east of the city of Bordeaux*, is considered the most picturesque of the wine villages, most of whch will strike you as rather flat and plain. This hamlet of 3,000 residents sits perched atop a lovely hill overlooking the Dordogne River Valley. Its finest reasure is the **Eglise Monolithe**, a 12th-century subterranean church carved out of the mountain by Benedictine monks.
- **Arcachon**, *60 kilometers (37 miles) southwest of Bordeaux*, is a fishing town of 12,000 people. It sits on a small peninsula jutting into the huge **Bassin d'Arcachon**. The massive triangular *bassin*, with the **Ile aux Oiseaux** (Island of the Birds) in the center, leaks out a small opening into the open sea.
- **La Rochelle** is a romantic port *about 200 kilometers (125 miles) north of Bordeaux*, famous for its lovely arcades, stately wooden homes and secutive nearby seascapes. Artists and aristocrats have long been drawn to this charming town of 80,000. Stroll along the **Old Port**, or sit for awhile in the welcoming cafés gazing across the tiny fishing harbor at the imposing **Tour Saint-Nicolas** and **Tour de la Chaine**

that guard the mouth of the port. From here you can also catch a boat to the lovely **Ile de Ré** and its tiny main hamlet of **Saint-Martin-de-Ré**.

• The **Dordogne River Valley** *to the east of Bordeaux* climbs for hundreds of miles to the high plains of the **Massif Central**. Along the way are some of the most important finds of prehistoric man, as well as memorable landscapes of rough water-hewn valleys, eerie caves and battered fortresses. The **Péreigueux** area is renowned for its cuisine, heavy with game, wild mushrooms, and tangy sauces. Worthy stops include: **Bergerac** with its 15th-century town center; the **Trémolat Meander** with its views of the river's sharp turns; **La Roque-Gageac** tucked into the cliffs overlooking the river; **Sarlat-la-Canéda** with its historic **Lantern of the Dead**; the castle keep and towers of **Rocamadour** clinging to the cliffs; and the underground river and limestone caves of the **Padirac Chasm**.

PRACTICAL INFORMATION

• **Bordeaux Office de Tourisme et Accueil,** *12 Cours 30 Juillet, 33000 Bordeaux; 56.44.28.41*

27. PROVENCE

INTRODUCTION

Ford Maddox Ford, the hailed though plodding British author of the early 20th century, fell head over heels in rapturous love with **Provence**.

Waxing poetic in *Provence: From Minstrels to the Machines* (1935), Ford concludes there can be no evil in Provence:

"Why should there be? The olive there gives its oil; the vine lets down the grape and its juices; the hills are alive with hares, boars and, in thousands, with the thrush, the partridge, and the ortolan ... Yes, why should anyone there sin? It would be superfluous. Life there is so pleasant, that if, as the Pilgrim Fathers, their Nordic ancestors and descendants held, to enjoy is to sin, all life is there one long breaking of commandments."

Sixty years later, the enormous popularity of Peter Mayle's delirious mega-seller, *A Year in Provence*, attests to the enduring allure of this region.

Provence is a relatively compact, though hugely varied area shaped somewhat like a lumpy triangle. Some say it begins as far north as Lyon, but Provence proper does not really take shape until roughly 100 kilometers (60 miles) north of the Mediterranean Sea along the banks of the broad Rhône River where you'll find the villages that produce such magnificent wines as **Hermitage** and **Châteauneuf-du-Pape** (stop by for free tastings).

The western border of Provence essentially runs along the Rhône, past **Orange**, **Avignon** (once home to the Popes), **Beaucaire** and **Arles**, then into the Mediterranean. It then moves east along the coast, past the humming port of **Marseille**, France's second largest city, to several miles past **Cassis**, a lovely seaside town. From the sea, the boundary arches north and then west, crossing the majestic **Mount Saint-Victoire**, then the rugged limestone outcroppings of the **Lubéron** range and the fertile valleys of the **Upper Vaucluse** before finally rejoining the Rhône.

Somehow, despite wave upon wave of malevolent invaders over the centuries and a crush of tourists in modern times, Provence remains idyllic, unhurried, and sumptuous.

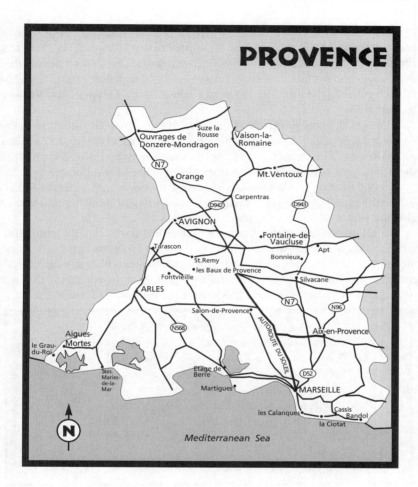

There are countless small villages perched on hillsides from which you can sip pastis (the refreshing licorice-flavored apéritif favored by the locals) and gaze out over huge fields of brilliant lavender, pastures sprinkled heavily with blazing red poppies, and countless rows of grape vines leading up to villas whose nearest neighbor is a half mile away.

No wonder, given its physical beauty and agricultural riches, Provence proved such an irresistible lure to vicious emperors, exalted holy men, and overwrought artists.

Beginnings

This land is steeped in history. Agricultural villages first sprang up thousands of years before Christ. It was the Phoenicians and early Greeks who first established a thriving port at **Marseille**.

The Romans, clearly the most influential of the early conquerors, arrived about 150 B.C., building wine-producing villages, arenas, baths, roads, aqueducts, and fortifications. They adored the land so deeply that they stayed on for another six centuries, and their presence is still visible in such relics as the amphitheaters of **Nîmes**, **Arles**, **Orange**, and **Vaison-la-Romaine**.

The great poets and troubadors were drawn in the Middle Ages to the virtually impregnable and breathtakingly handsome palace at **Les Baux de Provence**. The Papal Court adopted **Avignon** as its home for much of the 1300s – as evidenced by the imposing Palace of the Popes.

Paul Cézanne was a native of **Aix-en-Provence** and, in **Saint-Rémy**, Vincent Van Gogh spent his last years in a frenzy of painting and then a gloomy semi-existence in a nearby asylum.

In short, aside possibly from the fierce and frigid mistral winds that blow through during winter, Provence comes close to being paradise, blending a diverse heritage, a magnificent cuisine (liberally laced with garlic and olive oil), picturesque hilltop villages, and ripe fields that are reminiscent of northern Italy. It's a wonder we don't all move there.

FINDS & FAVORITES

- *The walled city of* **Avignon** *(see Avignon and Villeneuve)*
- **La Mirande hotel** *in Avignon (see Avignon and Villeneuve)*
- *The gardens of* **Fort Saint-André** *(see Avignon and Villeneuve)*
- *The village of* **Gordes** *(see Vaucluse)*
- *The* **Renaissance restaurant** *in Gordes (see Vaucluse)*
- *The village of* **Saignon** *(see Vaucluse)*
- *The* **Oustau de Baumaniäre hotel and restaurant** *(see Les Baux and Saint-Remy)*
- **Pont du Gard** *(see Roman Provence)*

AVIGNON & VILLENEUVE

Any trip to Provence must include the magnificent and historic walled city of **Avignon**, population 90,000, that hugs the banks of the Rhône. Avignon, where you should consider staying a night or two and which we consider the beating heart of Provence, was home to the Popes in the 1300s. In fact, the imposing **Palace of the Popes**, near the northwest corner of the city, is still Avignon's most-visited landmark.

It is also in the courtyard of the Palace that Avignon hosts the most important stagings of its internationally acclaimed arts festival, which has been staged here every July since 1947. The city is also known to many as the capital of the fine **Cotes du Rhône** wines, such as *Châteauneuf-du-Pape*, *Gigondas*, *Vacqueyras*, *Lirac,* and *Tavel*.

ARRIVALS & DEPARTURES

Avignon is 700 kilometers (435 miles) south of Paris just off of the A7 autoroute and about 100 kilometers (62 miles) short of Marseille. The first trick is to get into the walled city.

The massive ramparts, extending 5 kilometers (3 miles) around the city center, were constructed in the 14th century. There are seven original ports and a handful of other entrances that were added in the 19th century to provide greater access to the burgeoning town.

Having followed signs from the east toward Avignon, you will come up against the city at the boulevard Limbert or boulevard Saint-Lazare (it's the same road, but changes names as it circles the city along the outer side of the ramparts).

Going counterclockwise, you will begin to circle the city until you reach the upper northwest corner of the perimeter, where you will see the famous Pont Saint-Bénézet bridge. You'll recognize it because it stops well short of the opposite bank of the Rhône. Here, look for Porte du Rocher or Porte du Rhône.

There should instantly be a blue "P" sign (for Parking) that will lead you directly into a multi-tiered underground lot right in the center of things. If possible, drive to the highest level of the lot because that is closest to street level at the Palace of the Popes.

WHERE TO STAY

LA MIRANDE, 4 place Amirande, 84000 Avignon; 90.85.93.93, Fax 90.85.43.66. Rooms: 18. Double: 1,300-1,900FF. Restaurant.

A precious jewel of a hotel behind the Palace of the Popes, with a marvelous restaurant and several inviting salons. Quite luxurious.

CLOÎTRE SAINT-LOUIS, 20 rue Portail Boquier, 84000 Avignon; 90.27.55.55, Fax 90.82.24.01. Rooms: 73. Double: 750-850FF. Restaurant.

Charming hotel in the southern section of the old walled city, fashioned out of a 16th-century cloister.

GÎTES DE FRANCE DE VAUCLUSE, place Campana, la Balance, B.P. 147, 84008 Avignon Cedex; 90.85.45.00, Fax 90.86.86.08.

For bed and breakfasts in privates homes and on working farms in the Avignon area.

WHERE TO EAT

CHRISTIAN ETIENNE, 10 rue Mons, 84000 Avignon; 90.86.16.50, Fax 90.86.67.09.

A beautiful restaurant in a converted 14th-century home within an arm's reach of the Palace of the Popes. Pricey but special.

HÔTEL PALAIS DES PAPES, *1 rue Gerard Philipe, 84000 Avignon; 90.82.47.31, Fax 90.27.91.17.*
Located between the Place de l'Horloge and the Palace of the Popes, with a small outdoor dining patio with reasonably priced daily specials.

SEEING THE SIGHTS

After you've parked your car, it's time to have some fun.

Within a couple hundred yards you have a remarkable gathering of sights: the **Popes' castle**, the **Petit Palais** (a Cardinal's residence that also dates back to the 14th century and which now houses a museum with Italian paintings from the Middle Ages to the Renaissance), the **Rocher des Doms** (the rocky bluff and garden that once provided the city with natural protection against the sometimes wicked floods of the Rhône), the 12th-century **Notre-Dame cathedral** (with magnficent tombs of two popes inside), the **Saint-Bénézet Bridge** (first built in the 12th century, but ravaged many times by floods and war), and the **Place de l'Horloge** (a central square busy with cafés and surprisingly talented artists selling watercolors).

The **Palace of the Popes**, built during the papal leadership of Benoit XII and Clement VI from 1334 to 1352, was ultimately home to seven popes and two anti-popes (explained below).

The move from Rome was understandably rife with papal politics. Nonetheless, Avignon provided a perfect centrally-located seat from which the popes of the time could rule Europe. The switch was undone in less than 100 years when Pope Gregory XI returned the seat of Catholicism to Rome (though that move engendered a temporary split in the church, and two more unofficial, "anti-popes" continued to sit at Avignon).

The Palace, *open daily with an entrance charge of 32FF*, is well worth a tour. In the Salle de Consistoire you'll find portraits of the resident popes and anti-popes with brief descriptions of their reigns (in French). The **Grand Tinel** is an imposing hall with a massive arched and timbered ceiling and a fabulous Goeblins tapestry depicting Alexander the Great at Babylon. (You will see several magnificent Goeblins tapestries in the palace.)

The **Pope's chamber** is unexpectedly colorful, with a tile floor of ocher, green, and blue – colors echoed in the elaborate murals of ivy that blanket each wall.

Be sure to walk the **Promenades des Papes** around the exterior of the palace, where you can see how the walls rise out of the natural foundation of a rocky knoll and soar to the sky. You will also walk past **Le Mirande**, an exquisite hotel with several inviting salons and patios on the main floor. The restaurant is first-rate as well, with a menu that boasts such dishes as lobster ravioli, artichokes with corriander, mullet in crust, and roast pigeon swimming in garlic butter.

Stroll too through the park of the **Rochers des Doms** and down to the legendary **Saint-Bénézet bridge**. Legend has it that a shepherd boy named Bénézet was urged by an angel to begin the first span in 1177. Eighteen spans were said to have been washed away by horrendous floods in the 17th century. This bridge is the subject of the song *Sur le Pont d'Avignon*, in which all participants are urged to enjoy life and dance.

Take some time to sip a coffee in the **Place de l'Horloge** and watch the international collection of people parade by. And wander the narrow streets away from the bustling palace. You'll find lots of fascinating shops and get a better feel for the residential quarters.

When you're ready to leave Avignon and brave the local roads again, *cross the river on the Pont du Royaume* en route to **Villeneuve**. Literally, the name means "new city" and refers to the area built up in the 1300s by ambitious cardinals who wanted private estates outside the shadows of the Palace of the Popes.

Take a right turn on avenue Gabriel Peri just as you reach the opposite shore and you will come to the **tourist office** in less than a mile. There you can get more specific instructions to the sites of the cardinals' former homes.

A must-see here is **Fort Saint-André**, the magnificent castle dominating the hilltop. The ramparts provide protection for a Benedictine abbey, which in turn nurtures a lush garden where you will be mesmerized by fragrant roses, silvery olive groves, the tiny 11th-century **Chapelle Sainte-Casarie**, and the lichen-stained remains of a cemetery dating back to the 7th century.

Other Sights

- **Opéra House**, *on the Place de l'Horloge, 84000 Avignon.* A 19th-century opera house decorated with statues of Corneille and Molière.
- **Saint-Didier church**, *place Saint-Didier, 84000 Avignon; 90.86.20.17.* A Gothic style church built in the 14th century in the south central section of the walled city.
- **Saint-Pierre church**, *place Saint-Pierre, 84000 Avignon; 90.82.25.02.* An elaborate Gothic style facade from the 12th century, with handsome 16th-century carved doors.
- **Mireio Bateau Restaurant d'Avignon,** *allée de l'Oulle, 84000 Avignon; 90.85.62.65.* Boat tours (lunches and dinners too) up and down the Rhône.
- **Chartreuse de Val de Benediction**, *Villeneuve; 90.25.05.46.* This 14th-century monastery, with three cloisters, was founded in 1356 at the order of Pope Innocent VI and is one of the largest in France.

PRACTICAL INFORMATION

- **Palace of the Popes**, *6 rue Pente Rapide, 84000 Avignon; 90.27.50.00 or 90.27.50.71, Fax 90.86.61.21.*
- **Bureau du Festival d'Avignon**, *8bis rue de Mons, 84000 Avignon; 90.82.67.08.*
- **Avignon Office du Tourisme**, *41 cours Jean Jaures, 84000 Avignon; 90.82.65.11, Fax 90.82.95.03.*
- **Villeneuve Office du Tourisme**, *place Charles David, 30400 Villeneuve-les-Avignon; 90.25.61.33, Fax 90.25.91.55.*

THE VAUCLUSE AREA

Between the towering **Mont Ventoux** (from whose 6,000-foot summit one can see the better part of Provence to the southwest and the beginnings of the Alps to the east) and the **Lubéron** range are some of the most picturesque villages and captivating landscapes imaginable.

Apt, one of the larger towns in the valley fed by the gentle **Coulon** river, is all of about 12,000 people – a metropolis by this area's standards.

Though we wouldn't suggest to stay in Apt, this is an ideal area to find yourself a small villa on a farm and simply melt away, gazing out at the fields of lavender, strolling through hillside hamlets that have changed little since the Romans first set up shop, and indulging your appetites for fine cuisine.

Not a day goes by when one of the small villages in the valley doesn't host an open farmer's market. You'll find bins of ripe fruits, plump tomatoes, eggplant and squash, goat cheeses only two or three days old and suffused with garlic or herbs, black and green olives mingled with herbs and drenched in rich oils.

Freshly clipped herbs are everywhere (you're likely to get strange looks if you try to buy rosemary or thyme because both grow so profusely on virtually any property that no one needs buy them from a merchant).

Marinate a butterfly of leg of lamb in a blend of virgin olive oil and *Gigondas* spiced with rosemary, thyme, and garlic, then grill it on your outdoor terrace. Put a little Stan Getz on the CD player, pop open a vintage *Châteauneuf-du-Pape*, and you've found a slice of heaven.

On either side of the valley there are several villages worth a visit or overnight stay. On the north, moving west to east, you'll find **Gordes**, **Roussillon**, **Saint-Saturnin**, and **Rustrel**. On the south, there is **Ménerbes**, **Lacoste**, **Bonnieux**, and **Saignon**. If you have time, visit them all, wandering the narrow lanes, looking out over the vistas below, and sipping coffee or digging into a hearty lunch of sardines, rabbit, or lamb at one of the neighborhood cafés.

WHERE TO STAY

One option is a villa of your own. Bertrand Vacances publishes a phonebook-sized listing of villas all over France for 30FF. Most listings (private and agency) have photos and a description (the description is in French, but the words are usually easy to translate). *Contact Bertrand Vacances, 43 boulevard Barbes, 75880 Paris Cedex 18, France; 49.25.26.27 or Fax 49.25.27.49.*

Club Trianon also circulates listings for villas and apartments all over France. *Club Trianon, 21 avenue Pierre 1er de Serbie, 75116 Paris; 47.20.32.22 or Fax 47.20.03.39.*

LA MAYANELLE, *84220 Gordes; 90.72.00.28. Rooms: 9. Double: 315-420FF. Restaurant.*

A homey and comfortable little hotel with a view of the valley below.

BASTIDE DE GORDES, *84220 Gordes; 90.72.12.12, Fax 90.72.05.20. Rooms: 18. Double: 550-750FF. No restaurant.*

First-class and somewhat modern facilities in a world-class setting overlooking the valley floor beneath the Lubéron range. Small pool and terrace. (It's a shame that the once well-reviewed restaurant has closed.)

HÔTEL LES ROMARINS, *84220 Gordes; 90.72.12.13, Fax 90.72.13.13. Rooms: 10. Double: 380-650FF. No restaurant.*

Across a small gorge with a view of the village. Small pool. Request a room with a view.

HOSTELLERIE DU PRIEURE, *84480 Bonnieux; 90.75.80.78. Rooms: 10. Double: 350-595FF. Restaurant.*

Some of the rooms are a bit tired around the edges and the management isn't exactly warm and cuddly, but this converted nunnery has a wonderful garden and terrace where you can enjoy breakfast, lunch or dinner.

AUBERGE DU PRESBYTÈRE, *place de la Fontaine, 84440 Saignon; 90.74.11.50. Rooms: 10. Double: 170-300FF.*

A warm and friendly country inn in a captivating village that sprouts right out of the limestone hilltop.

WHERE TO EAT

LA RENAISSANCE, *Gordes, in the square by the entrance to the Hôtel de Ville.*

The Renaissance has a wonderful patio area, serving lamb, rabbit in a mustard cream sauce, and magnificent sardines in a Provenáal sauce.

DAVID, *place de la Poste, 84220 Roussillon; 90.05.60.13.*

On the small road into town, David is a good-sized restaurant with a splendid view of the valley in the distance and a cliff of shimmering ocher a hundred yards away.

LA GRASILLE, *seven kilometers west of Apt off route N100, Perrotet;*
90.74.25.40.

A sign about one kilometer west of the miniscule hamlet of La Chêne
will read "Perrotet, 2 km," asking you to turn right. The restaurant is a
couple hundred yards up the small road, offering all sorts of generous
portions of regional dishes (including a great appetizer bar). A favorite
with the locals.

SEEING THE VILLAGES

Below are the charming villages of Vaucluse:

GORDES

With all of 2,100 residents, **Gordes** is one of the most famous of these
villages. Wind your way up the slopes to this hillside perch and park in the
lot in the center of town. Like the other villages, Gordes is a nest of narrow
alleys meandering between earthen homes that are hundreds of years old.
From several vantage points (especially the **Théâtre des Terraces**) you
can also gaze out over the valley below, with its patchwork of vineyards.

A handful of galleries sell works by local painters. And make a quick
stop at the **Saint-Fermin** church to see its blue floral interior, trompe l'oeil
statues, and crumbling pulpit of faux marble.

ROUSSILLON

A bit further east, **Roussillon** sits atop a dazzling orange peak of ocher.
Once you leave your car in the center of the village, continue up the
orangish dirt path to the former mining site, where ocher was pulled from
the hillside and used as a tint in artistic and architectural projects of all
kinds. **Rustrel,** *further on,* is also the site of a former ocher quarry.

SAINT-SATURNIN

This village sits at the base of a 15th-century fortress, the disintingrating
walls of which are made of stones set in a herringbone pattern. At the top
of the ruins is a tiny chapel, underneath which is an eerie crypt with a
reclining figure whose face is turned away from the entrance and toward
the wall – almost as if in shame.

LACOSTE

Dominated by the château once owned by the Marquis de Sade,
Lacoste was the site where many of the youthful entertainments captured
in his writings were staged. The **Portal de la Garde** at the entrance to the
grounds has a particularly diabolical appearance – or is that just our
imagination?

BONNIEUX

A few kilometers east of Lacoste on the winding route D109, **Bonnieux** is somewhat like a wedding cake, layered with homes leading up to the 12th-century church and the surrounding park on the summit. At the end of the path past the church is a grassy knoll with a cross commemorating various local jubilees from the 1800s.

THE VILLAGE OF BONNIEUX

SAIGNON

Farthest east, just past Apt and up the hillside, is the entrancing hamlet of **Saignon**. From atop the massive cliff that juts outs into the air aside the village, you will wilt at the magnificent view of the hills and valleys around you. In the center of the village is a lovely auberge with an inviting patio, a small fountain, ancient public baths, and a ceramics shop with some very nice pieces.

Up the tiny road on the edge of town is the **Église Notre-Dame de la Pitié**, a broad-shouldered little church with muscular buttresses, handsome wood-carved doors depicting Christ and Mary, and a cemetery made colorful by ever-present garlands laid at the gravestones.

Other Sights
• **Fontaine de Vaucluse**, *on D25 in the foothills about 30 kilometers (18 miles) due east of Avignon.* Another small village, this one boasts the **Sorgue springs**, a pool of water fed by an underground river.

PRACTICAL INFORMATION
• **Départementale de Tourisme de Vaucluse**, *La Balance, Place Campana, B.P. 147, 84008 Avignon Cedex; 90.86.43.42, Fax 90.86.86.08.*
• **Gordes Office du Tourisme**, *O.T.S.I., Le Château, 84220 Gordes; 90.72.02.75.*
• **Apt Office du Tourisme**, *O.T.S.I., place Bouquerie, B.P. 15, 84400 Apt; 90.74.03.18.*

LES BAUX & SAINT-RÉMY

Approaching on sycamore-lined highways from Avignon about 24 kilometers (15 miles) to the north or from Cavaillon about 20 kilometers (12 miles) to the east, you will witness the plains of the Rhône basin give way suddenly to the jagged peaks of the **Alpilles**. Rushing past groves of fruit-heavy olive and cherry trees, you arrive in the chic village of **Saint-Rémy-de-Provence** and begin what is sure to be one of the more memorable days of your visit to Provence.

Saint-Rémy and **Les Baux**, which is hidden further up a small road into the mountains, combine the very finest of contemporary good living and historic exploration.

Saint-Rémy has in recent years become a home-away-from-home to such mega-celebrities as Caroline of Monaco, who can be seen on occasion strolling through the central marketplace with a woven basket of veggies perched on her hip. Terence Conran, chief of the Conran's and Habitat furnishings chains, has likewise sought haven in Les Baux.

They and others, newspapers and magazines report, seek to profit from the comfort, effortless grace, incontestable beauty, and fine cuisine of the region. The bustle of Saint-Tropez on the Côte d'Azur, they insist, no longer interests them. They would rather let the hours slip easily away at the ivy-bedecked **Café des Arts** in Saint-Rémy or indulge themselves with a lobster salad in basil cream at the **Oustau de Baumanière** in Les Baux.

WHERE TO STAY

DOMAINE DE VALMOURIANE, *Petite route des Baux, 13210 Saint-Rémy-de-Provence; 90.92.44.62, Fax 90.92.37.32. Rooms: 12. Double: 590-1,310FF. Restaurant.*

A transformed Provençal home in the heart of the Alpilles with a poolside grill, AC, and the works.

LES ANTIQUES, *15 avenue Pasteur, 13210 Saint-Rémy-de-Provence; 90.92.03.02, Fax 90.92.50.40. Rooms: 27. Double: 350-450FF. No restaurant.*

Modest, but nice hotel with a garden, comfortable salons, and proximity to the town center.

OUSTAU DE BAUMANIÈRE, *13520 Les Baux; 90.54.33.07, Fax 90.54.40.46. Rooms: 11. Double: 1,100-1,700FF. Restaurant.*

The finest. Stop for a lunch if nothing else (see *Where to Eat,* below).

LA CABRO D'OR, *13520 Les Baux; 90.54.33.21, Fax 90.54.45.98. Rooms: 21. Double: 550-800FF.*

A pool, garden and shaded terraces gazing up at the citadel.

WHERE TO EAT

OUSTAU DE BAUMANIÈRE (see *Where to Stay,* above).

In the elegant dining room or, on a sunny day or warm evening, on the expansive terrace facing the swimming pool, you can dine for hours on lobster cannelloni, baby duck with cherries, roast pigeon in a crust with foie gras and mushrooms, rabbit with basil, and a tempting list of fine Burgundies, Bordeaux, and Côtes du Rhônes.

The current chef in residence, Jean-André Charial, will drop by your table at some point to ask how you are enjoying yourself.

It's horribly pricey, but you came all this way, so why not indulge yourself for at least a lunch.

LA RIBOTO DE TAVEN, *13520 Les Baux; 90.54.34.23, Fax 90.54.38.88.*

A shaded terrace at the foot of the rocks. Lobster lasagna and a pie of lamb with thyme.

SEEING THE SIGHTS

Just a mile or so from this contemporary bliss, *on D5 en route to Les Baux,* you will be drawn to two impressive Roman antiquities, fittingly known as **Les Antiques**. One, a triumphal arch, celebrates Julius Caesar's conquest of Marseille in 49 B.C. The other, an unusual 40-foot tower, honors two of Emperor Augustus's grandsons, who died in battle.

Another hundred yards down the way, off the other side of the road, you can trod through the decapitated pillars that once supported a city named Glanum that was founded by Phoenician merchants 600 years before Christ.

While you are likely to spend more time roaming the shops and cafés of Saint-Rémy than its historic relics, Les Baux's history beckons loudly the moment you see the massive walls of the ancient fortress. They spring from a rugged stone plateau that soars over the landscape below and that provided the ideal natural protection for the inhabitants for centuries.

The history of civilization here goes back to the primitive peoples who sought shelter in some of the caves you now see in the sides of this startling plateau.

But Les Baux was best known for its medieval period, when the princes who occupied what was once a magnificent castle on the rocks were as brutal and unyielding as the rocks themselves. One ruler is said to have revelled in tossing people off of the highest castle wall to the rocks below and bellowing with laughter as his victims screamed in agony. Nice guy.

Les Baux was finally brought into the folds of France in 1481, when Louis XI ordered the castle demolished. The residents, an unruly lot, rebelled again against the crown in 1632, when Louis XIII ordered the rebuilt citadel torn down again. The locals were finally tamed and the plateau was largely abandoned as residents set up shop in the valleys below.

For all the violence that tore through this tiny corner of Provence, it was equally famous as a spawning ground for the troubadors, who came to Les Baux to woo princesses with poetry and song. The main path into the tiny city of shops and cafés at the foot of the plateau is named after the most famed of the local poets, Frédéric Mistral.

Park your car along the small highway or in the lot at the base of the plateau and meander up through the tiny stone walkways. There are several surprisingly good pottery and painting galleries, as well as a handful of cafés with views that are better than their food.

Follow signs to "The Citadel" and you will reach the entrance to the ancient abandoned city on top. There you will find several vantage points with detailed maps identifying the landscape below you. There are caves into the stone, and striking remnants of a 16th-century chapel dedicated to Saint Catherine, a dungeon going back several hundred years before that, and the **Paravel Tower** from which you can scan the entire remains.

Despite its legacy of savagery, Les Baux is now home to one of the finest hotels and restaurants in all of France: the **Oustau de Baumanière**. Opening in 1946 by the late artist-chef Raymond Thuilier, the Baumanière is tucked up at the end of the small valley below the citadel.

On a more prosaic note, Les Baux gave its name to **bauxite**, the mineral found here in 1822 that gave rise to the now-immense aluminum industry.

Other Sights
• **Saint-Paul-de-Mausole**, a former monastery and asylum where Vincent Van Gogh spent the last tormented years of his life. *Just to the south of Saint-Rémy.*

PRACTICAL INFORMATION
• **Saint-Rémy Office du Tourisme**, *place Jean-Jaures, 13210 Saint-Rémy-de-Provence; 90.92.05.22.*
• **Les Baux Office du Tourisme**, *near the entrance to the Citadel, 13520 Les Baux; 90.54.34.39.*

AIX-EN-PROVENCE

Like so many lovely spots in Provence, **Aix-en-Provence**, now a renowned city of arts and cafés, was spawned by war. A couple of centuries B.C., the Franks were harassing Greek outposts around Marseille. Finally, unable to cope anymore, the Greeks appealed to their Roman allies.

In 123 B.C., Sextius Calvinus and his troops arrived in force and made quick work of the barbarous Franks's stronghold at a place then known as Entremont. The spot where Sextius Calvinus set up camp, at a thermal spring located about 30 kilometers (18 miles) north of Marseille, became a village that would one day be known as Aix.

It was at about the same time that the Romans also stopped the Teutons from marching into Italy. That great victory was fought just a few kilometers east of Aix, beneath a magnificent peak now called Sainte-Victoire. Aix's golden era came with the reign of the beneficent King René, a true Renaissance man of the early and mid-1400s. It was under his regime that the city blossomed as an intellectual and arts center – a reputation it still holds.

WHERE TO STAY

HÔTEL VILLA GALLICI, *10 avenue de la Violette; 42.23.29.23, Fax 42.96.30.45. Rooms: 15. Double: 800-1,650FF. Restaurant.*

Just above the center of the old section, this former 18th-century mansion has its own gardens, a pool and a very good restaurant.

HÔTEL CARDINAL, *24 rue Cardinale; 42.38.32.30, Fax 42.26.39.05. Rooms: 30. Double: 250-390FF.*

Three very short blocks south of the Cours Mirabeau and very near the famous Place des Quatre Dauphins (Four Dolphins), as well as the Musée Granet, this charming spot was once a 17th-century apartment. Good sized rooms and unbeatable prices for the convenience.

WHERE TO EAT

CLOS DE LA VIOLETTE, *10 avenue de la Violette; 42.23.30.71, Fax 42.21.93.03.*

With pleasant outdoor service and a gourmet menu. Just a couple of blocks above the old town section.

VIEILLE AUBERGE, *63 rue Espariat; 42.27.17.41. Closed Wednesdays.*

Traditional and reasonably priced cuisine just between the Place Général de Gaulle and the Place des Augustins.

SEEING THE SIGHTS

Aix's already well-established cultural reputation gained ground this century when the city began sponsoring a huge **Festival of Lyrical Art and**

Music each summer and capitalizing on its heritage as the birthplace of Paul Cézanne, who died in 1906. The **Granet Museum** here houses several of his works, including the hugely famous *Bathers*, which plays a significant fictionalized role in the beginning of Zola's novel *The Masterpiece*.

Those who appreciate Cézanne's genius can also visit his birthplace *at 2 rue de l'Opéra*, and his studio *on rue Boulegon*, where he died.

Having said all that, Aix, with a population pushing 150,000, is enchanting not because of its distinguished history or even its thriving patronage of the arts. Aix is a wonderfully dreamy place, where one spends hour upon hour sipping espresso or pastis in a bustling café on one of the many charming squares. Or where one strolls through the tiny inner streets, poking occasionally into a shop or gallery, or simply admiring the sunny highlights illuminating a hotel tel or apartment that is hundreds of years old.

The first trick is to stow your car in one of the many parking structures that surround the inner city. Then find your way to the **Place du Général de Gaulle**, where you'll find the famous fountain at the western end of the **Cours Mirabeau**. This is where any walking tour should start (and not just because the **Office du Tourisme** is located here).

The tree-lined, fountain-studded Cours Mirabeau is virtually as well-known to the French as the Champs-Elysées – and, fortunately, the Cours is infinitely more picturesque and pleasant. The fountain, built in 1860 and known as **La Rotonde**, marks the spot where the roads converge from Avignon, Nice, and Marseille. The Cours, officially christened in 1651, was later named for Gabriel-Honoré, the Count of Mirabeau and a noted local writer and politician.

As you stroll west, you'll see on the right side of the avenue various splendid former hotels and a few stodgy businesses. And on your left will be one café after another, such as the **Café de Paris**, the **Café le Grillon** and, finally, the famous **Deux Garçons**, a large bistro with marble-topped tables and green wicker chairs where trendy, well-tanned customers watch one another come and go. This is Olympic-class people-watching.

Afterward, armed with a map you picked up at the Tourist Office, *wander around the corner and up into the oldest section of the city* toward the **Palais de Justice** and the **Église de la Madeleine**. The square outside the church is occupied by several more cafés and, on Wednesdays and Fridays, spectacular flower markets with brilliant cut blooms and whole potted plants.

The Madeleine, whose beginnings reach back to the 1200s, is well worth a quick visit. The Baroque church has a magnificent carved wood organ (not the pipes of course), as well as the *Triptych of the Annunciation*, a haunting work completed by an unknown artist in 1445.

Wander westward toward the 17th-century **Hôtel de Ville** with its Gothic clock tower topped by a Provence-style bell tower of delicate looking wrought iron. At the foot of the tower is yet another square busy with cafés.

Just a couple of blocks south, back toward the Cour Mirabeau, you'll come across the **Place Richelme**, which hosts an open market every morning with all kinds of fresh vegetables, fruits, herbs, cheeses, fish, and meat.

All through these streets you'll spy small signs directing you to pricey shops offering haute couture, perfume, jewels, and other baubles.

Inevitably, you will find yourself back on the Cour Mirabeau, sitting in yet another café, mesmerized by the traffic of young visitors helping themselves to another pastis and greeting one another with countless dramatic kisses.

Other Sights
• **Granet Museum**, *Place Saint-Jean-de-Malte. Open daily*, with ten works by native-son Cézanne, and many by other artists.
• **Atelier Cézanne**, *9 avenue Paul Cézanne. Closed Tuesdays*. A history of the artist and his works.
• **Saint-Sauveur church**, *rue Gaston de Saporta, near the north end of the old section*. A majestic church, though often criticized for the lack of symmetry and varying styles of architecture. Parts of the eerie but beautiful Baptistery dates back to the 4th century.

PRACTICAL INFORMATION
• **Aix-en-Provence Office du Tourisme**, *2 place du Général de Gaulle, 13100 Aix-en-Provence; 42.16.11.61, Fax 42.16.11.62.*

ROMAN PROVENCE

Virtually any town of any size in Provence can trace its history back to the glory days of the Roman empire. Here are a few stops circling Avignon where you can witness some of the more remarkable achievements of the empire – monuments that have bettered the destructive wrath of malevolent invaders, as well as the heavy weight of time.

ORANGE

Eons ago, **Orange** was a thriving Roman capital teeming with four times the current population of 27,000. Baths, temples, a circus, and many other structures stood here until disaster struck, first in the form of triumphant barbarians and much later, in the 13th century, under the name of Dutch royalty, which took possession of the city and used stone from various remaining Roman buildings to construct a defensive wall.

Still, Orange, *about 30 kilometers (18 miles) due north of Avignon on the A7 autoroute*, is home to two magnificent Roman antiquities: one, a great **arch** built in 49 B.C. celebrating one of Julius Caesar's many victories, and the two, a massive **theater** built by order of Augustus.

Performances are still held in the theater, which seats 7,000 and is touted for its crisp acoustics. This Roman theater is also said to be the only one of its kind in the world in which the massive 120-foot high back wall still stands.

Remains of an ancient Roman gymnasium have in recent years been exposed by archaeologists on grounds adjacent to the theater.

PONT DU GARD

Literally translated as the *Bridge of the Gard River*, the three-tiered Roman aqueduct that crosses the river here *about 25 kilometers (15 miles) due west of Avignon on route N100* is one of the most arresting Roman antiquities to be found anywhere.

Built just a few years before Christ, the aqueduct soars 130 feet above the river and spans more than 900 feet. Massive stones weighing as much as six tons were used to fashion the bridge and were fitted into place often with no mortar.

The distinctive design is composed of three tiers of different sized arches, stacked one on top of another. You can still walk across the river on two of the levels, and drive across on one.

NÎMES

Once referred to as "the French Rome," Nîmes was stripped from local tribes by Roman warriors who had previously stood by the side of Augustus when he defeated Antony and Cleopatra.

Those veterans, who were given Nîmes as a gift of thanks for their service, established a flourishing city with a perfectly oval arena capable of seating 24,000 people. Where gladiators once fought there are now bullfights and stage productions.

Also at Nîmes, *which is 40 kilometers (25 miles) southwest of Avignon on the A9 autoroute*, you will find the **Maison Carrée**, a Roman temple that was said to have been the inspiration for the Madeleine church in Paris. Indeed, the resemblance, with the Maison Carrée's 30 Corinthian columns and lack of windows, is striking.

The **Temple of Diana** in Nîmes is what is left of the Roman baths that were constructed near a spring dedicated to the god Nemausus.

ARLES

Arles, *40 kilometers (25 miles) south of Avignon along the Rhône on route N570*, first came under Roman influence when it lent Caesar a dozen ships with which to battle Marseille, whose rulers had unwisely shifted their allegiance from the Romans to Pompey. In gratitude, Caesar took Arles under his affluent wing, building it up with baths, an arena that rivaled most in the world, paved roads, canals, and other riches of civilized life.

Arles, which gained a reputation as "Rome of the Gauls," consequently thrived as a trading center for oil and wine. Unfortunately, it, like Orange, suffered mightily under the barbarian invasions that brought the collapse of Roman rule here in the mid-400s.

As in Nîmes, the prize here is the Roman **arena**, an ellipse seating 24,000 and is 450 feet long, with an upper perimeter of double-tiered arches. You should also take time to visit the Roman **theater**, which is quite beautiful even though it has been reduced to a vibrant lawn surrounded by lopped off columns and reduced seating. Several festivals and an annual July arts celebration are staged here.

The **Roman Lapidary Museum**, though housed in the 17th-century church of Sainte-Anne, has striking Roman mosaics, sarcophagi, and other archaelogical finds dating back to the 1st through the 3rd centuries. The mosaics are especially interesting, detailing scenes from Jason and the Argonauts, the zodiac, the seasons, and the myth of Orpheus.

28. CÔTE D'AZUR

INTRODUCTION

It's party time.

Just about everything you've heard about the **Côte d'Azur**, or French Riviera, is true. This is the land of bronze gods, naughty princesses, plushly-appointed yachts, casinos ablaze with fortunes won and lost, heaping plates of seafood, bluer-than-blue waters, hotter-than-hot discos, and hidden coves where you can strip down to your altogether and splash around in the sea just the way Roman warriors did two-thousand years ago.

But wait. There's more.

The coastal towns where royalty and Hollywood congregate to celebrate the good life get virtually all the publicity. But just a few miles inland, there is another universe – a mountainous one. Here, at the foot of the Alps, peaks blanketed in thick forests rise swiftly into the sky. Between them, raging rivers barrel down rocky canyons at breathtaking speed. And ski resorts are just an hour or two from the beaches.

We're still not done cataloguing the beauties of this region. Up in those hills, you will find **villages perchés**, or "perched villages," so named because they sit like stone nests atop mountainous crags.

Looking more Italian than French with their colorful gardens and red-tiled rooves, the clutch of homes in these villages are stained in a rainbow of earthy hues, ranging from brilliant ocher to dusty rose. And a steeple seemingly as old as time itself rises from the center of each tiny hamlet.

Here, too, crafty entrepreneurs and hoteliers have fashioned some fabulous hotels with first-rate menus and wine lists.

Strictly speaking, the Côte d'Azur is composed of two French *départements*: the **Var** and the **Alpes Maritimes**. Side by side, they hug the coastline between the smallish town of Bandol to the west and the border with Italy to the east.

Toulon, **Bandol**, **Saint-Tropez**, **Sainte-Maxime**, and **Saint-Raphaël** are the famous coastal towns of the Var. **Cannes**, **Juan-les-Pins**, **Antibes**,

Nice, **Villefranche-sur-Mer**, **Cap Ferrat**, **Monte-Carlo**, and **Menton** are situated in the eastern Alpes Maritimes *département*. The Alpes Maritimes is also home to many of the better-known "perched villages," such as **Eze**, **Saint-Paul**, **Vence**, **Tourrette-sur-Loup**, **Gourdon**, **Peillon**, and **Utelle**.

AN ADULT PLAYGROUND COMES OF AGE

The Côte d'Azur hasn't always been a happening place. The fabulous coves were always ideal for fishing and trading communities. But there are no river deltas and much of the coastal land sits at the base of very steep mountains, so there was very little room for larger, agriculturally-oriented towns to take hold and grow.

It was the Greeks, masters of their own jagged and rocky coastlines, who first flourished along the Côte d'Azur. Having settled Marseille 600 years BC, they set about founding a string of small trading ports to the east, including Saint-Tropez, with it's remarkable sheltered bay, Antibes, Nice, and Monaco.

Over the centuries, the Celts, the Romans, and various Barbarians arrived, with the Romans leaving behind several villages that are still in evidence today. The Grimaldi family, Prince Rainier III's ancestors, stormed the tiny nation now known as Monaco in 1297 and never left.

The bulk of the region was finally absorbed into the French empire in the late 1400s, though the eastern-most stretches, including the area around Nice, were not negotiated away from the King of Sardinia until 1860.

One tiny eastern corner of the Côte d'Azur was stripped once and for all from Italy after World War II, a fact that goes a long way to explain why Italian is almost as common as French in some of these villages.

The area played a key role in the Allied efforts to retake France during World War II. During the wee hours of August 15, 1944, troops parachuted behind enemy lines along the coastline from Saint-Tropez to Saint-Raphaël.

They were followed several hours later by American and French divisions who attacked the Germans from the sea, landing on the Hyères Islands and the now famous beaches around Sainte-Maxime. It took only 15 days to liberate the region.

The association of the Côte d'Azur with the good life didn't really take hold until the latter half of the 19th century, when famous Impressionist artists of the era began to capture the region's beauty and when a winter tourist business was established by wealthy foreigners seeking refuge from the bitter cold of England, Russia, and other northern nations.

To draw and entertain these well-heeled patrons, Monte-Carlo opened its fabulous Garnier-designed casino in 1878. (Charles Garnier was the same architect who dreamed up the famous Opéra Garnier in Paris.) Nine years later, a British writer and politician coined the phrase *Côte d'Azur*, or **Azure Coast**, in honor of the blue Mediterranean waters. It was a name that stuck.

Thanks to improved train lines, the **Riviera** flourished in the late 1800s, though still primarily as a winter resort. The summer season wouldn't blossom for another few decades, in the 1920s, when taking leisurely dips in the sea became increasingly popular. Really, it wasn't until after World War II that the area boomed as a summer resort region, where visitors could soak up enormous quantities of sun, crisp Provencal wines, and seafood.

When to Visit

Today, of course, the French Riviera is hugely popular, not just with foreigners, but with the French themselves. Virtually all the French take their holidays in July or August, and an enormous number of them head south. Which means this area is bumper to bumper on the roads, and shoulder to shoulder on the beaches (which may or may not be to your liking, depending on whose shoulders you're bumping into).

To find a bit of isolation or even relative quiet in July or August, you've got to know someone with big bucks and a private mansion with a boat sitting at the end of a private dock that's a few paces from a landing pad for their private helicopter.

Or you could visit in mid-June or late September, when the crowds have thinned, but the sun is still cooking and the waters are still blue and inviting.

Whatever you do, remember that the French Riviera is meant to be savored. Don't rush about. Dally over morning coffees and afternoon cocktails, snooze on a cushy beach-front lounge, listen to the water stroking the shore, and contemplate the brilliant colors in the sky as the sun sets over a spectacular cove. Luxuriate.

FINDS & FAVORITES

- *Hostelerie Le Baou* in *Ramatuelle (see Saint-Tropez)*
- *Saint-Tropez (see Saint-Tropez)*
- *Pavillon Eden Roc restaurant (see Cap d'Antibes)*
- *Nice (see Nice)*
- *Cap Ferrat (see Cap Ferrat)*
- *The pool of the Grand Hôtel (see Cap Ferrat)*
- *The Garnier Casino (see Monaco)*
- *D2565 through the Gorges de la Vésubie (see The Mountains)*
- *The village of Saint-Paul (see Perched Villages)*
- *The village of Sospel (see Perched Villages)*

ARRIVALS & DEPARTURES

The Côte d'Azur is a long haul from Paris. *It's more than 800 kilometers (500 miles) to the western fringes of the area*, which translates into a 10-hour drive or more, driving as fast as your rental car will take you and stopping only for gas, snacks and tolls. By the way, the toll roads will cost more than 200FF each way. (Yes, it's a lot, but the roads are in wonderful shape thanks to those tolls.)

If you're not up for the drive and want to preserve your energy, you can fly to Paris, then hop on a TGV train to Marseille, where your travel agent will have arranged a rental car. Or you can catch a commuter flight from Paris to Nice or Toulon, and rent a car there.

If you want to save the most amount of time, Delta Airlines will fly you direct from the United States to Nice, which is conveniently located near the center of the Riviera.

A last option: You can fly to Geneva or Milan, and drive or take a train the rest of the way through some very fetching country. From Geneva, you would pass through the French Alps or down the Rhìne River valley to the Côte d'Azur. From Milan, you would drive through part of the Italian Alps and see a section of the Italian Riviera.

THE WESTERN COTE D'AZUR

Aside from Saint-Tropez, the western half of the Côte d'Azur is not very well known to American tourists. But that doesn't mean there aren't some lovely stops in the **Var** *département*.

Bandol is a quaint port town of 8,000 people just on the western cusp of the Côte d'Azur. It's probably best known for its three beaches, its sailing facilities, and, most of all, the wine that carries its name and is among the best produced in the region.

Nearby **Castellet** is also worth a quick stop. The tiny hilltop village is picturesque, gives you a view of the valley below, and serves as home to Monsieur Laffargue, an award-winning chef based in the Castel Lumière inn (details below).

Toulon, with 170,000 people, is the largest of the Var cities. Well protected by a spit of land wrapping around the inner port, Toulon evolved into a busy commercial and military harbor. But the city has its charming side as well, especially in the narrow streets of the old part of town around the **Naval Museum** and the **Cathédrale Sainte-Marie**, whose beginnings date back to the 11th century.

On the east end of town near Cap Brun, you'll find a pretty residential area and a beautiful view of the harbor from the **Tour Royale**, with its 20-foot thick walls. For more breaktaking views, *climb avenue Saint-Roch north up out of the town center* to the crest of **Mont Faron**, near the top of which you'll also find a zoo.

Moving eastward down the coastline, you will quickly come to **Hyères**, which is a pleasant stop, but more importantly is the stepping stone to the **Hyères Islands**. There are four small islands, though only two are accessible to tourists. If you want a taste of unspoiled beauty, jot down the **Ile de Port-Cros** and the **Ile de Porquerolles** on your itinerary.

Though there are no cars and parts of the islands are protected for environmental reasons, each has lodging (see details below), restaurants, a couple of small beaches, and marvelous walking trails.

WHERE TO STAY

CASTEL LUMIÈRE, *1 rue Portail, 83330 Le Castellet; 94.32.62.20, Fax 94.32.70.33. Rooms: 5. Double: 330-380FF. Restaurant.*

Located 10 kilometers (6 miles) north of Bandol off the A50 autoroute on D226. This cozy former private home is as much a restaurant as a hotel. It's nestled inside the ramparts of the village, has lovely views of the village and mountains, is within easy striking distance of the Bandol beaches, and features cuisine impressive enough to earn a star from Michelin.

LES BASTIDIÈRES, *2371 aveneu de la Résistance, Cap Brun, 83100 Toulon; 94.36.14.73, Fax 94.42.49.75. Rooms: 5. Double: 550-650FF. No Restaurant.*

Tucked away in the exclusive Cap Brun neighborhood on the eastern edge of Toulon, this one-time private home offers large rooms, casual style, a pleasant pool, and small back garden. Not fancy, but comfortable, reasonable, and quiet.

The **MAS DU LANGOUSTIER** *(94.58.30.09) on Ile de Porquerolles* and **LE MANOIR** *(94.05.90.52) on Ile de Port-Cros* are said to be the best hotels. *You can reach the islands only by boat from Hyères or Le Lavandou, which is a little further east of Hyères.*

SAINT-TROPEZ

Saint-Tropez, Sainte-Maxime, Saint-Raphaël, and **Fréjus** are the four major resorts scattered *along the eastern half of the Var coastline.*

Fréjus is the most distinctive of the batch in that it has a Roman section complete with remains of an arena that once sat 10,000, a theater, defensive ramparts, and an aqueduct. But that doesn't make it the most interesting.

AN ARTIST SETS UP SHOP IN THE HARBOR OF SAINT-TROPEZ

Let's face it, **Saint-Tropez** is where it's at. Sainte-Maxime is very pleasant and has some lovely beaches and restaurants, and Saint-Raphaël has a busy waterfront and harbor jammed with pleasure boats. And if you prefer a bit of quiet elegance, but also want to be within easy reach of the action, you should consider staying near the adorable villages of **Ramatuelle** or **Gigaro** *just south of Saint-Tropez*. But Saint-Tropez is the star of the show, and with good reason. To begin with, it's name claims the most imaginative legend.

Supposedly, a Christian centurian by the name of Tropez was beheaded in his hometown of Pisa at the order of Nero. His body and head, as well as a rooster and a dog, were laid in a boat and cast adrift. (The rooster and dog were supposed to have gobbled up the warrior's remains.) Some time later, the lifeless Tropez, his body unharmed by the beasts, was swept ashore at the place now called Saint-Tropez.

Saint-Tropez also has the smartest shops and the best variety of restaurants (though beware of attempting a serious meal at some of the larger cafés right alongside the waterfront). It has a wonderful, homey, bustling **open market** *on the Place des Lices every Tuesday and Friday*. It has two adjacent ports with some of the most decadent sailboats you can imagine. They're a visual treat, even if you don't like to sail.

WHERE TO STAY/WHERE TO EAT

HOSTELLERIE LE BAOU, *avenue Gustave Etienne, 83350 Ramatuelle; 94.79.20.48, Fax 94.79.28.36. Rooms: 39. Double: 590-1,200FF. Restaurant.*

A wonderful spot where you can enjoy the relative quiet of Ramatuelle, reach the beaches with ease, read trashy novels by the pool, visit Saint-Tropez just minutes down the road, or just sit back on your own private terrace gazing out to sea (all rooms have a view). Gourmet restaurant.

LE FERME D'AUGUSTIN, *Plage de Tahiti, 83350 Ramatuelle; 94.97.23.83, Fax 94.97.40.30. Rooms: 34. Double: 580-1,600FF. No restaurant.*

Located just south of Saint-Tropez on the small road toward the famous Tahiti beach. A popular stop for those who prefer to hug the beaches by day and haunt Saint-Tropez by night. This renovated farmhouse is surrounded by gardens and its rooms overlook the sea. You can easily walk to the beach.

HOSTELLERIE DE LA BELLE AURORE, *4 boulevard Jean Moulin, 83120 Sainte-Maxime; 94.96.02.45, Fax 94.96.63.87. Rooms: 17. Double: 500-1,000FF. Restaurant.*

Right on the coast just on the edge of the town. Most rooms and the restaurant overlook the beach, the sea and, across the small bay, Saint-Tropez. Also has a pool and a small café on the beach.

HÔTEL SAN-PEDRO, *avenue du Colonel-Brooke, 83700 Saint-Raphaël; 94.83.65.69, Fax 94.40.57.20. Rooms: 28. Double: 650-750FF. Restaurant.*
Luxurious hotel set in a forested park at the foot of the Estérel mountains, but still only a couple of miles from the beaches. Quiet, air-conditioned, newish, with a pool, fitness room, sauna, lawn bowling, and a very passable restaurant. Golf and tennis nearby.

SEEING THE SIGHTS

The **harbor** and the narrow side streets of the old quarter provide a veritable feast for your camera – and some of the people aren't so bad either. A 16th-century citadel perched on a hillside behind the town looks down protectively on the village and the bay. There is a fine small museum – the **Annonciade**, with first-string works by Dufy, Seurat, Matisse, and other painters who were active in these parts around the turn of the century.

And it has the "beautiful people," including all manner of celebrity. Don't forget that this was Brigitte Bardot's home for years until the local politicians refused to back her on various animal rights issues.

The summer of 1994 was the Year of Jack Nicholson, who was photographed umpteen different times cruising along the docks on a small motorcycle with a cigar clamped in his teeth and his personal leading lady, Rebecca Broussard, holding on for dear life.

"The beaches?" you ask. There are some respectable beaches along the western edge of town. But what you really want to visit is the famed **Tahiti Beach**, which, along with **Bora-Bora**, **Moorea**, **Pago-Pago**, **Bahia**, **Coco**, **Tropicana**, and a dozen other connected beaches, are splashed along the **Baie de Pampelonne** *just to the southeast of Saint-Tropez.*

Really, it's all one long beach, parts of which are public and parts of which have been given over to "clubs" where you pay a daily fee in exchange for various benefits. Clubs like the Tahiti are set out on the edge of the sand and offer small cafés, service on the beach, showers, and other welcome features of civilization.

Yes, you pay on average about 70FF for a lounge chair and cushion, and another 25FF for a towel – but you get your own spot right next to the water and the adjacent café will serve you cocktails and lunch at your lounge chair. And if some yahoo steals your chair or knocks over your drink, the waiters are there to straighten things out.

The negative side: Summer crowds. Big, carniverous kinds of crowds. Amazingly, though, there is almost enough parking, both in Saint-Tropez (along the waterfront) and next to the beaches. But these are still some massive crowds and there will be times when you'll need to summon every ounce of patience you've got to cope with it all.

That is another reason to stake out a room in a place like **Le Baou** *in Ramatuelle*, where you can enjoy the peace of a hillside village, good dining, and a lovely pool set in an even lovelier garden on the terraced hillside. Each room has its own private terrace looking out on the vineyards and the sea beyond. So when you're not up for the crowds, just stay put and soak up some sun. In Ramatuelle, you'll also find a few nice little family-run restaurants.

PRACTICAL INFORMATION

- **Saint-Tropez Office de Tourisme**, *Gare Routiäre, 83990 Saint-Tropez; 94.97.41.21.*
- **Sainte-Maxime Office de Tourisme**, *promenade Simon-Lonrière, 83120 Sainte-Maxime; 94.96.19.24.*
- **Saint-Raphaël Maison du Tourisme**, *rue W-Rousseau, 83700 Saint-Raphaël; 94.95.16.87.*

CANNES

Take the coastal route from Saint-Tropez to **Cannes** and you'll get a good gander at the massive red-orange peaks that jut out of the **Massif de l'Esterel** range. It's a bit like Arizona by the sea.

Small roads and paths lead into the mountains and, if you're the hardy type, you can climb all the way to the top of **Mont Vinaigre**, which seems a great deal higher than its reported 1,060 feet. Peaks closer to the shore, such as the **Cap Roux**, will give you a stunning view of the sea and rocky coves.

ARRIVALS & DEPARTURES

From the west you enter Cannes through some pretty unremarkable semi-urban landscape and stretches of passable sandy beaches. Be patient and before long, you'll arrive at the eastern end of the Plage du Midi, where you will make a hard left at the port. This is where the Cannes you've heard about begins.

WHERE TO STAY/WHERE TO EAT

HÔTEL DE PARIS, *34 boulevard d'Alsace, 06400 Cannes; 93.38.30.89, Fax 93.39.04.61. Rooms: 45. Double: 550-750FF. No restaurant.*

Located just outside the heart of Cannes, this hotel gives you walkable access to the city and the beaches (about six blocks away). It is stylish, air-conditioned and soundproofed (because the hotel faces one of the city's busiest thoroughfares), with a lovely pool in the garden, and a jacuzzi and sauna on the ground floor. And for Cannes, this three-star won't cost you an arm and a leg.

HÔTEL SPLENDID, *4 rue Felix-Faure, 06400 Cannes; 93.99.53.11, Fax 93.99.55.02. Rooms: 63. Double: 500-850FF. No restaurant.*
Reasonably priced and well located.

MOULIN DE MOUGINS, *Notre-Dame-de-Vie, 06250 Mougins; 93.75.78.24, Fax 93.90.18.55. Rooms: 5. Double: 950-1,450FF. Extraordinary restaurant.*
Located 6 kilometers (4 miles) northeast of Cannes. A charming, tiny inn with five rooms. Owner Roger Vergé is an exquisite chef, who makes the most of regional dishes and has earned three Michelin stars.

MAS CANDILLE, *boulevard Rebuffel, 06250 Mougins; 93.90.00.85, Fax 92.92.85.56. Rooms: 23. Double: 650-900FF. Restaurant.*
Located 6 kilometers (4 miles) north of Cannes off N85. Another very pleasant alternative to staying right in the thick of Cannes, the Mas Candille is set in the midst of a 12-acre park and garden. The restored 18th-century house has fabulous views of the mountains, and there are two pools, a tennis court, and outdoor dining.

AUBERGE DE LA VIGNETTE HAUTE, *370 route du Village, 06810 Auribeau-sur-Siagne; 93.42.20.01, Fax 93.42.31.16. Rooms: 12. Double: 600-1,400FF. Restaurant.*
Located 10 kilometers (6 miles) northwest of Cannes off tiny D9 highway. Wild sort of a multi-leveled, rustic hotel on a hill overlooking the Siagne valley and centered around a large Roman-style pool. Lovely views, good dining, and tranquility.

CARLTON INTERCONTINENTAL, *on the beach at Boulevard de la Croisette (93.68.91.68, Fax 93.38.20.90). Very Expensive. Restaurant.*
Sumptuous marble lobby, off of which are a formal dining room and an exquisite café. Rooms, if you're inclined, begin at 2,000FF a night, though you're not likely to get a seaside view for such a pittance.

SEEING THE SIGHTS

The **central part** of Cannes, a town of about 70,000 people, *extends eastward a couple of miles from the port down the majestic, hotel-lined boulevard de la Croisette and its beach.* The local politicians, knowing which side their bread is buttered on, have done a remarkable job keeping this area clean and uncluttered. You won't find any of the usual T-shirt shops, fastfood stands, or other detrius common to beachfront communities. And you will find policemen seeded through the neighborhoods.

The beach itself is very carefully maintained and has both a general public section and a row of well appointed "clubs," where, for 60 to 100FF, you can enjoy your own lounge, a café, showers, and other amenities. You can stop by these lovely cafés for lunch, even if you don't want to loll around in the sand afterward.

Along the opposite side of boulevard de la Croisette are some magnificent hotels, most notably the Belle Epoque beauty, the **Carlton Intercontinental** (see above, *Where to Stay*). There are also the **Martinez**, **Majestic**, and **Nugo Hilton** hotels along the boulevard with beachfront views.

You should do some eye-popping window shopping along the boulevard as well. **Lanvin**, **Hermés**, **Gucci**, **Fred**, and others have tantilizing displays of jewels, cashmere, silk, and all manner of bauble and garment. You'll find several real estate offices here, too, each one touting the kind of glorious estates where only a Cary Grant would look truly at home.

Some more affordable, but still stylish shopping can be done *a couple of blocks north of the beach along rue d'Antibes, which turns into the rue Felix-Faure near the port.* This long avenue is home to lots of restaurants, some of which are pretty good and others of which offer second-rate meals to undiscriminating tourists.

Walk down to the western end of Felix-Faure and you'll find a typical bar-like café at the base of a narrow street that wanders up the hillside. That slim lane is **rue Saint-Antoine**, which is home to several nice small bistros and restaurants serving a variety of dishes at reasonable prices.

This road will also lead you up the spiky hill to a 12th-century **citadel** on top, where you can get a photographic view of the port, the beaches, and the town center.

GAMBLING ALONG THE RIVIERA

And as long as you've come all this way, you should pop into the **casino**. *Between the beach and the port, right at the front of the Palais des Festivals,* where the famous **Cannes Film Festival** is hosted every May, you'll find **Jimmy'z**, one of the biggest casinos in Cannes. (The other impressive gambling hall is the **Palm Beach Casino** *at the far eastern end of boulevard de la Croisette.*)

A few words about gambling here:

One, yes, you should gamble, if only a little bit, because it's fun. Set aside 50FF, play the slots, and, even if you lose, you won't have spent any more than you would for a cocktail before dinner. (And, who knows, you might win. We did.)

Two, *Machine à sous* refers to slot machines. Another fun and inexpensive game is *Boule*, which is a kind of roulette in which a cueball-sized ball is set adrift on a round table in the middle of which are a couple dozen dimples numbered from 1 to 9. You can bet on a single number or groups of numbers, just as in roulette.

Three, the *Salle des Joues*, or Hall of Games, is where the big-stakes players while away the hours with various card games. Like all the bigger casinos along the Riviera, there is an admission charge (70FF here). Yes, you have to pay even for the right to lose your hard-earned greenbacks.

And the odds in these *salles* are heavily stacked against you. Even with Blackjack, the house deals from a "shoe" packed with six decks of cards. There's no way you can keep track of what's been played (which is exactly why the casino does it that way).

PRACTICAL INFORMATION
- **Cannes Direction Générale du Tourisme**, *esplanade Président-Georges Pompidou, 06400 Cannes; 93.39.01.01.*

JUAN-LES-PINS, ANTIBES & CAP D'ANTIBES

For such a small pocket of space, there is a great deal of variety to be found here.

Juan-les-Pins is a tiny elegant cove, whose greatest claim to fame is its July **World Jazz Festival**. It's a lovely spot to stop for lunch and cruise local shops.

Cap d'Antibes, which technically refers only to the end of the narrow peninsula, is largely composed of beautiful estates, most of which you can only see from the roadside looking through iron gates.

The one open invitation to a life of luxury here is the **HÔTEL DU CAP** *(93.61.39.01, Fax 93.67.76.04)* with its separate seaside restaurant, the **PAVILLON EDEN ROC** *(93.61.39.01, Fax 93.67.76.04)*. Wow! Both the grand hotel and its smaller, but still château-like restaurant are set in a verdant park bordering a craggy cove where waves spatter on the rocks. What a spot for a movie. You half expect Scott and Zelda to pop out of the shadows and invite you to a lunch of lobster and champagne.

Continue along the eastern coastline of the Cap back toward the mainland and you will round a bend at Pointe Bacon and, there it is, **Antibes**. Stop for a photo of the blue waters, sandy beaches, and the town beyond.

Antibes' civilized history goes back to the days when the Greeks established a small trading post here. Today, it is sectioned largely into two parts: the more contemporary beach community, which is located south along the peninsula, and the original ancient city, much of which is still enclosed in ramparts guarded by the 12th- and 16th-century portions of the **Grimaldi Castle**.

It's tough going in the town center, with one-way streets and lanes so narrow even a compact car has trouble squeezing through. Still, Antibes is worth a visit. Park the car and walk through the winding core, and try to save time to visit the famous **Picasso Museum** set right beside the ramparts.

Picasso settled here for a time in 1946, producing a stunning volume of work, many pieces of which are on view in the museum. The museum also holds many of the master's ceramics, sculptures, tapestries, paintings, and drawings from earlier times.

PRACTICAL INFORMATION
• **Antibes Maison du Tourisme**, *11 place Général-de-Gaulle, 06600 Antibes; 93.33.95.64.*

NICE
Nice, the symbolic capital and commercial center of the Côte d'Azur, is an enormous, complex city of almost 350,000 people with all the challenges you might expect of a place that size. Also, to get the minuses out of the way, the beaches, though long and wide, are uncomfortable and pebbly. The prices are sky-high and the crowds can be overwhelming.

Having said all that, Nice is also a fascinating and colorful place to visit for a night or two, especially if you fly directly into Nice and need a day or so to catch your breath.

WHERE TO STAY/WHERE TO EAT
LA PÉROUSE, *11 quai Rauba Capeu, 06000 Nice; 93.62.34.63, Fax 93.62.59.41. Rooms: 62. Double: 580-1,180FF. Restaurant.*

If you want to stay in Nice, this is a smart and delightful choice. The hotel is big, but it's right on the coast at the eastern end of the principle beach in a surprisignly quiet spot (aside from normal workday traffic patterns on the road in front). Most rooms have views of the beach and the city. The hotel sits at the foot of the "Castle," the hill with a park and the ruins of a castle. Also a pool, sauna, sundeck.

HÔTEL NÉGRESCO, *on the Quai des êtats-Unis in Nice; 93.88.39.51, Fax 93.88.35.68. Very Expensive.*

With its decorative columns, ornamented dormers and signature dusty rose dome, the Négresco is the 83-year-old grand dame of all. The hotel boasts a center-stage location, antique furnishings from the 17th through the 19th centuries, and rooms beginning at 1,600FF a night.

MÉRIDIEN, *1 promenade des Anglais, 06000 Nice; 93.82.25.25, Fax 93.16.08.90. Rooms: 314. Double: 1,100-3,150FF. Restaurant.*

A heaping helping of elegance right in the heart of the Nice seafront. Terrace dining, views of the beach, and a pool help justify the price.

LE CAGNARD, *rue Pontis-Long au Haut-de-Cagnes, 06800 Cagnes-sur-Mer; 93.20.73.21, Fax 93.22.06.39. Rooms: 26. Double: 620-1,420FF. Restaurant.*

Located 10 kilometers (6 miles) west of Nice off of D36. Gives you the feel of being in an ancient village, even though you are just minutes from mega-Nice. You might imagine that your extraordinary meal on the terrace will be interrupted any second by a Medieval knight striding through in full armor. Tranquility, charm, views, and fine dining.

HÔTEL WELCOME, *1 quai Amiral Courbet, 06230 Villefranche-sur-Mer; 93.76.76.93, Fax 93.76.93.93. Rooms: 32. Double: 560-820FF. Restaurant Saint-Pierre.*

Right on the quai in the heart of this picturesque fishing port just east of Nice. Views from almost all the rooms, outdoor dining with some of the best food in town.

SEEING THE SIGHTS

Visitors inevitably begin their tour at the seaside, strolling the famous **Promenade des Anglais**, which turns into the **Quai des êtats-Unis** and stretches the length of the entire Nice waterfront. Along here you will find several palace style hotels from the grand old days near the turn of the century and even before, including the fabulous **Hôtel Négresco** (see above, *Where to Stay*).

The **port**, *located around the eastern corner of the beachfront*, is guarded by a mass of rock known as the "**Castle**," a 300-foot hill where today you'll find a lovely park and the ruins of an ancient fortress. Down below, in the harbor, are all manner of elegant yachts and a ring of red, orange, and yellow apartments that make for a stunning photo.

The seductive old part of town is set in a triangle just at the western foot of the "Castle," *between the beach and a long park that begins at the promenade and extends inland a dozen blocks or so* toward the bustling fish market at the **Place Saint-François** and further on to the stately 18th-century **Place Garibaldi** and the trés mod **Musée d'Art Moderne et Contemporain**.

COOL OFF IN NICE

Tucked into this triangle is a warren of narrow pedestrian streets lined on both sides by shops and cafés of all kinds. Don't miss the huge flower and vegetable **market** *on the Place Pierre Gautier between the Palais de Justice and the Promenade.*

In the middle stretch of the lengthy bordering park is the picturesque **Place et Espace Masséna**, a brilliant square surrounded by richly hued buildings with chic arcades below and embellished with a central pool with fountains that are lit up brilliantly at night.

A three-week **carnival** is held in and around this square every February. Various parades feature floats blanketed with flowers or populated by crazed cartoon figures and imaginative beasts. On the last night, all sense of decorum gives way to a wild, take-no-prisoners Mardi Gras.

Further north of the old town section is the **Musée Chagall** *off the hilly upper-crust boulevard de Cimiez* in an area where Romans first made camp Roman ruins can be found *just off the top of the boulevard*, where there is also the **Matisse Museum**.

Built in 1972, the Chagall musuem is said to possess the most important collection of Chagall's startling and often disturbing work. Included is his *Biblical Message*, a series of 17 paintings spread out in two rooms and depicting his somewhat bizarre vision of the Biblical texts.

Like so many prominent modern artists, Chagall came to the Côte d'Azur and found a great deal of inspiration in the natural landscape. He died in 1985 in the nearby hamlet of Saint-Paul.

Another must-see in town is the **Russian Orthodox Cathedral** *on the western side of the city just above the A8 autoroute off the boulevard Gambetta.* Its onion domes swirl with patterns of turquoise-colored tiles, and the interior is awash in gold, both in gilded woodwork and in the rich collection of religious paintings and murals.

The city is dotted with a variety of different museums, including a **Naval Museum** with models of ships and an enormous assortment of paraphernalia, a **Franciscan Museum** dedicated to frescoes and engravings, the **Matisse Museum** memorializing a great deal of his career, and a **Jules Chéret Fine Arts Museum** with a host of 18th- and 19th-century European masterpieces.

PRACTICAL INFORMATION

- **Nice Office de Tourisme**, *avenue Thiers (by the train station), 06000 Nice; 93.87.07.07. Or 5 avenue Gustave-V, 06000 Nice; 93.87.60.60.*
- **Villefranche-sur-Mer Office de Tourisme**, *square F.-Binon, 06230 Villefranche-sur-Mer; 93.01.73.68.*

CAP FERRAT

You don't see much written about **Cap Ferrat**, and so much the better for you because it's a lovely and largely unspoiled stop.

The tiny spit of land has been taken over in part by the same kind of elegant estates that are hidden behind iron gates on Cap d'Antibes. But here there is also a lovely little town, **Saint-Jean-Cap-Ferrat**, with a port, a little bit of shopping, and a couple of very good restaurants.

WHERE TO STAY

VOILE D'OR, *on the port, 06230 Saint-Jean-Cap-Ferrat; 93.01.13.13, Fax 93.76.11.17. Rooms: 50. Double: 900-3,200FF. Restaurant.*

First rate all the way, from the location to the decoration to the dining.

PANORAMIC, *avenue Albert 1er, 06230 Saint-Jean-Cap-Ferrat; 93.76.00.37, Fax 93.76.15.78. Rooms: 20. Double: 350-650FF. No restaurant.*

Nicely appointed, affordable small hotel on the hill with a view of the harbor below.

GRAND HÔTEL DU CAP FERRAT, *06230 Saint-Jean-Cap-Ferrat; 93.76.50.50, Fax 93.76.04.52. Rooms: 48. Double: 2,900-4,400FF. Gourmet restaurant.*

If you can afford it, you won't regret your stay. No expense was spared in building this virtual château, with its marble floors and antique furnishings, and gardens that terrace down the hillside to a spectacular pool whose waters seem to spill directly into the Mediterranean. (If you're lazy, you can take the hotel's own funicular down the hillside to the pool level.) The hotel has three restaurants: a somewhat informal one by the pool, a bar with snacks and very good cocktails called the Maugham (after novelist W. Somerset), and the Club Dauphin, with gourmet dining inside and out.

WHERE TO EAT

LE PROVENÇAL, *avenue Semeria, 06230 Saint-Jean-Cap-Ferrat; 93.76.03.97, Fax 93.76.05.39.*

Elegant preparations of seafood, quality meat dishes, delicate desserts, and selective, prepared with artistry and sophistication. Very smart wine list. It also has the advantage of a harborside view. Overpriced, but very good.

CLUB DAUPHIN, *Grand Hôtel* (see *Where to Stay*).

VOILE D'OR A very fine restaurant (see *Where to Stay*).

SEEING THE SIGHTS

An elbow of land juts off the eastern side of Cap Ferrat. Here, there is the tiny **Chapelle Sainte-Hospice**, with a small accompanying cemetery. Next to the chapel stands a striking bronze statue of a young queen and her child with a dedication to all those women who await the return of men who have gone off to sea.

If you want to soak up some sun, there are two small beaches, one just below the chapel at **Plage Paloma**, and the other on the western side of the narrow neck of the cape at **Plage de Passable**. A 14-kilometer (9-mile) walking path that is very well maintained almost completely encircles the cape, giving you a sea-level view of all the homes and coves.

You must visit the villa and gardens of the **Ephrussi de Rothschild**, a beautiful, Renaissance-style home completed in 1912 after seven years work. It was once the home of Beatrice Ephrussi de Rothschild and is as elegant as any estate you can imagine, with master artworks decorating the interior and seven gardens blanketing grounds that gaze out to sea. If you have time, take tea in the salon.

Last, but hardly the least of Cap Ferrat's attractions, is the **Grand Hôtel du Cap Ferrat**, situated on its own park at the southern tip of the cape. This, you will think, is as good as the good life gets (see *Where to Stay*, above).

PRACTICAL INFORMATION
· **Saint-Jean-Cap-Ferrat Office de Tourisme**, *avenue Denis-Semeria, 06230 Saint-Jean-Cap-Ferrat; 93.76.08.90, Fax 93.76.16.67.*

MONACO & MONTE-CARLO

At first glance, **Monaco** and **Monte-Carlo** are a bit difficult to grasp. Just which is which? Or are they the same?

Monaco is the principality – the famous one that beckons to rich people from all over the world because residents pay absolutely no income tax to anyone. But Monaco also refers to "The Rock," the old part of the city with the Palace that sits atop a massive stone shelf on the western edge of Monaco's small port.

Monte-Carlo is the eastern half of the principality. It resembles Manhattan, only its skyscrapers tower over a small beach and march up the steep slopes of a mountain. These are the chic apartments periodically called home by the people looking for the magic Monaco tax break.

In between the two communities is the port, called **La Condamine**, and another promontory, on top of which is one of the world's most famous casinos, designed in 1878 by none other than Charles Garnier, the architect who later masterminded the elegant Opéra Garnier in Paris. It's easy to see the similarities in the ostentatious ornamentation. The interior of the **Casino** is also well worth a look, even though you'll have to pay entrance and wear a coat and tie.

Sharing a square with the Casino is the remarkable **HÔTEL DE PARIS**, which is equally lavish and will put a sizable dent in your pocketbook whether you settle into one of the rooms or just sit down for dinner. Anything less than formal attire seems somehow inappropriate in the **IMPERIAL DINING ROOM**. Connected to the Casino is an ornate **opera house**. Gold seems to drip from the wall and ceiling decorations. The Sovereign's Box, centered in the back, is literally fit for a king.

In this case, of course, the king is really a prince: Prince Rainier III, the 26th ruler from the Grimaldi family that first occupied this tiny principality in 1297. He has done more than all who came before him in building a safe, clean, elegant hideaway for the very rich and very famous.

To indulge in a bit of cynical analysis, one of his greatest PR moves was to marry Grace Kelly, the unparalleled beauty from the American screen. From their marriage in 1956 until her death in a car accident on the nearby mountain roads on September 13, 1982, Princess Grace, more than the Prince himself, symbolized Monaco's allure.

Probably the most pleasant part of Monaco is **The Rock – Old Monaco**, where you wander tiny winding lanes, window shop, stroll through exotic gardens overlooking the sea, or visit the famous **Oceanographic Museum** and the **Palace** itself.

Even with its inner arcade decorated with frescoes of Hercules' triumphs, the York Room with its depictions of the four seasons on the ceiling, and the ornate throne room that oozes with a sense of grandeur and power, the most stunning object in the Palace is the portrait of Princess Grace, painted in 1974 by Ricardo Macaron.

PRACTICAL INFORMATION

• **Monte-Carlo Direction du Tourisme**, *2A boulevard Moulins, 98000 Monte-Carlo; 93.30.87.01.*

MENTON

A few kilometers further down the coast, on the cusp of Italy, is **Menton**, a largely middle-class town of 30,000 residents. There's nothing particularly fancy about Menton, but it has an easy, comforting appeal. Maybe that sense of normality stands out after all the highrises and glitz of Cannes, Nice, and Monte-Carlo.

WHERE TO STAY/WHERE TO EAT

PRINCESS ET RICHMOND, *617 promenade du Soleil, 06500 Menton; 93.35.80.20, Fax 93.57.40.20. Rooms: 44. Double: 390-520FF. No restaurant.*

A jacuzzi on the roof. A relatively modern, but comfortable hotel virtually on the beach.

LA BERGERIE, CASTILLON, *06500 Menton; 93.04.00.39. Rooms: 14. Double: 350-400FF. Restaurant.*

Located just inland from Menton, 12 kilometers (8 miles) up the winding D2566. Perched on a slope looking down a wooded valley to Menton and the sea, this three-star is nothing really fancy, but it is picturesque and homey, with a good and reasonably priced restaurant.

SEEING THE SIGHTS

The narrow **beach** *along the Promenade de Soleil* has none of the expensive beach clubs. The restaurants offer basic home cooking at decent prices, and the old port has as many working fishing boats as pleasure boats.

The center of town is at the eastern end, beginning with the **old port**. *Adjacent to the port are some lovely sandy beaches along the Promenade de la Mer*, where there are some of the typical beach clubs, which you can join for the day in exchange for café service and lounge chairs.

Cutting through the city center, the **Rue Saint-Michel** is a pedestrian street bracketed by shops, art galleries, and cafés. The **Place du Marché** is regularly tranformed into a humming fish market, and the tranquil **Place aux Herbes** has a couple of down-home, put-your-feet-up outdoor cafés, where you can sip a beer and watch the world amble by.

There is another lovely square facing the **Église Saint-Michel** just up the hill from the port with its distinctive dusty brick-colored tower.

And, of course, there is a **casino**, this one *a few steps from the sea at the foot of the Jardins Bioves that bisect the town.*

PRACTICAL INFORMATION

• **Menton Office de Tourisme**, *8 avenue Boyer, 06500 Menton; 93.57.57.00.*

THE MOUNTAINS

People forget that there is more to the region around the Côte d'Azur than topless starlets, casinos, and pleasure boats. The **French Alps** begin essentially at the water's edge and rise very quickly around raging rivers, rocky gorges, and dense forests.

One eye-popping tour of the interior *begins at Menton and winds its way up the coastal range on the D2566* to the heart-warming village of **Sospel**, where a gurgling, often frigid river, slices the town in two.

The serpentine road continues up the slopes, deep into heavy forests to a summit at **Col de Turini**, whose cafés provide warm refuge for winter skiers attracted to nearby slopes. *The road, now called D70, then turns down the opposite slope,* finally arriving at **Bollène-Vésubie**, another impossibly adorable village.

All along this route there are magnificent views of various ragged mountain ranges and green and gold forests. But possibly the most inspiring picture of all is found *along the D2565, which turns back south toward the sea* and leads you through the **Gorges de la Vésubie**. The landscape is like something out of the Wild West, with a torent of blue-green water slapping through the soaring walls of stone.

Another great drive is the **Route Napoleon**, *which is N85, trailing from Cannes all the way through the French Alps to Grenoble.* This winding highway covers almost 300 kilometers (185 miles) and retraces the route Napoleon took in 1815 when he returned from exile in Elba to wage a new round of wars. He was said to have braved the mountain passes because he felt hostile forces would turn him away if he took the easier path up through the Rhône valley. The road passes through several striking villages, but is most notable for its awesome landscapes.

THE PERCHED VILLAGES

These tiny hamlets date back hundreds of years. Most sit atop a rocky peak overlooking a valley below – the perfect defensive position from which to fend off unreasonable barbarians. Many are worth a quick visit or a lunch, and some are worth a night or two.

Our listing here begins, as above, in the west and moves eastward. There are dozens of perched villages, though we have chosen just a few to note here.

• **Le Castellet**, *near Bandol.* Worth a stay at the **Castel Lumière** (see above, *Western Côte d'Azur, Where to Stay*).

• **Les Arcs**, *12 kilometers (7 miles) south of Draguignan on D555, only a few kilometers above the N7.* Really more of a wine country village than a perched village. But there is a lovely hotel called the **LOGIS DU GUETTEUR**, *Place du Château, 83460 Les Arcs-sur-Argens; 94.73.30.82, Fax 94.73.39.95. Rooms: 10. Double: 450FF. Restaurant.* An amazing 11th-century stone castle that was transformed years ago into a three-star hotel. Panoramic views of the mountains in the distance and the valleys below. A good kitchen and a pool.

• **Trigance**, *99 kilometers (62 miles) northwest of Cannes, up the N85 Route Napoleon to Castellane, then west on D952 for 12 kilometers (7 miles), then south on D955.* Worth a stay at the **CHÂTEAU DE TRIGANCE**, *83840 Trigance; 94.76.91.18; Fax 94.47.58.99. Rooms: 10. Double: 480-680FF. Restaurant.* Feel what it was like to live in a castle in the 9th century – only experience it with modern amenities and a quality country-style kitchen. Way off the beaten track near the breathtaking Canyon du Verdon, this stone castle sits atop a hill overlooking the village below, and has a huge terrace and comfortable rooms.

- **Mougins**, *near Cannes*. Worth a stay at the **Moulin de Mougins** (see above, *Cannes, Where to Stay*).
- **Tourettes-sur-Loup**, *23 kilometers (14 miles) northwest of Nice, starting on N98, then turning north on D36 to Vence, then west on D2210.* Worth a visit for a stroll through the narrow lanes and a look at shops displaying the work of talented local artists.
- **Saint-Paul**, *20 kilometers (12 miles) northwest of Nice, starting on N98, then turning north on D7.* Worth a stay at **LE SAINT-PAUL**, *86 rue Grande, 06570 Saint-Paul-de-Vence; 93.32.65.25, Fax 93.32.52.94. Rooms: 15. Double: 750-1,250FF. Restaurant.* Tucked inside the ramparts of this marvelous village, the Saint-Paul has been very sucessfully transformed into a first-rate inn by new owner Olivier Borioo. All the comforts and service you could ask for. This is one of our very favorite stops.
- **Utelle**, *43 kilometers (27 miles) north of Nice, up N202, then D2565, then D32.* Worth a visit for the unparalled view of the mountains and the **Tinée** and **Vésubie** rivers.
- **Eze**, *11 kilometers (7 miles) east of Nice on N7.* Worth a stay at the **CHÂTEAU EZA**, *rue de la Pise, 06360 Eze; 93.41.12.24, Fax 93.41.16.64. Rooms: 11. Double: 1,350-2,500FF. Restaurant.* A renovated villa once owned by a Swedish prince, with stunning decor, breathtaking views of the coastline and the sea, and critically acclaimed dining.
- **Peillon**, *18 kilometers (11 miles) north of Nice by way of D2204, then D21.* Worth a stay at the **AUBERGE DE LA MADONE**, *06440 Peillon; 93.79.91.17. Rooms: 20. Double: 400-780FF. Restaurant.* A great place to get away from the mayhem of downtown Nice or Monaco, the hotel's terraces gaze out over the picture-postcard-pretty village of Peillon, as well as the surrounding valleys and hills. A very good restaurant and lots of nearby walking trails.
- **Sospel**, *15 kilometers (9 miles) from Menton on D2566.* Well worth a leisurely stroll and lunch at a local café.

INDEX

Unless otherwise noted, references below page 275 are for Paris.

LIST OF WINE SIDEBARS

A quick glance below will guide you to the sidebars featured in Chapter 8, *The Wines of France*, with the corresponding page number:

FROM THE PUBLISHER

Our goal is to provide you with a guide book that is second to none. Please remember, however, that things do change: phone numbers, prices, addresses, quality of food served, value, etc. Should you come across any new information, we'd appreciate hearing from you. No item is too small, so if you have any recommendations or suggested changes, please write to us.

Have a great trip!

Open Road Publishing
P.O. Box 20226
Columbus Circle Station
New York, NY 10023

TRAVEL NOTES

TRAVEL NOTES

TRAVEL NOTES

TRAVEL NOTES

TRAVEL NOTES

TRAVEL NOTES

TRAVEL NOTES

TRAVEL NOTES

TRAVEL NOTES

TRAVEL NOTES

TRAVEL NOTES

TRAVEL NOTES

TRAVEL NOTES

TRAVEL NOTES

OTHER TITLES OF INTEREST

BERMUDA GUIDE by Ron Charles. Relax in style, play a round of golf on championship tees, swim in beautiful azure seas – in short, come to Bermuda with Open Road's veteran travel writer and Bermuda connoisseur Ron Charles. Extensive insider shopping, watersports, hotel, and restaurant info is at your fingertips with this complete guide to Bermuda. **$14.95**

SOUTHERN MEXICO & YUCATAN GUIDE by Eric Hamovitch. Complete coverage of beautiful southern Mexico and the Yucatan peninsula. Discover terrific beaches, majestic Mayan ruins, great water sports, and the latest on hotels, restaurants, activities, nightlife, sports and more! **$14.95**

PLEASE USE ORDER FORM ON NEXT PAGE

ORDER FORM

Name and Address: _____

_____

_____

_____ Zip Code: _____

Quantity	Title	Price

Total Before Shipping _____

Shipping/Handling _____

TOTAL _____

Orders must include price of book <u>plus</u> shipping and handling. For shipping and handling, please add $3.00 for the first book, and $1.00 for each book thereafter.

Ask about our discounts for special order bulk purchases.

ORDER FROM: **OPEN ROAD PUBLISHING**
P.O. Box 20226, Columbus Circle Station, New York, NY 10023